An Introduction to Communication Studies

Sheila Steinberg

JUTA

AN INTRODUCTION TO COMMUNICATION STUDIES

First published 2007
Reprinted 2008
Reprinted 2009

Juta & Co.
Mercury Crescent
Wetton, 7780
Cape Town, South Africa

© 2007 Juta & Co, Ltd

ISBN 978 0 7021 7261 8

Typeset in $9\frac{1}{2}$ / 13 pt Stone Roman

Project Manager: Melanie Wagner
Editor: Sandy Shepherd
Proofreader: Angus Boswell
Typesetter: AN dtp Services, Cape Town
Indexer: Ethné Clarke
Cover designer: WaterBerry cc
Printed in South Africa by Mills Litho

The authors and the publisher have made every effort to obtain permission for and to acknowledge the use of copyright material. Should any infringement of copyright have occurred, please contact the publisher, and every effort will be made to rectify omissions or errors in the event of a reprint or new edition.

Contents

Part 2: Contexts of Communication Study

Chapter 7 – Intrapersonal communication   139

Chapter 8 – Interpersonal communication   160

Chapter 9 – Small group communication   192

Chapter 10 – Public speaking   218

Preface

The primary purpose of this text book is to provide a sound foundation in communication theory for undergraduate students at tertiary institutions in South Africa against the background of outcomes-based education. To achieve the learning outcomes related to knowledge, skills, competencies, and attitudes and/or experiences, the book combines the theory and practice of communication. Students are often puzzled by the need for a strong theoretical foundation in a subject as practical as communication. It is only with hindsight that they realise that the practice of communication is made more efficient by an understanding of the underlying theory. The approach in this book is first to provide knowledge and understanding of communication as a science, and then to relate this knowledge to their everyday experiences. The intention is to motivate students to learn about communication and to become actively involved in developing their personal and professional communication competence.

An informal style of writing has been adopted to produce an interactive text. In addition, the book contains a number of learning aids that should benefit students. Each of the twelve chapters begins with an overview which briefly outlines the contents and a list of outcomes that students should aim to achieve. Each chapter ends with a brief summary as well as an executive summary which provides a synopsis of the key elements in the chapter. The examples, scenarios and case studies throughout the text show that even the most abstract theory can be used to explain communication experiences and problems in real-life situations. A study guide, written by the Department of Communication Science at the University of South Africa, can be used in conjunction with this book to provide additional guidelines to the prescribed material. Readers who require additional information may wish to consult the Addendum at the end of the book for a list of electronic addresses.

This book replaces *Communication studies: an introduction* (1999). It takes into account the social and political changes that have taken place in South Africa during the last decade. New content includes chapters on the functions of communication, intrapersonal communication, public speaking, language and the specialisation areas that are being studied in communication research. Both content and practical examples have been updated to accommodate critical issues that communication scholars need to address in their contribution to national South African goals of social reconstruction and development. Although this text book includes a chapter on public speaking it does not replace *Persuasive communication skills: public speaking* (1999).

Chapter 1 contains a brief overview of the history of human communication from prehistoric times to today's information society and the new communication technologies.

Chapters 2 to 6 establish the foundation for a scientific study of communication. In Chapter 2 we discuss the functions of communication in terms of the needs they fulfil and the effects they have. We also emphasise the nature and importance of communication competence and explain that, to understand communication and its influence on society and on our lives, we need to study it scientifically as well as historically.

Chapter 3 introduces the concepts and models that are used to describe the process of communication as well as the settings in which communication occurs. Some theoretical approaches that assist an understanding of the complexity of communication studies are briefly introduced.

Chapter 4 deals with perception and listening. We explain the process of perception and illustrate the selective nature of perception with reference to the way in which works of art are expressed and interpreted. The importance of interactive listening in establishing relationships is emphasised as well as the role of appropriate feedback in the listening process.

Chapter 5 provides a framework for understanding the role and impact of nonverbal communication in our relationships and the interaction between verbal and nonverbal messages.

Chapter 6 explores the relationship between language and meaning. After explaining Jakobson's functions of language we introduce language as a system of signs. Some of the causes of misunderstanding in our communication are examined, including the way men and women tend to use language in different ways.

In Chapters 7 to 12 the theoretical principles that have been established are applied to the communication contexts introduced in Chapter 3. The most important concepts, models and theories in each context are presented. The importance of adopting a critical approach to the theories and their underlying assumptions is emphasised throughout.

Chapter 7 focuses on the intrapersonal communication context and its relevance in our lives. The concept of *self* is examined as well as the way we perceive ourselves and the world around us. The elements in intrapersonal processing and some of the intrapersonal variables that play in role in how we see ourselves and others are described.

Chapter 8 examines the interpersonal context by focusing on the relationships that we develop and maintain in our everyday lives. We discuss Martin Buber's *I-you* and *I-it* relationships and a model that describes the interaction stages of a relationship. We also consider some of the factors that influence the development and nature of our interpersonal relationships: self-disclosure, interpersonal needs and our communication style. Erving Goffman's theory of self-presentation illustrates communication behaviour in social relationships.

Chapter 9 is concerned with communication in small groups. Various characteristics of small groups are discussed as well as the stages in the formation of small groups and the communication networks that operate in small groups. The chapter examines the role of leadership and the ways in which groups discuss problems and reach decisions. Some strategies for resolving situations of conflict are also described.

Chapter 10 introduces the public speaking context. After explaining the importance of public speaking skills in professional and social situations, the steps in the speech-making process are discussed with reference to concrete examples. The sequence suggested is to determine the purpose of the speech, analyse the audience, select a topic, find the relevant information, write the speech and rehearse the delivery. By illustrating each step with examples from real speeches, the chapter helps to overcome some of the apprehension associated with addressing a group of people.

Chapter 11 deals with the mass communication context. The process of mass communication is illustrated by means of a model, followed by the functions of mass communication in society. The social effect of mass communication has been a topic of discussion, controversy and research since the first newspapers became available. The chapter focuses mainly on research studies and theories that attempt to explain the effect of mass media messages on society: gatekeeping, agenda-setting, spiral of silence, magic-bullet, two-step flow and uses and gratifications theory. We conclude with a discussion of technological or media determinism and the views of Marshall McLuhan (1911-1980), the Canadian literary and communications scholar.

Chapter 12 provides an introduction to the specialisation areas that students generally study in more advanced courses in communication. In this chapter, we provide a brief summary of some of the research that has been conducted and the theories that have been developed in the following specialisation areas: persuasive communication, organisational communication, intercultural com-munication, development communication and health communication. Each discussion is followed by a short case study in which the theoretical principles are applied to a practical situation.

In conclusion, I express my gratitude for the support, assistance and constructive criticism I have received over the past twenty years from the lecturers and administrative staff in Unisa's Department of Communication Science.

Sheila Steinberg
November 2006

Part 1

Foundations of Communication Study

1 A brief history of communication

Overview

"Hey Mom, I have a date tonight — can we be done with dinner by 7?"
"Sure, Dawn, who's the lucky guy?"
"Uh, you don't know him."
"So, someone new! What are you two going to do?"
"Oh, we're just going to talk. I can spend hours talking with him. It's like we're real soul mates. He really seems to understand me."
"And what's this fellow's name?"
"Well, I call him J.T."
"What does the 'J' stand for?"
"What difference does it make?"
"None, really. So is he picking you up at 7?"
"No . . ."
"So you're meeting him somewhere."
"Yes, I guess that's right — we're 'meeting' somewhere."
"And what time do you expect to be back?"
"Back? Well, I won't, because, you see, I'm not really going anywhere."
"Wait a minute — you have a date, your date is not coming to pick you up, and you're not coming back because you're not really going anywhere. Can you see why I'm a bit lost here?"
"Oh, Mom, get with it. This is the 21st century. I have a cyberdate with J.T., who lives in Sweden. I met him in a chat room the other day, and we're scheduled to 'meet' at 7.15 tonight. So can you please get dinner ready?" (Verderber & Verderber 2001:398)

As a student at the beginning of the 21st century, you probably have no problem identifying with Dawn in the above scenario. However, like Dawn's mother, an older person would probably feel somewhat bewildered by the concept of her daughter having a 'cyberdate'. The way in which we communicate has undergone dramatic changes in the past century and even more so in the last decade or two. The study of communication is of particular interest today because of rapid developments in new technologies for producing and transmitting (sending) information. But communication scholars agree that, despite the proliferation of communication technologies, the human communication problems we have today are not basically different from those that people experienced hundreds of years ago. The consensus of opinion is that we are not going to solve communication problems by teaching people to master technology, but rather by helping them to gain insight into the phenomenon of communication (cf Trenholm 1991).

We begin our exploration of communication by looking back and briefly examining the way in which prehistoric people communicated and how communication developed into its modern forms. We do so by discussing the major stages in the history of human communication: the age of speech and language, the age of writing, the age of print and the age of electronic mass media. To conclude the section on the history of communication, we briefly discuss the new communication technologies. We end the chapter with a scenario based on an issue of communication ethics in the modern organisation.

Learning outcomes

Our primary aim in this introductory text is to motivate you to learn about communication and to become actively involved in developing your communication competence. By the time you reach the end of this book we want you first to have obtained theoretical knowledge and understanding of communication. Second, we want you to think about what you have learned and relate your new knowledge to your own everyday experiences of communication. Third, we want you to demonstrate your competence, for example, by improving your relationships with other people. In each of the 12 chapters that comprise this text, we have designed the list of learning outcomes to **help** you to achieve these aims.

At the end of this chapter you should be able to:

1. List the five stages in the history of communication in chronological order, name the medium or technological development that characterised each age and describe the most important outcome of each new age.
2. Think about the relevance of modern means of communication in your own life.
3. Answer the questions based on the case study at the end of this chapter.

Introduction

Have you ever thought about what your life would be like if you were not able to share your thoughts about the day's events with your best friend, write a letter to a family member who lives far away, send an e-mail congratulating a friend on her birthday, put up your feet and watch your favourite television show, relax to soothing music on the radio or CD player, send a fax to a business associate, get onto the Internet to look for information for an assignment, or read a newspaper to find out what is going on the world? We take our ability to *communicate* — to make contact and share meanings with others — very much for granted. We also take for granted the technology that makes much of this communication possible. Yet there was a time when we did not have television or newspapers, and computers and cellphones belonged in science fiction stories. In fact, there was a time when communication through speech was not possible because our prehistoric ancestors did not have our well-developed language systems. To fully understand the nature of communication, we need to have some idea of how it evolved and made possible the techniques and technologies that we refer to as 'communication' today. The history of communication also gives us insight into the way it influenced the development of civilization and still exerts an influence on modern societies.

In your history lessons at school you probably learned about the different stages in the development of the human species, such as the Stone Age, the Bronze Age, the Iron Age, and so on. These names refer to periods thousands of years ago during which people made tools from different materials and developed ways to produce food or make weapons. Eventually, human civilization as we know it would develop from these early inventions.

A similar series of 'ages' can be used to define the stages in which our ancestors made advances in their ability to communicate. It was equally important for the development of civilization that our ancestors be able to exchange information, record it, recover it and disseminate (spread) it. Communication enabled the inventions and solutions that marked the stages of human civilization to be shared and passed down to following generations (De Fleur & Ball-Rokeach 1989).

Without some means of recording information, we would not have been able to trace the development of civilisation. An example of how knowledge of the past has been acquired is the cave paintings, dating from 25 000 to 10 000 years ago, that were discovered by archaeologists in southern Africa, Spain and France. The paintings depict animals, geometric signs and human figures that describe scenes of hunting and rituals. We do not know exactly what purpose they served at the time, but their importance to us is that they are the oldest surviving records of human communication. Today, we use technological means to exchange, record, recover and disseminate information. What is of interest to communication scholars is how techniques and technology that made modern communication possible developed over the ages. We ask questions such as the following: How did people communicate before speech and language? How did they record information? How did they transport it? What changes did the mass media and technology make in society and in the life of the individual?

Figure 1.1 Cave painting

1.1 The stages of human communication

The following account of the history of communication is based on discussions in Schramm (1988), De Fleur and Ball-Rokeach (1989), DeFleur (1994) and Fang (1997).

The stages in human communication are associated with the development of speaking, writing, printing and the mass media (newspapers, magazines, radio, film and television). The most recent stage is the Information Age, the outcome of the development of computer technology. As we discuss each of these stages, you should be aware that each successive communication development did not replace the one that preceded it. Rather, it gradually built on what was already there. Our ancestors first learned to communicate by means of signals, and we still use them today (for example, waving your hand to greet someone). Then speech and language were added, followed by writing and mass communication. Today, we use all of these means of communication in addition to the rapidly spreading use of computers.

Another point to bear in mind is that the developments we discuss cannot be measured in terms of hundreds of years. They cover a period of more than 500 000 years. The time span between speech and the invention of writing, and between writing and the invention of print, for example, was thousands of years, a concept difficult to convey in a short account such as this. The consequence is that there are necessarily many gaps in our 'story'. We have selected what we consider to be the most significant highlights in the history of communication.

The story of human communication begins some half a million years ago with small groups of prehistoric hunters who lived in caves. These people did not walk upright and were physically incapable of producing speech. They could produce vocal sounds, but their voice boxes had not yet developed sufficiently to generate and control the intricate sounds of speech. Although we have no records, scientists assume that their communication was similar to animal communication. That is, prehistoric people received and exchanged information about the environment (for instance, the presence of danger or food) through their senses: sight, smell, taste, touch and hearing. They also communicated with each other through gestures, posture and facial expressions, and expressed a limited number of sounds such as grunts and cries. Over time, people began to move out of the caves and settle in small communities. The need to communicate played an increasingly important role in their ability to participate in community life. The development of speech and language was the first major revolution in the means of communication available to human beings.

1.1.1   The age of speech and language

Scientists estimate that speech and language originated some 40 000 years ago among people who had evolved to physically resemble human beings today. Not much is known about the origins of speech. One view is that it was a divine gift. Another view assumes that, as the human speech organs developed, recognisable words gradually developed from the basic sounds emitted by prehistoric people, and speech and language evolved. What is important, is that speech gave people the ability to think and plan, to hunt and defend themselves more effectively, to invent ways of preserving food and keeping warm in winter, and to learn to cultivate the land. It was during this era that people also began expressing their creativity in the form of art — the cave paintings that have been discovered in different parts of the world. The development of speech and language thus had consequences for both individuals and society. While the ability to use language did not cause great changes, it made possible the transition from a hunting way of life to an agricultural way of life.

Some of the earliest agricultural communities settled along the fertile banks of the Tigris and Euphrates rivers, the shores of the Mediterranean and the banks of the Nile River. As these agricultural areas grew and developed over the centuries, people needed to find ways to record such matters as boundaries and land ownership. And, as their towns grew in size and commercial activities and trading increased, they also needed to keep records of buying and selling, and other transactions. It was needs such as these that prompted the invention of writing in about 3500 BC.

1.1.2   The age of writing

The cave paintings produced by prehistoric people mentioned in Section 1.1 are our earliest attempts to record ideas in graphic (in the form of pictures) form.

They clearly depict animals, people and hunting scenes. However, we do not understand the purposes for which they were used and the meanings they held for the people who made them. Only the original artists could answer such questions accurately. What is important is that cave paintings provided people with a way of recording customs, traditions and ceremonies for succeeding generations that was more accurate than using the spoken word alone. For this reason, scientists regard cave paintings as the precursor to writing. The significant point about writing is that it enabled people to standardise and share the meanings of signs (words) because each language system has its own set of rules (such as grammar) to which everyone conforms.

The earliest forms of writing were cuneiform and hieroglyphics (an ancient Egyptian writing using picture symbols carved into stone). Although the invention of writing allowed people to record and store information, the problem with hieroglyphics and cuneiform (an ancient system of writing with wedge-shaped characters in clay tablets) was that clay tablets and stone 'documents' were difficult to transport. The first advances towards a more portable writing medium were made by the Egyptians, who invented the papyrus-making process in about 2500 BC. Later, animal skins and parchment (a kind of paper made from animal skins) replaced papyrus (a kind of paper made from water plants), and paper made from wood pulp was finally invented by the Chinese in about AD 100.

The importance of light and portable media is that it provided the conditions for far-reaching social and cultural changes. Of prime importance is that it was no longer necessary to rely on the human memory to retain information and to pass the culture (the language, traditions, art, rituals and lifestyles in a particular society) of a society to following generations by word of mouth. In Egypt, for example, papyrus was used to record the affairs of government and to write down legal, literary, scientific, medical and religious ideas. Libraries were opened and schools were established to teach a class of clerks, known as scribes, to write. It took many centuries, however, before a large number of people could read and write. In fact, it was not until the invention of printing in the 15th century that literacy started to spread.

1.1.3   The age of print

The printing process is traditionally attributed to the invention of movable metal type by Johannes Gutenberg of Mainz, in Germany, in 1450. Prior to this time, manuscripts and books were produced by craftsmen and monks who copied and recopied them by hand — a slow, laborious and expensive process. Gutenberg's invention revolutionised book production. The printing press spread rapidly throughout the world and by the beginning of the 16th century, thousands of books were being produced. The importance of Gutenberg's invention is that it permitted the storage of large amounts of information. Printing is said to have marked the start of the modern world because it changed the way information was conveyed and, for the first time, literacy came within reach of the masses. De Fleur (1994) makes the important point that the new medium of communication did not displace earlier ways of communication. Then, and now, spoken language remains the primary mode of communication. Writing, and then printing, supplemented oral communication, but never replaced it.

As techniques were developed for more rapid printing and improved road and postal systems made distribution easier, news-sheets — an early form of newspaper — began to flourish and their circulation increased rapidly. While the early news-sheets of the 17th and 18th centuries were aimed at the educated elite, the mass newspapers of the 19th and 20th centuries were designed to appeal to the growing numbers of literate artisans and merchants in the rapidly developing urban-industrial cities of Europe and America.

The social significance (ie how society was influenced or changed) of printing is that with the spread of books, information became available to a greater number of people. For the first time in history, they were able to share knowledge that had previously been denied to them. As more and more people learned to read and write, their thinking was freed from the restrictions of church and government. New political and religious ideas began to circulate in society, and throughout Europe and America, revolutionary movements emerged, making use of print to disseminate their ideas to increasingly receptive publics. Particularly with the spread of newspapers, public opinion became something that political leaders had to take into account. Although it came after book production, the great success and wide distribution of the newspaper made it the first true mass communication medium.

1.1.4   The age of electronic mass media

Scientific discoveries and technological inventions during the 19th century (such as electricity and the telegraph) laid the foundations that would eventually lead to mass electronic media. Towards the end of the 19th century, people were able to send telegrams and cables and talk to each other on the telephone. It is important to note that the advent of electricity created the 'wired world' and, for the first time in history, it became possible to separate communication and transportation. Until then, the medium that carried the information had to be physically transported from one place to another. Books and newspapers had to move from place to place in much the same way as clay tablets in ancient times. Information travelled only as fast as the messenger who carried it. With the invention of the telegraph and the telephone, information could be transmitted rather than transported. Communication over vast distances was no longer dependent on the available means of transportation. The effects of this 'revolution' are still in evidence today. E-mail, for example, can transmit a letter speedily without the need for mail delivery. It is also important to note that, while the telegraph facilitated the sending of information that could be collected at a distance for later use, the telephone was an immediately interactive medium (Crowley & Heyer 1991). In other words, there was no longer a time delay between the transmission of information and its reception by the person to whom it was addressed.

☐ **Radio** Towards the close of the 19th century, Guglielmo Marconi invented the first 'wireless telegraph' which permitted signals to be transmitted without the use of electric wires. By Christmas of 1906, a Canadian professor, Reginald Fessenden, was able to broadcast a musical programme from his experimental laboratory in Massachusetts. In 1908, another American inventor, Lee de Forest, demonstrated the transmission of the human voice from the Eiffel Tower in Paris, and the signals were picked up by radio operators some 800 km away. Technological inventions and public interest in the possibilities of using radio for commercial purposes followed, and by 1912 the first licensed radio station transmitting news and music was operating in California. After the end of the First World War, the idea of using radio to broadcast messages to large audiences emerged, and by 1928 a number of commercial networks were operating across the United States of America.

The British Broadcasting Corporation was established in 1922 and similar developments took place in other industrialised countries. By the 1930s, radio achieved a central position as a mass medium providing news and entertainment to an increasing number of audiences. During the Second World War, radio was the primary means for keeping people informed on the progress of the war.

☐ **Film** The invention of photography and developments in optics and chemistry in the late 19th century made it possible to record images on film. In 1895, the first projected images (10 short films that lasted about 20 minutes) were demonstrated in France by the Lumière Brothers. By the early 20th century, the movie camera and projector were available and motion pictures became an important means of providing entertainment. The early films were offered as an attraction at fairgrounds but, from 1905, permanent cinemas were being built in Europe and the United States. The most important person associated with the first full-length (silent) movies was David Wark Griffith, an American film-maker who directed films such as *The Birth of a Nation* (1915) and *Intolerance* (1916), which are still regarded as classics today. The first sound film, *The Jazz Singer*, was made in 1927 and colour was widely used in films from the 1950s. Since then, increasingly sophisticated technology has created the type of films we as audiences have come to expect when we visit the cinema.

The golden age of film in the United States was from 1930 to the late 1940s, when thousands of films were made. The content of most of these films was sufficiently bland to provide excellent and inexpensive family entertainment, especially during the Depression (the world-wide economic depression of the early 1930s). While most films still seek to amuse or entertain by providing diversion and entertainment, films are also socially significant in other ways. For example, many documentaries seek to educate people and most propaganda films have a persuasive influence. Most films reflect the society that produces them and thereby enrich our cultural experiences as well. Botha (1997) argues that, while film is an important part of any country's culture, this is particularly true in a country like South Africa, where film can make an important contribution to the democratisation and development that need to take place. For example, during the last few years, many people have been the victims of violent crime, and a film such as the Oscar-winning *Tsotsi* dramatises South Africa's social problems in an attempt to illuminate the roots of crime and violence. However, in the past, apartheid policy and ineffective subsidy structures contributed to the fragmentation of the South African film industry so that, for most of its history, it has reflected apartheid ideology and ignored sociopolitical turmoil as well as the realities experienced by black South Africans (cf Botha 1997).

☐ **Television** Developments in film and radio prompted attempts to transmit images and sound over the air, and so television was born. Television was demonstrated in London in 1926, and, as early as 1936, the British Broadcasting Corporation offered a regular daily broadcast. In the United States, television began operating in 1940. However, its growth was halted by the outbreak of the Second World War, and it was not until the 1950s that development started again. The expansion of television was rapid. For example, in 1950, there were only about one million television sets in American homes. Within 10 years their number rose to about 60 million, and less than 20 years later television was being used in approximately 90 percent of American homes (cf Schramm 1988). The discussion about the social significance of film is relevant to television as well. In most societies, even though it may be primarily used for entertainment and information (eg news and discussion programmes), television is also part of the culture of the society.

The mass media are so deeply embedded in modern society that we cannot imagine life without them. Not only would we be deprived of the source of much of our entertainment, but the incredible flow of information that we accept as 'natural' would not be available. A significant social outcome of developments in the mass media is the increase in the speed of communication, and the increase in the volume (amount) of communication and information brought about changes that created the information society (discussed below). Equally significant is what Fang (1997:138) describes as the creation of the Communication Toolshed Home, which has transformed the average person's home into the central location for receiving information and entertainment. The Communication Toolshed Home is equipped with 'tools' such as radio, television, VCRs (video cassette recorders), CDs (compact discs), DVDs (digital video discs) newspapers, books, magazines, fax machines and computers, all of which perform a variety of communication functions that make it unnecessary to leave the home in order to obtain entertainment and information.

1.1.5   The Information Age

Scientists agree that we are well into a new stage in the development of communication: the **Information Age**, also called the computer age or the digital age. There is no clear-cut distinction between the age of mass media and the Information Age. The Information Age is the inevitable outcome of the new technologies of the second half of the 20th century. The significance of the Information Age is that it has created 'information societies', societies that depend for their economic survival on immediate access to large amounts of information on a global scale.

We can trace the beginnings of global communication — the worldwide network of communication — to the introduction of computer and satellite technology after the Second World War. In 1945, a futurist writer, Arthur C. Clarke, predicted that three satellites positioned in orbit over the Earth could provide a global network for communication. By 1962, the first satellite, Telstar, was in orbit around the Earth. In the 1980s, more than 40 satellites were orbiting the Earth and it has become difficult to estimate just how many more satellites are in orbit today. Most of the satellites are used for broadcast services, that is, television and radio signals are sent up to the satellite and are then relayed to different stations all over the world. Important news events happening in one country can be broadcast around the world via satellite as they are happening and be seen simultaneously by millions of people in many countries.

The remainder of this section is based mainly on information from Dominick 1999; Verderber and Verderber 2001; Verderber and Verderber 2002; and Tubbs and Moss 2003.

☐ *The Internet* While the invention of the printing press made possible the sharing of large amounts of information on a massive scale, computer technology has made this process even more efficient. Computers are basically machines capable of processing and storing information. Originally used in large organisations to perform complicated mathematical calculations and aid administration, they are used today in industry, medical research, the military and the exploration of outer space, to name but a few examples. Computers are the basis of the *Internet*, the worldwide network that carries information and entertainment along what has become known as the Information Highway. The Internet has revolutionised the computer and communications world like nothing before. It is at once a world-wide broadcasting capability, a mechanism for the dissemination of information and a medium for collaboration and interaction between one individual and another, or between one organisation and another, regardless of geographical location. Every day, several billion pieces of e-mail (electronic-mail) are carried by the Internet, and millions of people log on to computerised chat lines, check bulletin boards, visit web sites, shop online, read the news, play trivia and other games, engage in online conferences and transfer information files.

While scientists are yet to find a satisfactory definition of the Internet, it is not difficult to explain how it works. The Internet is an international 'network of computer networks'. In simple terms, the Internet is a system that combines thousands of computers from all over the world into one big computer that you can access from your personal computer at home. The idea of linking computers together began in the mid 1960s, and by 1983 this network of computer networks became known collectively as the Internet. Some computer networks are run by government agencies, others by universities, libraries, businesses, and so on. A person using a computer connected via a telephone to another computer anywhere in the world can send and receive large amounts of information on almost any imaginable topic. Being connected to the Internet allows you to find out, for instance, the latest cricket score in a match being played in Australia, what courses are offered at Unisa, stock exchange prices in New York, or weather conditions in Paris. The stage for this unprecedented integration of capabilities was set by the invention of the telegraph, telephone, radio and computer.

☐ **E-mail (electronic mail)** IDC, a subsidiary of the International Data Group (IDG), the premier global provider of market intelligence for the information technology and telecommunications industries, predicted that the total number of *e-mail* messages sent daily will have exceeded 60 billion worldwide by 2006. They expect that e-mail volume will continue to grow as person-to-person e-mails are joined by rapidly growing numbers of spam, e-mail alerts and notifications. IDC predicted that more than half of all messages sent in 2006 will have been person-to-person e-mails (www.idc.com).

Surveys also report that 90 percent of all people on the Internet use it for e-mail. E-mail has become an essential part of communication within and between organisations and has also changed the nature of relationships between individuals. For many people, messages sent via e-mail have replaced letters, faxes and telephone calls in both their business and personal lives. E-mail is generally fast, cheap and reliable. Because physical distance between communicators is irrelevant, relationships are created through connection rather than through physical proximity. It is, however, important to remember that electronic mail is not necessarily private and that people other than the intended receiver of your messages can access them.

☐ *The World Wide Web* A part of the Internet in which information is presented in a multimedia format, is the World Wide Web (WWW). The WWW was created in 1989 by Tim Berners-Lee at the CERN Particle Physics Laboratory in Switzerland. Berners-Lee's intention was to create a system that could exchange papers and other scientific information between CERN and the Stanford Linear Accelerator Center in California (http://www.isoc.org/internet/history/brief.shtml). Because of the cost and slowness of using traditional media, computers networked via the Internet provided the best means of publishing and delivering this material (Straznitskas 1998). Since then, the WWW has become the most popular Internet service, just behind e-mail. The WWW combines words, graphics, video and sound, adds colours, and includes advertising and downloadable text and programmes. It is possible to search for information on almost any topic using a key word or phrase. Information in the WWW is presented on 'web pages', rather like the pages in a book. A collection of pages belonging to the same organisation or individual is called a 'web site'. It is estimated that there are more than a million web sites in operation. Each WWW site welcomes you with a 'home page' that includes a table of contents (see Figure 1.2 below). The home page

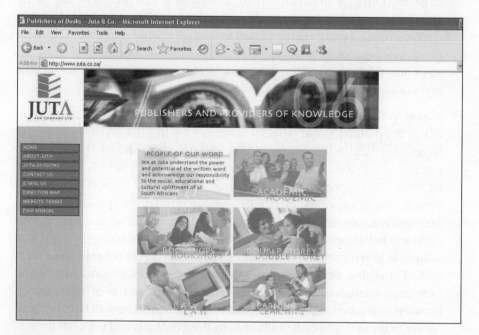

Figure 1.2 Juta's home page

acts as a 'front porch' for the many rooms of the 'house' inside (Fang 1997:219). The WWW is nonlinear which means that you do not have to start at the beginning of a document and work through it. Using *hypertext*, a navigational tool that allows you to link one piece of information, either text or graphics, to another, you can jump from the middle of one document into the middle of another. Another tool that enables you to quickly find the information you are searching for is a *browser*. A browser is a software programme that enables you to look over the information on a topic on thousands of web sites on the WWW. Microsoft's Internet Explorer, Safari and Mozilla are among the most popular browsers.

❑ ***Newsgroups and chatrooms*** An increasing number of people all over the world are communicating with people they don't know, but with whom they share a common interest, through *newsgroups* and *chatrooms*. A newsgroup, or bulletin board, is "an electronic gathering place for people with similar interests" (Miller 1999:187). The information, or 'articles', that make up a specific topic are written by people interested in the topic. Others read the articles and comment on them and so the newsgroup grows and becomes an ongoing discussion in which a few or hundreds of people may participate. There are thousands of different newsgroups on the Internet, with topics ranging from nuclear physics to Elvis Presley's life and music.

Verderber and Verderber (2001; 2002) describe Internet chat as "an interactive exchange between two or more people". Instead of posting articles on a bulletin board, in a chatroom typed responses appear instantly on all the participants' personal computer screens. As few as two or three people can hold a conversation or it may include several hundred participants. Internet chat resembles face-to-face conversation in that feedback is relatively instantaneous. Of course, you do not know the other participant(s), nor can you interpret any meaning that is normally transmitted nonverbally. You must also bear in mind that the people you are talking to in a chat room may use pseudonyms and represent themselves as something they are not. You will never really know whether they are young or old, male or female, rich or poor. In the scenario at the beginning of this chapter, for example, 'J.T.' may be an elderly woman rather than the young man that Dawn assumes she is chatting with. What is rather scary is that most probably she will never know.

❑ ***Teleconferencing*** is a way to hold a meeting with people who are in different, often distant locations. ***Audioconferencing***, which uses telephone technology, is a substitute for face-to-face communication that allows businesses and other organisations to cut down drastically on business expenses as well as providing for a rapid exchange of ideas and information. For example, a banking institution with branches all over the world may conduct a daily briefing through audioconferencing. ***Videoconferencing*** is accomplished through both audio and video links and allows people in different locations to see as well as hear each other. Inserts in a television news broadcast, for example, often show the news reader speaking to a politician in Pretoria and another in Cape Town about a current event. The people being interviewed answer questions, express their views and may even speak directly to each other. For the viewer, it is interesting to see the participants 'live' and to be able to observe their appearance, facial expressions and other nonverbal behaviour. Business organisations increasingly use videoconferencing for diverse purposes, such as meetings, sales presentations, teaching and training, and even job interviews.

☐ **Telecommuting** literally means that people commute to work via the Information Highway. They may, for instance, work at home two to three or even five days of the week, and be connected to the main office by computer, fax, voice mail, e-mail and videoconferencing. Using e-mail, documents can be exchanged almost instantaneously and meetings can be arranged at a suitable time on a daily basis. Telecommuting is becoming increasingly widespread, particularly in the United States, and will certainly have an impact on business, family and social relationships. It is estimated that, in addition to cutting costs, telecommuting can increase productivity by five to 20 percent.

1.1.6   Implications of the Internet

While the Internet undoubtedly provides for an unprecedented amount of information exchange, an important question that has become the subject of ongoing debate and research among communication scholars is: Is the Internet isolating people or does it extend social contact and enhance communication? Early studies suggested that people who used the Internet at home (including the most social forms, such as e-mail and chatrooms) showed higher levels of loneliness and depression than people who did not. Recent studies suggest a more positive view, in that Internet use actually enhances social and family relationships, particularly through e-mail, although it does increase stress. A dissenting view is that, with the growing use of the Internet, people are spending more time at work and less time with their family and friends. The same study expresses concern that telecommuting will diminish social contacts at work, resulting in further isolation. The study suggests that there is no replacement for the immediacy and warmth of face-to-face communication which affects individual wellbeing and our sense of connection with others.

Another issue that concerns communication scholars is the digital divide or technology gap. There is a growing concern that technology is creating a gap between those who can use, afford and understand it, and those who cannot. In South Africa, as in other countries, for instance the United States, it is a select group of people at the higher socioeconomic levels who have and understand how to use state-of-the-art technology at work and in their homes.

There are other implications of the latest technological developments, for example, the prospects for an electronic global community. We discuss some of the issues in Chapter 11, which deals with mass communication and the views of Marshall McLuhan.

In conclusion, we point out that, in contrast to the thousands of years that elapsed between the development of speech and language, writing, and finally print, the most remarkable achievement of the 20th century was the speed with which communication developments occurred. However, today's media still perform the same functions as the clay tablets and hieroglyphics of centuries ago — they move information across time and space. The difference is that information reaches unlimited numbers of people over vast distances at breathtaking speeds using incredibly sophisticated technology.

Developments in mass communication in particular created a need for a deeper understanding of communication and its influence on society and on our lives. Hence scientists began to study communication in an orderly and systematic way. In other words, they engaged in the scientific study of communication. In the next chapter we introduce you to the way in which academics study communication as a scientific discipline.

Scenario 1.1

An issue of communication ethics
Blurred lines

The increasing use of new kinds of communication technologies has meant that it is more difficult to draw the line between organisational time and private time. Even on vacation many executives find that they are in constant communication with their offices. One Chicago executive suffered from ulcers, leading his physician to prescribe rest at a vacation cottage. Still, the fax, modem and telephone kept him in touch with work continually, even at the cottage. The ulcers subsided only when he found a location in Mexico remote from all electronic communication devices. He was probably lucky to be high enough in the organisation to have control over his time in this way. What does a more junior employee do or say when a boss orders him or her to carry a pager seven days a week, 24 hours a day?

Many people have welcomed the freedom to be able to work at home in 'virtual offices', communicating through fax, modem and personal computer. Still, problems arise in such arrangements stemming from the difficulty of separating work life from personal and home life. Telecommuters report feelings of isolation, and some experience more work pressure at home than in the office. The social setting of a regular office allows many people to let off steam and relax by sharing the pressure with co-workers. Many telecommuters find that they work longer hours with fewer breaks than they otherwise would. The intrusive nature of computer and personal communication technologies raises the ethical issue of how far an organisation can go in communicating that a member is on call just about any time of day or night. Organisations must also confront the issue of providing social and other support for the growing number of telecommuters and home workers (Neher 1997:163).

Having studied this scenario, please think about the issue of communication ethics discussed by the author and then come to some conclusions about how you would handle a situation in which you found yourself having to carry a pager or keep your cellphone switched on seven days a week, 24 hours a day in order to secure your job.

Summary

This chapter has been largely concerned with the history of human communication. It began by examining the way in which prehistoric people communicated and how communication developed into its modern forms. It discussed the major stages in the history of human communication: the age of speech and language, the age of writing, the age of print and the age of electronic mass media. The section on the history of communication concluded with a brief discussion of the new communication technologies. The chapter ended with a scenario based on a question of communication ethics in a modern company.

Test yourself

1. Five major stages of the development of human communication are distinguished according to different 'ages'.
   (a) List each age in historical order.
   (b) Write down the medium or technological development that characterised each age.
   (c) Briefly describe the most important social outcome(s) of each new development.
2. Write down the number of times you use a mass communication medium in the course of a typical weekday and over the weekend. For what purpose do you use it? How different would your day be if you did not have access to one or more of these media?

3. Has the Internet and the opportunities it offers for information, entertainment and communication made an impact on your life? Explain how and why. For instance, has personal interaction become more or less important in your everyday life? Has the Internet made a difference in the way you research material for assignments? If you are working, has the nature of oral communication in your organisation changed?

EXECUTIVE SUMMARY
History of communication

1 The age of speech and language
2 The age of writing
3 The age of print
4 The age of the electronic mass media
   ☐ radio
   ☐ film
   ☐ television
5 The Information Age
   ☐ the Internet
   ☐ e-mail
   ☐ World Wide Web
   ☐ newsgroups and chatrooms
   ☐ teleconferencing
   ☐ telecommuting

2 The functions of communication

Overview

In this chapter, we take a brief look at the functions that communication performs in our lives. These functions, or purposes, of communication are described in terms of the needs they fulfil and the effects they have. We then consider two theories that examine our needs and explain the relationship between communication and the satisfaction of needs, using the examples of Maslow's hierarchy of needs and Packard's hidden needs. As a preparation for your formal study of communication, we introduce you to the way in which academics study communication as a scientific discipline. In the next part of the chapter we explain how communication scientists use theory and research to reach an understanding of an aspect of communication. We follow this by bringing to your attention the nature and importance of communication competence. We end the chapter with a scenario based on Maslow's theory.

Learning outcomes

At the end of this chapter you should be able to:
1. Define and explain five purposes of communication, using examples from your own experience of communication.
2. Explain the relationship between the purposes and effects of communication.
3. Identify and give an example of each component of Maslow's hierarchy of needs.
4. Choose five advertisements from different magazines and try to identify whether the advertised products appeal to emotions associated with needs of which you are not even aware.
5. Explain the meaning of the terms 'scientific study', 'theory', 'theories', 'concept', 'model' and 'research'.
6. Reflect on the importance to yourself of becoming a competent communicator.

Introduction

Why do we communicate? What does communication do for us? Look again at the everyday experiences of communication we discussed in the Introduction to Chapter 1 and you will see that each one performs a function in our lives — we communicate with some purpose in mind.

2.1 Purposes of communication

It is generally agreed that we communicate with some purpose in mind and that the most important purpose is to satisfy a personal or social need. Theorists in many disciplines have established the idea that needs are the driving force behind human behaviour. Needs are generally described as requirements of life, which can range from the physical need for food and shelter to the overall sense of wellbeing that is derived from knowing, for instance, that you have achieved success at work or in an examination.

Sometimes we need the active co-operation of others to achieve the purpose, for example, asking a patient to 'breathe deeply' enables a doctor to examine for a lung infection. Reaching a decision at a meeting to introduce a new sales policy requires the co-operation of a number of people. Sometimes the purpose is achieved without the direct participation of others. Some of us are able to satisfy our need for self-expression, for instance, by sharing our ideas and feelings through our creative abilities — in art forms such as literature, painting, photography and music (cf Verderber & Verderber 2002; Tubbs & Moss 2003).

2.1.1 Physical and psychological needs

We communicate with others because we have basic physical needs to fulfil in order to survive (food, water, air and shelter). We need to communicate in order to obtain food or rent a house, for example. But we also communicate to satisfy psychological needs. Psychologists have established that people need contact with other people just as they need food, water, air and shelter. Without at least some contact with others, most of us would suffer serious consequences, including hallucinations and a loss of our sense of time and space. It has been shown that socially isolated people die at a younger age, that the likelihood of death increases when a marriage partner dies, and that poor communication skills contribute to coronary heart disease. Often the topic of the conversation is unimportant: the purpose it serves is the interaction with another person. We discuss a theory about needs in Section 2.3.

2.1.2 Relationships

One of the prime purposes for communicating is to develop and maintain relationships with others. Relationship in this context means any connection, involvement or association between two people, regardless of its source.

Relationships can be permanent, such as by blood, or transitory, such as a work relationship with a colleague. We need the love and friendship of friends and family, and the co-operation of those in our work and social groups to feel secure about ourselves. We discuss interpersonal relationships in more detail in Chapter 8.

2.1.3   Our sense of self

We also communicate to gather insight into ourselves. Through our communication with others and the way they respond to us, we develop a sense of who we are (a self-concept) and how other people react to how we behave. Do you do your job well? Did you give an effective speech at your 21st birthday party? Do other people respect you? You learn the answers to these questions in part from the responses you receive from the people with whom you form relationships. We explore the development of self-concept in Chapter 7. The link between our need to form relationships and acquiring a sense of self is succinctly expressed by Hora (Gamble & Gamble 1998a:15) as follows: "To understand oneself, one needs to be understood by another. To be understood by another, one needs to understand the other." Understanding others takes place through interpersonal communication.

2.1.4   Information

We cannot function in our society without information. We communicate to obtain and share information for a number of purposes. We obtain some of our information through observation, some in conversation, and some through the mass media. For example, observing the way an experienced colleague performs a task may give you more information about improving your work skills than studying a manual. Should you need to find out the time a train leaves, you would ask the station master or consult the timetable. You read newspapers because you want to know and understand what is going on around you and in other parts of the world. You may gain useful information about the topic of the assignment you have to submit by watching an educational programme on television or surfing the net.

2.1.5.   Decision making

Some of our decisions are made unconsciously — we do not go through an internal debate about whether to brush our teeth in the morning or avoid an oncoming car in the traffic. Other decisions are made together with others. Whatever the context, we communicate to obtain and share information that enables us to make informed decisions. Buying a house, or deciding which school your children should attend, for instance, are usually mutual decisions made after discussion by both parents based on information they have obtained about these concerns. Sometimes we need specialised information to arrive at a decision. For example, the management of a supermarket requires accurate facts and figures to discuss the viability of opening a new branch before taking such a decision. Ways of obtaining information and reaching decisions are discussed in Chapter 9.

2.1.6   Persuasion

In many situations, we communicate to persuade others to think the way we think or to change an attitude or behaviour, as well as to have them understand what we are saying. The teenage girl earnestly explaining to her mother that wearing trendy clothes does not mean she is a member of a gang is trying to persuade her mother to let her choose her clothing as well as trying to change her mother's attitude to modern fashions.

In today's word of high technology, the mass media are used extensively for persuasive purposes. Political leaders, for instance, have learned the value of using the mass media, particularly television, to influence our voting behaviour. We are bombarded with persuasive messages on a daily basis by advertisers who make a determined effort to persuade us to change our buying habits through constant exposure of their goods and services. Persuasion is discussed in Chapter 12.

2.2   Effects of communication

We said earlier that the outcome of communication can have consequences that are intentional or unintentional. The effects of communication are thus linked to the purposes of communication.

Intentional effects are the direct and predictable changes in the behaviour, opinion, attitudes or feelings of people in response to communication messages. In addition to example 2.1 below you will find further examples in Section 3.2.4.

Example 2.1

John is finding it difficult to concentrate on his work because he is upset about the argument he had with his girlfriend, Marie, the previous evening. He rushes off to Marie's office in his lunchbreak and presents her with a bunch of flowers. Her response is a smile and a friendly greeting. John's purpose was to patch up their argument without going through a heated debate about who was at fault. The effect it had on Marie was exactly as he intended; he achieved his goal.

Sometimes our messages do not have the outcome or effect that we intended. **Unintentional effects** are the indirect influences and unpredictable results of the communication. A mother, for example, who is worried that her son sits at a desk all day and gets little exercise, may try to persuade him to start jogging in the morning before leaving for work. To her surprise, he becomes angry and tells her to get off his back and stop nagging — her good intentions certainly had an unintentional effect.

 The relationship between purpose and effect can also be illustrated by means of an example from mass communication. One of the purposes of television, for example, is to provide entertainment. The intended effect is that viewers should be able to relax in their leisure time. A negative, unintended effect is that television entertainment often has the effect of inhibiting conversation between family members. On the other hand, a positive unintended outcome is that television entertainment sometimes stimulates interest in previously unknown topics, such as the study of wild life.

2.3   Maslow's hierarchy of needs

Each of us has our own sets of needs that motivate our communication and our responses to messages. While not everyone's priorities are identical, our needs resemble one another's sufficiently for scholars to have developed theories that establish the relationship between needs and communication.

☐ Maslow, a well-known psychologist, distinguished a **hierarchy** of five basic levels of need in 1954: survival, safety, social, esteem and self-actualisation, which are depicted as a pyramid in Figure 2.1. Maslow maintained that needs have to be aroused and remain unsatisfied for them to motivate behaviour. As you study the hierarchy (a sysem of persons or things arranged in a graded order), think about how each of the needs motivates your own communication behaviour (cf Wilson, Hantz & Hanna 1989; Kreps 1990; Bredenkamp 1996).

Maslow's hierarchy of needs

☐ **Survival** Maslow contends that the most basic of all needs is the physical wellbeing or survival of the individual. Our physiological needs include the need for air, food, water, sleep and reproduction of the species.

☐ **Safety** or security is the next level of needs in the hierarchy. We need to feel secure and free from danger. We also have a need for structure, predictability and law and order in our lives. Such needs are fulfilled by having shelter, a job, and feeling protected against bodily harm. For example, rising crime rates in our neighbourhood may lead us to install a burglar alarm system in our homes.

☐ **Social** The third level of needs, the social need, is the need to develop meaningful relationships with others. This category is related to the need to be accepted by others, to have friends, to belong to a group and to be appreciated and loved by others. Social needs usually remain dominant until they have been satisfied, for instance in marriage, in close relationships with friends or by joining a sports club or trade union.

☐ **Esteem** The fourth level of needs, the esteem need, is the need to respect yourself and be respected by others. Enhancing your self-respect or self-image may lead to activities such as private study or practice in a sport or skill, whereas needs pertaining to the regard of others lead to activities which will increase your prestige and power, for instance being promoted at work, or your socioeconomic status. In other words, it is the need not only to feel successful in what you do, but to receive public recognition for your efforts.

☐ **Self-actualisation** The most difficult need to satisfy is self-actualisation, the need to fulfil your potential as a human being and achieve all that you are capable of being. Self-actualisation includes learning more about yourself and the world around you, excelling in the activities you perform (such as your studies or work responsibilities), becoming more satisfied with yourself, expressing your creativity (whether in art or cooking), and generally feeling that you are growing as an individual. On this level, we find, among others, writers, composers, artists, innovators and campaign leaders.

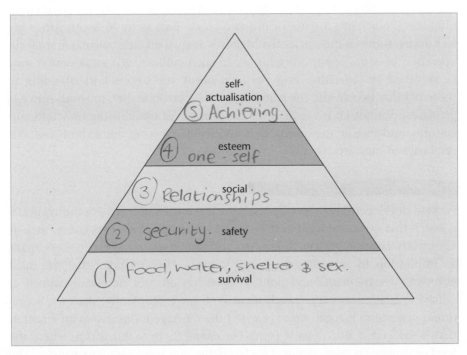

Figure 2.1 Maslow's hierarchy of needs

Maslow contends that these needs follow a hierarchical order and that people have to satisfy lower-order needs, such as hunger and thirst, before higher-order needs become important. The importance they attach to particular messages reflects these needs. For example, Maslow would say that when you are in physical danger, messages about safety usually take priority over others. However, if you were starving, you might decide to risk your physical safety to obtain food. The person who has been retrenched and is worried about how he is going to pay the rent (a safety need) is more concerned to find a job than with the admiration of his friends (esteem need). According to Maslow, self-actualisation only becomes important to people who feel secure in the knowledge that they have gained the respect (esteem need) and companionship (social need) of family, friends and colleagues.

While the hierarchy illustrates how our inner needs motivate us to communicate with others, Maslow's views also have shortcomings. The most important is that the hierarchy reflects the society and culture of which he was a part. People from other cultures do not always agree with the hierarchical order in which he has placed the needs. Also, as Burton and Dimbleby (1995) explain, Maslow's highest need in the hierarchy is the product of a Western, industrial, individualised culture where the highest value is placed on self-actualisation — being able to fulfil your personal physical and emotional needs and desires, and ultimately to achieve a sense of independence. But, as we in South Africa are well aware, some cultures place the highest value on qualities such as mutual co-operation or equal opportunity for all. In such cultures, self-actualisation may be achieved by repressing your personal needs and desires and attending to those of other people and the community. We conclude that, in South Africa, a great deal of research is required for the purpose of establishing how different cultures understand the needs that motivate our communication and our responses to messages.

2.4   Packard's theory of needs

Packard developed his theory by studying the results of intensive motivational research that was conducted in the 1950s to determine how persuaders, such as advertisers, political leaders, fundraisers and public relations practitioners, make an impression by appealing to people's needs. He concluded that the most effective advertisements and political speeches are not necessarily aimed at satisfying basic needs (the needs identified, for example, by Maslow). Sometimes, persuasion is more effective when the message is directed at an emotion that is associated with a basic need. For example, in South Africa, where the level of violence is high, political leaders delivering speeches often associate the emotion of fear with the need for safety. They promise us 'peace of mind'. By associating peace of mind with a political party, they hope to persuade us to vote for them. Packard called such associated needs 'hidden needs'. He identified eight hidden needs which we discuss below.

We would not like to give the impression that all communication is aimed at persuasion. Persuasion is but one of the functions of communication. We discuss Packard's theory because it provides an example of the relationship between theory and research which we discuss in Section 2.5 below. Packard's research has generated a theory which has an outcome in the real world — it is used in the field of advertising. At the same time, studying Packard's theory should make you aware of how the persuasive function of communication motivates your own behaviour. In spite of the time that has elapsed since Packard conducted his investigations, we can see how many persuasive messages today, especially those contained in advertisements, are aimed at his eight hidden needs (cf Larson 1989; Larson 2004). The following discussion is based on Larson's interpretation of Packard's work.

2.4.1   Need for emotional security

Packard found that people have a need for emotional security as well as physical safety. Larson suggests that we live in one of the most insecure periods of human history. War and terrorism are on the increase. Many countries are unable to control inflation and recession. The environment is becoming more and more polluted with potentially deadly wastes. The traditional family unit is breaking down. AIDS is causing the deaths of millions of people. People feel unsafe on the streets and in their homes. Packard maintains that living in such circumstances poses threats to our emotional security, and we react by buying products that symbolise or promise physical safety. In the 1950s, he found that Americans bought home freezers, for instance, because it allowed them to think that they might survive a nuclear attack or another depression. Air-conditioners allowed people to feel their homes were secure because they could keep the windows locked. The need for emotional security identified by Packard still exists and is still being appealed to by advertisers, politicians and demagogues.

2.4.2   Need for assurance of worth

Packard noted that in the increasingly competitive and impersonal society in which we live, people need to feel valued for what they do. In the 1950s, and still today, many women who work as homemakers see themselves as mere drudges. Product advertisers frequently appeal to the homemaker's need to feel appreciated to sell their products. Think about advertisements on television urging women to use a particular brand of washing powder. The appeal is often less to the qualities of the washing powder but to the implication that if she switches to Brand X she will be a better wife and mother, and her family will be happier. Similarly, many advertisements promise that you will be appreciated if you 'remember her with flowers' or enrol for a self-improvement course.

Larson finds it disconcerting that many Americans today seem to find reassurance of worth in material goods rather than in their relationships with the people in their personal and public lives.

2.4.3   Need for ego gratification

Packard found that many of the consumers he studied not only needed to be reassured of their basic self-worth but also to have their egos stroked as if they were really special — a step beyond mere self-worth. Ego-gratification — the feeling that 'I'm OK' — can come from within ourselves or from the people with whom we come into contact. As with the reassurance of worth, in today's world it is often provided by products, services or ideas which promise us 'OK' feelings if we use them. Many financial institutions, for example, stroke our egos by promising to tailor an account that specifically meets our individual needs. The implication is that 'you're somebody special'.

2.4.4   Need for creative outlets

In modern technological societies, more and more of the work formerly done by individuals is now being done by technology. With mass production and the assembly line to increase productivity, many workers feel merely like a cog in the wheel of the machine they operate. Packard found that people need a substitute for expressing the creativity for which there is no longer an outlet in their work. As technology increases, people seem to need to demonstrate their own handicraft skills. Given this need, Packard concludes that it is no wonder that gourmet cooking, flower arranging, pottery and jewellery-making classes are popular, and that home-improvement tools and other hobby-type products sell successfully. You can probably think of many situations in which advertisers use the need for creative outlets to get you to buy their product or idea.

2.4.5   Need for love objects

Packard's interviews established that people have a need for a love object. Those whose children have left home cope with the 'empty nest syndrome' by replacing the child love object with a pet. Advertisements for pet foods play on this need by humanising pets and suggesting that the food is like our own, is of the highest quality, and that it contains all the minerals and vitamins needed to promote healthy growth. Larson draws our attention to the fact that some homes for the elderly are using pets as therapy for their patients, many of whom have a profound need for a love object. Would you agree with Larson's suggestion that the popularity of movie stars with sex appeal could be that they act as love objects for people who have the need to replace the lover who has not yet appeared on the scene?

2.4.6   Need for a sense of power

Packard found that Americans, more than any other culture, seem to be programmed to chase power and to gratify the need for this symbolically. Think about the number of advertisements that appeal to the sense of power by showing a motor car speeding along an open road. Whether the product is a motor car, lawnmower, electric drill or a cellphone, power is the emphasis. Larson notes that even advertisements for spare parts appeal to the need for power by featuring the phrase 'heavy-duty' to convince you that you are a getting a powerful replacement part.

2.4.7   Need for roots

Packard found that in an era of increasing mobility, people need replacements for the traditional roots that offer a sense of security and permanence. People whose jobs require that they move to new places tend to overcome their feelings of insecurity by looking for their favourite supermarket chain or the brand names they used 'at home'. Advertisers appeal to these feelings by marketing products that are made in the 'old-fashioned way' or that suggest a sense of family — home-baked apple pie, cereal made only from natural ingredients, grandma's rusks. A South African banking institution promises that, should you move to a new town, you will retain the same account number — a 'piece of home' that you can bring with you.

2.4.8   Need for immortality

The eighth hidden need is the need for immortality — the belief that life will go on in much the same way as at present. Packard suggests that the fear of dying and the need to believe in an ongoing influence on the lives of others underlies many insurance appeals. The breadwinner is made to feel that by buying insurance, he buys 'life after death'. His wife will be able to continue living in the family home and his children will be educated even if he is not there. Other products make a similar appeal to the fear of ageing and death — margarine that contains no cholesterol, face creams to make you look younger, vitamins that make you feel as energetic as you did 10 years ago. Larson maintains that we are not buying the margarine or the face cream or the vitamins. We are buying hope — hope for youth and immortality.

Having made you aware of the appeals that persuaders make to our needs, we leave you with the following question: Do you sometimes buy services or products because they appeal to a hidden need?

2.5   Communication as a scientific discipline

Generally speaking, a demand for scientific knowledge is characteristic of the modern age. The scientific study of communication is undertaken for various reasons. The need for more effective communication in institutions such as schools, factories, hospitals and banks for instance, is often emphasised. To be able to determine whether communication takes place in the most effective way, we need to understand how it may contribute to or interfere with the efficient operation of such institutions. Or, as is the purpose of this book, we may want to acquire knowledge and understanding of what communication is, how it works and how it influences people's lives. Unless we understand why we and other people act in the way we do, we will hardly be able to explain why communication sometimes goes wrong, how communication problems may be solved and how communication between people may be enhanced.

Since we are constantly involved in communication in our everyday lives, we have naturally developed some notions about it and what it is all about. Our knowledge not only derives from our intuition, or from what we personally think or feel about it, but from other sources as well. For example, we may have asked someone whom we consider to be knowledgeable to explain something about communication to us, or we may have read about it in a book or magazine. Other sources of knowledge include folklore, traditional wisdom, people in authority and common sense. The problem with this type of knowledge is that we cannot be sure that it offers a true picture of communication in real life. Our knowledge and assumptions about communication need to be tested by comparing them with real-life examples of communication encounters to determine whether they are indeed 'true'. For this purpose we need scientific study.

2.5.1   Scientific study of communication

Scientific study involves a special way of acquiring knowledge, a way that requires the use of the so-called **scientific method**. In contrast to the other ways of gaining knowledge mentioned above, the scientific method follows a systematic and disciplined approach. This type of study is carefully planned and is conducted by generally accepted procedures and rules which guide the investigator in observing people engaged in communication. The results of scientific study, that is, the results of **scientific research**, are assessed with reference to generally accepted standards applied by all investigators.

The results of communication research have provided knowledge and under-standing of what communication is, how it works and how it influences people's lives. Unless we understand why we and other people act in the way we do, we will hardly be able to explain why communication sometimes goes wrong, how communication problems may be solved and how communication between people may be enhanced.

You might well ask how communication researchers begin their studies. The simplest answer is that any scientific study begins with theory.

2.5.2   Theory and theories

Theory is the basis of the scientific understanding of any phenomenon in any discipline. You theorise all the time. You decide to visit a friend, and hearing music coming from her bedroom, you open the door and say, "Hi, Carol!" She doesn't return your greeting. You might explain her apparent rudeness in one of the following ways: perhaps Carol doesn't want to see me today and I should come back another time; perhaps I have offended her in some way and she is deliberately ignoring me; or, because the music is rather loud, perhaps she did not hear me. These are all **theories** that you have formed about the situation. You think that your third theory is the most likely explanation so you test it by repeating your greeting a little louder. She turns around, smiles and says, "Hi, Nomsa, how nice to see you." You can now discard your other two theories in the knowledge that you are welcome and that you have not offended her in any way. Your prediction about her unusual behaviour was correct. Communication theorists also have ideas about a situation and test them in different ways to find out whether or not they are valid.

Bear the example about Carol and Nomsa in mind as you continue reading. First, it is important to understand the difference between the concepts of 'theory' and 'a theory' (or theories). In the example above, Nomsa was drawing on the knowledge that she had about her relationships with other people to arrive at three different ideas about the situation she found herself in. The body of knowledge we have about a particular subject is called **theory**. In our discipline, communication science, we need theory to help us to understand, explain, predict and improve communication because communication is vital in every aspect of our lives — as individuals or in the groups and organisations that constitute our society.

When planning scientific research, the researcher first reviews existing scientific knowledge (communication theory) about the matter or matters in which she or he is interested. Such knowledge could direct the researcher's attention to a particular aspect of communication which she or he may be interested in investigating. Communication is, however, a complex, multifaceted and ever-changing phenomenon. Existing knowledge may therefore be represented in different ways. These different ways of looking at communication are **theories of communication**.

Theories suggest to us what real-life communication looks like. Each theory describes an aspect or a number of aspects of communication. A theory is in fact a way of making sense of a situation in order to explain how or why something occurs. Theories have been described as maps of reality. Like a map, they guide us through unfamiliar territory because they are designed to describe, explain and/or predict reality.

As in Nomsa's experience, theories often represent tentative solutions to a problem. But the view offered by any theory must be tested by research. The research results may show that a particular theory does not offer a true representation of those aspects of communication it describes (in which case the theory is revised or a new theory is formulated) or that it does offer an accurate picture of the matters studied. As you study the theories in this textbook, remember that theories are not just abstract ideas. They provide a basis for application in real situations. A theory about improving communication in hospitals might suggest that nurses, for instance, require different types of communication skill in order to perform their tasks more effectively. In practice, this theory could be used to train nurses to communicate in different ways with patients, doctors, social workers, administrators and so on.

2.5.3   Concepts

Theories are made up of different concepts. Think of them as the building blocks of theory. A **concept** is a word to which all scientists in a field of study assign the same meaning so that they can understand each other. We always formulate our thoughts in concepts. We cannot think of an object (a motor car), an event (a funeral) or a person (a well-known political leader) without forming a mental image or concept of the object, event or person. Concepts are as indispensable to scientific study as they are in our everyday conversations. In scientific study, scientists deliberately try to avoid confusion by consistently using concepts with the same meanings. At school, for example, the concepts or terms you learned in order to make sense of mathematics were very different to the concepts you learned about in biology or history, but you all ascribed the same meanings to the words. Scientists use communication concepts to explain their theories by arranging them in a logical way to show the relationships between them.

2.5.4   Models

Scientific concepts are not only used to build theories. They also occur in communication models. **Models** are usually presented in the form of diagrams. Their basic purpose is to capture the essential features of a real situation in a simplified form so that it can be described, explained and understood more easily.

☐ A model can explain the process of communication between two people by showing the relationships between various concepts. In this way they help us to visualise communication more clearly.

☐ Models often fulfil a predictive function. They allow us to answer 'if . . . then' questions. For example, a model can simulate the expected growth projections of an organisation. If we employ two additional telephonists, will we then have eliminated delays in connecting clients to the relevant departments? In this way, models help us answer questions about the future.

☐ Models can also fulfil a control function. They help us recognise and diagnose problems by showing us how to control certain conditions that impede effective communication. For instance, a model of intercultural communication can help pinpoint at which stage of the process misunderstanding occurs between employees of different cultural backgrounds. Steps can then be taken to change the relevant conditions.

Although they aid understanding, models also have drawbacks. Perhaps their greatest limitation is that they are necessarily incomplete. Models simplify a complex phenomenon such as communication by trying to capture its essence in a one-dimensional diagram. As a result, a model usually represents only the aspect of communication a particular theorist wishes to emphasise and eliminates other aspects. Nevertheless, while models cannot fully represent what happens in reality, they serve a useful purpose in providing a simplified representation of a complex process, thereby making it easier for us to understand. Think about an architect's plan for a house. It makes it easier for us to picture what the house will look like and to visualise the relationship between the different rooms in the house. But it cannot give us a complete picture of what the house will look like when it has been built.

2.5.5 Communication research

We said earlier that theories often represent tentative solutions to a problem or a communication issue. But the view offered by any theory must be tested by research to establish the validity of the theory. Remember that Nomsa tested her theory that Carol did not hear her greeting because the music was too loud by repeating her greeting. The following is a brief overview of five different research methods in communication science: historical research, survey research, content analysis, field research and experimental research (cf du Plooy 2002).

☐ *Historical research* is concerned with events and people of the past. But as such information is no longer available to us for direct observation, we have to read and interpret the written documents, records and artefacts people have left behind. Thus, historical research involves studying the messages and interpreting the significant communication of people in past societies. A study of the development of film production in South Africa from 1960 to 2000 to discover how a particular genre changed in response to the needs of a changing South African society is an example of historical research.

❏ **Survey research** involves collecting information from a group of people to describe their abilities, opinions, attitudes, beliefs or knowledge with regard to a particular topic or issue. A questionnaire sent by the South African Broadcasting Corporation (SABC) to all its licence holders to find out whether subscribers are satisfied with programming on SABC1, for instance, is an example of survey research.

❏ There are many definitions of **content analysis** as a research method in the social sciences. In communication research, content analysis is a method whereby the researcher can measure the amount of something (eg violence or racial discrimination) found in a representative sample of a mass communication medium, such as newspapers or television. Content analysis is the method chosen when the researcher wants to determine, for example, whether the portrayal of women in soap operas is more stereotypical than the portrayal of women in detective series.

❏ **Experimental research** is a rigorous and highly controlled method of research. It attempts to account for the influence of one factor or multiple factors on a given situation. For instance, a researcher in communication science might want to ascertain the impact of noise on the recall of radio news. The researcher would select two similar groups of people and expose them to the same radio broadcast. The only difference is that one group is exposed to the broadcast in a quiet environment and the other in a noisy environment. The two groups are then measured and compared for their recall of the content of the news.

❏ **Field research** is particularly suitable when the researcher wants to make observations (eg of people, cultural groups, organisations, families) in their natural settings. The research is conducted at the place where the phenomenon occurs. Field research allows the researcher to understand the world from the perspective of the people being studied and to learn about their attitudes and behaviour and the meanings they attach to that behaviour. Field research can be conducted in various ways. One of the methods is by means of focus groups. A focus group usually consists of six to 12 people who are interviewed simultaneously. A discussion leader guides the participants in a relatively free discussion about a topic, such as consumers' preferences about the packaging of a new product or the attitude of employees in an organisation towards affirmative action.

2.6   Communication competence

What is **communication competence**? Think about the two definitions that follow.

> Larson *et al* (1978:16) define communication competence as "the ability of an individual to demonstrate knowledge of the appropriate communication behaviour in a given situation".
>
> "Communication competence is the impression that communicative behaviour is both appropriate and effective in a given situation" (Spitzberg 2000:375).

Despite the more than 20 years that have elapsed between the two definitions, they are very similar. Verderber & Verderber (2002) explain that communication behaviour is effective when it achieves its goals and it is appropriate when it conforms to what is expected in a given situation. In addition, Larson's definition stresses that knowledge and the ability of the individual to demonstrate it are essential determinants of competence. We demonstrate communication competence through the verbal messages we send and the nonverbal behaviour that accompanies them. In other words, we develop communication skills. But competence also requires knowledge about the theoretical principles on which a particular action or behaviour is grounded (cf Dickson, Hargie & Morrow 1989:13). Taking these arguments into account, the approach to communication competence in this text book is a combination of 'knowing that' and 'knowing how' or, to put it simply, a combination of understanding and skills.

Communication competence is not a natural ability but, like any other skill, it can be learned. We will only be able to improve our communication competence if we are motivated, that is, if we want to acquire the necessary knowledge and skills. Your personal commitment to spending time and energy — your *motivation* — will determine the measure of success you derive from studying this introductory course in communication. The remainder of this book provides you with the theoretical knowledge on which communication in various contexts is based, as well as practical advice on how to perform specific communication skills. We encourage you to use whatever opportunities you can to practise these skills. Remember that, as your communication skills improve and other people begin to perceive you as a competent communicator, so your confidence in your abilities and your motivation to succeed will increase.

You might be interested in the following information provided by Tubbs & Moss (2003:7): A 10-year study conducted by researchers at Carnegie Mellon University identified the most important skills that differentiated between average job performers and outstanding job performers. They found that interpersonal communication, relationship building, leadership, teamwork, networking and persuasion were some of the most important skills for job performance and career success.

As you will see, all these topics are covered in this book.

Scenario 2.1

In Section 2.3 we said that people from other cultures do not always agree with the hierarchical order in which Maslow placed basic human needs. Write down the hierarchy that you feel reflects your culture's understanding of basic needs. Then compare your list with those of fellow students of different cultures and take note of the differences. If there are indeed differences, do you think your investigation helps your understanding of how other people communicate their needs?

Summary

The first part of this chapter looked briefly at the functions communication performs in our lives. It described these functions or purposes of communication in terms of the needs they fulfil and the effects they have. The chapter then considered two theories that examine our needs and explained the relationship between communication and the satisfaction of needs: Maslow's hierarchy of needs and Packard's hidden needs. As a preparation for your formal study of communication, it then introduced you to the study of communication as a scientific discipline by explaining how communication scientists use theory and research to reach an understanding of an aspect of communication. The last part of the chapter brought to your attention the nature and importance of communication competence. The chapter ended with a scenario based on Maslow's theory.

Test yourself

1. Define and explain five purposes of communication, using examples from your experience of communication.
2. Explain the relationship between the purposes and effects of communication.
3. Identify and give an example of each component of Maslow's hierarchy of needs. Does Maslow's hierarchy help you better to understand the needs that motivate your behaviour?

4. List the eight hidden needs identified by Packard and provide an example of how advertisers appeal to the emotions associated with at least two of these needs. Does Packard's theory help you to understand how persuasive messages appeal to needs of which you are not always consciously aware?
5. Explain the meaning of the terms *scientific study, theory, theories, concept, model* and *research*. Use your own examples to illustrate your answer.
6. Write down as many communication skills you can think of that you would like to improve. For example, "I would like to feel less nervous about having to speak to people I meet for the first time". At the end of this course, come back to this list and see whether you have indeed achieved your goals.

EXECUTIVE SUMMARY
Functions of communication

1 Functions
   - ☐ physical and psychological needs
   - ☐ relationships
   - ☐ sense of self
   - ☐ information
   - ☐ decision making
   - ☐ persuasion
2 Maslow's hierarchy of needs
   - ☐ survival
   - ☐ safety
   - ☐ social
   - ☐ esteem
   - ☐ self-actualisation
3 Packard's hidden needs
   - ☐ emotional security
   - ☐ assurance of worth
   - ☐ ego gratification
   - ☐ creative outlets
   - ☐ love objects
   - ☐ sense of power
   - ☐ roots
   - ☐ immorality
4 Scientific study of communication
   - ☐ theory and theories
   - ☐ concepts
   - ☐ models
5 Communication research
   - ☐ historical research
   - ☐ survey research
   - ☐ content analysis
   - ☐ experimental research
   - ☐ field research

3 The communication process

Overview

The study of human communication is over two thousand years old. In the 4th century BC, for example, the ancient Chinese philosopher Confucius, and the classical Greek philosopher Aristotle, were both formulating ideas about communication. The study of communication is of particular interest today because of rapid developments in new technologies for producing and transmitting (sending) information. But communication scholars agree that, despite the proliferation of communication technologies, the human communication problems we have today are not basically different from those that people experienced hundreds of years ago. The consensus of opinion is that we are not going to solve communication problems by teaching people to master technology, but rather by helping them to gain insight into the phenomenon of communication. One way of understanding communication is to study it scientifically in order to come closer to answering the question: What is communication?

In this chapter we provide the foundation on which the scientific study of communication is based. We begin by discussing the complex nature of communication. We first consider three definitions of communication and then gain further insight by examining the following dimensions of communication: verbal and nonverbal communication, oral and written communication, formal and informal communication, and intentional and unintentional communication. In the next part of the chapter we explain the components that comprise the process of communication. We then discuss various models which illustrate different views of the communication process. The development of communication models and theories over the years reflects the increasingly broad range of topics covered in communication studies. We provide a brief overview of some of the theoretical developments in the field to help you gain an understanding of the complexity of communication studies. The last section of this chapter introduces you to the different contexts in which communication is studied today: intrapersonal communication, interpersonal communication, small group communication, public speaking and mass communication.

Learning outcomes

At the end of this chapter you should be able to:

1. Define communication in three ways and explain how each definition provides a different view of the concept, using examples from your own experience of communication.
2. Explain how the dimensions of communication contribute to its complex nature.
3. Define and explain each of the components that comprise the process of communication, using examples from your own experience of communication.
4. Describe the various models in this chapter, explaining the differences between them.
5. Define five contexts in which communication takes place. Explain the basis on which we differentiate between the contexts, illustrating your answers with examples from your own experience of communication.
6. Apply the principles you have learned in this chapter to everyday experiences of communication.
7. Answer the questions based on the scenario at the end of this chapter.

Introduction

We would probably all agree that we know what communication is and that we can recognise it when we experience it. However, words are used in many different ways by different people. Some people immediately think about a conversation between friends, a politician making a persuasive speech, a minister delivering a sermon or even the exchange of glances between lovers. Others immediately associate communication with mass media, such as newspapers, radio and television. To some, communication brings to mind computers, cellphones and satellites. Communication is also used to describe traffic signals, Morse code, the sign languages of the deaf, uniforms, flags and telephone calls. A child's cry, a mother's kiss, a facial expression, graffiti on the wall of a public restroom, even silence, are also referred to as 'communication'. It is equally difficult to describe why we use communication. People communicate to establish relationships with others, to express feelings and opinions, to share experiences, to work together efficiently, to be entertained, and to persuade others to think as they do. What is very clear is that communication is used to describe many things. For this reason, it is difficult to arrive at an exact definition of communication.

3.1   Defining communication

As a student of communication, you may already have turned to your favourite dictionary to find a clear definition of the term. The *Oxford English Dictionary*, for example, will provide you with not just a single definition, but 12 different meanings! Should you search further in different books on the subject, you would find that there is little agreement among communication scholars about a definition — nearly every book on communication offers its own definition. In a survey of the literature on communication, Dance and Larson (1973) found that there were 126 definitions, and since then even more definitions have been formulated.

One of the reasons for the proliferation of definitions is that there is no single approach to the study of communication. Definitions differ according to the theorist's views about communication. In the scientific study of communication, there are two general and basic views about communication: a **technical view** and a **meaning-centred view**.

Theorists who adopt a technical view are concerned with how accurately and efficiently messages can be transferred from one person to another along a channel such as a telephone wire or the airwaves that carry sound and pictures to radios and television sets. They attempt to identify ways of increasing the clarity and accuracy of the message and concentrate on improving the tools and techniques that promote efficient communication, such as clear telephone lines or faster computers. Communication is seen as a linear (one-way) sequence of events from Person A to Person B. From a technical point of view, communication can be defined very simply as 'sending and receiving messages', or 'the transmission of messages from one person to another'. However, solving technical or engineering problems does not tell us much about the complexity of communication or the human aspect of communication.

A second and more complex view of communication is that, in addition to the transmission of messages, it involves their interpretation and meaning. This view considers communication as a human phenomenon and the central aspect of human existence. Our ability to communicate is what distinguishes us from other forms of life. Meaning-centred theorists concentrate on issues such as what motivates people to communicate in the first place, how they give meaning to each other's messages, what happens between them during communication, and how they use language to create and exchange meaningful messages. The emphasis is on the interaction between the participants in communication. From this point of view, communication can be defined as 'a dynamic process of exchanging meaningful messages'.

Defining communication as a process brings us closer to an understanding of its complexity. In contrast to the technical view, considering communication as a process means that it is not a fixed, static thing; rather, it is dynamic, never-ending and ever-changing. It does not have a beginning or an end, nor does it follow a fixed sequence of events.

The use of the term 'process' also tells us that communication is characterised by continuous evolution and change. We change others and are changed by them when we communicate. All the communication encounters you have had in the past, as well as all the information, ideas and opinions you have gathered, gradually change you and your behaviour, and consequently the way you communicate with others. According to Dimbleby and Burton (1985:31) "everything that we learn, every bit of information that we acquire changes our behaviour to some extent in the end. Every piece of communication which we experience may affect our attitudes and beliefs in some small way".

A process is also irreversible, which means that each communication encounter you have influences the one that follows. How you communicated with someone in the past can help or hinder your communication with them in the future. Should you have an argument with your partner before going to work, for example, your feelings may cause you to lash out at a colleague who asks an innocent question. The problem is that the next day, you and your colleague are unable to communicate as comfortably as before. Your reaction to the argument of the previous day has had an effect on your future communication with your colleague (cf Barker & Gaut 1996).

An extension of the process definition is the **transactional definition** of communication. Contemporary theorists regard communication not only as an interactive process of exchanging meaningful messages, but as a transaction between the participants during which a relationship develops between them. A transactional process is one in which the people communicating are mutually responsible for the outcome of the communication encounter as they transmit information, create meaning and elicit responses. The focus is on the quality of the relationship that develops between them, as well as on the transfer and interpretation of messages. Communication becomes a reciprocal process in which meaning is negotiated through the exchange of messages. From this perspective, communication is defined as a transactional process of exchanging messages and negotiating meaning to establish and maintain relationships (cf Verderber 1990). We prefer this definition because the concept of 'transaction' suggests that the participants must arrive at some mutual agreement about the meaning of their messages for communication to be effective and for their relationship to be satisfying.

3.2   Dimensions of communication

The definitions we have discussed so far make it clear that the communication process is more complex than one person sending a message to another person. Considering questions such as the following brings us closer to an understanding of the nature of communication: Are we communicating when we do not use words? To what extent is communication intentional? In the next section, we gain further insight into the complexity of communication by examining the dimensions of verbal and nonverbal communication, oral and written communication, formal and informal communication, and intentional and unintentional communication. The discussion is based largely on Barker and Gaut (1996).

3.2.1   Verbal and nonverbal communication

When we think of communication, we tend to think about spoken messages. But the way in which we understand messages depends on more than words. The tone of voice, gestures, use of space and touch, facial expressions, accent and dress of the communicator all influence our understanding. For example, when we give someone directions, we often point and use other gestures to clarify our spoken instructions. Communication scholars divide the 'language' of communication into two primary categories: verbal and nonverbal communication.

Verbal communication refers to the spoken or written signs called words which make up a particular language, such as English or isiZulu. People who speak the same language understand one another because they usually ascribe similar meanings to words. **Nonverbal communication** refers to all human communication that does not use written or spoken signs, such as a smile or a nod of the head. Although nonverbal signs have socially shared meanings, such meanings are not always universal. In traditional African society, for example, it is generally considered rude for someone to be higher than a person he or she respects. While a teacher entering the room in a Western school would expect the class to rise and greet her, most rural African pupils would remain seated with castdown eyes and not speak until spoken to (cf Finlayson 1991). When we study communication, we cannot separate the two categories because our clothing or tone of voice, for example, communicates a message even as we speak. Verbal and nonverbal signs thus work together to convey the meaning of a message. We discuss nonverbal communication in more detail in Chapter 5.

3.2.2   Oral and written communication

Oral and written communication both involve the use of words. **Oral communication** refers to messages that are transmitted aloud. We constantly participate in oral communication in our daily lives by speaking and listening.

We may have a conversation with friends, watch a programme on television, listen to some music on the radio, attend a lecture or telephone a classmate. From these examples, we can conclude that oral messages generally involve both verbal and nonverbal communication.

Written communication is taking place right now as you read this book. Although this type of communication involves mainly words, it also has a nonverbal dimension. A hand-written birthday message, for example, usually evokes a different response than a printed card that was bought in a store — it communicates a somewhat more personal message. The graphics or diagrams that accompany the words in this book also communicate information nonverbally. Oral and written communication are sometimes used together. Many advertisements use graphics to make the oral message clearer. You may have seen an advertisement for toothpaste, for example, that uses graphics to reinforce the oral message that plaque causes damage to our gums if we do not brush our teeth regularly. Although oral and written messages differ in a number of ways, what is important is that they both involve the creation and sending of messages.

Figure 3.1   Using graphics and words in an advertisement

3.2.3 Formal and informal communication

Two speakers debating an issue at a political gathering, the news reader on television, a group of students chatting on campus, or some children playing games together, are all involved in communication. Whether we communicate formally or informally depends largely on the situation in which we find ourselves. When we are involved in **formal communication**, such as a job interview, we pay more attention to both our verbal and nonverbal messages. For instance, we tend to avoid using slang in our conversation, try to express ourselves clearly when answering questions, and pay particular attention to grammar. We are also more concerned about the image our nonverbal communication conveys. For example, we would dress carefully for a job interview, make sure that our hair is neat and consciously sit up straight to create the desired impression.

When we are involved in **informal communication**, such as talking to friends at a party, we are more at ease and can communicate more naturally. You are probably aware from your own experience that, when you communicate informally, your verbal messages are less structured and you pay less attention to nonverbal messages, such as clothing and posture. While you might feel that you are being yourself by sitting on the floor at a friend's house, for example, it is unlikely that you would do so in your boss's office — you would not be communicating the desired image.

3.2.4 Intentional and unintentional communication

All communication has a purpose — we communicate for a reason. However, we are not always aware that we have communicated a message.

- ❑ *Intentional communication* occurs when we communicate with a specific goal in mind. For example, at your graduation ceremony, you intentionally thank your parents for all the help and support they have given you over the years. You reinforce your message nonverbally with a smile and a hug. Or, you engage in conversation with someone at a party because you want to come across as friendly. You also know that the speaker at a wedding, for instance, deliberately includes several jokes in his or her speech to get the guests to relax and enjoy themselves. You turn on the radio with the intention of catching up on the latest news. However, there are times when we communicate messages we never intended.

- ❑ *Unintentional communication* refers to the occasions when communication takes place without the communicator being aware of it. A friend might tell you that he is not upset by the fact that you forgot to call on his birthday, but the look on his face tells another story. While our verbal communication is almost always intentional, our unintentional messages are usually nonverbal. The way that people use gestures, tone of voice and other nonverbal signs often speaks louder than words. Then there is another type of unintentional communication. Consider the following example: a young man whistling cheerfully passes you on the street. You think to yourself, 'He's in a good mood today'. The young man, of course, is totally unaware that he has communicated a message to you, a complete stranger. The point to remember is that communication has occurred, whether it was intended or not.

3.3   Components of the communication process

The definitions and dimensions we have discussed thus far have probably given you the impression that communication is not an easy topic to study. One way to understand the communication process is to study it as a system. A **system** is any entity that is composed of interdependent parts working together to achieve an intended goal. An example of a system is the human body. The individual parts such as the heart, lungs, liver, kidneys and so on, all work together to keep the body functioning efficiently. Should something happen to prevent the lungs, for example, from obtaining oxygen, it is not only the lungs that are affected. The heart is put under strain and this in turn affects the blood supply to all the other organs. We can study communication in much the same way by identifying its components, or elements, and analysing how the components affect one another during the communication process. We should then have a better idea of what happens when we communicate and perhaps be able to improve our communication knowledge and skills.

We use communication terms or concepts to identify and explain the components of the process. The definitions we give to the components in the communication process turn them into concepts. As we discussed in Chapter 2, a **concept** is a word to which all scientists in a field of study (such as psychology, law, medicine, communication) attach the same meaning so as to enable them to understand each other. Later in this chapter we will see that concepts are indispensable for describing communication models.

Figure 3.2 gives us a visual representation of the communication process. Take note that, although we discuss the components separately for the purpose of analysis, they are not isolated entities, but occur almost simultaneously as the process evolves. The discussion that follows is based mainly on Verderber (1990); Hybels and Weaver (1995); Barker and Gaut (1996); and Verderber and Verderber (2002).

3.3.1   People

The people involved in the communication process are usually referred to as the 'message source' and the 'message receiver'. However, source and receiver sound like technical terms, and as we are discussing human communication, we prefer to call them 'communicator' and 'recipient'. Because communication is a

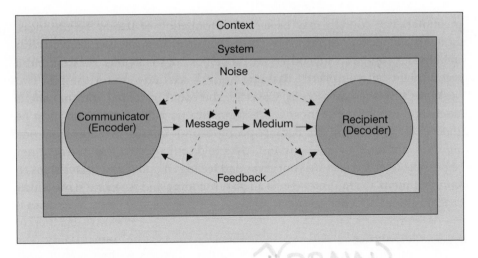

Figure 3.2 The communication process

dynamic process, people are never exclusively communicators or recipients. Each participant in the interaction plays both roles.

❑ As a *communicator*, you intentionally form purposeful messages and attempt to express them to others through verbal and nonverbal signs. You usually use both words and gestures to put your message across. Your purpose may be the need to share your thoughts and feelings, or perhaps to persuade someone to change an attitude, opinion or behaviour. Or, your purpose may simply be to entertain a group of friends by telling a joke.

❑ As a *recipient*, you do not merely receive messages. You are an active participant in the communication process in that you intentionally and consciously pay attention to the message in order to understand and interpret it.

❑ When you respond to the message, you become the communicator and your partner is the recipient. In fact, you are usually *communicator–recipient* — both receiving and sending messages at the same time. For example, while you listen to your best friend tell you about the bad news she received last night, you may instinctively put out a hand to touch her because she is upset — you are listening to her and communicating a message of sympathy at the same time. When you come across the terms 'communicator' and 'recipient' (or 'sender' and 'receiver'), remember that they are used more as a convenience than as an accurate description of the roles of the participants in the communication process.

3.3.2   Message

Communication takes place through the sending and receiving of messages. The **message** has a content which is conveyed during the communication encounter. The content may be factual information or it may be the ideas, thoughts and feelings expressed by the participants. Some messages have a clear and obvious content, while others are hidden or not so obvious. For example, a friend might tell you overtly that she has not seen anyone for the past two weeks because she has been ill. Covertly, she could be telling you that she is lonely and wants your company. Messages thus have a meaning that must be understood and interpreted. Because people cannot transfer meaning from one mind to another, they use signs and codes to formulate messages. It would not be possible to communicate your ideas and feelings if you did not have signs to represent them. Communication is all about sending and receiving signs which have meanings attached to them.

diction ← donnotive   Connotive → emotion.

3.3.3   Sign and code

A **sign** is something that stands for something else — a particular thing or idea. Smoke is a sign of fire. The South African flag is a sign that represents or stands for South Africa. The words and diagrams in this book are also signs. **Verbal signs** are spoken and written words and sounds, whereas **nonverbal signs** are cues or signals that are transmitted without the use of sound. As you speak, you choose words or verbal signs to convey your meaning. But, as we discussed in Section 3.2.1., your verbal message is accompanied and given additional meaning by nonverbal signs — your body movements, facial expressions, tone of voice and hand gestures. When you listen to others, the nonverbal signs they use affect the meaning you assign to the verbal signs. For example, a friend who says, "Yes, I'm interested in what you are telling me", but flips through the pages of a magazine while you are talking, is actually conveying a different message.

Signs are combined in a systematic way according to codes. A **code** is a system for using signs. The system is based on rules or conventions shared by those who use the code. For example, speech is made up of a sequence of sound signs (words). But the act of speaking involves knowing which sign goes where. Grammar is the code for the use of speech. We combine words to form sentences according to the rules of the language we use. Unless we agree on these rules, we would not be able to communicate at all. The practice of using and combining certain signs becomes established over time as a social convention or fixed pattern in society. Bear in mind that language is not our only means of communication. We are also familiar with traffic signs or pictorial signs, for instance. We can regard such groups of signs or sign systems as 'languages', each made up of special types of signs with its own special code. For example, we know how to behave at the traffic lights because the traffic code in our society provides the rules by which we understand the combination of the colour signs red, green and amber. The traffic code is a social convention.

3.3.4   Encoding and decoding

Encoding is the process of taking the ideas in your mind and transforming them into verbal and nonverbal signs so that they can be transmitted as messages to someone else. **Decoding** on the other hand is the process of taking the verbal and nonverbal messages that you receive from others and giving them meaning. In other words, we encode or create messages, and decode or give meaning to other people's messages. We are usually not aware of either the encoding or decoding process because we have been communicating since childhood. We do not consciously think about each word and gesture that we use. However, a teacher preparing a lesson may go through a conscious encoding process to select the best words to explain a difficult topic to his or her pupils. Likewise, should you choose to learn a foreign language, you would consciously be aware of both the encoding and decoding processes — such as the rules of grammar — until you become proficient in that language.

3.3.5   Medium and channel

After a message has been encoded by the communicator, it has to travel to the recipient. The medium and the channel are both links between the communicator and the recipient. The **medium** is the physical means by which messages are transmitted between people in communication. Your voice and body movements, as well as technological and electronic means of communication, such as the telephone, a loudspeaker, newspapers, a book, a photograph, or the TV, are mediums (media) of communication. Think back to the dimensions of communication we discussed in Section 3.2 and you will realise that different media have different requirements of which we, as communicators, must be aware. Whereas the physical appearance of a radio presenter will not influence the recipients of the message, the personal appearance of the speaker at a seminar could influence the way in which the audience (recipients) receives the message.

When we use more than one medium to encode a message — for example, by accompanying our words with body movements — we increase the redundancy (repetition) and, to a certain extent, the accuracy of the message. Excessive redundancy, however, could make some recipients feel that you think they are stupid.

The **channel** is the route by which the messages travel. The light waves that carry the television image or the airwaves that carry the sound of your voice are channels of communication, as are your five senses — hearing, sight, smell, touch, and taste. We may hear a musical programme on the radio, watch a soccer match on television, smell fresh coffee as we walk down the street, hug a friend we have not seen for some time, or taste the flavours in a dish of curry. The channel has little to do with the meaning of the message and has become largely the concern of technical theorists (refer to Section 3.1) whose interest in communication is to measure and maximise the capacity of a given channel to convey information.

3.3.6   Meaning

Meaning is an extremely difficult term to define because of its abstract nature. O'Sullivan et al (1989) suggest that, rather than try to define the term, we should regard meaning as the product or result of communication. In other words, the act of communication produces meaning. To enable us to better understand the concept, we could say that messages contain two types of information to which we attach meaning: content information and relational information. The **content level** refers to factual information about the topic of the message — what it is about. The **relational level** determines how the participants understand their relationship — it provides information about the feelings of the communicator and how the content should be interpreted. For instance, the message, "Let's discuss this problem" could be a request when a friend is talking to you, but a command when it is your lecturer or tutor who conveys the message. The content is the same, but the tone of voice and the way in which the message is delivered serve to define your relationship. Often, it is the relational level of a message rather than the content that tells you whether a person is expressing affection or dislike, and whether or not a comment is humorous or sarcastic. We also need to be aware that meaning is not fixed. People are unpredictable and we cannot always be sure that they will react to a message in the way we intended.

3.3.7   Interpretation

The meaning in a message must be interpreted. **Interpretation** involves more than a literal understanding of the signs in a message — it means that you add your own individual meaning to what is being conveyed. Interpretation depends on both social (shared) meanings and individual (personal or subjective) meanings. 'Social' in this sense indicates that, to be able to begin communicating, we must have something in common. For example, we must share some basic understanding of verbal signs — we must speak the same language. We usually also share an understanding of what certain words mean in our culture, such as 'democracy' or 'justice'. But the way in which we use these words and what we understand by them is expressive of our personal and individual character (refer to the discussion of abstract words in Section 6.5.2). Should you and I attend the same political meeting, for instance, we may well ascribe different meanings to the ideas expressed by the speaker because each of us is the product of our individual background, past experiences, gender, attitudes, feelings, ideas, values, occupation, religion and culture. For example, if you have been discriminated against in the past because you are a woman, or black, or Muslim, the meaning you assign to the word 'justice' would differ from that of someone who has never experienced discrimination. We would say that your **frame of reference** influences your interpretation. The important point is that interpretation is never right or wrong. There may be different, but equally valid, interpretations for individual recipients of the same message.

3.3.8 Noise

Any stimulus that interferes with the transmission and reception of messages so that the meaning is not clearly understood creates a barrier between the communicator and the recipient. We call such barriers noise. **Noise** is more than distracting physical sounds, such as traffic noises or the yells of children that could make it difficult to hear the message. It is anything that interferes with the success of the communication by distorting the message so that the meaning received is different from that which is intended. The outcome of your encounter often depends on how you cope with external, internal and semantic noise.

- *External noises* are stimuli in the environment that distract your attention. A bad odour, for instance, a cold room, an uncomfortable chair, the static on a telephone line or even a pair of sunglasses can interfere with the transmission and reception of messages. You could be attending a lecture in a hot overcrowded room and become so uncomfortable that you cannot concentrate on what the lecturer is saying. Blurred type or creased pages create noise in written communication because they interfere with the clarity of the communicator's message. Think about the following examples: Do you hear the announcements at stations and airports clearly? If not, why not? What happens to the conversation when you communicate with someone who has a stutter or other speech impediment?

- *Internal noises* are the thoughts and feelings in people that may interfere with communication. Your moods and personal prejudices, as well as the amount of attention you pay to others, are all internal noises that influence the way you interpret messages. For instance, a student doesn't hear the lecture she is attending because she is thinking about the dance she is going to that evening. A man may be so resentful about having a woman appointed as his manager that he does not fully concentrate on what she is saying. If his bias (thoughts) prevents the accurate reception of her messages, then internal noise has occurred.

- *Semantic noises* are interferences that occur when people have different meanings for words and when these meanings are not mutually understood. For example, if at the airport you ask your departing friend about his itinerary, and he replies that he hasn't packed one, then you know that he has not understood your message because he does not know what an itinerary is (cf Barker & Gaut 1996). Semantic noise also occurs when your doctor uses unfamiliar medical terms to explain why you are feeling ill. The result could be that you will be uncertain of what the problem is because he or she has created semantic noise by using words you do not understand. Similarly, other people may react in a way that you did not intend to your use of slang, ethnic slurs, foreign words, sexist remarks or profanity, thereby distorting the interaction between you. Semantic noise can also be caused by social and cultural differences between communicator and recipient because they may use different words to denote the same object or idea. One way of overcoming noise is by means of feedback.

3.3.9   Feedback

Feedback is the response of participants to each other. During communication, the participants continuously send messages or feedback to each other. Feedback can be verbal or nonverbal. For instance, you tell me a joke and I smile. The smile is feedback. Or, I explain a problem to you and you ask for more information. The information I give you is also feedback. A shrug of the shoulders in response to a message is feedback, as is the applause of the audience to a speaker at a meeting. Feedback is important because it lets the participants know whether they have ascribed the same meaning to a message. In the examples of semantic noise described above, for example, feedback between the participants would have helped to clarify the misunderstandings.

Feedback also gives communication its dynamic nature by making it an *interactive process* rather than a *linear process*. Feedback is the means whereby we negotiate ideas and exchange meaning. Without feedback, it is not possible to discuss an issue or a feeling, exchange opinions or arrive at a mutually satisfactory conclusion to the communication encounter. It also allows people to monitor their performance by telling them how they are 'coming across'. A smile from your partner is positive feedback and encourages you to continue a conversation. Should you, however, receive negative feedback, such as a sarcastic remark, you may decide to terminate the conversation. It is therefore important to pay attention to the responses and reactions of others.

3.3.10 Context

Communication does not take place in a void. People always communicate within a situation or setting. **Context** refers to the environment, the place or conditions in which the communication encounter takes place. A doctor's office is a context, as is the manager's office in an organisation. Communication is always contextual and is influenced by factors such as the time, place and physical properties of the meeting place, as well as the roles, status and relationships of the participants. People express themselves differently depending on, for instance, how well they know each other, whether they are at home or at work, and what their formal position is. Although the school hall is a good place for giving speeches and presenting scholastic awards, it is not conducive to intimate conversations. In the same way, the school principal and a teacher will communicate more formally during working hours than when they meet socially at a party.

Researchers have increasingly become aware of the importance of the **cultural context** in which communication occurs. The cultural context includes the beliefs, values, attitudes, meaning, social hierarchies, religion, notions of time and roles of a group of people (Samovar & Porter 2000). Because South Africa is a multicultural country, its citizens are culturally diverse and participants in communication may experience difficulties when they do not understand one another's customs and traditions, let alone their home language. Most people think about cultural diversity in terms of race and ethnicity, but cultural diversity in communication also takes into account differences in gender, age, sexual preference, class, education and religion. (There is a brief introduction to intercultural communication in Chapter 12.)

Putting all the components of the communication process or system together, we could say that a communicator encodes a message, using verbal and nonverbal signs and codes, which is carried by a medium along a channel to the recipient who decodes the message to understand it, interprets it to give it personal meaning, and responds via feedback. The presence of noise in any part of the system could affect the outcome of the encounter. Each component in the process influences and is influenced by every other component. Should your nonverbal behaviour, for example, create noise because the recipient perceives you as arrogant, she may decide to terminate the conversation by withholding feedback, and the relationship between you would not have a chance to develop.

3.4   Models of the communication process

One of the ways in which scholars have sought to understand the nature of communication is by means of **models** which describe and explain the communication process. (It would help you at this point if you revised the introduction to models in Section 2.5.4.) We used a simple model in Figure 3.2 to help you visualise how the components in the communication process relate to one another. Models are visual diagrams of abstract ideas. The basic purpose of a model is to capture the essential features of a real situation in a simplified form so that it can be described, explained and understood more easily. In the same way that an architect's plan, for example, helps us to see what a house will look like upon completion, communication models help us to visualise the process of communication more clearly. Communication theorists use models to identify relevant components of the process and to provide a picture of how the components relate to each other during a real communication encounter. Models can be said to reflect the view of communication presented by a particular theorist.

A limitation of models is that they often provide simplified pictures of communication because they present only the aspect of the communication process a particular theorist wishes to emphasise. For example, one theorist may be interested in explaining how persuasion is used to change people's attitudes towards a social problem, while a second theorist may want to describe how a group of people reaches consensus about a problem that has arisen in the organisation where they work. In each case, certain aspects of the communication process will be emphasised and other aspects will be omitted. Despite the fact that they present a simplified view of communication, models are useful 'tools' in that they allow us to start thinking more critically about communication. The models we have selected illustrate the different views of communication expressed in the definitions in Section 3.1.

Communication was established as a field of study at universities in the late 19th century, but it was mainly housed in departments of English literature. In the early part of the 20th century, individual communication departments began to emerge and, in the late 1940s, the first attempts at describing the nature of the communication process began to appear in the literature on communication. Some of the earliest views of communication were those of Lasswell, Shannon and Weaver, and Schramm. The models they created reflect the development of communication from a linear to an interactive process.

3.4.1   Lasswell's view of communication

Harold Lasswell was an American political scientist whose main interest was in the area of propaganda. In 1948, he described a view of communication that emphasises the effect of a message on the recipient(s). He said that the communication process could best be explained by asking the following questions: Who? Says what? To whom? In what channel? With what effect?

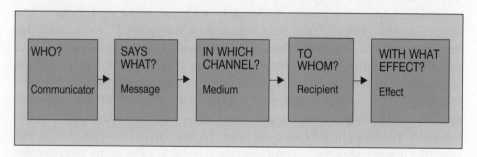

Figure 3.3 Lasswell's model of communication (after Lasswell 1948)

In the model, 'who' refers to the communicator who formulates the message; 'what' is the content of message; 'channel' indicates the medium of transmission; and 'whom' describes either an individual recipient or the audience of mass communication. 'Effect' is the outcome of the message which, for Lasswell, should be that the recipient will be persuaded to adopt a particular point of view. Note that the model focuses our attention on the individual components of the communication process and emphasises that the components occur in a sequence that begins with the communicator and ends with the recipient. In other words, communication is a one-way process in which the communicator influences others through the content of the message. It therefore assumes that only the communicator is an active participant in the process, and that the recipient plays a passive role. Please note that, although it does not provide for feedback, Lasswell's is not a technical model of communication because he draws our attention to the importance of the content or meaning in the message. In fact, Lasswell emphasises that, for a message to have the intended effect on the recipient(s), for example, a message to vote for a particular politician, it is important for the source of the message (eg the advertising agency co-ordinating the election campaign) to consider, from the recipients' point of view, who the best person would be to actually communicate the message, what sort of content would most appeal to the intended recipients and which medium would be the most effective means of transmitting the message. In South Africa, for example, when the African National Congress advertises an appeal for votes, the party would consider using different messages, different media and different communicators to reach different segments of the population. A rural community, for instance, may not be able to access television readily, whereas radio would reach most potential voters. And a message that largely addresses the concerns of urban dwellers would be of little interest to them.

By asking "With what effect?", Lasswell suggests that there could be a variety of outcomes or effects of communication, some of which may be unintentional (refer to Section 2.2 for a discussion of the unintentional effects of communication).

3.4.2 Shannon and Weaver's view of communication

Shannon and Weaver worked for the Bell Telephone Laboratory in the United States. They were primarily interested in finding engineering solutions to problems of signal transmission. They concentrated on how the channels of communication could be used most efficiently — how to send a maximum amount of information along a given channel. Think about the model in terms of how a telephone message is transmitted. An information source (communicator) encodes a message which is converted by the transmitter (telephone) into a signal which is sent through a channel (telephone line) to the receiver.

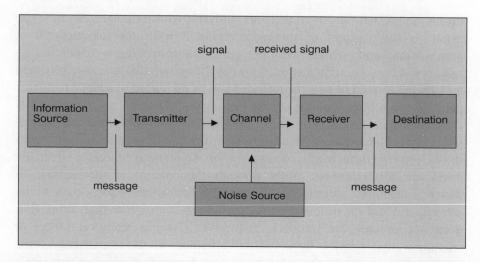

Figure 3.4 The Shannon and Weaver model (after Shannon & Weaver 1949)

The signal is received at the other end (telephone) and converted back into a message which is heard by the recipient (destination). Shannon and Weaver concentrated on which kind of communication channel carries the maximum amount of signals or sounds, how much of the signal is lost through noise (eg static on a telephone line) before it reaches its destination, and how to eliminate distortion caused by noise.

Bittner (1985) points out that the model describes mass communication as well. In radio broadcasting, for example, the announcer (information source) says words (the message) that are transmitted in the form of a radio wave (signal) to a radio receiver (receiver) which in turn changes the signal to an audible voice (the message) to be heard by the listener (destination) at home.

Like Lasswell's model, Shannon and Weaver's model depicts a sequential process in which each component of the communication process is clearly defined. Although not indicated by means of a label, Shannon and Weaver's model also draws our attention to the effects of the message — that is, the effects of noise on the reception and understanding of the message by the recipient. This is because Shannon and Weaver's greatest concern was the efficient transmission of information from communicator to recipient and the clarity of the message that is transmitted. They did not consider the content of the message or the meaning conveyed and interpreted by the participants.

For this reason, Shannon and Weaver's model is often referred to as a transmission or **technical model** — it depicts the relationship between the communicator, message and recipient as a linear (one-way) process. Many subsequent theorists have maintained that the most important aspect of communication is the transmission process because, if the communicator's message reaches the recipient with distortion, then little communication can take place between them (cf Ellis & McClintock 1994). Theorists who adopt a technical view of communication concentrate on improving the transmission process — the tools and techniques that help us to communicate more efficiently.

Although it is technical, the model is considered important because it provided a basis for developing other models which deal more specifically with the process of human communication. When applied to human communication, Shannon and Weaver's model has several limitations or drawbacks. First (and perhaps the greatest limitation), is that there is no channel for feedback (compare Lasswell's model). Second, it assumes that noise arises only in the channel — that is, it depicts only physical or external noise as a distortion in the communication process (refer to the discussion of noise in Section 3.3.8). The third limitation follows from the second: the model is concerned only with the clarity of the message and not its meaning. In other words, nothing in the model suggests that 'something' occurs inside people when they engage in communication behaviour or that successful communication requires at least two people to share experiences and goals (cf McQuail & Windahl 1981; Gibson & Hanna 1992). The scholar who first described communication as an interactive process was Wilbur Schramm, who depicted communication as a circular process that includes feedback.

3.4.3   Schramm's view of communication

Schramm was aware that, for a message to be understood by the recipient in the manner intended by the communicator, the participants must share a common language, common backgrounds and a common culture. Schramm is suggesting that if people do not have some common background or frame of reference, noise (such as internal prejudices) may be introduced and cause misunderstanding or different interpretations of the message by the participants. It is therefore essential to make provision for feedback in a model of communication.

In his description of the model, Schramm (1954:9) says that "feedback tells us how our messages are being interpreted". The communicator can adjust his or her message, or provide additional information should the recipient not be clear about the intended meaning. Schramm's model moves away from the technical view of communication to the issue of the content of messages and the meaning that is exchanged between the participants. Schramm and other theorists who follow this approach to the study of communication regard meaning, not transmission, as the most important aspect of the communication process. They maintain that, even if a message is transmitted and received clearly and accurately, its meaning may not be understood in the same way by the participants because they may not share similar circumstances (cf Ellis & McClintock 1994). Unlike Shannon and Weaver, they do not believe that there is only one correct meaning for a message. The meaning is determined by the person who is interpreting it (refer to the discussion of interpretation in Section 3.3.7).

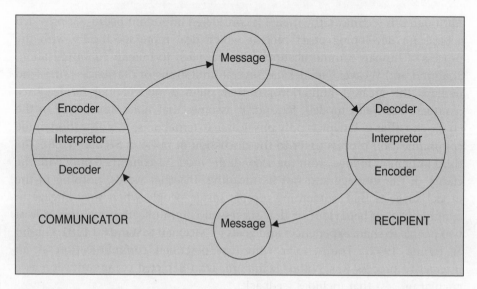

Figure 3.5 Schramm's model of communication (after Schramm 1954)

Schramm's view of communication is more complex than previous views and adds substantially to our understanding of the communication process. Schramm's model describes communication as a dynamic interaction in which meaningful messages are exchanged by two active participants. Communicator and recipient both encode, transmit, receive, decode and interpret messages. That is, both play the roles of communicator and recipient. By highlighting the importance of feedback, the process becomes two-way instead of linear. The model thus moves away from emphasising the channel through which messages are transmitted to the **interpretation of meaning** by the people in the process.

3.4.4   A transactional model

By identifying the components and relationships basic to the communication process, the early models we have discussed laid a foundation on which future scholars could build. The model below (Figure 3.6) uses all the elements in the previous models and builds on them to show that communication does not only involve the transmission of messages from one person to another, nor is it simply an interaction between two people. The communication process becomes a **transaction** during which the meaning of a message is negotiated (refer to the definitions in Section 3.1). At the same time, the transactional model overcomes the major limitation in Schramm's model — that is, the suggestion that communicator and recipient take turns to express and interpret messages.

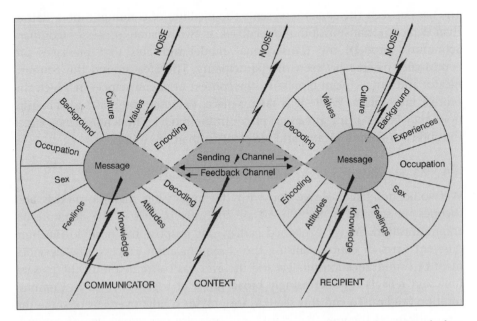

Figure 3.6 A transactional model of communication (adapted from Verderber 1990; Verderber & Verderber 2002)

The model is not substantially different from the circular model. It also depicts communication as a dynamic process in which both participants are actively engaged in encoding, transmitting, receiving and decoding messages. The main difference is that communication is seen within the context of a relationship between two participants who are simultaneously involved in the *negotiation of meaning*. 'Simultaneous' implies that, instead of a two-way flow, both people are constantly encoding and decoding messages. For example, even as I talk to you, I am watching your nonverbal reactions and interpreting them so that there is, in fact, no longer a separation between the two communicators (cf Tubbs & Moss 2003).

The transactional model also highlights that the creation of meaning is negotiated between the participants. The two circles represent the communicator and the recipient. In the centre of each circle is the message: the thought, idea or feeling that is communicated using verbal and nonverbal signs. Surrounding the messages are the participants' values, culture, background, occupation, gender, values, interests, knowledge and attitudes. These factors (the frame of reference of the participants) influence the meaning that is expressed and the meaning that is interpreted. The outcome of the encounter is determined by the mutual involvement of the participants in negotiating the meaning of the messages.

The bar between the circles represents the medium of communication. Rather than depicting transmission and feedback as two separate processes (compare Schramm's model), the transactional model indicates that messages are continually passing between the participants. The area around the communicator and the recipient represents the context or circumstances in which the process takes place. While it is taking place, external, internal and semantic noise may be occurring at various places in the model. These noises may affect the ability of communicator and recipient to share meanings.

3.5   More advanced communication theories

We would not like to leave you with the impression that the models and theories we selected in Section 2.4 are the only models in the literature on communication. As we explained earlier, our purpose has been to illustrate different ways of conceptualising the communication process. The development of communication models and theories has continued until the present time and reflects the increasingly broad range of topics covered in Communication Studies. To end this section, we provide a brief overview of some the more advanced theories that clarify and organise our knowledge of communication. You do not study all these theories or the models that illustrate them in this introductory course, but we hope that this brief overview will make you aware of developments in the field and help you to understand other models and theories that you will come across during your Communication Studies. The following overview is based mainly on Littlejohn (2002).

Many communication theories originated in the physical and natural sciences. **System theory** is a good example and is particularly relevant to the study of communication in organisations. System theory rests on two main principles. First, that all the parts of a system (in our case, an organisation) are interdependent. Thus, if one part changes, all other parts of the system are affected. Second, that of synergism, which is the interaction of the parts of the system where a result greater than the sum of its parts is created. An important goal of the system is to maintain itself in balance, or equilibrium, in order to remain viable. The control mechanism that maintains all the parts of the system in a state of equilibrium is cybernetics — that is, by acting on feedback information from the often rapidly changing environment (society) in which it exists, the system maintains awareness of environmental changes and adjusts and readjusts to maintain itself in a state of balance. You could think about how almost every organisation in South Africa has had to adapt to rapidly changing social circumstances in the past two decades in order to survive or close down.

Another trend in the study of communication was the importance of signs and symbols, language and discourse in human life. In general, the study of signs is referred to as **semiotics**. We introduced you to the concept of signs and codes in Section 3.3.3. Signs and codes are the basis of the language we use to communicate in our everyday life. We also use signs to communicate nonverbally, that is to communicate without the use of words. You will learn about nonverbal communication in Chapter 5 of this book and we introduce you to language as a system of signs in Chapter 6.

The term 'discourse' is used in Communication Studies to refer to verbal utterances of greater magnitude than a sentence (O'Sullivan et al 1983:72). Its scope of study includes, for example, television discourse, political discourse and, of course, conversations between people. One of the popular theories about discourse is that language is a game because people follow rules to generate meaning and make themselves understood. Following from this idea is that conversations and arguments can be analysed through the careful examination of sequences of talk between two or more people. To reach an understanding of the meaning of a conversation, theorists ask themselves what speakers are doing as they communicate — possibly asking and answering questions, managing turn-taking, and protecting their feelings. However, a more modern approach to the study of discourse comes from a group of theorists known as poststructuralists, who reject the idea that conversation is primarily a tool of communication. Jacques Derrida, for example, maintains that language cannot express a definite meaning or truth. Using his method of deconstruction (taking meaning apart), he shows that there are always alternative meanings in a text (whether it is spoken or written) and texts therefore cannot have a fixed meaning or truth. Other poststructuralists maintain that meaning is determined by the historical and social forces of a particular era. In other words, the power structures at the time determine the rules by which we use language and understand texts. You could give some thought to the question of why black pupils in the mid-1970s rejected Afrikaans as a medium of instruction in their schools.

There is a group of theories that concentrates on **message production and reception** — how messages are created and processed, and how information is produced and shared. Some of these theories focus on relatively stable characteristics of individuals and predict that, if you have a certain personality trait, you will communicate in certain ways or produce certain types of messages. Other theories concentrate on the behavioural characteristics of individuals and determine how certain behaviour is associated with the feelings, thoughts and traits that influence the way messages are produced and processed. A third approach in this group of theories is more concerned with what happens in the mind during message production and reception. These are **cognitive theories** and focus, among others, on the following aspects: how information is acquired and organised in the mind to make sense to the individual; how people use memory; what makes people decide to act in particular ways; and how messages are created to achieve certain goals.

In contrast to cognitive theories, there is a group of theories that approach communication from the standpoint that meaning is created and understood in the context of the social group in which the individual interacts. The best-known approach in this group is **symbolic interactionism**.

Symbolic interactionism emphasises that we use symbols (language) to negotiate meaning in interaction with others. During this process we learn the rules and norms of our society and also to behave in ways that our social group prescribes. In Chapter 7 you will learn about the ideas of the sociologist, Erving Goffman. His theory about the way people communicate in everyday encounters is based on symbolic interaction. Theories of **social** and **cultural reality** extend the ideas laid down in symbolic interactionism. These theories suggest that, not only meaning, but our conception of reality — including how we understand ourselves — is constructed by the social and cultural influences around us. You will learn more about the construction of the self in Chapter 7.

Communication theorists are also interested in the role of communication in understanding the nature of human experiences. The central assumption of these theories is that people actively interpret their experiences by assigning meaning to them. Because each individual has a personal frame of reference, any message — whether it is heard or read or observed — can be interpreted in a variety of ways. Therefore, the meaning in a message can be different for different people — meaning can never be fixed. Such theories emphasise the recipient's subjective participation in interpreting and understanding the world. Two of the important approaches in this group of theories are phenomenology and hermeneutics. **Phenomenology** studies people's perception and inter-pretation of objects and events from their subjective experiences of them. **Hermeneutics** is mainly concerned with understanding how individuals interpret written texts, such as the Bible and literature, and also mass media messages. Some theorists have extended hermeneutics to also explain how people arrive at subjective interpretations of social actions.

The final group of theories we introduce you to is critical theory. **Critical theory** has a Marxist foundation and is concerned with the social conditions that influence the way people interpret their circumstances. Critical theory attempts to reveal the oppressive power arrangements under which people come to understand their conditions of existence. Critical theorists are particularly interested in how messages reinforce oppression and subvert the interests of certain groups and classes. For this group of theorists, language is the primary tool of oppression because the power groups in society use language in a way that makes it difficult for the working classes to understand their situation and to change it. They see the solution to domination and oppression in **conscientisation** — making people aware of the injustices in society — and thereby empowering them to change social conditions and emancipate themselves.

Cultural studies and feminist studies are usually classified as contemporary or poststructuralist critical theory. **Cultural studies** are mainly concerned with the ways that culture is produced among competing ideologies and the influence that it exerts on society. Studying the mass media is extremely important because the media communicate the ideas of the dominant ideology. **Feminist studies** have become increasingly popular in the study of communication and explore the meaning of gender in society. Feminist theorists maintain that every aspect of life, including language, work, family roles, education and socialisation, are experienced in terms of the masculine and the feminine. They emphasise that the nature of gender relations in a patriarchal society are oppressive to women. Feminist theory challenges the prevailing gender assumptions of society and aims to achieve more liberating ways for men and women to exist in the world.

3.6   Contextual approaches to communication

As the focus of Communication Studies broadened, the way in which communication was studied also began to change. One of the important developments was a move away from general models and theories to an approach that deals with specific contexts of communication. In the next section, we introduce some of the contexts that are receiving attention from communication scholars today.

Think for a moment about your own experience of communication. For example, in a single day you may have a conversation with a friend, engage in deep thoughts, listen to the radio, read the newspaper, look at an illustrated pamphlet, participate in a seminar, make a speech to a business or social group, watch TV, surf the Internet or go to the cinema. Each of these experiences occurs in different situations, involves different numbers of people, uses different means of communication and creates different relationships.

Contexts are different types of communication situation classified according to the number of people in the interaction and the degree to which they are able to interact. The contexts are: the intrapersonal, interpersonal, small-group, public speaking and mass communication contexts. The contexts are not mutually exclusive and the distinctions among them are not clear-cut. Note that the degree to which people are able to interact refers to the immediacy of feedback they are able to provide. In other words, is feedback possible and, if so, is it immediately available or delayed?

3.6.1   The intrapersonal communication context

The term 'intra' means 'within' or 'inside'. **Intrapersonal communication** occurs when an individual sends and receives messages internally: in other words, you communicate with yourself. The distinguishing characteristic of intrapersonal communication is that you are the only participant — you are the communicator-recipient. The message is made up of your thoughts and feelings which your brain processes and interprets. Feedback occurs in the sense that, as you 'talk' to yourself, you make decisions or discard some ideas and replace them with others (cf Hybels & Weaver 1986). Intrapersonal communication is an ongoing process that is taking place even while you are communicating in all the other settings. For instance, you are probably doing it right now, since thinking about what you are reading is a form of intrapersonal communication. Intrapersonal communication is the foundation on which interpersonal communication is based. To communicate effectively with others, you first have to be able to communicate with yourself. Communication theorists have investigated the way people make sense of the world through their intrapersonal communication. We discuss intrapersonal communication in more detail in Chapter 7.

3.6.2   The interpersonal communication context

The term 'inter' means 'between'. **Interpersonal communication** occurs between people in a face-to-face situation. They are able to see each other and observe facial expressions and other nonverbal behaviour while they are exchanging verbal messages. A characteristic of interpersonal communication is that the participants continually provide feedback or respond to each other's messages. Conversing with your sister, discussing a movie with your friends, or talking to your boss or your lecturer are examples of interpersonal communication. This kind of communication is usually between two people, though it may include more than two. We use the term **dyadic communication** to distinguish an encounter between two people from a small group of people. It is in the interpersonal context that meaningful relationships are formed and maintained in our daily interactions with others. Relationships are the focus of study in the interpersonal context. We discuss interpersonal communication in more detail in Chapter 8.

3.6.3   The small-group communication context

Small-group communication refers to communication within a group of between three and 12 people. The group must be small enough so that each member is able to interact with all the other members. We all belong to a number of groups: the family, work groups, social clubs, church groups, study groups and so forth. People in groups usually share a common purpose or goal which brings them together, such as the need to solve a problem. Small-group communication is also interpersonal because the members of the group are able to interact with each other by providing feedback, but it is more complex than communication between two people because groups have unique dynamics that affect the way people interact. Small-group communication is the topic of Chapter 9.

3.6.4   The public speaking context

When the group becomes too large for direct interaction between the members, we talk about the **public speaking context**, or oral presentation. In public speaking, one person addresses an audience in a public setting, such as a lecture hall or auditorium. Public speaking is more formal than interpersonal or small-group communication. Usually the event is planned in advance, the speaker is introduced, and delivers a speech that has been prepared to meet the goals of the particular situation. It could be a persuasive political speech, a presentation by a salesperson to promote the company's products, a lecture to students or a speech at a wedding. Participants are still face-to-face but the audience does not usually participate directly until the end of the speech when questions are invited. However, they can send nonverbal messages or feedback. An audience that is not enjoying a speech, for instance, often becomes restless and stops paying attention. They can also provide positive feedback in the form of laughter or applause. We discuss the process of public speaking in Chapter 10.

3.6.5   The mass-communication context

Mass communication is communication to large masses of people who do not know each other and who are usually not in the same place. A distinguishing characteristic of mass communication is that it is *mediated* — that is, the message reaches you through a mechanical or electronic medium, such as print or television. When you read a book, watch a movie or listen to the news on the radio, for instance, you are part of a mass-communication audience. Mass communication differs from interpersonal and group communication in many ways. An important difference is that it provides little or no opportunity for you to interact directly with the person or people conveying the message, due to the difficulty of providing feedback. Areas of study include the influence of mass communication on people's behaviour and the way exposure to the mass media shapes our perceptions of the world. You will learn more about mass communication in Chapter 11.

Scenario 3.1

The chairperson at a business meeting looks at her watch and sees that there are only five minutes left before she has to leave for a lunchtime appointment with the bank manager. She frowns because there are still two items on the agenda that have not been dealt with. Aware that it is too late to begin a discussion, she says, "Let's call it a day", in a frustrated tone of voice. Some members of the group look surprised because meetings in that organisation usually carry on until all business has been completed, regardless of the time. Others smile because, for a change, the meeting is not going to run into the lunch hour. Most people gather their notebooks and pens and begin leaving. John, however, looks confused — he has been thinking about the argument he had with his girlfriend the previous evening (cf Verderber 1990).

Having studied this scenario, answer the following questions.

1. Identify the context in which the communication takes place.
2. Is the context formal or informal?
3. How many communication codes are used? Substantiate your answer by means of examples.
4. Identify the channel(s) of communication.
5. What message is the chairperson communicating?
6. Do you think there is an example of unintentional communication? Explain your answer.
7. Give three examples of feedback by the recipients.
8. Has noise interfered in the communication process? Explain.
9. Does the case describe a technical or meaning-centred view of communication?

Summary

This chapter started by describing communication as a complex phenomenon and considered three definitions of communication — technical, interactive and transactional. It then extended understanding of the complex nature of communication by examining the following dimensions of communication: verbal and nonverbal, oral and written, formal and informal, and intentional and unintentional. The next part of the chapter described, with the aid of examples, the components or elements that comprise the process of communication. This was followed by a discussion of communication models to illustrate three different ways of conceptualising the communication process: linear, interactional (process) and transactional models. You were then given a brief overview of some of the theoretical developments in the field to help you gain an understanding of the complexity of Communication Studies. The last section of this chapter introduced you to the different contexts in which communication is studied today: intrapersonal communication, inter-personal communication, small-group communication, public speaking and mass communication. This chapter ended with a scenario that describes the communication process among the participants in a business meeting.

Test yourself

1. Think about a serious conversation or an argument you have had recently with a friend or family member. Write down your experience using all the components discussed in Section 3.3 to describe the interaction. Then answer the following questions:
   (a) Did you both participate actively in the encounter?
   (b) Did you both make yourselves understood?
   (c) Did your partner's nonverbal communication help you to understand him/her more easily?
   (d) Did your encounter have a satisfactory outcome? (Why or why not?)
   (e) Was it disturbed by any kind of noise? (What kind of noise and what effect did it have?)
2. Working either on your own, or with a fellow student, develop an original model of the one-to-one communication process. Try to include all the components that comprise and influence the process, and label each part.
3. Think about the different views of communication described and how each changes the way in which the concept of communication is understood. Then formulate your own definition, emphasising the aspects of communication you consider to be important. Would you say that your definition offers a technical or a meaning-centred view of communication?
4. Define five contexts in which communication takes place. Explain the basis on which we differentiate between the contexts, illustrating your answers with examples from your own experience of communication.

EXECUTIVE SUMMARY
The communication process

1 Definitions of communication
   - ❏ technical definition
   - ❏ process/meaning-centred definition
   - ❏ transactional definition
2 Dimensions of communication
3 Components/elements of the process
   - ❏ communicator and recipient
   - ❏ message
   - ❏ denotative/connotative meaning
   - ❏ sign
   - ❏ encoding/decoding
   - ❏ medium and channel
   - ❏ content level/relational level
   - ❏ interpretation
   - ❏ noise
   - ❏ feedback
   - ❏ context
4 Theories and models of communication
   - ❏ Lasswell's model
   - ❏ Shannon & Weaver's model
   - ❏ Schramm's model
   - ❏ transactional model
5 Advanced theories of communication
   - ❏ system theory
   - ❏ semiotics
   - ❏ message production and reception
   - ❏ symbolic interactionism
   - ❏ social and cultural reality
   - ❏ phenomenology
   - ❏ hermeneutics
   - ❏ critical theory
   - ❏ cultural studies
   - ❏ feminist studies
6 Contextual approaches to communication
   - ❏ intrapersonal
   - ❏ interpersonal
   - ❏ small group
   - ❏ public speaking
   - ❏ mass communication

4 Perception, listening and feedback

Overview

Have you ever been lost because you did not correctly follow the directions someone gave you? Have you missed an appointment because you got there at the wrong time? Are the notes you take in a lecture so detailed that you cannot identify the main points? When was the last time you jumped to a wrong conclusion or felt you were misunderstood? Have you ever said, "I don't want to discuss it" when you really mean "I don't want to hear your point of view"? Have you ever had the feeling that there is a hidden message behind the words someone is saying to you? (Hybels & Weaver 1989).

These examples involve your ability to listen efficiently and also illustrate why listening plays such an important role in the communication process. It is not only in interpersonal communication that we need to listen efficiently. As you can see from the above examples, the ability to listen plays an important role in almost every aspect of our lives. The problem is that we tend to assume that, because people are able to hear us, they are also listening to us. Researchers have shown that this is not the case. In the same way that we are taught to read and write, we also need training and practice to listen well.

Listening is one of our perceptual processes. People are equipped with five senses through which they receive information — sight, hearing, touch, smell and taste. We use these senses to make sense of the world around us. That is, our understanding of our circumstances and other people depends on the way we perceive the events that take place around us. In this chapter we emphasise the importance of perception and listening in the communication process. We begin by explaining the process of perception: the ways in which we select, organise and interpret the information that reaches us through our senses. We offer suggestions on how to improve the accuracy of your perceptions and, to illustrate how perception 'works' in our lives, we briefly discuss Gombrich's theory of perception. We then pay attention to the differences between hearing and listening and explain the process of listening. We continue by describing the types of listening that are appropriate in different situations. We point out some poor listening habits and discuss the external and internal barriers that impede efficient listening. After offering some suggestions for improving your listening skills, we show the relationship between listening and feedback and the importance of appropriate feedback in the process of communication. We end the chapter with a scenario based on a practical exercise to illustrate how the relationship between listening and feedback influences the nature of a communication encounter.

Learning outcomes

At the end of this chapter you should be able to do the following:
1.   Define 'perception'.
2.   Explain the process of perception by referring to selection, organisation and interpretation.
3.   Provide examples of the way selective exposure and selective attention influence your perceptions.
4.   Distinguish between active and passive listening.
5.   Name four types of listening and provide an example of the situation in which each occurs.
6.   Define internal and external listening and give two examples in each category.
7.   Identify at least three skills that must be developed to improve one's perception and three skills that must be developed to improve one's listening.
8.   Explain the function of feedback in the listening process.
9.   Apply the knowledge you gain in this chapter to do the following: improve your perception of events and people in the world around you, sharpen your listening skills, avoid giving inefficient feedback to others and improve your ability to offer appropriate feedback in your interpersonal communication.
10.   Answer the questions based on the scenario at the end of this chapter.

Introduction

Studies show that we spend most of our communication time in listening. Certainly, we use the communication skill of listening more than the skills of reading, writing and speaking. "From 42 to 60 percent or more of our communication time is spent listening, depending on whether we are students, managerial trainees, doctors, counselors, lawyers, or nurses" (Purdy 1996:4).

Although so much of our communication time is spent in listening, studies also reveal that the average adult listens at no better than 25 percent efficiency. Think about this statistic — it means that we often do not hear as much as 75 percent of a message! And after about 48 hours many people can remember only about 25 percent of what they heard. The reason is probably because most of us take the ability to listen so much for granted and do not think about it as a skill that we must learn.

In order to be in a position to improve our listening skills we need to first understand the process of perception and the role it plays in our understanding of the world.

4.1   Perception

Ellis and McClintock (1994:1) define **perception** very broadly as "information which is taken in by the senses, processed by the brain, stored in memory and produces some form of physical or mental response". Perception is therefore the process whereby we acquire information about our environment through our five senses. We gain information about ourselves and the world we live in through the interaction of these senses with the environment. The first time you touched a hot stove, you reacted instinctively by withdrawing your hand (a physical response). The information that heat burns the skin was processed by your brain and stored in your memory so that you would not repeat the action in future.

We perceive through a frame of reference — a set of interlocking facts, ideas, beliefs, values and attitudes. This frame of reference provides the basis for our understanding of people, events and experiences because it filters our perceptions. As we take in new information, we evaluate it in terms of our frame of reference and either reject it because it doesn't fit our frame of reference (our ideas, values, beliefs and attitudes) or we make use of it to support or expand our existing frame of reference (cf. Wilson, Hantz & Hanna 1989).

A feature of perception is that it is a personal process which provides each of us with a unique view of the world. It does not, however, always provide us with an accurate representation of the world. The result is that our understanding of many situations can be distorted. Some people distort the information that comes to them through their senses to such an extent that their perception of themselves, others and the events around them has little resemblance to reality. The two major causes of perceptual distortions are perceptual inaccuracies and the element of subjectivity in the perception process.

4.1.1   Perceptual inaccuracies

To illustrate that our sense organs can create perceptual inaccuracies, look at the two figures below. Which appears longer?

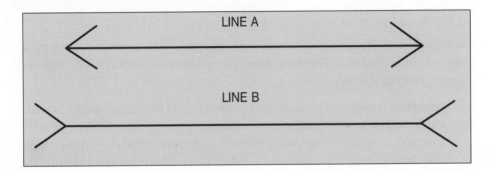

Figure 4.1 The Müller-Lyer illusion

This is a well-known phenomenon called the Müller-Lyer illusion. If you've never seen the figure before, you would probably trust the evidence of your eyes that line B is longer than line A. Those who have seen it before will know that the two lines are the same length. Measure them to make sure!

A similar effect can be seen in Figure 4.2.

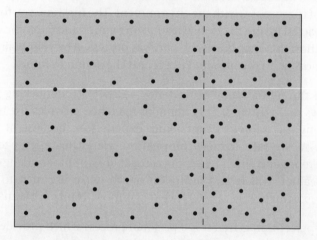

Figure 4.2 Illusion of quantity related to space

At first glance it looks as though there are more dots on the right side than on the left. In fact, there is the same number on each side but those on the right are packed into a smaller space.

A second contributor to perceptual distortions is the element of subjectivity in the process of perception. Perception is not merely a physical or mechanical act. People play an active role in the process. As a result, the image they have of themselves and others can be distorted. Let's see how this happens by briefly examining the perception process.

4.1.2 The perception process

The process of perception occurs in three principal stages: selection, organisation and interpretation. The three stages take place relatively unconsciously and almost simultaneously.

☐ **Selection** There are sensory stimuli around you all the time — sights, sounds, smells, textures — yet you focus your attention on very few of them. We select only some aspects of information from the environment — those which attract our attention at a given time. When you are deeply engrossed in a book, for example, it is unlikely that you will hear the ticking of your alarm clock or the traffic noises in the background. It is only when your attention lapses that you pay attention to these sounds. This phenomenon is often explained by comparing the sense organs to receivers that are tuned to pick up all sorts of information, and the brain to the control mechanism that makes the information meaningful. The first stage in the perception process is that, from the variety of information your senses receive, your brain selects what is relevant in a particular situation.

Two factors that influence the selection process are selective exposure and selective attention. A key factor in the way we view the world is the extent to which we are open to stimuli and experiences. From all the sensory stimuli that compete for our attention, we tend to select only those that reaffirm our frame of reference — our existing attitudes, values and beliefs. This is **selective exposure**. We likewise tend to ignore those experiences that are incongruent with our existing attitudes, values and beliefs (cf Gamble & Gamble 1987;1998a). That is why, for example, most people buy newspapers whose editorial policy confirms their existing political views. They expose themselves to information with which they already agree and disregard information that contradicts their political views. When we communicate with others, we make a similar choice, allowing ourselves to be open to some stimuli and excluding others. Limiting our exposure to some messages or parts of messages may create inaccurate perceptions of what is happening around us.

Selective attention is related to selective exposure. It describes how we see what we want to see and hear what we want to hear. Apart from the physical limitations of our senses (such as a hearing or sight impediment), factors that influence selective attention are our *interests* and *needs*. If you are interested in soccer, for example, you will hear all the statistics that are presented during a radio sports broadcast, whereas someone who is not interested may hear only the sound of the broadcaster's voice. The driver of the bus that you board needs to pay attention to traffic lights, pedestrians and other vehicles, whereas you, the passenger, may be unaware of these sights as you have no need to notice them. A similar process occurs during communication. In a meeting, for example, you may selectively attend to only those points of discussion that directly concern your work and lose concentration when matters that are less important to you are discussed.

❐ *Organisation* Once the brain has selected the relevant material, it arranges its selections into meaningful patterns according to our frame of reference. This is known as *perceptual organisation*. The organisation of what we perceive is largely affected by our *expectations* and our desire to form a whole image (a phenomenon called closure). The following two perception tests illustrate how expectations and closure affect the organisation of information.

Read the three phrases in Figure 4.3.

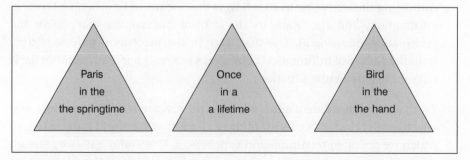

Figure 4.3 Perceptual expectation

Did you notice that in each sentence the article (*the, a*) appears twice? If you did not, your expectations may have affected the organisation of what you perceived — you expected to see correct sentences and thus read them 'correctly'. Now look at the shapes in Figure 4.4.

You probably had no difficulty in identifying the shapes because your mind unconsciously completed or closed the incomplete shapes to provide you with a whole image.

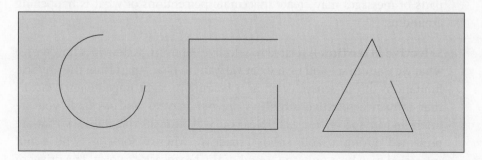

Figure 4.4 Perceptual closure

❑ **Interpretation** After sensory stimuli have selected and organised information, we give meaning to it by means of our frame of reference in what is called *perceptual interpretation*. Interpretation is the process of explaining and evaluating what has been selected and organised. Because people are individuals, they are unlikely to select the same sensory information or organise it in the same way. They are thus unlikely to arrive at the same interpretation of events or other people. Even if they attend to similar parts of the experience, they may still interpret it differently. For example, you may believe that you see two friends arguing, whereas another observer may see them as sharing a joke. You cannot know which perception is correct without investigating further. The example is often given of three bystanders who witness the same road accident, yet provide three different accounts of the sequence of events that led to the accident. All three saw the same events, but interpreted them in terms of the information they had selected and organised. Think about the following example:

Example 4.1

You and a friend are watching the news on television while enjoying a drink in the local pub. The first item on news shows members of the police service armed with batons and rubber bullets breaking up a peaceful demonstration. Your friend says, "Another example of police brutality!" The stranger sitting next to you says, "It's good to see the police doing their job so efficiently — demonstrations should be banned!"
What do you think accounts for the difference in the two ways of interpreting the same event?

4.1.3   Improving the accuracy of your perceptions

Although our perceptions influence our understanding of the world, we rarely consider ways to improve our perceptual accuracy. The suggestions that follow should help you improve your perceptual skills and provide you with a more accurate interpretation of the events and people around you.

Throughout this chapter we have emphasised that perception is a personal process. Your perception of a person, object or event is different from the actual person, object or event. In other words, you are the major actor in the perception process (Gamble & Gamble 1998a). By recognising that you have biases and that you are not always open to the information around you, you can increase the probability that your perceptions will provide you with accurate information about the world around you and the people in it.

Because of the subjective element in forming perceptions and the resulting inaccuracies, you need some means to check or validate the accuracy of your perceptions and to sharpen your ability to take in and interpret information from your environment. Apart from making the conscious effort to pay attention and concentrate on what is happening around you, Verderber and Verderber (2002) suggest two methods that you should learn to use: multi-sensory cross-check and consensus.

☐ **Multisensory cross-check** Perceptions are often based on information that you receive through one sense — what you see or hear or feel or taste or smell. By cross-checking the interpretation through another sense, you can some-times validate the accuracy of your perceptions. For example, a rock in your friend's nature collection may look coarse and heavy, but proves to be soft and light when you touch it. In fact, it is not a rock at all, but has been made from synthetic material to resemble a rock. In this instance, your perception has been influenced not only by what you saw, but the context or environment in which you interpreted what you saw. Similarly, you can cross-check your initial perception that the amber liquid in a glass is apple juice and not beer by tasting and smelling it.

❑ ***Consensus*** means that you validate a perception by comparing your interpretation with that of others. You ask others what they think the liquid in the glass is, or how they interpreted an event or someone's behaviour. In this way, you become aware of factors that you may have missed and which have distorted your interpretation.

4.1.4   Gombrich's theory of perception

The art historian, Ernst Gombrich, developed a theory which shows the relationship between perception and the way in which works of art are expressed and interpreted. Earlier in this chapter, we defined perception as the process by which we acquire information about our environment through our senses. We also said that this information is selected, organised and interpreted through a frame of reference. Another way of explaining this process is to say that we *represent* such information to ourselves by creating a mental image of what we know. Artists have the ability to communicate their mental images or interpretations of the world, by using the medium in which they are best able to express themselves — literature, poetry, music, painting and so on.

Gombrich (1978) was interested in the fact that different artists represent the world in different ways. He suggested that the diversity of representations comes about because the artist's eye is never 'innocent'. When painters, for instance, begin to depict a scene, they do not simply begin painting what they see. Their frame of reference filters what they see and how they represent it. Their expectations, as well as the selection, organisation and interpretation of the scene, play a part in the way they communicate their image of the world. Their frame of reference also contains definite schemata, that is, rules, conventions and styles of art, which they have inherited from their culture and from previous artists. These schemata provide a framework which guides the artists' interpretation of reality and the style they use to express their interpretation in a work of art.

The viewers of the work of art also interpret the work according to their frame of reference. That is why their understanding of the work of art need not necessarily coincide with that of the artist or with that of other viewers. In other words, perception plays a role in the way we express ourselves in art and the way we interpret it. Gombrich's theory confirms the view proposed at the beginning of this section that our perceptions do not always provide us with an accurate picture of the world. The importance of Gombrich's theory is that, by providing us with insight into the communication of art, we are better able to understand the role of perception in our everyday communication encounters.

We discuss perception again in chapters 7 and 8 which deal respectively with intrapersonal and interpersonal communication because our perception of ourselves and of other people forms the basis of our interpersonal relationships.

4.2   Listening

One of the most important perceptual processes in communication is the ability to listen efficiently.

There is no doubt that we spend a great deal of our time listening. We listen to the sounds of nature, to traffic noises and to people. Researchers report that one of the major limitations in establishing and maintaining relationships is the inability of the partners to listen efficiently. And it is not only in interpersonal communication that we need listening skills. During the course of each day we are constantly called upon to listen in a variety of situations. We use the telephone, attend lectures and meetings, participate in arguments, give and receive instructions, listen to the news on the radio or television and make decisions based on oral information (cf Gamble & Gamble 1987; 1998). Yet, as we pointed out in the Introduction to this chapter, most of us do not listen actively.

Listening is often explained by distinguishing it from hearing. **Hearing** is a passive process. Most of us are born with the ability to hear — hearing is the physical act of receiving aural stimuli (sounds). When soundwaves vibrate against the eardrum and the brain registers these sounds, we hear. Listening, like all acts of perception, is a dynamic, active process involving the communicator and the recipient. Listening occurs when the signals or sounds sent to the brain are processed and used — that is, when we attend to what is being said, select what is relevant and then understand and interpret it for ourselves. (Refer to Section 4.1.1 if you need to revise the process of perception.) Efficient listening also requires that we remember what has been conveyed to us and that we respond to the communicator.

The listening process becomes even more complex when we communicate with others. *Interactive listening* requires that we listen or pay attention to what is said (the verbal or content level of the message) and the manner in which it is conveyed (the nonverbal or relational level of the message). (Content and relational messages are discussed in Section 3.3.6.) We have to listen to the words that are being spoken and, at the same time, 'listen' to the nonverbal cues that accompany the words. The reason is that the nonverbal part of the message carries the feelings and emotions of the speaker, and often 'says' more than the words that are used. Active, efficient listening therefore helps us interpret messages and responses more accurately and thereby gain a better understanding of the people with whom we come into contact. In fact, poor listening is one of the major causes of misunderstanding in our personal and professional relationships.

4.2.1　The listening process

We have said that listening is more complex than merely hearing. It is a process that consists of four stages: sensing and attending, understanding and interpreting, remembering and responding (see Figure 4.5). The stages occur in sequence but we are generally unaware of them.

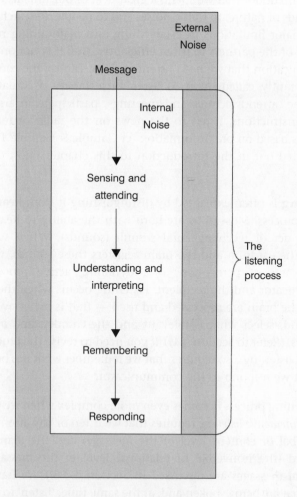

Figure 4.5 The listening process

- ***Sensing and attending*** In the physical part of listening, or *sensing*, sound vibrations must reach the hearing part of the brain before you can complete the listening process. You then *attend* to the sounds your brain has identified. You will remember from the discussion of perception in Section 4.1 that you do not pay the same amount of attention to all the stimuli you receive — you perceive selectively. In the listening process, selective attention allows you to concentrate on what the other person is saying or on the book you are reading and ignore background noises, such as loud noises or the sound of the rain. But selective hearing also has a negative consequence. We sometimes ignore not only background sounds, we block out or fail to attend to important parts of the other person's message — verbal information and nonverbal cues, such as the expression on her face. When this occurs, selective attention contributes to poor listening.

- ***Understanding and interpreting*** The next stage in the listening process is to understand and interpret the meaning of the message. In the listening process, *understanding* implies that you are able to assign the intended meaning to the content or verbal part of the message. *Interpretation* in the listening process implies that you are able to ascertain the emotional meaning the speaker attaches to the message by his or her use of nonverbal signs, such as tone of voice and body movement. Understanding and interpreting a message is an important stage in listening because it enables you to evaluate its meaning for correctness and validity and respond to the other person.

- ***Remembering*** is the process of storing the meanings that have been received so that they may be recalled later. A good reason for taking notes in a lecture or meeting, for instance, is that it is easier to forget than to remember. Studies show that we tend to forget a great deal of what we hear almost as soon as we hear it. In the same way that you listen selectively, you remember some messages more easily than others, perhaps because some messages are more important to you than other messages. *Selective remembering* creates problems when you forget a message or part of a message that later turns out to be important.

- ***Responding*** The fourth stage in the listening process is that of *responding* to the message. At this stage you complete the process of listening by providing feedback to the speaker. Feedback is a prerequisite for efficient listening. It consists of all the verbal and nonverbal messages that you consciously or unconsciously send to the speaker in response to the message. The importance of your feedback is that it is the way the communicator knows you have sensed (heard) the message, understood, interpreted and evaluated it — in other words, that you have been listening.

4.2.2   Types of listening

The stages of the listening process follow one another whether you listen actively or passively. Your degree of involvement in a given interaction and the amount of energy you expend in listening distinguishes active from passive listening. You work harder to absorb the contents of the news on the radio, for example, than listening to a DJ announcing your favourite piece of music. You also work harder at listening to a friend sharing a problem than listening politely to your grandmother telling you how different things were when she was young. The following types of listening provide an idea of the different levels at which we listen.

☐ **Listening for enjoyment** occupies a good deal of our listening time — we listen to music, our favourite television programme, or a friend sharing an interesting titbit of gossip or telling a humorous story. At such times we may suspend our critical faculties, relax and enjoy the stimulation (cf DeVito 1989). At other times, for example, at a concert or at the theatre, we may listen for enjoyment, but we nevertheless respond intellectually or emotionally to the music or the words of the play. The response is to ourselves rather than to the performers.

☐ **Comprehensive or discriminative listening** is one of the primary means of obtaining information. The more efficient our listening skills, the more accurate will be the information we gather. Naturally, we listen for different sorts of information. The student taking notes in a communication lecture or the worker receiving instructions about how to perform a new task is listening for information or listening discriminately. The purpose is to understand and remember the information by following the logic of the lecture or message and concentrating on identifying and separating the main ideas from the supporting material that relates to them. The business world also requires people to listen for information. The assistant listening to his or her supervisor's instructions, the customer listening to the salesperson's description of a new product, or the shipping clerk listening to an order to ship 100 containers to Cape Town, are all listening for information. Information is frequently also exchanged over the telephone in the business world — appointments are scheduled and products are ordered. In the business world, listening is often seen in terms of rands and cents. Errors due to inefficient listening cost money. Imagine what the total cost to the economy would be if every worker in a company like Anglo American made a R10 listening error every day for a month.

☐ **Critical listening** is the type of listening you engage in when you suspect that the source of the information may be biased — for instance, an advertisement on the radio, or a friend who is telling you why your political beliefs are not sound. Critical listening requires skills to analyse, evaluate and challenge the content of the information. The field of persuasion offers you the greatest opportunity to use critical listening skills. Advertisements, political slogans and persuasive messages from friends and family should be critically analysed and evaluated before you act on them.

❐ *Conversational and reflective listening*. Conversational listening implies a constant exchange between the participants. You and your partner are expected to concentrate on each other's messages and to provide appropriate feedback. In close relationships, you engage in a different type of conversational listening by showing affection, caring and warmth to your partner. This is called *reflective* or *empathic listening*. Sometimes the situation arises where, for example, a friend in distress may need to talk to someone and you provide the necessary support by listening. In this situation, you are not usually required to listen for information or to be critical, but to listen for feelings. And you know that some feelings are often expressed nonverbally rather than verbally. Sharing feelings, whether they are of sorrow or joy, enables people to cope with them better. You have probably noticed how your distress over an incident is lessened after you have 'poured your heart out' to an understanding listener. Similarly, feelings of joy are often increased when they are shared.

4.2.3   Inefficient listening behaviour

The problem in all types of listening is that some of our listening behaviour hampers our effectiveness as listeners. The following are some examples of behaviour of which we may not be aware but which impede efficient listening.

❐ *Fidgeting* while someone is talking shows impatience, tells the communicator that you are distracted or not interested in the conversation, and discourages him or her from continuing. Think about the nonverbal messages you are conveying to the speaker when you scratch your head, pull on your earlobe or swing your feet while he or she is talking.

❐ *Lack of concentration* is a prime cause of inefficient listening. If you allow your mind to wander during a conversation and perhaps think about what you are going to do later on, you are unlikely to pick up the ideas that are being expressed or remember them. You are also unlikely to provide your partner with the feedback that tells him or her that you are listening and are interested in what is being said.

❐ *Inaccurate listening* means that you either pay too much attention to the communicator's ideas and forget to interpret the emotions that are being expressed, or that you pay too much attention to emotional messages and neglect the ideas that are being expressed. Every message has two parts: the ideas that are spoken and the emotions that are conveyed through body movements and tone of voice. The exception is that in reflective listening we purposefully concentrate on feelings.

4.2.4   Barriers to listening

As well as poor listening behaviour, there are other barriers to listening that have an equally negative effect on our ability to listen efficiently

The general term used to describe anything that interferes with the communication process is **noise** (refer to Section 3.3.8). With respect to listening, noise refers not only to loud sounds, but to anything that distracts us from listening. We call such interferences **listening barriers**. They can be categorised as external barriers and internal barriers (cf Abrams 1986).

- **External barriers** to listening are distractions in the listening environment. They include background sounds, such as doors slamming, telephones ringing or jack-hammering in the street outside. The activities of people nearby, interruptions from others and physical discomfort such as an uncomfortable chair or a hall with poor acoustics are also external barriers to listening. If you have ever tried to pay attention to instructions while your head of department constantly stops speaking to answer the telephone, you will know the extent to which environmental barriers can affect attention and remembering.

  We cannot place all the blame for inefficient listening on external barriers. Some of the difficulties we encounter stem from within ourselves. Distractions in the listener's mind are the personal prejudices that we call internal barriers to listening.

- **Internal barriers** are the physical and psychological conditions we bring to the communication situation that may inhibit active listening. These include feelings such as anger, anxiety and fatigue, as well as personal prejudices about the communicator's appearance, status, style of speaking and subject matter. Our attitudes often have detrimental effects on our communication. If, for instance, you see yourself as cleverer than other people, with nothing to gain from listening to them, you have created a psychological barrier. Similarly, if you make judgements based on stereotypes — perhaps that a man wearing an earring is a dropout, or that a woman knows nothing about economics — you will evaluate them on the basis of preconceived ideas about their appearance instead of listening to them. Other internal barriers that impede active listening include jumping to conclusions about what the communicator will say, the tendency to ignore topics that are regarded as difficult, and the listener's inability to understand some of the words and ideas expressed by the communicator.

4.2.5   Developing efficient listening skills

Active listening seems difficult to people who have never tried it. Because so many of the problems associated with listening have negative consequences, practise the techniques described below to listen more efficiently (cf Gamble & Gamble 1987; Hybels & Weaver 1989; Rensburg & Bredenkamp 1991).

❏ *Focus your attention* The first step in learning to listen more efficiently is to consciously make the effort to overcome your poor listening behaviour as well as the external and internal barriers that may be impeding your listening ability. Being an effective listener requires that you put aside daydreams and distractions and focus your attention on what the communicator is saying. Remember that your feelings and attitudes are as much a drawback to effective listening as distracting sounds.

❏ *Show that you are listening* It is important not only to pay attention to others, but to show active signs of attentiveness. You can achieve this by offering them verbal and nonverbal cues. Verbal cues can be comments such as "I see", or "Go on", or "Tell me more". Nonverbal cues also show that you are listening, for example, by maintaining eye contact, smiling, frowning or nodding. Such feedback encourages the other person to give you the details necessary for better understanding and lets him or her know that you are involved in the interaction. At the same time, it is important to suppress what you want to say until the communicator has finished talking and not to interrupt.

❏ *Listen to understand ideas* Since it is not possible to remember every word of a complex message, work towards identifying only those concepts that are most important — in other words, those ideas that comprise the main points of the person's message. Thus, when you listen to understand, you actively concentrate on identifying the key words and phrases that will help you accurately summarise the concepts being discussed.

❏ *Listen to retain information* Listening to retain information also requires attention and concentration. Some of the methods that help retention include the following:

Anticipate what is coming: For example, if the speaker says, "The following five points are important", prepare yourself to listen to and remember five points.

Form associations: Some people remember names, places and numbers by associating what was heard with something that is familiar, or by associating it with a visual image.

Take notes: When messages are complex, and accurate retention of information is important, note-taking is probably the most reliable method for recalling information. In other words, paraphrase what has been said by writing down the main ideas and points.

Construct mnemonics: Mnemonics is a word used to describe any artificial technique that aids memory or helps you remember a list of items. One simple way of forming a mnemonic is to take the first letters of a list of items to form a word that you will easily remember, for example, 'potjie', to remember the list **p**otatoes, **o**nions, **t**omatoes, **j**am, **i**ce-cream, **e**ggs. When you have to remember items in a specific sequence, you could try to create a sentence that is easy to remember. As a child, when I first learned to play the piano, my teacher taught me to remember the lines of the treble clef (EGBDF) by using the sentence: '*E*very *g*ood *b*oy *d*eserves *f*ood.' For the spaces in the treble clef (FACE), I simply had to remember the word 'face'.

☐ *Listen to analyse and evaluate content* Listening critically calls for even greater skill than identifying and remembering ideas. Try to establish the communicator's motives and credibility by challenging and questioning the ideas expressed. To evaluate the validity of a message and then accept or reject it involves being able to separate fact from opinion, determine if an argument is based on logic or emotion, and detect ambiguities in the argument (Barker 1984). You also need to recognise your own biases and prejudices about the topic. Hybels and Weaver (1989:65) express evaluation as follows: "We must learn to suspend judgement — delay taking a position — until all the facts and other evidence are in, we have had a chance to test the facts in the marketplace of ideas, or they have been chewed over sufficiently for digestion."

☐ *Listen reflectively* The best way to listen reflectively is to try to understand what other people are feeling *from their point of view* and reflect these feelings back with empathy. It requires that you put aside your own feelings and opinions and make the effort to recognise the emotions being expressed and to encourage other people to come to terms with their feelings. We do this by paraphrasing the communicator's statements and reinforcing those statements with nonverbal cues — eye contact, touching and facial expressions.

Example 4.1

The following is an example of a reflective listening response in which the listener paraphrases the speaker's words and feelings.

Thandi is confiding to Sipho about her studies.

Sipho replies: "You keep telling me how well everything is going and how pleased you are that your assignments are up to date. But every time you bring up the subject of credit marks for examination entrance your tone changes and you sound less enthusiastic. Is something bothering you?"

It is important to remember that it is not your task to judge the situation. You help the other person reach a solution without offering advice in the form of, "You shouldn't feel that way", or "Why don't you look for another job?", or "You must tell her you won't tolerate such behaviour". These are poor responses because they do not help the other person to address the feelings that are the cause of the problem.

4.3   Listening and feedback

In our discussion of the listening process in Section 4.2.1 we said that the last stage in the process is responding, or giving feedback, to the communicator. In Section 3.3.9 we defined feedback as the response of the participants to each other. Verbal feedback (eg questions or comments) and nonverbal feedback (eg a puzzled look or a nod of the head) by the partners in communication indicate the level of understanding or agreement between two or more people in response to the original message. Feedback tells us whether our message is being understood, whether it is being received positively or negatively, or whether we should change our communication style altogether. The point we emphasise is that, in order for successful communication to take place, the communicator and recipient must take mutual responsibility for giving and receiving feedback. If the participants in communication are not aware of each other's feedback or do not pay attention to it, there is a strong possibility that their communication will be ineffective. We therefore have to listen attentively to the verbal and nonverbal elements of a message and respond to them. In this regard, we need to remember that even silence is a form of feedback. If a tutor asks a question and no one in the class responds, she needs to consider whether the students have understood the topic she was explaining, or perhaps whether they are too afraid of possible sarcasm or anger if they give the incorrect answer.

Think back on the years in your life when you were growing up. What would have happened to your understanding of the world and the people in it, as well as your understanding of yourself, if no one had praised your first efforts to walk and talk, or to learn to swim? Or if no one had warned you to look out for cars before crossing the road or not to touch a hot iron? Or if your mother had not comforted you when you fell or laughed at your immature jokes? What would have happened to your values and morals if no one had taught you, for instance, that it is wrong to steal other children's possessions? (cf. Barker & Gaut 1996).

4.3.1   Inappropriate and effective feedback

We can conclude from the few examples given above that feedback is an essential element in the process of communication. A problem that arises in connection with feedback is that, if we are not listening attentively, we often give **inappropriate feedback** — responses which do not encourage effective communication or show concern for the needs of the communicator. Some examples of inappropriate feedback are the following:

❑ *Irrelevant responses* do not apply to the situation that is being discussed because the listener has not been paying attention or has heard only part of the conversation. If you were telling a friend about your forthcoming holiday in Europe and he replied that the local weather forecast for tomorrow is that it will be extremely hot, the impression you would get is that he is not interested in your conversation.

☐ *Interrupting responses* occur when one of the participants breaks into the conversation without allowing you, the communicator, to finishing speaking, thereby interrupting your train of thought. The implication is that what he or she has to say is more important than what you have to say. You start telling a friend that you heard on the radio that . . . and before you can finish, she says, "Oh yes — the Oscars will be screened live on TV tonight."

☐ *Tangential responses* sidetrack the topic of a conversation. When one person is talking about a burglary at her house and the other responds by talking about his motor insurance policy, the interaction gets off track. The response indicates that the recipient is not really listening to what the communicator is saying.

☐ The *impervious response* occurs when a person fails to acknowledge your attempt to communicate, even though you know that she has heard you. At best, you may feel a sense of awkwardness or embarrassment or, at worst, such a (non)response may undermine your self-image and self-esteem.

On the other hand, **effective feedback** improves the process of communication and the understanding that is reached between the participants. When you give a supportive response to someone who expresses her disappointment with a test result, for example, or you compliment a friend on an award she has received, you are not only showing that you have been listening, you are also confirming the value or worth of the other person. There are many ways of giving effective feedback in interpersonal communication, some of which we describe below.

☐ *Focus* on what you actually see and hear and do not make inferences about what someone has said or done. For instance, the reason someone does not greet you as enthusiastically as you would like, may not be that she is annoyed with you, but that she is worried about a personal problem that has cropped up in her life.

☐ Be *descriptive* rather than judgmental. Because the purpose of constructive criticism is to be helpful, it is appropriate to provide a suggestion that can lead to a positive change in behaviour. A teacher who tells you, "I think your marks would improve if you spent more time at home revising what we do in class" is being more constructive than one who says, "You are the laziest person in the class".

☐ Give *immediate* feedback because it will be more specific and accurate than feedback given at a later stage. Also, it is generally better to deal with negative feelings immediately and discuss them with the other person rather than to allow them to grow out of proportion. The exception is, of course, occasions when you know that your feelings and emotions will result in your giving feedback that you will later regret.

☐ **Limit** your feedback. Particularly in dyadic situations, if you constantly smile and nod your head, your partner will not be sure whether you are really listening or listening superficially. Similarly, if you continually interrupt the flow of your partner's conversation with comments, he or she may start feeling uneasy because you seem to be trying to control the direction that his or her thoughts are taking. Limited feedback is not, however, the same as no feedback! (cf Barker & Gaut 1996; Beebe, Beebe & Redmond 1999).

Scenario 4.1

The scenario is based on Johnson (1997).

In the course of the day, you often find yourself in a position where someone, a close friend perhaps, or even an acquaintance, talks to you about a situation he or she has to deal with. You are expected to listen attentively and then respond. Here is such a scenario.

Peter: "I'm really depressed. I have a good job and I earn a reasonable salary, but I'm not happy. I realise now that working is not as great as I thought it would be when I gave up my university studies in order to be financially independent. I have some money saved. Even though I did not do particularly well at university before, I think I should quit work and start studying again. Actually, I don't know what I should do."

There are five possible feedback responses you might make in trying to help Peter solve his problem. Each response illustrates a different technique of listening and responding. The five techniques are:
1. Advising and evaluating
2. Analysing and interpreting
3. Reassuring and supporting
4. Questioning and probing
5. Paraphrasing and understanding.

These are the responses:
1. How long have you felt this way? Have your negative feelings started only recently, or have you always felt depressed about what you are doing?
2. In other words, you're depressed and puzzled because your job isn't fulfilling, but neither were your studies, and they are the only two alternatives you see yourself as having.
3. Depression is often anger turned against yourself. Perhaps you are angry at yourself for not feeling fulfilled by what you are doing.
4. You don't know that you will do any better at university now. You really should stop complaining and thank your lucky stars that you have a good job. There are lots of people out there who don't and who would gladly swap places with you.

5. Lots of people have trouble making up their minds. There are hundreds of people who don't like their jobs and would not go back to university even if it was for free. You don't need to feel depressed.

Each of these ways of responding communicates certain intentions and all of them may be helpful. We would not label any of them as good or bad, ineffective or appropriate because the purpose of all of them is to help someone solve a problem. We do, however, believe that some of the responses are more helpful than others in building relationships and helping people to examine their feelings and thoughts in a different way.

After you have studied the scenario, answer the following questions, giving reasons for each answer.

1. Identify each response in terms of the five alternatives listed at the beginning of the case.
2. Explain the effect you think each response would have on:
   (a) the nature of your relationship with the communicator
   (b) helping the communicator to see the problem in a different way.
3. If the communicator was a close friend, which response do you think would be the most appropriate and which the least effective?
4. If the communicator was an acquaintance, would your answer to question 3 change?

Summary

This chapter discussed the importance of accurate perception and active listening in the communication process. Our understanding of our circumstances and those of other people depends on the way we perceive the events that take place around us. The chapter began by explaining the process of perception: the ways in which we select, organise and interpret the information that reaches us through our senses. It offered suggestions on how to improve the accuracy of perceptions and, to illustrate how perception 'works' in our lives, it briefly discussed Gombrich's theory of perception with reference to works of art. It then looked at the differences between hearing and listening and explained the process of listening. It continued by describing the types of listening that are appropriate in different situations. It pointed out some poor listening habits and discussed the external and internal barriers that impede efficient listening. The last part of the chapter showed the relationship between listening and feedback and described appropriate and ineffective types of feedback. The chapter ended with a scenario based on a practical exercise to illustrate how the relationship between listening and feedback influences the nature of a communication encounter.

Test yourself

1. Briefly explain the process of perception by referring to selection, organisation and interpretation.
2. Cut out some pictures and scenes from a magazine and ask three of your friends to write down their perceptions of what they see. Then compare notes and discuss the differences between your perceptions. Can you account for the differences?
3. With reference to Gombrich's theory, explain why you and a friend who see the same work of art at an exhibition interpret it in different ways.
4. Describe in your own words how we distinguish listening from hearing.
5. Think about some different situations in which you are involved in listening. Identify the types of listening you are engaged in.
6. Think of a situation in which you let a personal prejudice interfere with your listening. How did this prejudice interfere with your communication encounter? Explain.
7. Watch yourself carefully in your next lecture. Take note of how many times your attention wanders and for how long. How effective do you think your listening was?
8. Explain the function of feedback in the listening process.
9. Explain the types of verbal and nonverbal feedback you can use as a good listener.
10. Write down three examples of ineffective feedback and three examples of appropriate feedback based on your own experiences of interpersonal communication.

EXECUTIVE SUMMARY
Perception, listening and feedback

1 The process of perception
   ☐ selection
   ☐ organisation
   ☐ interpretation
2 Gombrich's theory of perception
3 The listening process
   ☐ sensing and attending
   ☐ understanding and interpreting
   ☐ remembering
   ☐ responding
4 Types of listening
   ☐ enjoyment
   ☐ comprehensive
   ☐ critical
   ☐ conversational
   ☐ reflective
5 Listening and feedback
   ☐ inappropriate feedback
   ☐ effective feedback

5 Nonverbal communication

Overview

It's the first day of a new job and you want to make a good impression. You have set the alarm clock for earlier than usual so that you will have plenty of time to prepare for the day. After a shower, you take particular care about the clothes you choose — not too casual, but not too smart either. You don't want your new colleagues to think that your appearance is more suitable for a cocktail party than for a day at the office. As you leave, you check your hair in the mirror and collect the articles you have selected to put in your office — a photograph taken at your graduation ceremony, a dictionary, a pencil box and a pot plant.

The description we have outlined may seem pretty routine, but as Staley and Staley (1992) point out, your actions reveal a great deal about yourself without a single word being uttered. Your concern about being punctual, the care you have taken to make a good first impression, and even the items you place in your office, all communicate nonverbal messages that speak as loudly as words. To arrive at a better understanding of communication and to develop skills that allow more effective participation in the communication process, you need to be aware of the range of nonverbal signs you are conveying and receiving at a particular time. The ability to analyse nonverbal messages enhances your understanding of other people's meaning and helps to eliminate communication problems. In addition, how people are perceived as communicators is based partly on their use of nonverbal skills.

In this chapter, we provide a framework for understanding the role and impact of your own and other people's nonverbal communication. After defining the term 'nonverbal communication', we explain the functions of nonverbal communication and then go on to discuss some of the factors that influence our understanding of our own and other people's nonverbal behaviour, such as the context of the communication encounter and the culture of the participants. We continue with a discussion of six categories of nonverbal behaviour and then suggest how you can apply what you have learned to your own communication. We end the chapter with one scenario based on examples of nonverbal communication in a printed publication, and another which demonstrates that nonverbal communication and culture are inseparable.

Learning outcomes

At the end of this chapter you should be able to:
1. Define nonverbal communication and identify the reasons for studying it.
2. Describe five functions of nonverbal communication using examples from your everyday experience of communication.
3. Explain three factors that influence your understanding of nonverbal communication.
4. Describe the relationship between verbal and nonverbal communication.
5. Explain the meaning of the following categories of nonverbal communication and illustrate each with an example from your own experience: kinesics, proxemics, haptics, chronemics, personal appearance, the environment and paralanguage.
6. Apply what you have learned about nonverbal communication in everyday experiences of communication.
7. Be more sensitive to your own use of nonverbal messages.
8. Answer the questions based on the scenarios at the end of this chapter.

Introduction

The term nonverbal is commonly used to describe all intentional and unintentional messages that are not written or spoken. But nonverbal communication is not only concerned with the image that people present through personal appearance or interior design as described in the chapter overview. It is also concerned with messages we send through our body movements, gestures, facial expressions, tone of voice and eye movement, as well as our use of space, time and touch. In fact, researchers report that, in face-to-face communication, more than 65 percent of the meaning in a message is conveyed by nonverbal behaviour (Mehrabian 1981; Stewart 1990). Your own experience tells you that, at times, you are at a loss when you need words to express feelings and emotions. When a person needs comforting, for example, a touch or a smile is often more effective than words. Nonverbal communication also has an effect even when the participants are not in each other's presence. In a telephone conversation, for example, some of the meaning of a message is carried by the speaker's tone of voice. Very often, the success of your communication and relationships depends on how well you 'read' these silent messages from others. To gain greater insight into the complexities of nonverbal behaviour, we begin by discussing the functions that nonverbal communication serves.

5.1   Functions of nonverbal communication

Essentially, a nonverbal message functions in one of five ways: it reinforces, complements, contradicts, replaces or regulates a verbal message (cf Knapp 1990; Verderber 1990).

☐ A nonverbal message **reinforces** or **accents** the verbal message when it adds to its meaning. In the same way that underlining or *italicising* written words emphasises them, saying "Come here **now**" conveys a more urgent message than "Come here now". Pounding your hand on the table when saying, "Listen to me", conveys a more effective message than the words alone. While your gesture may be redundant, it adds emphasis to your statement and captures the listener's attention. Very often, reinforcing the message is not deliberate, it is done without conscious thought or intent on your part.

☐ A nonverbal message **complements** the verbal message when it conveys the same meaning. If you tell someone, "I'm pleased to meet you", and accompany your words with a warm smile, your tone of voice and facial expression are complementing the verbal message.

☐ A nonverbal message may **contradict** the verbal message. People often say one thing, but do another. For example, a student about to make an oral presentation to a class may say, "I'm not nervous", despite his trembling hands and perspiring forehead. Research has shown that, in most cases, people tend to believe the nonverbal cues rather than the words that are spoken. Nonverbal messages are highly credible, perhaps because they often convey feelings and emotions. The voice may also contradict the verbal message. A change in pitch, for example, can tell us that someone is perhaps telling a lie or being sarcastic or merely teasing. Research has shown that when we are attempting to conceal the truth, our pitch tends to change in a upwards direction and lets others know we are contradicting the verbal message (cf Barker & Gaut 1996).

☐ A nonverbal message may **replace** the verbal message. Gestures, facial expressions and other nonverbal cues generate meaning without the use of words. You wave your hand to someone instead of saying hello, or give someone a hug instead of saying thanks for helping me — your message is clear. Similarly, the expression on the face of a dejected person who comes home after a hard day at work, substitutes for the statement, "I've had a rotten day".

☐ Nonverbal behaviour functions to **regulate** the flow of verbal interaction. Your eye contact, tone of voice, nodding of the head, slight hand movements and other nonverbal behaviour tell your partner when to talk, to repeat a statement, to hurry up or to finish the conversation. Good public speakers learn to adjust what they are saying and how they are saying it on the basis of such cues from the audience. The same applies to group communication. The chairperson at a meeting, for example, uses eye contact or hand gestures instead of words to indicate whose turn it is to speak.

5.2   Aspects of nonverbal communication

The potential for misunderstanding a nonverbal message is greater than for misunderstanding a verbal message. To begin with, nonverbal communication is often beyond our control. Whereas we can plan what we say very carefully and stop talking at will, we cannot simply 'switch off' nonverbal behaviour. Even if we consciously control our facial expression and hand movements to hide the fact that we are nervous, for example, our strained voice or shaking knees may give us away. We call such nonverbal cues **leakage** because we are, in fact, leaking information about ourselves that we cannot hide (cf Burton & Dimbleby 1995). Nonverbal behaviour confirms the axiom (a generally accepted statement) that, "One cannot *not* communicate" (Watzlawick, Beavin & Jackson 1968:51). Even your silence communicates a message, and you cannot tell your body not to leak information by way of your posture, for example, or the clothes you are wearing.

Another factor that has to be taken into account is that nonverbal behaviour is **contextual**. Verbal and nonverbal signs work together to convey the total meaning of a message. Whereas verbal communication primarily conveys content information, nonverbal communication primarily conveys relational information (emotions and feelings), depending on the circumstances or context in which it occurs (refer to Section 3.3.10). The tone of voice of the communicator, for example, can convey sincerity or sarcasm depending on how the message is related to the circumstances. "Nice work" is a compliment when you have completed a difficult project, but a reprimand when you submit a careless piece of work. Similarly, you know from your own experience that smiles, nods and winks can convey different meanings depending on the context in which we find ourselves.

Whether the context is formal or informal also plays a role in determining nonverbal behaviour. You might watch television at home with your feet up on a table, but you are unlikely to do so at someone else's home unless invited to "make yourself comfortable". Similarly, you might pick up some food from your plate with your fingers at home, but are less likely to do so at a dinner party. We hope that some of you reacted spontaneously to the latter example by saying, "That's not a valid statement. In my culture, it's perfectly acceptable to eat with one's fingers at a dinner party". One of the major causes of misunderstanding between people of different cultures is the assumption that nonverbal cues have the same meaning for all people.

We are often unaware of the pervasive influence that **culture** has on the meaning we attach to nonverbal communication. Each culture provides its members with a code of behaviour that is acceptable in different situations. It is not only through language that culture is transmitted. Some of the behavioural codes we learn are communicated nonverbally, as we illustrate in Scenario 5.2 at the end of this chapter.

Research results suggest that some aspects of nonverbal communication seem to be fairly consistent regardless of race or culture. For example, studies have shown that facial expressions to convey emotions such as fear, surprise, happiness or anger are relatively constant across cultures and are thus fairly easy to recognise and interpret. But more subtle facial expressions like disgust, surprise or embarrassment may vary across cultures (cf Ellis & McClintock 1990). In North America, for instance, embarrassment is normally shown by blushing. In Japan, embarrassment is shown by laughter and giggling. Arabs show embarrassment by sticking out their tongues slightly (cf Hamilton & Parker 1990). Similarly, the signs given by clothing may be personal or influenced by the culture of the individual. As a result there may be more variation in the way such signs are interpreted. In South Africa, a woman dressed entirely in black is signifying that she is a widow, whereas a woman wearing a black pinafore is communicating the loss of a child. Attaching fixed meanings to nonverbal signs without taking the cultural context into account often results in misunderstanding and the creation of **stereotypes**. (We discuss stereotypes in more detail in Section 7.5.1.) In a multicultural country such as South Africa, it becomes even more important to be aware that all nonverbal communication conveys information that must be evaluated or interpreted within the context in which it occurs.

5.3   Categories of nonverbal communication

It could be extremely misleading to try to make a list of nonverbal signs and attach a single meaning to each, as many popular books on 'body language' tend to do. There is no dictionary for understanding nonverbal behaviour. Because nonverbal messages are more ambiguous than verbal messages, they do not always mean what people think they do. The real reason someone constantly glances at the clock during a meeting, for example, may not be that he is bored, but that he is expecting an important phone call.

We discuss the following categories of nonverbal communication: kinesics, proxemics, haptics, chronemics, personal appearance and paralanguage. The discussion is based largely on research published in North America and Britain. Therefore, many of the assumptions and examples of nonverbal communication pertain to Western cultures. As you read the discussion, please feel free to disagree with any assertions we make if they do not coincide with the meanings of a particular nonverbal sign in your culture.

5.3.1 Kinesics

Body movement, gestures, posture, facial expressions and eye contact fall within the broad field of nonverbal study called **kinesics**. The term was coined by Ray Birdwhistell (1952; 1970), a pioneer in the field of study. He was among the first theorists to suggest that communication is not restricted to verbal language and that there is a significant connection between physical behaviour and spoken language. Birdwhistell concluded that body movements could be studied and understood like a language, such as English or seTswana, and he made an intensive study of how people infer or attribute meaning to physical signs in their communication encounters.

Body movements are strong indicators of how you feel. Have you ever considered how much you communicate about yourself simply by the way you walk? Watch the people walking down a busy street. Some, for example, walk as though they are in a daze and seem oblivious to what is going on around them, whereas others stride along as if they are determined and confident about where they are going. An interesting study conducted in the United States shows that people in the first category are more likely to be mugged than those in the second! Their body movements seem to communicate to potential muggers that they could be easy prey (cf Wilson, Hantz & Hanna 1989).

On a more scientific basis, researchers Ekman and Friesen (1969) have classified body movements into five classes: emblems, illustrators, regulators, affect displays and adaptors.

☐ *Emblems* are nonverbal signs that have a direct translation into words, for instance the manual languages of the deaf, the extended thumb of the hitchhiker and the two-fingered peace symbol. Unlike much of our nonverbal behaviour, emblems are intentional and are most often used when verbal channels or blocked or impractical, for example when people are too far apart to make themselves heard. In other words, they substitute for or replace the verbal message. For example, you knock on your neighbour's door, and, because she is on the telephone, she waves a greeting to you and then gestures for you to come in and sit down. However, some emblems are not universal and their meanings have to be learned within each culture. For example, an investigation which tested 20 emblems revealed that a gesture that was intended to signify good luck/be well (*sterkte/voorspoed*) was interpreted differently by Afrikaans-, seTswana- and Southern Sotho-speaking respondents (cf Terblanche 1994).

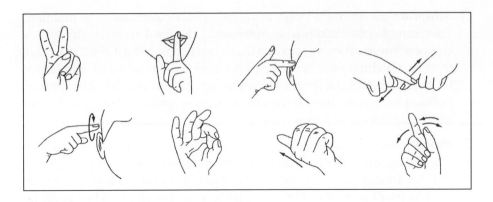

Figure 5.1 Can you understand these signs?

☐ *Illustrators* are the aptly named nonverbal sketches or pictures that accent, emphasise or reinforce words. Examples are gestures that illustrate the shape or size of an object, such as the large fish that you caught, as well as the hand movements that illustrate the directions you might give someone about how to reach a particular destination. They are usually intentional and are often used in situations where the verbal code alone is unable to convey meaning accurately — they help to make communication more exact. Because illustrators are more universal than emblems, they are less likely to cause misunderstanding.

☐ *Affect displays* are facial expressions of emotion. The face is a constant source of information to those around us. Facial expressions communicate emotional states or reactions to a message and generally mirror the intensity of people's thoughts and feelings. Examples include smiling, frowning, lifting the eyebrows and pursing the lips. Although it is not always possible to interpret all facial expressions correctly, they can be a more accurate cue to interpreting people's emotions than the words they use. Apart from the universal facial expressions of anger, fear and happiness discussed above, it has been estimated that the face is capable of producing more than 20 000 expressions (cf Staley & Staley 1992). Combinations of emotions — anger plus fear, for example — make matters even more complicated. Unlike emblems and illustrators, affect displays are almost impossible to control, making your face the primary means for communicating emotions.

☐ *Regulators* are the subtle signs we use to control the give-and-take of conversation (refer to Section 5.1). These signals are sent quickly and almost unconsciously, and are an effective means of assisting the exchange of listening and speaking roles in a communication encounter. Regulators include head nods, puzzled looks and changes in posture. The teacher who points to the child she wants to answer the question is using a regulator.

❑ *Adaptors* are nonverbal ways of adjusting to a communication situation. They can also be described as movements designed to meet physical or emotional needs. Have you noticed that when people feel self-conscious, they tend to straighten their clothes and pat their hair? It seems to help relieve tension, or reduce the stress experienced by, for example, a public speaker. Rubbing your eyes, jingling the change in your pocket, fiddling with your jewellery or biting your fingernails are also examples of adaptors.

❑ *Posture* also communicates a great deal of information about yourself. The way you sit, stand, slump or slouch provides information about your gender, status, self-image, attitudes and emotional state. Slouching or sitting with your head in your hands often indicates that you are feeling low, whereas sitting with your feet on the desk may be interpreted by others as a sign of your feeling of superiority.

❑ *Gestures* are movements of hands, legs, arms and feet. People vary in the amount of gesturing they use. Hand gestures are commonly used to describe or emphasise a verbal description or to communicate attitudes. For example, in a conversation, crossing your arms generally conveys a less aggressive attitude than putting your hands on your hips. Similarly, leaning forwards usually conveys a positive attitude towards the other person, whereas leaning backwards could be interpreted negatively.

❑ *Eye contact* is another aspect of nonverbal communication which helps us interpret meaning. Eye contact refers to the way we use our eyes to regulate and monitor the effects of communication. For example, public speakers who never look up convey the impression that they are nervous. Speakers who do look at their audience during a speech come across as confident and in control. However, unlike some facial expressions, the use of eye contact is a less universal convention. In some traditional African cultures, for example, dropping your eyes in conversation with a superior is regarded as a sign of respect, whereas in Western cultures little or no eye contact is often interpreted as an indication of boredom, a lack of concentration or a feeling of inferiority. Even though conventions in eye contact may differ, it plays an important part in nonverbal behaviour and is something we learn in childhood as part of our cultural experience (cf Ellis & McClintock 1990).

Example 5.1

ALLAN: *The most useful professional development seminar I have ever taken taught me how to sit and look at people to show I'm interested. Our instructor told us that a lot of times men don't show their interest with head nods and eye contact. That explained to me why some of the women I supervise complain that I never seemed interested when they came to talk to me. It wasn't that I wasn't interested. I just didn't show it with my nonverbal behaviour* (Wood 2002:165).

Allan's story illustrates the importance of being aware of how your body movements influence your communication with others.

5.3.2 Proxemics

The study of how people's perception of space communicates information is known as **proxemics**. The term was invented by Edward Hall (1959), who conducted cross-cultural studies on the use of space in personal and social situations. Proxemics includes the messages people convey when, for instance, they choose to sit at the front or back of a classroom, or whether they sit near to or far from the head of the table at a meeting. Most teachers will tell you that the mischief-makers dash to the back of the classroom and that the more serious students choose a front seat. Similarly, the general interpretation of people who sit far from the head of a table at a meeting is that they are reluctant to participate in the proceedings by voicing opinions. The danger of such fixed interpretations is that we often attribute the same generalisation to the person who may simply be late and occupies the only remaining empty seat.

Degrees of status are also communicated through the use of space. Heads of companies, university principals and high government officials usually have large, well-furnished offices, whereas their employees occupy smaller, more sparsely furnished spaces. In a household, children have smaller bedrooms than their parents, and often have to share that space with other family members.

The distance between people in communication conveys information about their relationship. Hall (1959) identified four spatial zones of interpersonal communication: intimate distance, personal distance, social distance and public distance. The basic premise of his theory is that when we observe the distance that people maintain between themselves and others in interpersonal communication, we can tell which people have close relationships and which have formal relationships. Hall found that the use of space depends on your nationality and culture. The findings below apply to the meanings that most Western cultures ascribe to space.

In **intimate distance**, people are in direct contact with each other or are no more than 45 centimetres apart. It is the zone reserved for lovemaking and only those who are very close to you are allowed into it. Most people feel apprehensive when those who have no right to be there intrude into it. In **personal distance** people are between 45-120 centimetres from each other. This is the distance most often reserved for interactions with friends or family members. It is close enough to see each other's reactions, but far enough away not to encroach on their intimate zone.

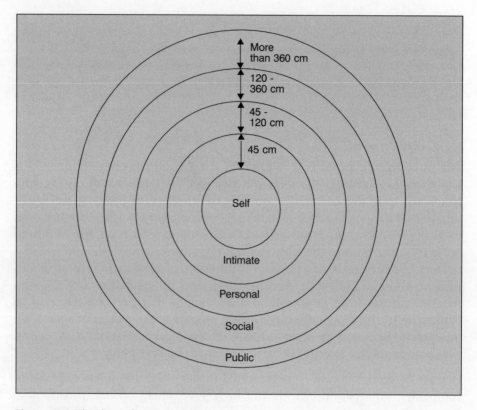

Figure 5.2 The four distance zones

When people do not know each other very well, they tend to maintain a **social distance** of 120-360 centimetres. This is the distance most often used at social gatherings, business meetings or interviews. A distance of more than 360 centimetres, or **public distance,** is typically used in public speaking situations. It indicates a formal occasion, such as a politician addressing a gathering. At this distance, there is little opportunity for mutual involvement in the communication encounter.

Look at the photograph reproduced in Figure 5.3. What does it tell you about the distances people maintain in personal and social situations?

Space influences what we talk about with others. You would be considered rather odd and certainly very rude if you entered someone's intimate zone to ask the time. Likewise, it would be difficult to have a conversation of a personal nature with someone at a social distance. Apart from the fact that everyone else in the vicinity would be able to overhear your conversation, the distance is too great to provide a setting which is conducive to exchanging confidences (cf Hybels & Weaver 1989).

Figure 5.3 Personal distance zone (reproduced with the kind permission of Robben Island Mayibuye Archive)

While all individuals have spatial zones, Hall established that the distance of the zones varies across cultures. People of different cultures have different notions about, for example, what is considered an appropriate distance between strangers. Generally, Latin-Americans, Arabs, Turks and Italians converse at a closer distance than British people or North Americans (cf Shuter 1984). In South Africa, black people in queues typically stand much closer to the next person in the queue, whereas this measure of social distance might offend a white person (cf Finlayson 1991). The way different cultures use space could create problems if, for instance, you feel crowded by someone of another culture whom you feel is too close for comfort, whereas she might interpret your use of space as an indication that you are cold and distant.

Within a culture as diverse as South Africa, various subcultures may develop their own proxemic norms. In research on intercultural communication, a distinction is often made between **high-contact** and **low-contact cultures** (cf Tubbs & Moss 2003). Members of high-contact cultures touch each other more often, sit or stand closer to each other, make more eye contact, and speak louder. Members of low-contact cultures touch each other less often, maintain more interpersonal distance and are more indirect in facing each other and in their eye contact. They also tend to use a lower, softer tone of voice. French, Italian, Latin-American, Russian, Arab and African cultures are some high-contact cultures, whereas German, Danish and East Asian cultures include those seen as low-contact. Moderate-contact cultures include the United States, New Zealand, Australia and Canada (Ting-Toomey 1999; Tubbs & Moss 2003). You might like to observe people of different cultures in communication encounters and draw your own conclusions.

Example 5.2

JERRY: *Last summer I had an internship with a big accounting firm in Johannesburg and space really told the story on status. Interns like me worked in two large rooms on the first floor with partitions to separate our desks. New employees worked on the second floor in little cubicles. The higher up you were in the hierarchy of the firm, the higher up your office was — literally. I mean, the president and vice-presidents — six of them — had the whole top floor, while there were forty or more interns crowded onto my floor* (Wood 2002:167).

Jerry's story illustrates how space expresses power relationships.

Example 5.3

SANDY: *I was so uncomfortable when I travelled to Mexico last year. People just crammed into buses even when all the seats were taken. They pushed up together and pressed against each other. I felt they were really being rude, and I was uptight about having people on top of me like that. I guess it was a learned cultural difference, but it sure made me uneasy at the time. I never knew how territorial I was until I felt my space was being invaded* (Wood 2002:168).

Sandy's story illustrates how the norms for personal space vary from culture to culture.

5.3.3   Haptics

The field of study that examines messages that are conveyed by our use of touch is called **haptics**. Physical contact with others is the most basic form of communication and a lack of touch in certain situations often communicates that there is a problem. Social workers, for instance, know that something is wrong in a relationship when a mother avoids touching and hugging her child. Lack of contact in childhood often may also contribute to physical and psychological problems in adulthood. As with distance, touch communicates information about the nature of the relationship between people. Lovers usually touch each other more frequently in conversation than do friends. People who have just been introduced shake hands more formally than relatives. We often pat someone on the back to calm them down when they are angry. We may grab someone's elbow to attract his or her attention. Most of us also get pleasure from touching material objects — stroking the smooth leather of a pair of gloves or the silky fabric of a dress or shirt.

Whether or not you often reach out to touch other people is frequently determined by cultural influences. Before making inferences about other people's use of touch, you should bear in mind that the kind of touching behaviour that is permissible in interpersonal communication depends largely on the individual's culture. Finlayson (1991) notes that, in South Africa, white people generally prefer to maintain a social distance and often tend to feel somewhat embarrassed when touched. However, among black people, touching is considered normal. The practice often extends to two people of the same gender holding hands when walking down the street, a practice frequently misunderstood by others who assume that they are homosexuals. Staley and Staley (1992) point out that we need to be especially careful about how we use haptics in an organisational environment. Aside from handshakes or the occasional pat on the back, touching your colleagues — no matter how innocently — may be misinterpreted as a sign of romantic attraction and could result in a charge of sexual harassment.

Example 5.4

WILL: *One of the neatest things about my parents is the way they are always connecting with each other. I don't mean with words. It's more like looks and touching. If Mom says something, Dad looks at her. Whenever either of them comes into a room the other's in, they have to touch — just brush a shoulder or scratch the other's back or whatever. It's like they're always reaching out to each other* (Wood 2002:166).

   Will's story describes how a young man interprets the close relationship between his parents by observing their touching behaviour.

5.3.4   Chronemics

Chronemics is the field of study concerned with the use of time. Should your doorbell ring at three o'clock in the morning, for instance, your first thought is probably that something must be wrong. You have interpreted the meaning of the ringing doorbell in terms of time. If you leave a message for a friend to return a telephone call and she does not respond for three days, how do you interpret her action? Perhaps you think that your friendship is not as valuable to her as you thought. Again, time affected your interpretation of a message. Time influences the way we interpret many messages and forms of behaviour. Time is often a reflection of status: the higher our status, the more control we have over time. Parents control when their children will eat, bath and go to bed. Professionals in our society often control how long we wait for an appointment. As a student, you have little control over the date of an examination or the time of a particular class.

In most industrial societies (such as North America, Japan, Germany, South Africa) time is money and high productivity features prominently in the way of life of the society. People are intolerant of others who are consistently late for work or for appointments and consider them to be rude and irresponsible. But this inflexible conception of time does not apply to every society.

Some cultures have a more flexible attitude to time. Generally, these societies emphasise social relationships more than productivity and tend to be less concerned about being 'early' or 'late'. Central and South America, and much of the Middle East, operate on flexible time (cf Barker 1984). In many African countries, time is relative to the occasion. The correct time to celebrate a wedding, for instance, is when the preparations have been completed.

Misunderstandings can arise when people of different cultures conduct business and do not understand one another's assumptions about appropriate timing. In the same way, employers and employees of different cultures are often confused by the other's conception of punctuality.

Time also operates differently within one country. In South Africa, people in metropolitan areas, such as Johannesburg, Pretoria or Cape Town, are more restricted by time than people in small towns or rural areas. People from small towns who come to the big city report that they experience tension because city dwellers' lives are dominated by the clock and they cannot get used to the emphasis on punctuality in almost every aspect of their lives.

Example 5.5

In the example below, take note of the different conceptions of work time and personal time in different countries.

How much time does a good worker invest in his or her work? That may depend on where one works. The typical job in Germany requires 37 hours a week, and stores close on weekends and on four of five week nights so that workers can have leisure time. Personal time is considered so precious in Germany that it is illegal to work more than one job during holidays, which are meant to allow people to restore themselves.

In the United States, jobs typically require 44 to 80 hours a week. Vacation time is also limited in the United States. Many workers can't take more than a week's leave at a time or two weeks total per year. Many other countries have laws that ensure more vacation time for workers. According to the Economic Policy Institute (Robinson 2000), laws guarantee the following numbers of vacation days: Spain, 30; France, 30; Ireland 28; Japan, 25; Portugal, 25; Belguim, 24; Norway, 21; Germany, 18; United States, 0 (Wood 2002:182).

Example 5.6

This example continues the theme of time by describing how work time intrudes on home life in the United States where, it would seem, time increasingly goes into paid jobs to the detriment of family life and relationships. Do you think the situation described in the scenario is acceptable? What should people do about it?

Sociologist Arlie Hochschild claims that time is the central issue in corporate life today. In her recent book, *The Time Bind: When Work Becomes Home and Home Becomes Work* (1997), Hochschild reports that many professionals today feel compelled to force home and family time into an industrial, time-saving model that, ironically, is less and less endorsed in workplaces. Children often are allotted 20 or 30 minutes of time at the end of the day when two working parents get home. Dinner is restricted to 15 minutes so that there is enough time to drive the kids to their soccer game. Breakfasts are made and eaten assembly-line style. Tasks that families used to share are increasingly outsourced as harried, hurried parents hire a birthday party service, a personal shopper, and a cleaning service. There just isn't enough time for parents to do all of the homemaking and child-rearing activities themselves (Wood 2002:183).

5.3.5   Personal appearance

Why do people spend large sums of money each year on beauty products, weight-control pills, makeup, skin lighteners, new hairstyles and clothes? Some even resort to plastic surgery to increase their physical attractiveness. Why do most (Western) advertisements portray young, thin, attractive women and well-built, handsome men? Simply because we are judged by the way society has determined we should look. Physical appearance influences first impressions, job interviews, consumer buying behaviour and even courtroom decisions.

Although we may have no control over elements such as height or premature balding or the shape of our nose, elements over which we do have some control include clothing, hairstyle, jewellery and so forth. Your appearance provides visual clues to your age, gender, status, personality and attitudes. For example, if you are inappropriately dressed at a job interview, the interviewer may pay little attention to your qualifications because your appearance conveys the wrong message: jeans and a T-shirt indicate that your attitude is not right for the job! The interviewer, of course, is guilty of stereotyping and may be entirely wrong, but the damage has been done.

Appearance is considered so important in the business world that many large organisations have a strict dress code that lays down rules for the style and colour of clothing that may be worn, as well as the personal grooming of their employees. Others require their employees to wear uniforms that communicate to the public the image the organisation would like to portray.

Since your appearance conveys messages, you need to be aware of what is considered appropriate and what will be of most benefit to your image in both work and social situations. However, 'appropriately dressed' in any situation must be interpreted in its cultural context. At a social event such as a wedding reception, appropriate apparel for Western men may be a suit and tie, but at a traditional African wedding, this attire may appear to be inappropriate.

Artifacts are the personal items we wear or keep close to us and are another important aspect of physical appearance. Your jewellery, car, watch and makeup all communicate a message about whom and what you are. In the work context, it has been suggested that, until you learn what is considered appropriate at your place of employment, women should keep jewellery to a minimum and that men should avoid earrings and bracelets altogether in a conservative organisation.

Example 5.7

Thembi in a South African teenager. Her comments show that not all cultures prize or encourage thinness in women.

Thembi: *I hear white girls talking all the time about their weight — wanting to lose weight, thinking they're too fat, working out for hours to drop some kilos. I almost never hear this kind of talk when I'm with black girls in the township. We've got to worry about keeping our grades up, doing part-time work to help out at home, and just surviving in a mainly white private school. Weight just isn't important relative to the real issues in our lives* (Wood 2002:174).

5.3.6. The environment

The **environment** in which we communicate sends another powerful nonverbal message because our surroundings influence how we feel and how we will react to people and situations (cf. Gibson & Hanna 1992). When you are looking to buy a house, for example, you might say something such as, "I like most things about the house we have decided to buy, but the living rooms are so small they make me feel claustrophobic. We will have to knock out some of the interior walls before we move in". Attractive and pleasant surroundings have been shown to play a part in effective communication. Most people seem to feel better about themselves and others when they are in a bright, sun-filled room, and tend to communicate more easily. Many department store managers play soft background music to provide a positive atmosphere for their customers. They report that people tend to stay in the store longer and spend more money when they are in a pleasant environment.

The arrangement of objects in an environment also sends a message. How do you react when you visit a home that is so neat and tidy that you feel that it would be a 'crime' to accidentally drop a crumb on the carpet? Or when you go into your lecturer's office and she cannot find your assignment in the clutter of papers, books and files that are heaped up on the desk? Perhaps you wonder if her communication and teaching are as disorganised as her professional space.

You might also have noticed that, in a business setting, some executives sit behind a formal desk and offer you a stiff, upright chair on the other side of the desk. Some more modern executives get up from behind their desks when you come in and conduct you to a coffee table around which are some comfortable armchairs. The first arrangement puts across a message of formality and power relationships, whereas the second suggests that conversation and an open exchange of ideas will be welcomed. What does the arrangement of furniture in your living area suggest to strangers? Would they feel like talking freely or have you unintentionally created communication barriers by the location of objects in your personal environment?

Three other elements in the environment that influence communication by sending messages are temperature, lighting and colour. These elements mainly influence the attention and mood of the participants in communication. Teachers will tell you that it is difficult for children to concentrate in either a hot stuffy classroom or a very cold classroom. The reason that a library is well-lit and a restaurant has dim lighting is precisely because bright light encourages good listening and comfortable reading, whereas dim lighting creates an atmosphere that encourages intimate conversation. Colour may stimulate both physical and emotional responses. That is why interior decorators use reds and yellows in a playroom — these colours elevate people's mood — whereas they use shades of blue to create a peaceful, serene atmosphere in a living room. You might be interested in the report of a research project which shows how colours influence mood (Verderber & Verderber 2002; Wood 2002).

red	exciting, stimulating
blue	secure, comfortable, soothing
orange	distressed, upset, disturbed
brown	dejected, unhappy, melancholy
green	calm, serene, peaceful
black	powerful, strong, defiant
yellow	cheerful, joyful, jovial
purple	dignified, stately

Example 5.8

Fast-food restaurants are usually brightly lit and have fast music. More expensive restaurants tend to have dim lighting and soft, slow music, which encourages diners to stay longer and spend more on wines and desserts. The effect of restaurant atmosphere on diners was verified by the following experiment.

Over a 16-day period, researchers played music in a cafeteria. On the first day, the researchers played music with 122 beats per minute. They next day they played slow instrumentals with 56 beats per minute. On the third day they played no music. The researchers repeated the sequence for 16 days while they observed diners. The results confirmed the relationship between the pace of the music and the pace of eating. When no music was played, people averaged 3.23 bites per minute. When slow music was played, customers ate slightly more quickly: 3.83 bites per minute. But when the fast music with 122 beats per minute was played, diners sped up their eating to 4.4 bites per minute (Bozzi 1986:16 in Wood 2002:179).

5.3.7 Paralanguage

The vocal signs that accompany spoken language are termed **paralanguage**. It is concerned with the sound of the voice and the range of meanings that people convey through their voices rather than the words they use. The study of vocal phenomena or paralanguage refers to something beyond or in addition to language itself. The two main categories of paralanguage are vocal characteristics and vocal interferences.

❑ *Vocal characteristics* are the pitch (the highness or lowness of your voice), volume (how loudly or softly you speak), rate (the speed at which you speak) and quality of the voice (how pleasant or unpleasant your voice sounds). Each characteristic influences the impression others have of you. For example, a loud voice is often associated with aggressiveness whereas people who speak quickly are said to be nervous.

☐ ***Vocal interferences*** are the sounds and words we use when we hesitate or are not sure of the right word. We all use the occasional 'uh', 'er', 'well' and 'you know' to indicate that we are searching for the right word. But such interferences become a problem when they are excessive and interrupt your listeners' concentration and comprehension.

Written communication cannot, of course, express additional meaning to that contained in the written message. Many people add nonverbal cues to their text-based messages when they are online (Jacobson 1999; Hancock & Dunham 2001). To express feelings or convey variations in tone and volume, they use capital and lower-case letters differently, exclamation and other punctuation marks, as well as emoticons (also called smileys) together with their verbal messages. For example:

:)	smiling	:')	crying
;)	winking	:D	laughing
:(	frowning	:P	Sticking out tongue

You can see the effect more clearly if you turn your head to the left.

Example 5.9

HESTER: *I got so many funny looks for my accent when I went on holiday to England. I never thought of myself as having an accent because everyone on the Cape Flats talks the way I do. I really stood out. People also made assumptions about my intelligence because they couldn't understand me. It was really hard to get anyone to judge me on my merits.*

Hester's story illustrates how a regional accent can stereotype a person. In some cases, people with foreign accents (eg a French speaking person using English) are falsely perceived as less intelligent than native speakers (Wood 2002: 184).

Example 5.10

This final example encourages you to think about the effects of silence on your own relationships. For example, silence between people who know each other well generally communicates contentment. On the other hand, silence between new acquaintances can communicate awkwardness. Have you ever experienced the negative effects of silence as described by Ginder?

GINDER: *Silence is the cruellest thing you can do to a person. That was how my parents disciplined all of us. They told us we were bad and then refused to speak to us — sometimes for several hours. I can't describe how awful it felt to get no response from them, to be a nonperson. I would have preferred physical punishment. I'll never use silencing with my kids* (Wood 2002:186).

5.4   Nonverbal skills

The greatest problem with nonverbal communication is that most of us don't pay sufficient attention to our own and other people's use of it. The best way to improve your understanding of the nonverbal cues you receive from others is to make a conscious effort to interpret both their verbal and nonverbal communication — what they say and how they say it. We emphasise again that nonverbal messages cannot be viewed as fixed and unchanging — as they are influenced by context and culture. People who ascribe rigid meanings to nonverbal signs are prone to stereotyping. They allow their personal biases and feelings to influence their communication encounters. In the same way that different people ascribe different meanings to words on the basis of their attitudes, background, feelings and beliefs, so too do they attach different meanings to nonverbal cues.

How to improve your nonverbal communication

The best way to improve your own nonverbal communication — the way you send messages without the use of words — is to consider the effects created by each of the categories we have discussed and relate them to your own behaviour. The following four techniques may help.

1. Pay careful attention to the feedback you get from others. If you find that people regularly misunderstand your meanings and feelings, it could be that your verbal and nonverbal messages are incongruous (that is, they do not convey the same meaning). Use their feedback to try to improve your nonverbal communication.

2. Ask your friends and family to tell you about any distracting mannerisms of which you may not be aware and make a conscious effort to avoid them. People often do not know that they are playing with a strand of hair, swinging their feet or saying "OK" or "Well, you know . . ." too often.

3. Observe the nonverbal communication of others. If you find some of their nonverbal behaviour irritating or distracting, make sure that you are not doing the same things!

4. Try to record yourself on audiotape or videotape, and study the results critically to identify some of the nonverbal habits of which you may not be aware. You can then work on improving aspects such as the tone of your voice, posture, appearance or hand gestures.

Scenario 5.1

Even in this age of international travel and trade negotiations, we are sometimes not aware of the meaning of the nonverbal communication of people who visit South Africa, or the host nation we are visiting as tourists or on business. This scenario also illustrates the point we made in Section 5.2 that some of our cultural behaviour is communicated nonverbally.

The wai in Thailand

In Thailand, the wai is a nonverbal gesture used to communicate greeting, farewell, deep and sincere respect and appreciation (Smutkupt & Barna 1976). The palms of both hands are placed together and held vertically slightly under the chin followed by a slight bow, chin towards the fingertips. Rarely is the gesture accompanied with eye contact or verbal communication.

The wai is consistent with other elements of Thai culture. Children absorb its nuances along with learning the spoken language. The first nonverbal teaching the Thai child receives is this gesture of obeisance. The mother holds her infant, puts its palms together between her own, and raises them to the chin or forehead, depending upon the degree of deference that is called for. Before the child is taken from the house, its hands will be put in the proper position to greet guests. When its mother takes the child to the temple, she raises its palms to pay homage to Buddha. The child is constantly directed to wai in every appropriate occasion until it becomes a regular component of behaviour. Children never fail to wai the family's elders before leaving for school in the morning. In the classroom, children stand and perform the wai upon their teacher's arrival. When school ends, they wai to thank their teacher. On returning home, they greet all their elders with the wai. The day ends with paying homage to Buddha by performing the wai in front of the family's altar.

Thus the wai is a representation of the cultural values, including respect for elders, that the child learns while learning the nonverbal code. By understanding the wai we can also understand part of the Thai culture (Jandt 1995:89-90).

Scenario 5.2

Prior to the adoption of *The Constitution of the Republic of South Africa* (Act 108 of 1996) a pamphlet was issued, designed to answer the sort of questions people were asking about the Constitution, especially with regard to how it was going to affect their lives. The pamphlet is reproduced below.

Study the pamphlet, paying particular attention to the drawings that include people, and then make notes of which of the six categories of nonverbal communication are represented in the drawings.

This pamphlet was issued prior to the adoption of The Constitution of the Republic of South Africa (Act 108 of 1996). The pamphlet was designed to answer the sort of questions people were asking about the Constitution, especially with regard to how it was going to affect their lives. We reproduce the pamphlet below.

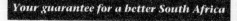

Your guarantee for a better South Africa

The new Constitution has taken months of negotiation. It is a very important document that is going to affect all our lives. Many people are asking all kinds of questions about it. This pamphlet is there to answer some of them. We hope it answers yours too.

I keep hearing about the new Constitution, but I don't understand it. What is it all about?
It's not so complicated, really. A Constitution sets out the basic rules of a country. Everybody has to obey them — the President, Parliament, every man and woman.

What's so special about the new Constitution?
It says everyone is equal, black and white, whatever language you speak, whatever part of the country you come from.

What have the elections to do with the Constitution?
The Constitution says that every permanent resident in

THE NEW CONSTITUTION IS THE SET OF RULES ON WHICH THE COUNTRY WILL RUN

South Africa, who is 18 years or over, shall have the right to vote. The more votes a party gets, the more seats it will have in Parliament.

What will happen to the present Parliament?
It will be completely replaced by the new one.

And the government?
It will also be new. The National Assembly will choose the President and Deputy Presidents.

And all the Cabinet Ministers? The Minister of Law and Order, or Education?
The President will have to choose Cabinet Ministers from all parties in Parliament. The more support

these parties have, the more ministers they will have.

Is that what they mean by a Government of National Unity?
Exactly. For five years all the parties, except the very tiny ones, will be entitled to a place in government.

Maybe my home language is the one I not only prefer to speak, but the one I'd like my children to read and write in. How is that going to be possible now?
Very easily — because this is such a basic right that it's one of the strong points of the Constitution now. All South African languages will be official — that means they'll be spoken, taught and communicated.

If I want to protest against something will I be able to march or speak my mind?
Under the new Constitution everyone has the right to assemble and demonstrate peacefully. Your fundamental rights cover things like free

speech, political rights, trade union rights etc.

What recourse do I have if any of my rights aren't respected?

You use the law — the Constitutional Court, after April 27th 1994, will make sure your fundamental rights are protected and respected.

What about land or ownership and the rights that govern them?
Everyone will have the equal right to own property according to the new Constitution. Even the people who lost their land or property will be attended to.

Who will make the laws?
The National Parliament will make laws about issues that affect the whole country. Each Province will also have its own Provincial Parliament which will pass laws dealing with matters that affect the Provinces.

What matters are these?
Take health. The National Government will deal with the overall health programme for the country and the qualifications of doctors and nurses. The Provincial Government will deal with health promotion in the province, where hospitals and clinics should be located, who should be appointed to staff them, etc.

I keep hearing that the elections are going to be "free and fair" — but I want to know who checks where my vote is going?
It's not possible for anyone to check.

Does anyone see my name during voting?
No — it works like this — after you've shown your ID or voter's card, you go to vote in secret.

Why must I have my ID or voter's card?
Just to allow you to vote as a permanent resident of this country. It's got nothing to do with the actual voting procedure — that's your private

concern and nobody need ever know — except if you decide to tell them.

What's going to happen to the defence and police forces?
There'll be a new defence force and a new police force that work for a new nation. They'll both be there to serve the community.

Is there really going to be no discrimination whatsoever?
Discrimination has become a rather dirty word and you'll be able to use the law to protect you against any of it — whether it be linguistic discrimination, religious or cultural.

Lots of people haven't been able to be educated before. What will happen now?
Now everyone will have the right to a basic education and equal access to that education. And wherever reasonably practical, you'll have it in the language of your choice.

Are women's rights going to be protected?
Of course — the new Constitution even provides for establishing a Commission on Gender Equality. Just to ensure women are respected and their rights protected.

What can we expect South Africa to look like — and how will it operate according to the Constitution?
There'll be 9 new provinces and each one will have it's own Constitution so it'll be quite different. The provinces will govern themselves and make their own laws on issues such as agriculture, own language policy, education except universities and technikons, housing, health policy and welfare.

When do all these things come into effect?
On the 27th April 1994. After that, no government will be able to pass laws that conflict with our Constitution.

You have the right to know. In the interest of democracy the Trasitional Executive Council wants you to be an informed voter. Published by the TEC, Private Bag 878, Pretoria 0001.

OUR NEW CONSTITUTION

Source: National Archives of South Africa

Summary

This chapter established that communication is not merely a matter of exchanging verbal messages. People also use a large number of cues or signs to send messages to each other. The chapter discussed the following functions of nonverbal communication: to reinforce, complement, contradict, replace or regulate a verbal message. It then emphasised that there is no 'recipe' for understanding nonverbal communication. This type of communication is influenced by factors such as context and culture and is often beyond our control. The chapter continued with a discussion of the following categories of nonverbal behaviour: kinesics, proxemics, haptics, chronemics, personal appearance, the environment and paralanguage. Some hints were provided for improving our nonverbal skills in everyday communication and the chapter ended with two scenarios: one based on a constitutional pamphlet and the other demonstrating the relationship between nonverbal communication and culture.

Test yourself

1. Define the five functions of nonverbal communication. Illustrate your answer with examples from your everyday experience of communication.
2. Describe the relationship between verbal and nonverbal communication.
3. Briefly explain the meaning of the following categories of nonverbal communication and illustrate each with an example from your own experience: kinesics, proxemics, haptics, chronemics, personal appearance, the environment and paralanguage. Do not write more than 10 lines for each category.
4. How important is proxemics in your everyday life? Provide an example and explain why it is important.
5. Choose an example from a recent situation when vocal inflection provided you with important information. Why did inflection give you this information?
6. What effect does posture have on your perception of people that you meet for the first time?
7. Study Figure 5.4 below and list the nonverbal codes that are represented.
8. Study Figure 5.5 below and suggest what differences in meaning the weapons would have for the two soldiers in the background and the students in the foreground.

Figure 5.4 Nonverbal communication 1 (reproduced with the kind permission of Robben Island Mayibuye Archive)

Figure 5.5 Nonverbal communication 2 (reproduced with the kind permission of Robben Island Mayibuye Archive)

EXECUTIVE SUMMARY
Nonverbal communication

1   Functions of nonverbal communication
 ❑   to reinforce
 ❑   to complement
 ❑   to contradict
 ❑   to replace
 ❑   to regulate
2   Kinesics
 ❑   body movement
  — emblems
  — illustrators
  — affect displays
  — regulators
  — adaptors
 ❑   gestures
 ❑   posture
 ❑   facial expressions
 ❑   eye contact
3   Proxemics
 ❑   intimate distance zone
 ❑   personal distance zone
 ❑   social distance zone
 ❑   public distance zone
4   Haptics
5   Chronemics
6   Personal appearance
7   Paralanguage
 ❑   vocal characteristics
 ❑   vocal interferences

6 Language and communication

Overview

We can define language as the whole body of words (vocabulary) and ways of combining them (grammar) that are used by a nation, people or cultural community (Burton & Dimbleby 1995). Although this definition provides us with an accurate description of the word, it does not convey the importance of language in our lives. Heath and Bryant (2000) suggest that language allows us to describe and evaluate the objects, emotions and ideas we experience. By using signs (words) we create, share and interpret meanings about the world around us. For society to function, people use words to create and co-ordinate their social, political and economic activities. A second and more comprehensive definition of language is that it is a unified system of signs (words) that allows people to think, share meaning and define reality.

Our language skills (for instance, the way we convey meaning to others or our ability to think through a problem) depend largely on the way we use words. We take our ability to use language so much for granted that we rarely recognise the role it plays in our lives until a situation arises when it cannot be used — for example, when you have difficulty in finding the right words to express yourself or when your meanings are misunderstood by others.

This chapter is largely concerned with the relationship between language and meaning, or between language and thought. Knowledge about this relationship should help you understand why words sometimes create barriers or misunderstandings when we communicate.

We begin by discussing George Orwell's views on the relationship between language, meaning and thought. We continue with the uses of language in our everyday communication and then explain the specific functions of language identified by Roman Jakobson. We follow this with a discussion of language as a system of signs and illustrate this view with a well-known theory about language: the Triangle of Meaning. We then turn our attention to some of the reasons why language sometimes causes misunderstandings in our communication. We do so by considering the denotative and connotative meanings of words, and the differences between concrete and abstract words. One of the aspects of language that has become the focus of attention of many researchers today is the way men and women use language in different ways. After a short discussion on language and gender and the misunderstandings that occur between men and women in communication, we introduce the Sapir-Whorf hypothesis. This theory shows how language not only provides members of a community with a means of communication, it transmits and perpetuates the perceptions that the community has of the world. In the final section of the chapter we provide some guidelines for improving your language skills. We end with a scenario based on some of the misunderstandings that language creates in interpersonal communication.

Learning outcomes

At the end of this unit you should be able to:
1. Define the term 'language'.
2. Briefly explain the relationship between language, meaning and thought with reference to the views of George Orwell.
3. Describe how you use language in your everyday communication.
4. Apply Jakobson's functions of language to an advertisement from a newspaper or magazine.
5. Use the Triangle of Meaning to explain why we say that meaning resides in people, not in words.
6. Show your understanding of denotative and connotative meanings, and concrete and abstract words by providing examples of each from your everyday experiences of communication.
7. Explain how language shapes our view of the world by referring to the Sapir-Whorf hypothesis.
8. Become more aware of differences in the way men and women use language.
9. Apply the suggestions for improving language skills to your everyday communication encounters with others.
10. Answer the questions based on the scenario at the end of this chapter.

Introduction

In Chapter 1 we discussed how the development of speech and language played an extremely important role in the history of human civilisation. Communication by means of speech facilitated the formation of social groups and, with the invention of writing, the traditions and culture of a society could be perpetuated and recorded for future generations. The ability to speak and read well is also important to the individual, not only to become educated, but in our daily activities and contact with people. Think for a moment about the role your language skills play in your ability to 'get on with others' and the extent to which progress in your job is determined by your oral and writing skills. In fact, even when you are not speaking out loud, you are using language to think and to create meaning — that is, to communicate intrapersonally. Without language, thought is not possible. Like many philosophers and theorists before him, the eminent British writer George Orwell (1903-1950), understood the important connection between language and thought, and also between thought and humanity.

6.1 Orwell's views on language

In the novel *1984*, Orwell expresses his concerns about how the manipulation of language curtails our freedom of thought and expression. Written in 1949, the novel describes a future world where the Party (or government) controls the masses through a language called 'Newspeak'. **Newspeak** contains a limited number of words chosen in such a way that any idea not in line with party principles cannot even be thought about, let alone expressed out loud or discussed. All words that threaten political unity, such as 'honour', 'justice', 'morality', 'democracy', 'science' and 'religion', have ceased to exist, and words such as 'free' have been stripped of undesirable connotations. Because words no longer have shades of meaning, people are not able to evaluate or criticise the status quo. Newspeak is frightening because its distortion of language is dehumanising — it not only diminishes the range of human thought but controls how we think so that only one 'correct' interpretation of any word or event is possible. To reinforce the desired image of reality, the Party has also reinterpreted history by falsifying historical (written) records and replacing facts with accounts of the Party's past successes and expectations of its future achievements. Orwell's novel has been interpreted as a criticism of the control over society that some totalitarian states exercised during the rise of Stalinism and Fascism, and a plea for freedom of expression by autonomous individuals (cf Jansen & Steinberg 1991; Trenholm 1995).

6.2 Uses of language

Language is our primary means of exchanging messages. In a general way, we use language to tell each other who we are and how we feel about each other. We describe our experiences of the world by using language. Language allows us to think about the past and anticipate the future. We also use language to transmit our culture. The general uses of language are so varied that we cannot discuss them all. We list some of the purposes for which we use language below (cf Barker 1984; Shuter 1984; Benjamin 1986; Verderber 1990; Verderber & Verderber 2002).

❐ *We use language to label and define* Labelling means that we identify an object, act or person by giving it a name so that we can talk about it. Once something is named, it is simultaneously defined — that is, it takes on the characteristics that people associate with its label. There is a difference, for example, between calling a classmate a 'student', a 'friend', a 'young adult' or a 'soccer player'. Whichever label you choose, you are drawing attention to some particular aspect of that person. You are also suggesting how others should define that person.

☐ **We use language to evaluate** Evaluative language is any word or phrase that judges the rightness or wrongness of an activity or behaviour. Evaluative language includes words like 'clever', 'stupid, 'wonderful', 'good' and 'bad', and expressions such as "you could do better", and "this is a first-class piece of work". Without evaluative language we would not be able to be critical or supportive of others. But we have to be careful how we use evaluative language. We can create a negative or positive impression of people, places or actions simply by talking about them inappropriately.

☐ **We use language to discuss things outside our immediate experience** Language enables us to talk about the past and the future, and to communicate about people who are not present. Through language we can learn about other people's experiences, weigh up different alternatives to problems and plan for the future. We can also use language to substitute for direct experience. For example, we may not be able to visit foreign countries, but we can read travel books and thereby vicariously experience foreign travel.

☐ **We use language to entertain** We entertain ourselves and others by telling jokes, doing crossword puzzles, watching movies and reading poetry and novels. In other words, a great deal of our entertainment and socialising takes place through language. Even the pleasure of an activity such as watching a sports event is enhanced by the cheers of the fans and the commentary of the television sports announcer.

☐ **We use language to talk about language** Using language to talk about communication is called *metacommunication* and serves, for example, to help us judge our own communication skills. We can discuss with someone how we expressed an idea and whether better phrasing would have resulted in a clearer formulation. In this instance, the content of your communication is communication itself.

The uses of language are so varied that we have not been able to discuss them all. Language can be used, for example, to lie, to be aggressive, or to destroy a relationship. We encourage you to think about all the uses for which you use language.

6.3   The functions of language

In Chapter 2 we described the functions of communication in terms of the needs they fulfil and the effects they have. But we also have to consider the specific communicative functions of language. These functions have been identified by the linguist Roman Jakobson (1958) as follows: referential function, expressive function, conative function, phatic function, poetic function and metalinguistic function. Most messages contain combinations of these functions (cf Hawkes 1985; Fourie 1996; Hartley 2002). Please study Figure 6.1 before you continue reading.

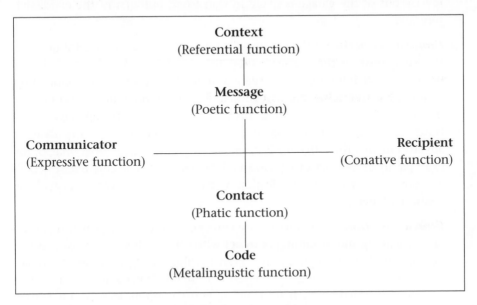

Figure 6.1 Jakobson's model of the functions of language
(adapted from Jakobson 1958)

☐ **Referential function** If the communication is oriented towards the **content** or subject matter ('context' in the diagram) then the referential function dominates. The referential function conveys concrete, objective information about the content of the message or 'what the message is about'. The referential function is prominent in news reporting, science writing and courtroom testimony, for instance. It is the referential function that enables us to inform others about something in our world or to describe it. If you say "the distance from Pretoria to Cape Town is about 1 500 kilometres", you are using the referential function of language.

☐ **Expressive function** If the communication is oriented towards the **communicator** of the message, then the expressive function dominates. The expressive function refers to our ability to use language to communicate our emotions, beliefs and opinions as well as our attitude towards the subject matter of the communication. If your home is in Cape Town but you are presently living in Pretoria, and you tell me, "Pretoria is a long way from home", you are revealing your emotional response to the situation, rather than a purely referential description of it. Similarly, in a debate about the advantages and limitations of a new law that has been promulgated, the communicators would use the expressive function of language to explain their attitude towards the new law. The expressive function operates even when an audience is not present. For example, denting the bumper of your car as you reverse out of the garage is likely to lead to an outburst of the expressive function.

❏ *Conative function* If the communication is oriented towards influencing the **recipient** of the message, then the conative or regulatory function dominates. Such messages are usually intended to persuade the recipient by means of instructions, requests, commands or other more subtle acts of verbal persuasion. The conative function is well illustrated by the language of air-traffic control, political speeches and advertisements. In the case of advertisements, the language is often accompanied by pictorial images, for example in newspaper or television advertisements. The conative function also dominates your communication when you say to someone, "Listen!" or "Now, look here. . ."

❏ *Phatic function* We frequently use language not just for articulating ideas, but for making and sustaining **contact** with others. This use is known as the phatic function of language and often involves using ritualistic formulae which are almost meaningless. For example, idle chatter, comments about the weather and greetings such as "How are you?" communicate to others that you welcome their participation in conversation. When you say, "It's a nice morning", you are not offering information about the weather but getting the conversation going. The purpose of your comments is to make sure that the contact between you is working properly. Similarly, in response to your question about the recipient's health, you are quite likely to be told, "Fine", even though your friend has fallen off a ladder and broken an arm. You are also using the phatic function when you say, "Hello, can you hear me?" during a cellphone conversation when the connection between you and your partner is breaking up.

❏ *Poetic function* Language may also be used as a source of intrinsic pleasure. Young children play with the sounds of language as they learn to speak purely for the pleasure of hearing different sound combinations. When the communication is oriented towards the form of the **message** or, to put it another way, when the message fascinates by its own form, then the poetic function dominates. We could also refer to this function as the 'aesthetic' function because it is intended to draw attention to the sound patterns, diction, syntax and so on, of the language used in the message. Rhyme, alliteration, punning, ambiguity and even grammatical rule-breaking are examples of the poetic function. The poetic function is not restricted to poetry. Many proverbial sayings (eg "finders, keepers, losers, weepers") illustrate this function and advertising uses language in its poetic function as much as it does in the conative function.

❒ **Metalinguistic function** The use of language to explore and reflect upon itself is known as the metalinguistic function of language. This means that the communication is oriented towards the **code** or the act of communication between the participants. We could say that this function of language is used to communicate a message about the message. For example, when you want to check that the code being used has the same meaning for both you and your partner, you might use phrases such as "understand?", "see?", "do you get my drift?" The television interviewer who says, "Is what you are saying then, Mr President . . .?" or "Would you repeat that, please?", is using the metalinguistic function to ensure that the viewers understand the message the President is conveying. Grammar books and dictionaries rely heavily on the metalinguistic function, as does a text book such as this one.

6.4   Language as a system of signs

We defined language earlier as a unified system of signs and the grammatical rules that permit a sharing of meaning. In using language to share meaning, we construct messages that are made up of linguistic signs, or words, using the rules of the language that we speak. Your teachers at school emphasised the view of language as a system when they taught you the differences between nouns, verbs, adjectives and adverbs, and the rules for constructing grammatically correct sentences. All spoken or natural languages (as opposed to artificial languages, such as computer languages) like English, isiZulu, German, Japanese and so on, are classified as language systems.

6.4.1   Natural and symbolic signs

Languages consist primarily of words. But what is a word? In Chapter 3 we noted that a word is a sign — that is, it stands for or represents something else. We call the things it represents or refers to the 'referent'. The referent can be an object such as an animal, table or chair, or an idea, feeling or need. It is very important to understand that words stand for things but are not the things themselves. Words are spoken sounds or the written representation of sounds that people have agreed will stand for something else. In the simplest terms, the word 'dog' is not the dog in reality, but stands for the hairy canine we have as a pet in our home.

We pointed out in Chapter 3 that not all signs are linguistic (word) signs. For example, we also use nonverbal signs, traffic signs and pictorial signs. All these signs have been created by people. But some signs are natural signs. Examples of **natural signs** are the smoke that indicates fire or a sneeze that represents hayfever. In these examples, the relationship between the smoke or the sneeze and the fire or hayfever has not been created by people — the connection is natural. Signs, such as words, that people have created are called **symbolic** or

arbitrary signs. For example, we use the word 'tree' to represent a species of vegetation. The word 'tree' is an arbitrary sign because there is no natural connection between the idea of tree and the signifier 'tree'. There is nothing particularly treelike about the word 'tree'. In Latin, the signifier *arbor* is used to signify the same idea, and in isiZulu the signifier also represents the idea of 'tree'. Think about a different sort of example: even though the word 'six' is physically smaller than the word 'three', the quantity that six represents is greater — there is no natural connection (this time, its size) between the word and its meaning.

These examples also explain why arbitrary signs are **conventional**. The word 'tree' is conventional because its meaning depends on social agreement. Speakers of English have agreed to use the word 'tree' to represent something that speakers of other languages have not. In English, the sound sequence t-r-e-e has meaning, whereas in isiZulu it does not. But the sounds made by the letters t-w-e-e do not constitute a word in English because they do not stand for anything. Thus, by mutual consent we could make any sound stand for anything. It is this agreement that distinguishes a word from a random sound and gives it meaning.

The arbitrary nature of symbols shows that words do not depend on reality for their meaning. It is not things that determine the meaning of words, but words that determine the meaning of things. We use words to help create meaning in our communication. However, important as words are in describing objects and ideas, they have no meaning in themselves. As Gamble and Gamble (1987:100) express it, "the meaning of a verbal message is not stamped on the face of the words". Meanings reside in people, not in words. There is no reason, for example, why a tree should not have been called a twee (or for that matter, a flower), other than that the people who speak English have assigned that meaning to the sign 'tree'.

Because meanings reside in people, not in words, meanings can differ. You have your meaning and other people have theirs. Even a simple word like 'cat' can bring to mind meanings ranging from a common alley cat to a lion or a cat made from wire. To understand each other, our meanings have to overlap. If not, language becomes a barrier to effective communication, rather than an aid. It is precisely because the word is not reality that we sometimes experience communication difficulties. If I tell you that I am getting a new pet tomorrow and that it is a dog, you will know that my new pet is not a cat or a bird or a fish. But the dog I picture in my mind might be a big black Labrador, whereas the dog you picture might be a small white poodle.

The Triangle of Meaning (see Figure 6.2) developed by the communication theorists Ogden and Richards in 1923, helps to explain how language works as a system of signs.

The triangle is meant to illustrate how words are related to thoughts (meanings) and things. The dotted line connecting **word** (a sign) and **thing** (a referent) indicates that the word is not the thing and that there is no direct relationship between the two. The only direct relationship between words and the things they represent are in people's minds, indicated by the solid lines between **thought** and **word** and between **thought** and **thing**. For example, when we hear the word 'apple' or see an apple, it calls up a mental picture of a particular fruit (a thought) in our minds. Ogden and Richards emphasise that words are arbitrary, or indirect, signs that members of a culture agree to use to represent the things they sense and experience. It is because meaning does not reside in the word that different cultures can also agree that *hond, chien, injha, mpya* and *dog* will be used to talk about the same animal (cf Ogden & Richards 1930; Stewart & D'Angelo 1990; Wood 2000).

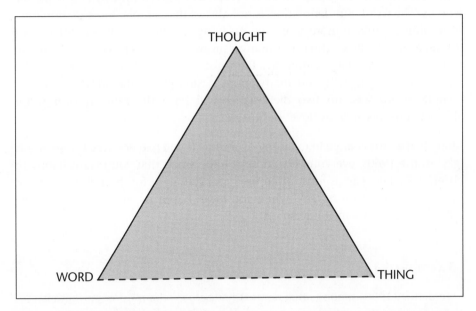

Figure 6.2 The Triangle of Meaning
(adapted from Ogden & Richards 1930)

6.5   Causes of misunderstanding

One of the strengths of the Triangle of Meaning is that viewing language as a system of arbitrary signs helps us understand why two people may understand a word differently — the thought or meaning associated with a word by one person may or may not be the same as the meaning associated with that word by another person. As a result, our use of words can cause misunderstandings. Your own experience tells you that we sometimes fail to convey the meaning we intend and, at other times, we misunderstand other people's messages. When we talk about 'misunderstanding' in this chapter, we are not referring to the problems that arise when people speak indistinctly, or use a dialect that is unfamiliar, or have a limited vocabulary in which to express themselves, or make grammatical errors. Rather, we are concerned with the fact that we tend to assume that the words we use have exactly the same meaning for the other person as for us. Despite the fact that people agree that a word will stand for a particular thing, words have more than one meaning. To help understand and overcome the reasons for some of our misunderstandings, we look at the differences between denotative and connotative words, and between concrete and abstract words.

6.5.1   Denotative and connotative meanings

The **denotative meaning** of a word is the explicit, literal meaning that is provided in a dictionary and which is accepted at a given time by all the people who use the word. But denotation is not always that simple. Most dictionaries, for example, provide more than one meaning for the same word. 'Strike', for instance, has at lease three denotative meanings: workers go 'on strike' to negotiate better working conditions. But we also 'strike a match' or 'strike up the band'. In fact, you will find many more meanings for the word 'strike'. To complicate matters, no two dictionaries will have the same meanings for abstract concepts such as 'love' or 'justice'.

Moreover, words change in meaning over time. If you had described someone as 'gay' in the 1960s, everyone would have understood that you meant happy or cheerful. Today, 'gay' is most often used as a synonym for 'homosexual'. So, if you describe someone as 'gay' when you mean happy or cheerful, you run the risk of being totally misunderstood.

Example 6.1

Verderber (1990) suggests that context has perhaps the most important effect on the denotative meaning of a word. The position of a word in the sentence and the other words around it are likely to change the denotation. Wenburg and Wilmot (1973: 93) provide the following example:
The stone stuck in the bird's **crop**.
She carried a riding **crop** in her hand.
The shepherd watched the sheep **crop** the grass.
The farmer reaped a **crop** of barley.

The connotative meaning of a word generally cannot be found in a dictionary. Connotation refers to the emotions and evaluations that an individual associates with a word. It is the personal or subjective interpretation that is attached to a word as result of one's background and past experiences. In other words, our connotative meanings vary according to our feelings for the object or concept we are considering. Research has shown that gender, for example, influences connotative meanings. A 1970 study investigated male and female responses to sex-related words. Not surprisingly, it was found that women tend to respond much less favourably than men to words such as 'wife-swapping', 'husband-swapping', 'whore' and 'prostitute' (Tubbs & Moss 1991). We discuss gender differences in more detail in Section 6.6.

An awareness of **connotative meaning** is also essential if we are to avoid misunderstandings in our communication encounters. We need to be aware, for instance, that a particular word may evoke a positive connotation in one person but a negative connotation in another. Consider the word 'communism'. According to the dictionary, its denotative meaning is a theory or system of social organisation based on holding common property. However, for some people, the word 'communism' has the negative connotation of revolutionary threat and upheaval, whereas for others the idea of common and shared property has a positive connotation. Try it out for yourself. Ask five people of different backgrounds and personal beliefs for the meanings of the following words: 'abortion', 'democracy', 'cancer', 'mother-in-law', 'love', 'AIDS'.

6.5.2   Concrete and abstract words

We said earlier that words are not directly related to the things and experiences they describe. Language is thus an abstract system of sounds. There are, however, levels of abstraction. For example, calling a cow a 'cow' is less abstract and conveys a more precise meaning than calling it an 'animal' or 'livestock'. So does identifying someone as 'Daniel' rather than referring to him as 'friend' or 'man'.

Words can be loosely classified as concrete and abstract. A dictionary will tell you that **concrete words** are signs that name a thing, or a class of things, as opposed to naming a quality or attribute. Examples of concrete words are 'father', 'sailor', 'radio', 'church' and 'pencil'. In each instance the referent is the thing which being named.

In contrast to concrete words, **abstract words** are the names for qualities and attributes. Such words as 'love', 'humanity', 'justice', 'clever' and 'worship' do not denote an actual object. You can see from these examples that concrete words carry more specific meanings than abstract words. Since the referent for the former is perceptible to the senses — it can be seen or heard or felt — there is a smaller margin of meaning error than in the case of abstract words. Hence there is likely to be less misunderstanding between communicator and recipient.

Abstract words have feelings, emotions, attitudes and ideas as their referents. Since the referent is a concept rather than a thing, words such as 'democracy', 'ethics', 'honest', 'coward' or 'freedom' are likely to be different for different people. There is thus more likely to be a breakdown in communication (cf Andersch, Staats & Bostrom 1969).

In summary, the main problems that have been identified in connection with denotation and connotation, and concrete and abstract words are the following:
1. The connotative meaning of a word may overshadow and distort its historical (denotative) meaning.
2. The referent of a word may be different for different people.
3. The referent of abstract words are highly individualised because they do not exist in reality (Andersch, Staats & Bostrom 1969:123).

The most easily understood words are those that describe concrete reality: 'this pen', 'my DVD collection', 'her red hair'. But we need to be careful of abstract words like 'love', 'democracy', 'honesty', 'safety' because they may or may not represent the same reality to your partner in communication as they do to you. For instance, what does the word 'safety' mean to you? A bank vault perhaps, or a seat belt or a safety pin? (Stewart & Logan 2002).

6.6   Genderlects

Some researchers (Tannen 1990) have argued that there are significant differences in the way men and women speak. In recent years, language and communication scholars have drawn our attention to the way language reinforces gender stereotypes. Words like 'mankind', 'chairman', 'policeman', 'businessmen' create the impression that men are more prominent and numerous than women. Similarly, we do not often hear the following combinations of words: 'male doctor', 'male lawyer', 'male police officer'. Yet it is common practice to talk about a 'lady dentist', 'female lawyer' or 'woman scientist'. These examples highlight the way that language exerts a powerful influence on the way we perceive women in society. According to Gamble and Gamble (1999:93), "Women are thus defined as exceptions to a norm established by males".

The communication practices of men and women also demonstrate wide differences in the way each gender uses language. People who speak the same language sometimes fail to understand each other because they speak different dialects. A dialect is a local or regional variation of a language which has its own unique pronunciations, vocabularies, grammar rules and usage norms. In recent years, some communication and language scholars have suggested that men and women also have 'dialects' because they use language in different ways. These scholars have coined the term **genderlects** to describe linguistic variations based on gender. According to such scholars, genderlects account for some of the misunderstandings that arise between men and women in communication.

Such scholars also believe that the misunderstandings occur because men and women grow up in different cultures. Women's culture values intimacy and relationships, whereas men's culture places a greater emphasis on autonomy and individual achievement. The outcome is that men generally use language to assert themselves or to achieve something, whereas women use it to create and maintain relationships. Also, men use language to attract and keep an audience, whereas women use it to indicate they are listening by saying things like, "Carry on" or "Tell me more". Men tend to use language to compete, women use it to collaborate. Importantly, for women, communication is the very core of a relationship, whereas for men it is a means to achieve conversational dominance (Gamble & Gamble 1999).

Example 6.2

Study the following examples which illustrate the differences in the way the genders view communication.

On the way to visit friends in another part of the city, Juan and Denise get lost. Denise suggests that they stop and ask the way, but Juan refuses. He feels uncomfortable asking for help and believes there's no guarantee a stranger will give accurate information anyway. He'd prefer to drive around until he finds the way. This doesn't make sense to Denise, who isn't at all embarrassed about asking for information and believes that anyone who doesn't know the way should admit it.

Maria can't wait until Tom gets home from work, so that they can talk about the day. As Tom enters the house, Maria begins a barrage of questions. What did he do? How was his presentation? Where did he and his colleagues go for lunch, and what did everyone order? She is interested in every detail and his evasive answers hurt her. He, on the other hand, feels overwhelmed by Maria's 'third degree' about details he barely noticed.

Michael's friends ask if it's OK to come over and watch the game on Friday. Michael says 'sure'. When he tells his girlfriend, Alyssa, she's upset — not because the friends are coming, but because Michael didn't consult her first. Had the situation been reversed, she would have asked. In fact, "I have to check with Mike" would have been a way for her to let others know that she's part of a couple. For Michael, however, asking Alyssa implies he needs to get permission. As a result of these differences, Michael thinks Alyssa is unreasonable, and she sees him as insensitive (Trenholm 1995:103-104).

6.6.1   The development of gender differences

Psychologists and social scientists maintain that, from the moment of birth, baby boys are seen to be stronger and more forceful than baby girls. As children grow up, their behaviour tends to match these expectations. Studies have shown that children's games are a primary agent of gender socialisation. There are notable differences between the games boys and girls tend to play and these differences teach boys and girls specific rules for formulating their own messages and interpreting the messages of others. The rules taught through childhood play seem to shape the way we communicate as adults.

Games that are traditionally favoured by girls, such as playing 'house', 'school' or 'hospital', require few players and have few fixed rules. Communication is used to encourage intimacy and status equality and to negotiate how to play so that everyone will 'get a turn'. There is an emphasis on co-operation and sensitivity between the players. Girls tend to say, "Let's try this" rather than, "You do this". Boys, on the other hand, tend to play rule-bound games with winners and losers. Typical boy games, like soccer, cricket and war, are highly competitive, both between the teams and for individual status within the teams. Boys' games involve more players and, because they have clear goals and rules, less talk is needed. Generally, girls' play is less physically active and more verbal than that of boys.

As adults, men continue to bond through shared physical activity like working on cars, watching sport or playing games. Women tend to bond through communication. Most women see talk as essential to the foundation of close relationships. Their talk is generally more expressive and focused on emotions and personal issues, whereas men's talk seems to be more instrumental and competitive. Typically, if a woman confides in a man about a problem, his response is to offer advice or a solution. His primarily instrumental use of language leads him to show support by doing something. But women usually expect expressions of empathy and discussion of feelings before they listen to advice. As a result, women often interpret responses from men as uncaring and insensitive. On the other hand, men often feel irritated when women offer empathy and support instead of advice for solving problems. Generally men are less comfortable making personal disclosures, whereas women regard personal talk as the way to intimacy and the enrichment of relationships. That is why when women say, "Let's talk about us", they want to communicate to enhance a relationship, whereas most men interpret the request as meaning that there is a problem in the relationship (Trenholm 1995; Wood 2002).

The table below summarises some of the rules of feminine and masculine speech communities.

Feminine Communication Rules	Masculine Communication Rules
1. Include others. Use talk to show interest in others and respond to their needs.	1. Assert yourself. Use talk to establish your identity, expertise, knowledge, and so on.
2. Use talk cooperatively. Communication is a joint activity, so people have to work together. It's important to invite others into conversation, wait your turn to speak, and respond to what others say.	2. Use talk competetively. Communication is an arena for proving yourself. Use talk to gain and hold attention, to wrest the talk stage from others; interrupt and reroute topics to keep you and your ideas spotlighted.
3. Use talk expressively. Talk should deal with feelings, personal ideas, and problems and should build relationships with others.	3. Use talk instrumentally. Talk should accomplish something such as solving a problem, giving advice, or taking a stand on issues.

Figure 6.3 Communication rules of gender speech communities

Source: Wood 2002: 144

According to Adler, Rosenfeld and Proctor (2001), a growing body of research indicates that there are factors other than gender that account for the differences. For example, in Western societies, it has been found that feminist wives talk more than their husbands do, whereas nonfeminist wives talk less. Sexual orientation rather than biological sex may influence speech mannerisms: in gay and lesbian relationships the power relationship between the partners (eg who is earning more money) is often reflected in speech patterns. And the speaker's occupation also plays a role in speaking style. For example, the speech of male day-care nurses resembles that of mothers' speech rather than fathers'. Male patients interrupt female physicians more often than they do male physicians. A study of trial transcripts shows that the speaker's occupation and experience on the witness stand has more to do with language use than biological sex. The researcher concluded that "So-called women's language is neither characteristic of all women nor limited only to women" (O'Barr 1982).

While there are differences in the way men and women speak, we need to be aware that these differences may be caused by factors other than gender. Nevertheless, we still need to try and resolve some of the problems that arise between men and women in communication.

6.6.2   Adapting to gender differences

Is there a way to resolve misunderstandings that arise because of differences between men's and women's use of language? Firstly, we have to remember that the differences we have described are not absolute dichotomies, but matters of degree. Some women use words instrumentally and men sometimes use talk expressively. Not all women are sensitive and not all men are competitive. Some men actually listen actively when women talk to them. Secondly, the gender differences we have been discussing are generally culturally determined and, as in all communication that is culturally based, we need to acquire a sensitivity to the intentions and meanings that underlie messages from the opposite sex. Men need to learn that wanting to talk about relationships does not always indicate that women are communicating that there are problems in the relationship. Women need to learn that dealing with conflict and controversy does not necessarily undermine a relationship. Both men and women also need to be more flexible in their communication styles and not respond unthinkingly in a single genderlect. By becoming aware of our ways of talking and how effective (or ineffective) they are, we can adapt our habitual styles when they do not serve us well (Tannen 1990; Trenholm 1995).

6.7   Sapir-Whorf hypothesis

The close relationship between language and thought has led language and communication scholars to consider the nature of their interrelatedness. They pose the question: Do we think first and then use words to express our thoughts, or do the words we use influence the way we think? According to two American linguists, Sapir and Whorf, the language we use shapes our thoughts and does not merely reflect them. Their theory, the **Sapir-Whorf hypothesis**, suggests that because different cultures use different languages, the world is perceived differently by different cultures. The implication is that language restricts each language community to a particular view of the world. The word 'snow' is often used as an example. English has only one word to describe all types of snow. But Inuit Eskimos, for whom the ability to describe and talk about fine distinctions between different types of snow could make the difference between life and death, use several words to describe, for example, snow on the ground, falling snow, snow drifts, hard snow, soft snow and so on. Likewise, many African languages do not even have a word for snow because snow does not fall on most of the African continent. Whorf (1966) suggests that Inuit perceive different types of snow because their language allows them to do so. Other scholars have reversed this view by arguing that Inuit have many words for snow simply because there is a need (survival) for them.

A second type of example that Whorf uses to substantiate his theory relates to his study of the Hopi language used by some North American Indian communities. The Hopi language has limited tenses and makes no distinction between time and space. There is, for example, no word for 'future'; time is always 'approaching'. English, however, has many tenses and it is common to look at events from the point of view of when they happened. It has been suggested that, because of his or her chronological orientation, an English speaking child could more easily understand history, whereas the Hopi language would enable a child to understand the theory of relativity better (Hybels & Weaver 1995).

If we accept the Sapir-Whorf hypothesis, then learning a language is not simply a matter of mastering the mechanics of speech or acquiring a list of concepts. By learning a language, a child acquires words that have meaning in his or her culture and which shape the way he or she thinks and behaves. The child also learns to direct its attention to particular aspects of the environment that are important for its culture. Language thus not only provides members of a community with a means of communication. It transmits and perpetuates the perceptions that a community has of the world.

6.8   Improving language skills

It is not possible to provide you with a list of rules to improve your oral communication. It is possible, however, for you to think about and consciously practise improving your use of language. We consider two points below: the clarity of your language and the appropriateness of your language. Being conscious of these two aspects should improve your interactions with people in the interpersonal, small-group and public speaking contexts we discuss later in this book.

6.8.1   Clear language

Clarity is important in all communication settings. Unclear language results in misunderstandings between people that could have been avoided by the use of more specific and precise words. For instance, because meaning is affected by denotation and connotation, you can never be completely sure that your use of a word will create a meaning in the minds of others that is exactly the meaning you intend. Being able to choose the precise words you need should help to make your meaning clear. Take the word 'said' as an example. Notice the changes in meaning when you substitute another word such as 'stated', 'averred', 'growled', 'indicated', 'intoned', 'suggested', 'pleaded', shouted', 'purred', 'answered' or 'asked' (cf Verderber (1990). Each word invokes a slightly different, but more precise meaning, in the mind of your listener.

Substituting concrete words for abstract words often succeeds in conveying your meaning more clearly. For instance, instead of saying, "I bought a car", you could describe the car as "a new red Toyota". To clarify an abstract idea, it helps to use a concrete example to make your meaning clearer to the listener. For instance, if you use the word 'loyalty' which can evoke different associations in your listener's mind, you could avoid ambiguity by adding a phrase that explains exactly what you mean: "Jan is very loyal to his company — he always buys their products" expresses the abstract concept of loyalty in terms of a concrete example.

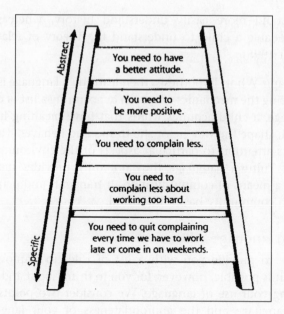

Figure 6.4 Abstraction ladder. A boss gives feedback to an employee about career advancement at various levels of specificity

Source: Adler, Rosenfeld & Proctor 2001:137

Figure 6.4 is an abstraction ladder that shows how we can describe the same idea at various levels of abstraction. Reading down the ladder, can you see how much more specific each statement becomes?

6.8.2   Appropriate language

It doesn't matter how accurately a word you select expresses your meaning if your recipient cannot comprehend it. If you want to be understood, you must make the effort to choose words that are meaningful to your listeners. Appropriateness means that you adapt your language so that it is suitable for the people you are communicating with and to the context of the conversation. Generally, you need to take demographic factors, such as the age, educational level, background, gender, interests and needs of your recipients into account, as well as the occasion of the encounter. These factors are discussed in more detail in Chapter 10.

Appropriate language also requires you to keep your use of jargon words to a minimum. Two doctors in conversation, for instance, will understand that 'cephalagia' means a headache or that 'agrypnia' is insomnia, but these terms are meaningless to the patient. Slang may be understandable to your peers, but not to people younger or older than you. You also need to be sensitive to the feelings of others when you choose words. You may think that describing a colleague as a 'workhorse' is a compliment; she may feel offended by your comment. Likewise, telling a joke that you find amusing may end up offending someone because it has racial insinuations. Today, most of us are especially sensitive to sexist language and make a conscious effort not to use words that imply that a manger or a scientist, for example, is always male, or that women are not capable of changing the wheel on a car.

6.8.3   Vocabulary building

The clarity and appropriateness of your language can be improved by increasing your vocabulary. The more words you have at your command, the more precisely you will be able to express yourself. You will also be able to avoid overused words such as 'nice', 'good', 'bad'. Check the unfamiliar words other people use, or that you hear on radio and television, or that you read in a book, in a dictionary and make a conscious effort to remember them and to use them in your conversation (when appropriate) and to make your meanings clearer.

Keeping these guidelines in mind as you interact with others should help to improve your communication skills and go a long way to achieving mutual understanding with your listeners. Keep in mind that, every time you communicate with others, you stand the risk of being misunderstood — you will then be more likely to become sensitive to the way your words affect those with whom you relate.

The following scenarios illustrate problems in the use of language. Study each scenario and then answer the questions based on each one. Try to identify the cause of the differences in understanding between the communicator's message and the recipient's interpretation

Scenario 6.1

When do words make a difference? When you give someone your 'word', what does that imply? Have you ever seen communication difficulties arise over the use and assumed meaning ascribed to certain words?

Hillary Rodham Clinton called her involvement in an Arkansas real estate deal 'minimal'. *Newsweek* stated that it was about an hour a week for 15 months. What word would you use to describe that amount of work?

When General Motors exported the popular Nova model into Spanish speaking countries, it had disappointing sales. *No va* means "does not go" in Spanish — not a particularly good advertisement for a car. How could this have been avoided?

When Telkom lays off 40 000 employees, it is called 'downsizing' or 'restructuring'. What do you think it would be called if 40 000 people were permanently put out of work by an act of nature? (Tubbs & Moss 2003:76)

Scenario 6.2

Study the following conversation between a father and his teenage daughter:
"Daddy, I need your advice about a car. I mean, it's clear that I'm going to have to get one pretty soon, and . . ."
"Yes," interrupts father, "I agree that it's time. In fact, I was thinking that you might have the old Corolla."

What the father was thinking	What the daughter was thinking
❐ My Toyota Corolla would be good	❐ I want a Toyota RunX
❐ It's already paid for and has low maintenance	❐ It's sleek and fast and has a great sound system
❐ It gets 10 kilometres per litre	❐ It has electric windows
❐ It's reliable transportation	❐ It represents freedom and privacy
❐ It's no hassle and relatively safe	❐ It would make me feel powerful
❐ It's inconspicuous and conservative	❐ Boys would flock to my car

(adapted from Gibson & Hanna 1992)

The word 'car' is a concrete word, yet look at the differences in meaning that father and daughter ascribe to the word in their conversation.
1. Which of the causes of misunderstanding you have studied is illustrated in this scenario?
2. Do you agree that the meaning of language is determined by the people who use it? Give reasons for your answer.

Scenario 6.3

This scenario is based on the Sapir-Whorf hypothesis.

Stoltz (1997) cites brain research that shows that the language we use can shape our perception of success, and even our ability to be successful. Those individuals who tell themselves that their shortcomings are long lasting tend to have more failures than those who see setbacks as temporary. Similarly, those who see setbacks as a result of their lack of abilities tend to have more failures than those who see their failures as a result of not having given their best effort. This research has major implications for helping people to improve their career and life successes (Tubbs & Moss 2003:81).

Do you think that the above scenario illustrates the view that language shapes our ideas, or do you think language is merely an instrument of thought? Give reasons for your answer.

Summary

This chapter deals with various aspects of language as a medium of communication. It first paid attention to the relationship between language, meaning and thought with reference to the views of George Orwell. It continued by pointing out the uses of language in everyday communication and then explained Roman Jakobson's six functions of language: referential function, expressive function, conative function, phatic function, poetic function and metalinguistic function. It followed this with a discussion of language as a system of signs and with reference to the Triangle of Meaning. The chapter then examined some of the reasons why language can cause misunderstanding in our communication. Two major reasons are the ambiguities caused by denotative and connotative meanings of words, and the differences between concrete and abstract words. In the next section the chapter discussed genderlects, or the way men and women tend to use language in different ways, and the misunderstandings that ensue. The Sapir-Worf hypothesis was then used to show how language not only provides members of a community with a means of communication: it transmits and perpetuates the perceptions that community has of the world. The final section of the chapter provided some guidelines for improving your language skills. It ended with scenarios based on some of the misunderstandings that language can create.

Test yourself

1. Define the term 'language' in two ways. Explain which definition you prefer.
2. Briefly explain the relationship between language, meaning and thought with reference to the views of George Orwell.
3. Describe the situations in which you use language in your everyday communication.
4. Select an advertisement from a newspaper or magazine and identify the various functions of language it contains.
5. Use the Triangle of Meaning to explain why we say that meaning resides in people, not in words.
6. Provide an example from your own experience in which you and a friend or parent misunderstood one another because of differences in the denotative and connotative meanings of words.
7. Provide an example from your own experience in which you and a friend or parent misunderstood one another because of differences in concrete and abstract words.
8. Listen carefully as friends of both sexes talk about fashions, cars, music or current affairs. Take note of any differences in how men and women use language in these conversations. What are the differences and how do you account for them?

9. Do you think that communication breakdown between people of different languages can be explained by the Sapir-Whorf hypothesis? Why?

10. Make the following statements clearer by using more precise/concrete/ appropriate words.

"You know how much I love soccer. Well, I'm practising a lot because I really want to get better."

"That concert I went to the other day was real cool, man."

"The government's attempt to cover up was a total fiasco."

"I've just bought a beautiful new outfit — I mean it's really great — you'll just love it."

"Man has always been threatened by those who are different to him."

11. Make an effort for several days to apply the suggestions for improving language skills to your everyday communication encounters with others. Try to judge for yourself whether or not people seem to understand your meanings more easily.

EXECUTIVE SUMMARY
Language and communication

1 Orwell's views on language
   ❏ Newspeak
2 Functions of language
   ❏ referential function
   ❏ expressive function
   ❏ conative function
   ❏ phatic function
   ❏ poetic function
   ❏ metalinguistic function
3 Language as a system of signs
   ❏ natural signs
   ❏ symbolic or arbitary (conventional) signs
4 Triangle of meaning
5 Causes of misunderstanding
   ❏ denotative and connotative meanings
   ❏ concrete and abstract words
6 Genderlects
7 Sapir-Whorf hypothesis

Part 2

Contexts of Communication

7 Intrapersonal communication

Overview

Ayanda stretched lazily as she woke one morning and thought, "Good, it's Saturday and I'm meeting Amos for lunch. I'm going to wear my new outfit — it makes me look even sexier than usual and I want to make a really good impression on him." She opened the curtains to check the weather and decided that, as it was overcast, she had better take an umbrella with her. "I don't want to ruin my new clothes." She joined her dad for a cup of coffee in the kitchen, but found it difficult to concentrate on what he was telling her because she was planning what she would say to Amos during their lunch date. She had heard from mutual friends that he had won a scholarship to an overseas university, and was concerned that she was not clever enough to talk to him about topics that would capture his interest.

In the first few moments of the day, Ayanda was already engaging in the mental activity of talking to herself, or intrapersonal communication. Her thoughts ranged from her appearance to her lunch date and the weather, to the conversation she was going to have with Amos. Although we are not always conscious of the fact that we are constantly engaged in 'self-talk', communication scholars have become increasingly aware of the important role intrapersonal communication plays in the nature of our relationships. In this chapter we discuss the most important ideas that have emerged from research into the intrapersonal communication context.

We begin by examining the concept of 'self' and its various parts: the private and public self as well the physical, emotional, intellectual and moral self. Our communication with ourselves and others depends to a large extent on the way we perceive the world around us. We first consider the way we perceive ourselves with reference to two theories: the looking-glass self and social comparison. Because the element of subjectivity in interpreting sensory information can result in inaccurate perceptions of oneself, we examine the role of self-fulfilling prophecies in the process, and then suggest some guidelines for improving one's self-concept. Intrapersonal processing is the basis of self-concept, so we then discuss the five elements in intrapersonal processing: decoding, schemata or integration, perceptual sets, memory and decoding. In the next part of the chapter, we look at the way we perceive other people and form impressions of them and why some of our impressions are inaccurate. The next section deals with some of the intrapersonal variables that play a role in how we see ourselves and others. These variables are mainly concerned with values, attitudes and beliefs. In the final part of the chapter we suggest some intrapersonal skills that could lead to greater insight about your self and your interpersonal relationships. We end the chapter with a scenario which is based on the way perception influences our concept of ourselves.

Learning outcomes

At the end of this unit you should be able to:
1. Describe the concept of 'self' and its various parts.
2. Explain how one's self-concept develops.
3. Explain how the concept you have of yourself influences your communication with others.
4. Apply the five elements in intrapersonal processing to a message that has influenced your self-concept in a negative or positive way.
5. List four factors that influence our perception of others.
6. Apply what you have learned about intrapersonal communication to your everyday communication experiences.
7. Answer the questions based on the scenario at the end of this chapter.

Introduction

Because we are human, we are constantly involved in planning, dreaming, thinking and worrying about what is happening in the world around us. In other words, we are constantly engaged in **intrapersonal communication** — communication within the self to the self. Research conducted into intrapersonal communication confirms the view that, "The first step towards effective communication with others is successful communication with yourself" (Barker & Gaut 1996:111). But what is the 'self' with which we communicate?

7.1   The self

The concept of **self** is used to describe who and what we think we are — that is, our personal identity. Stewart (1990:115) defines the self in two dimensions: "The self is an **internal** thing — a composite of personality characteristics, attitudes, values, beliefs and habits that make us unique." It is also a **social** thing — "it grows out of contacts with others and functions primarily to guide our communication". Note that the self and communication are closely related — the self is shaped in relationship with others and, in turn, the self guides our communication and relationships with others.

Even before reading this, you might already have expressed a similar view about the two dimensions of the self by saying that you have a **private self** and a **public self**. The private, or inner, self is often at variance with the public, or social, self that we display to others. The complexity of modern society demands that we in fact display a variety of public selves, for example, as friend, employee, bank clerk, spouse, parent, student or soccer goalie. The well-known theorist Erving Goffman (1975) (see Chapter 8 for a discussion of his theory) maintains that we are constantly engaged in playing roles or staging performances in order to create the desired impression on other people. It is in internal conversation that we can discard the masks we wear in public and get to know the private self.

We learn to monitor the public and private dimension of our selves. Picture yourself going up on stage at graduation to receive your degree or diploma. To the audience, you will appear composed and serious. Internally, your heart will be thumping and your emotions will be getting the better of you. But it is probably only after you return to your seat that you will allow tears of joy to fall.

We are in fact many selves (cf Burton & Dimbleby 1995; Barker & Gaut 1996).

☐ The **physical self** is the material body with its internal functions and outward appearance. The number of advertisements for preparations that will make you lose weight, look more beautiful, build stronger muscles or improve your resistance to disease is indicative of our awareness of the physical self. The physical self — the part that others see — is often referred to the material self because many people identify themselves in terms of what they have — their material possessions, such as their car, house, clothes and so on.

☐ Another self is the **emotional self**. Some people are regarded as more emotional than others because they respond 'from the heart' (emotionally) rather than with the brain (rationally) to a variety of situations, especially those involving fear, tension or conflict. (Physiological changes, such as rapid heartbeat, tensed muscles or crying for no reason make us aware that our emotions are taking control.) It is important, however, that we or others do not assume permanent characteristics from a temporary condition. Our emotional responses to situations are often fleeting and should not be the basis of stereotypical generalisations. So, if you occasionally lose your temper in trying circumstances, you(self) and others should not label your(self) as unstable.

☐ The **intellectual self** is associated with our mental processes and has to do with problem-solving, reasoning, analysis and logical thinking. Our education plays a role in how we view our intellectual self. Reading this text is an attribute of the intellectual self and your existing view of your intellectual abilities may determine the attitude with which you approach this text — with confidence or a measure of apprehension.

☐ Finally, we have a **moral self**, consisting of our values, the principles we uphold and our ethical beliefs. Our morals are learned in interpersonal communication and from observing the behaviour of others. Morals play a prominent role in social behaviour or social accountability. For example, if you hit your neighbour's fence while backing out of your garage, even if there is no damage, you may hold yourself morally responsible and immediately report the incident to him or her. If you do not see yourself as responsible, you will simply ignore the incident and not even bother to apologise. The question of values, beliefs and opinions in intrapersonal communication is discussed in more detail later in this chapter.

There are two important features regarding the self. First, we cannot separate the parts of the self — in reality they all work together. We see ourselves as a whole and our communication reflects the whole self. Second, the self is not inborn or static, but rather active and dynamic. It grows and changes throughout our lives. You will recall that Ayanda's concept of her physical self is that she is sexy, while her concept of her intellectual self is that she might not be clever enough to hold Amos's interest. How did she form these impressions? To answer the question, we need to refer back to the process of perception described in Chapter 4. We said that perception is the process whereby we acquire information about ourselves and our environment through our five senses. Perception is a subjective process in which we select information from the stimuli around us, organise it into a meaningful whole and then interpret it. The way in which people perceive themselves creates the mental image or self-concept they have of themselves. However, because of the subjective element in the process, we often form inaccurate perceptions of ourselves and others.

7.2   Self-concept

In the literature on intrapersonal communication you will come across the terms 'self-concept', 'self-image' and 'self-esteem'. Although some theorists argue that there are slight differences between each of these terms, in this chapter we use the terms synonymously. **Self-concept** can be described as everything that people think and feel about themselves. It includes appearance, physical and mental capabilities, attitudes and beliefs, strengths and weaknesses — that is, it includes the whole self. It is this mental image that is communicated to others through the way you behave in a particular situation (cf Verderber 1990).

When we feel good about our achievements and our relationships we also tend to value and feel good about ourselves. The more we value ourselves, the more likely we are to meet the challenges that come our way and perform well in a variety of situations. Success tends to breed success. People who think well of themselves generally think well of others and are more successful in their private and professional lives. When we perceive ourselves as failures, we are more likely to behave in ways that cause us to fail and our relationships often suffer as a result. It is important to understand, however, that in building a positive self-concept, it does not help to merely praise yourself. A great deal depends on the way others evaluate you and your achievements. You therefore have to make the most of opportunities that will help you to develop your skills and abilities to their fullest potential. The Danish philosopher, Soren

Kierkegaard, expressed it this way: "To venture causes anxiety, but not to venture is to lose one's self" (Gamble & Gamble 1999:52).

7.2.1   The development of self-concept

How does self-concept develop? We said earlier that our self-concept is shaped by our relationships with others. The way we perceive ourselves depends to a large extent on how we believe others see us. The link with others is communication. From the moment we are born, we become aware of how others see us through their verbal and nonverbal communication. As we interact with parents and siblings, and later with peers and teachers, employers and colleagues, we internalise their views about us so that they become part of how we see ourselves. Think about the effects the messages of others have on you, especially those you respect. You will probably agree that positive messages make you feel accepted, worthwhile, valued, lovable and significant, whereas negative messages tend to make you feel inferior, worthless, left out, unloved or insignificant. In general, the more positive you feel about factors such as your physical appearance, capabilities and the impression others have of you, the more positive your self-concept and your communication about yourself. The more negative you feel about yourself and the impression others have of you, the more negative your self-concept and the way you communicate about yourself.

Messages do not have to be overtly positive or negative to have an effect on you. Think back to what we said about the content level and relational level of messages in Section 3.3.6. Assume that you ask me how I am feeling today, and I say "Fine, thanks". On the content level, I offer some information. At the same time, I also convey a relational message. If I smile as I answer, I tell you that I am happy to continue the conversation. If I respond sharply, then I imply that you are bothering me and I don't want to continue the conversation. In both cases the content is similar but the relational information differs. If you constantly receive negative relational messages, the way you see yourself will be undermined. On the other hand, frequent positive relational messages will reinforce your self-concept.

7.2.2   Theories about self-concept

Looking-glass self A theory about the development of self-concept that is based on the feedback you receive from people around you is the **looking-glass self.** This theory maintains that we evaluate ourselves on the basis of how we think others perceive and evaluate us. These reflected perceptions are formed during our interactions with others and are combined to make up what Mead (1934) calls the "generalised other". The generalised other is made up of impressions formed during our interpersonal relationships and also from our interactions with society. The perspectives of the generalised other reflect the values, experiences and understanding of a particular society. Some of these perspectives are learned during interpersonal communication, but others are communicated to us through the mass media and other social institutions that reflect cultural values. For instance, when we read popular magazines, watch TV, or go to the movies, we are inundated with impressions of how we should look, behave and feel. Even though these impressions vary across cultures, mediated communication in any society tells us over and over how we should be and provides us with criteria for assessing ourselves. The media also reinforce the values that our social institutions weave into the fabric of our culture — values regarding, for example, the law, marriage and education. Reflecting on social values allows us to make choices about which ones we will accept for ourselves (Tubbs & Moss 2003; Wood 2002).

Social comparison Whereas the looking-glass self is based on reflected appraisals from others or how others view us, **social comparison** suggests that, in forming a self-concept, we use others as a measuring stick to assess ourselves. In other words, we compare ourselves with others, especially our peers, to form judgements of our talents, abilities, qualities and so on. In this process, we use social comparisons in two ways. First, we make comparisons to decide whether we are like others, or different from them. Are we the same sex, age, colour, religion? Do we have friends in common? Are our social and economic backgrounds similar? What about political beliefs, values and ethics? Research has shown that people generally feel more comfortable with others that are like them, so we prefer to socialise with people who are similar to us. But this tendency limits our view of ourselves because we lose out on perspectives of people whose experiences and beliefs are different from our own. Our understanding of the world can be so limited that our judgements of ourselves and others are often inaccurate. People in this category are often referred to as 'insular' — that is, narrowminded and not responsive to changes or new influences in their lives.

The second way we use social comparison is to measure ourselves in relation to others. You must know people who regard themselves as 'superior' and others who have what is commonly called an 'inferiority complex' because they are constantly underrating themselves and their abilities. We decide whether we are superior or inferior by comparing ourselves with others. Am I as pretty as Alida? Am I as clever as Thabo? Do I play chess or soccer as well as David or Loyiso? By comparing ourselves with others, we form an image or concept of ourselves based on how we measure up on various criteria. Although this is a normal and necessary process in forming a realistic self-concept, we should not undermine ourselves with constant comparisons to fashion models or professional athletes, for example, because then we are setting unreasonable standards and are bound to underrate ourselves. The power of social comparison to shape identity can be illustrated with practical examples. A child who is interested in the birds she sees around her and would like to find out more about birdlife may live in a family and community who label such an interest as odd or weird. In time, because there is no support from parents or friends, she might begin to accept this label and turn her attention to something that is considered more conventional in her community. Similarly, couples who want to improve the quality of their relationship, but are surrounded by friends who deride the idea of marriage counselling, may begin to think of themselves as oddballs and drop the idea altogether.

Table 7.1 summarises some important differences between people with positive and negative perceptions of themselves (Adler, Rosenfeld & Proctor 2001:73).

Table 7.1 Characteristics of communicators with positive and negative self-esteem

Persons with Positive Self-Esteem	Persons with Negative Self-Esteem
1. Are likely to think well of others.	1. Are likely to disapprove of others.
2. Expect to be accepted by others.	2. Expect to be rejected by others.
3. Evaluate their own performance more favourably.	3. Evaluate their own performance less favourably.
4. Perform well when being watched; are not afraid of others' reactions.	4. Perform poorly when being watched; are sensitive to possible negative reactions.
5. Work harder for people who demand high standards of performance.	5. Work harder for undemanding, less critical people.
6. Are inclined to feel comfortable with others they view as superior in some way.	6. Feel threatened by people they view as superior in some way.
7. Are able to defend themselves against negative comments of others.	7. Have difficulty defending themselves against others' negative comments; are more easily influenced.

An important characteristic of self-concept is that it is not a fixed entity, but changes with your age and the situations you find yourself in. For example, do your colleagues at work or at college see you in the same way as your family or social friends? Do you see yourself differently in different situations? The important point is that the concept you have at any particular time is the outcome of perceptions that have been provided by your parents, teachers, friends and others since birth. But, if you think again about the process of perception we discussed in Chapter 4, you can understand why the image you have of yourself can be distorted. The element of subjectivity in interpreting sensory information can result in inaccurate perceptions of yourself. A problem is that such inaccuracies often cause self-fulfilling prophecies.

7.2.3   Self-fulfilling prophecies

Have you ever made assumptions about what sort of person a new acquaintance is? And then found that he or she in fact behaves in the way you predicted? It is equally true that all of us also interpret messages in ways that confirm what we already think of ourselves. What we believe about ourselves often comes true because we expect it to come true. We refer to this as a **self-fulfilling prophecy.** Self-fulfilling prophecies occur when our expectations of an event help create the very conditions that allow the event to happen. If you think that you will fail a science examination because you believe that you are not good at science, then you will most likely begin to act the part. Poor study habits and low marks reinforce your negative feelings and a vicious circle of events begins. Then you will have to overcome not only your deficiency in science, but also your low expectation of yourself. On the other hand, if you expect to do well at something, you often do well because — without being aware of it — you have prepared yourself for success. People who consistently perform well in job interviews, for example, report that they make the effort to keep their emotions under control, dress appropriately and mentally rehearse the sort of questions they expect to face and the answers they will give. As a result, they are more confident in the interview than people who tell themselves that they are going to botch the interview — and usually do.

Example 7.1

In *My Fair Lady*, the filmed version of Bernard Shaw's play *Pygmalion*, Professor Henry Higgins transforms a Cockney flower girl, Eliza Doolittle, into a fine lady by teaching her how to dress, behave and speak like an upper-class lady. Eliza herself indicates that she understands the principle of self-fulfilling prophecies when she says to Colonel Pickering: "... the difference between a lady and a flower girl is not how she behaves, but how she's treated. I shall always be a flower girl to Professor Higgins because he always treats me as a flower girl, and always will: but I know I can be a lady to you, because you always treat me as a lady, and always will" (Gamble & Gamble 1998a:41).

Studies on critically ill patients have also shown that patients who have a positive, co-operative spirit are more like to recover from illness more quickly than those who assume the worst. Beebe, Beebe and Redman (1999:51) cite a well-known American heart specialist who says, "Optimism is a good thing. When people give up and feel they are not going to make it, it is usually a self-fulfilling prophecy".

The media may also influence the self-fulfilling prophecies we create. In many soap operas, for example, there are more male characters than women. Women are still portrayed largely as homemakers whereas men portray most of the characters with high-powered jobs. When women do have jobs, they are often depicted as subordinate to their male counterparts. Television's portrayals of men and women in particular types of roles can influence the roles that people will seek to fulfil. A research project reported that, when asked what he would like to be when he grew up if he were a girl, a young boy said that if he were a girl, he'd have to grow up to be 'nothing' (Tubbs & Moss 2003).

Because the self-concept reflects the image of who we think we are, not necessarily who we really are, we are usually not very objective about ourselves. Very few people can make an honest inventory of how they perceive their strong and weak points, or their social assets and liabilities. In order to improve one's self-concept it is important to develop a measure of self-awareness.

7.2.4   Improving self-concept

Even though it is more secure to maintain an established image of ourselves, most people would like to improve their self-concept. However, too often people decide they are going to change their behaviour overnight and are then disappointed when they fail. Change is a gradual process and requires a great deal of self-discipline. It is helpful to set realistic goals for yourself and encourage someone close to you to monitor your efforts. Pick one area in which you would like to improve yourself and see if you can work out why you have had problems in this area. Are you perhaps living out a self-fulfilling prophecy? It also helps to try to visualise how a more positive view of yourself would influence your relationships and your career. Visualisation can act as a strong incentive to change.

Try to deliberately become aware of your communication behaviour to determine how it has been influenced by other people's messages. Do the people in your environment support you in your endeavours or do they deliberately try to hold you back? Has someone else defined the roles you play? For instance, many husbands control the way their wives behave as spouse or parent, or whether they continue in their profession after marriage. Such situations often lead to poor interpersonal relationships. Can you change such circumstances so that you are in control?

Learn to monitor the positive and negative feedback that others send you and adjust your behaviour accordingly. Some individuals who were raised by overly critical parents, for example, find it difficult to accept the positive comments about themselves they receive from others. Others simply choose to ignore the negative feedback they receive.

It is important to be aware of how accurately you perceive the context in which you are communicating. You may regard yourself as a humorist because people usually laugh at your jokes. When you are being interviewed for a job, however, you are expected to answer certain questions carefully rather than relate anecdotes that would go down well at a party.

7.2.5   Intrapersonal processing

Earlier in this chapter we said that people develop a concept of who they are by internalising positive and negative messages from others. Internalising messages is a complex process that involves taking in information and 'shifting' it around to various parts of the brain to make sense of it, and then either acting on it or storing it for future use. There are five main elements in intrapersonal processing, all of which overlap to some extent. These are decoding or cognition, integration, memory, schemata or perceptual sets, and encoding (Burton & Dimbleby 1995). As you study the five elements, remember that we are describing the internal communication process through which we give meaning to the positive and negative messages that influence our image of ourselves.

❑ *Decoding* is that part of the process through which messages (information) are taken into the brain and made sense of.

❑ *Integration* refers to that part of the process during which the various bits of information are put together. We relate one piece of information to another, make comparisons and analogies, draw distinctions, and then categorise or make a decision about which piece of information belongs with what.

❑ *Memory* is the storehouse of intrapersonal communication. In it are kept facts and events, attitudes, previous judgements and beliefs. When we think about who we are, we collect some of these messages and organise them into a pattern we call self-concept. Memory involves the ability to store information and to retrieve it. But both these processes are selective (refer to Section 4.4.1) and help to account for the inaccurate perceptions we may have about ourselves.

❑ *Schemata,* or *perceptual sets,* describe structures of thinking or ways of organising information. They provide us with frameworks we have built up over the years for making sense of what we have experienced. We might have, for instance, one schema for organising how we perceive feminine and masculine traits, another for evaluating beauty, another for assessing friendship, and so on. What happens in the intrapersonal process is that information being dealt with is assigned meaning and organised according to these frameworks or cognitive structures.

☐ **Encoding** is the final organising part of the process, in which meaning has been assembled and signs (words) arranged to produce meaningful communication. In the intrapersonal process the encoded communication is to ourselves. It is our internal response to the message we decoded in the first stage of intrapersonal processing. Even when the message is audible (we do sometimes talk out loud to ourselves), the element of encoding in intrapersonal processing describes the mental activity that takes place in order to put a message together from the pictures in our mind and the words in our head. The encoded communication determines whether the initial message we received will have a negative or positive effect on our self-concept.

7.3   Intrapersonal variables

Throughout this section we have emphasised that perception is a personal process: you are the major actor in the perception process. By recognising that you have biases and that you are not always open to the information around you, you can increase the probability that your perceptions will provide you with accurate information about the world around you and the people in it. There are a number of other intrapersonal factors which also create biases in our interpretation of ourselves, others and the events around us. Barker and Gaut (1996:123) refer to these as the 'intrapersonal variables' that influence communication. Among others, they include your personality traits, past experiences and the defence mechanisms you use to resolve conflicts and anxiety. For example, the experiences of someone who has recently been divorced will no doubt affect that person's communication on the subject of marriage. Similarly, some of us deal with our failures by repressing them — that is, keeping certain thoughts and feelings below the conscious level so that we do not have to think about them. Others deal with the same situation by attempting to justify their failures, a process known as rationalisation. Some of these variables assist communication, and others create barriers to communication by interfering in the transmission and interpretation of messages. There are so many intrapersonal variables that influence our communication that we cannot discuss them all. For the purpose of this course, we have limited our discussion to values, attitudes, beliefs, opinions and prejudices.

7.3.1   Values

Values are the moral and ethical judgements we make about things that are important to us. "World peace ought to be our highest goal" and "Cleanliness is next to godliness" are examples of values. All of us learn a value system as we develop from childhood to adulthood. Our values are instilled in us from our earliest interpersonal relationships. For most of us, the most important influence is our parents. Because values are enduring concepts of right and wrong, good and bad, we don't give them up easily. Values are central to our behaviour and our concept of who we are in that they provide standards by which we may assess experience, including communication from others.

The word 'standards' of course suggests that values are relative (Burton & Dimbleby 1995). What people value in one culture may not be so valued in another. What is valued at one time may not be valued at another. Differences in values occur because we have different needs and our social and physical circumstances change over time. For example, most Western cultures accept as 'right' that the elderly should go to retirement homes, whereas in most African cultures, where family values include the belief that the elderly should be looked after at home, this is seen as 'wrong'.

We also need to take into account that contradictory messages about values may cause conflict in the development of self-concept in young people. A father may instil in his children the value that honesty is always paramount, yet they hear him smugly tell his wife how he cheated on his income tax to save a few rands.

Spranger's value systems

Edward Spranger, a German scholar, argues that we each have one predominant value system drawn from the following six major value types (Gamble & Gamble 1998a:264-265):

Theoretical: Values the pursuit and discovery of truth, the intellectual life
Economic: Values what is useful, practical
Aesthetic: Values form, harmony and beauty
Social: Values love, sympathy, warmth and sensitivity in relationships with others
Political: Values competition, influence and personal power
Religious: Values unity, wholeness and a sense of purpose above human beings.

As well as being a determinant of self-concept, values also have an effect on our relationships. They can be a source of conflict within us as well as a barrier between people who have opposing standards. For example, should you value both friendship and honesty, you would try, at all times, to remain loyal to your friends and be as honest as possible. But how would you resolve the inner conflict that arises when given the choice between telling the truth to a friend who has asked your opinion about something, and lying in order not to hurt that person? Think about what your answer to the question tells you about your value system.

Gamble and Gamble (1998a:265) sum up the discussion on values with the following insightful comments:

> Our values provide us with a relatively persistent framework for deciding what we think is right or wrong, which goals to aspire to, whom to listen to, and how to live. They provide us with criteria for evaluating people, ideas and actions. Our values indicate what we find desirable and to what extent, and, consequently, what we are willing to strive for.

7.3.2   Attitudes

Related to values are **attitudes**. An attitude is a learned reaction to a person or situation. It implies a positive or negative evaluation of someone or something. A person who believes that pornography is detrimental to society would have a negative attitude towards any magazine or film, for instance, that contains and promotes pornography. In our relationships, people come to expect a pattern of behaviour from us based on what they have learned about our attitudes. Should we behave differently, they might say that we are acting out of character, and they might also revise their opinion of our attitudes and values.

Where do we learn our attitudes? They develop mainly from our family, religion, education, economic and social class, and culture. We communicate our attitudes in our verbal and nonverbal interactions. Every time we communicate, we display our attitudes. Facial expressions, postures and gestures often reveal our attitudes more clearly than words, even when we remain silent because, perhaps, we disapprove of someone's views.

7.3.3   Beliefs, opinions and prejudices

Beliefs are the building blocks of attitudes. They provide the basis or foundation for the attitudes we hold. A belief is anything that is accepted as true without a negative or positive judgement. For example, you might believe in life after death, but your belief does not involve a positive or negative judgement of that idea. However, should you say that, because you believe in life after death it would be in our best interests to prepare for a life hereafter, you would be voicing an **opinion** on the subject.

Where do our beliefs come from? Sometimes we believe information because it comes from a reliable source. For example, you believe that flossing your teeth after each meal will prevent tooth decay because your dentist told you so. He or she does not have to provide proof. Sometimes we believe information because we read it or hear it on television, without realising that the source of the information may be biased. Because we don't require proof in order to believe the things we do, our beliefs are often not necessarily logical. Instead, we often allow our beliefs to influence our interpretations of events and people. We sometimes distort what we see and hear and then behave in ways that are consistent with what we think is true.

Some of our beliefs are about the self and influence our relationships because the more positive our beliefs about ourselves, the more confident our communication becomes. If you believe that you have good communication skills, for example, the more likely you are to communicate with confidence and, in turn, the more strongly that belief will be reinforced. Unfortunately, some people's abilities do not match their beliefs and they may fool themselves into believing that they are good communicators. Burton and Dimbleby (1996:16) point out the correlation between beliefs and behaviour is that "we try actively to get others to behave in ways which accord with our main beliefs about ourselves".

Some of our beliefs and opinions are based on preconceived ideas and not on our own experiences. Such beliefs and opinions are the basis of the stereotypes, or preformed judgements about a person, group or thing, which we discuss in Section 7.5.1. When stereotypes become deeply entrenched, we refer to them as prejudices. **Prejudices** are extremely dangerous because they are very resistant to change and are accompanied by strong emotional reactions (cf Ellis & McClintock 1994). Think about people who have strong racial prejudices and the emotional reactions these produce. While none of us is entirely free from prejudices, some are more harmful to our communication and relationships than others.

7.4   Cultural and gender differences

Verderber and Verderber (2001) refer to research that shows that culture influences perception and one's view of oneself. The Western view of self is that the individual is an independent entity with distinct abilities, traits, motives and values that cause behaviour. People with this view regard the individual as the most basic social unit. This individual builds a positive self-concept by being independent from others and discovering and expressing individual unique-ness. Other cultures, mainly African and Eastern, have a different set of values regarding self-concept. They see the family, not the individual, as the basic social unit. These cultures value interdependence among individuals, so that someone from an African or Eastern culture would view the characteristics that Westerners value so highly as shortcomings. Whereas Western children are taught the values of independence and develop high self-esteem from them, in other cultures children are socialised towards greater interdependency and develop higher self-esteem when they perceive themselves to be co-operative, helpful and self-effacing.

Similarly, one's culture creates perceptions of men's and women's roles in society. If women are expected to be homemakers and nurturing mothers rather than pursue careers, then women who perceive themselves to have the skills to attend to family life feel good about themselves. Women who do not have these attributes are likely to be less confident about their role in society and are likely to have a more negative self-concept.

7.5   Perception of others

The interaction between the senses and the environment not only provides us with information about ourselves but also about the people with whom we come into contact. When two people meet, they form initial impressions of each other, which will be reinforced or changed as they continue to interact. You are introduced to Nikiwe at a conference, for example, and would like to find out which company she represents. Before you even start a conversation, you form an impression of her. This impression influences your reactions to her and determines what you will say and how you will say it. If you perceive her as arrogant and self-centred, your communication will be different than if you perceive her as friendly and outgoing. It is difficult to explain how such impressions are formed, but they are certainly related to your perception of her.

Nonverbal behaviour plays the most important role in the way our first impressions are made. Of all the nonverbal codes you studied in Chapter 5, the most relevant in this respect are, in this order: race, gender, age, appearance, facial expressions, eye contact, movement, personal space and touch (Verderber & Verderber 2001). These characteristics help us to categorise people as friendly, intelligent, laid-back and so on, or their opposite. We could say that we perceive others in order to make sense of their social behaviour. Of course, your initial impression could be entirely wrong. The smile that first attracted you to Nikiwe could be a characteristic that she deliberately displays at conferences in order to attract people and make new business contacts.

We can conclude that verbal and nonverbal communication are extremely important in the process of perceiving others because we obtain information about their attitudes, personality and emotional state. We need this information to make sense of their behaviour and to deduce meaning about what they may be thinking and feeling. This information, in turn, helps us to plan our own communication behaviour. Nikiwe's nonverbal communication — her tone of voice or the manner in which she shook your hand — could have created the impression you formed of her. Perhaps her clothing or her posture contributed to the impression. Your interpretation of the information about Nikiwe your brain selected and processed has been influenced by your past experiences of people, and creates your perception of her.

7.5.1   Perceptual inaccuracies

There are so many factors influencing perception that we cannot take our perceptions for granted. We have to consider whether they are correct. At times our impressions are so inaccurate that our understanding of people and situations is distorted. An awareness of how inaccuracies in our perception of others occur can help to improve our relationships.

☐ ***Emotional state*** The feelings people experience at a particular time affect the nature of perception. First impressions are especially vulnerable to fluctuations in mood. When you are feeling low or irritable, your perception of others is generally more negative than if you are having a good day. Think about how your feelings may have affected your perception before acting on first impressions.

☐ ***Selective perception*** Selective perception refers to the fact that people choose information according to their existing attitudes, values and beliefs. Briefly, it means that people see what they want to see and hear what they want to hear (refer to Section 4.1.1). For instance, you tend to think highly of a person you like and perceive only the positive side of his or her personality. The negative traits of that person, which may be apparent to other people, are often overlooked or ignored.

☐ ***Fundamental attribution error*** Fundamental attribution error refers to the fact that we sometimes attribute cause and blame to people rather than to circumstances. We tend to assume that someone who says or does something we do not like has negative feelings about us instead of taking into account the external causes that might have prompted their behaviour. We need to find out about the circumstances in which people are behaving in a particular way before forming judgements about them. Wood (2002) cites the example of a woman who accused her boss of gender bias when he transferred her to another branch. In fact, he proved that he had a pressing need for staff in the new location and she was the most suitable person to take up the position.

☐ ***False consensus*** Most of us tend to believe that other people agree with the views we express and, as a result, we mistakenly project our own values and beliefs onto them.

☐ ***False consistency*** False consistency refers to the fact that we prefer people to be predictable. We therefore tend to believe that their behaviour is more consistent than it is. It gives us more confidence in dealing with them if we believe that we can predict what they will do and say next because we expect consistency in their behaviour.

☐ The ***primacy effect*** refers to a tendency to fix first impressions in one's mind and to build on these rather than to be open to changing our views of others. The ***recency effect*** refers to the alternative tendency for people to perceive others in terms of the last thing they have said or done. You may have had a pleasant conversation with an acquaintance you have just met, but an unfortunate remark about your occupation or someone's appearance, for example, at the end of the conversation is probably what will have the greatest influence on your impression of that person.

☐ *Halo effect* The halo effect occurs when we form perceptions of people based on the observation of a single characteristic which they display. We allow that characteristic to influence our impressions of that person without first verifying them. In an experiment described by Tubbs and Moss (1991), half the students in an economics class at the Melbourne Institute of Technology were given a note in which they were told that their new lecturer was considered to be a rather warm person, industrious, critical, practical and determined. The other half were given a note which told them that he was considered to be a rather cold person, industrious, critical, practical and determined. After the lecturer had finished speaking, the students were asked to rate him on 15 different characteristics. Those who were given the 'warm' note usually described the lecturer as social, popular and informal. Those who read the 'cold' description felt he was formal and self-centred. It appears that a halo effect can work to a person's advantage or disadvantage, depending on whether the perception is favourable or unfavourable.

☐ *Stereotyping* As we form impressions of other people, we tend to classify them into categories on the basis of their characteristics. We put them into groups based on their race, religion, occupation, age, gender, physical disabilities, accent or socioeconomic level. Thus we think about a teenager, a foreigner, a lawyer, a trouble-maker or the elderly and assume that they will display all the characteristics we have come to associate with that type. Furthermore, the way we communicate with them will be based on the way we expect them to behave, rather than responding to each person as an individual.

7.6   Improving the accuracy of your perceptions

Knowing yourself is perhaps the most important intrapersonal skill you can acquire — to recognise your own strengths and weaknesses. It is then possible to build relationships with others as well as to develop a positive but accurate self-image of yourself.

Improving the accuracy of your perceptions of others is largely a process of being mentally aware that your initial perceptions are not always correct and that they may need to be revised.

Aiming for a realistic impression

Verderber and Verderber (2002) provide guidelines for constructing a more realistic impression of others and for assessing the validity of your own perceptions.

☐ **Actively question the accuracy of your perceptions** Many people act on their perceptions as though they were reality, saying "I know what I saw". Recognising the possibility of error motivates you to seek further verification and avoids erroneous impressions.

☐ **Withhold judgement until you have more information to verify your perceptions** Taking the trouble to gather more information about people you meet helps to determine whether your original perception is accurate.

☐ **Talk with the people with whom you are forming perceptions** The best way to get information about people and to get to know them is to talk with them. Some perceptions may still be inaccurate, but the likelihood of accuracy is increased.

☐ **Realise that perceptions of people need to change over time** People's attitudes and behaviour often change, and your perceptions of them need to change accordingly. It may be easier to hang onto your original perceptions, but communication based on outdated, inaccurate perceptions can be more costly than revising your perceptions.

☐ **Check perceptions verbally** To avoid drawing the wrong conclusions from other people's nonverbal behaviour, it is important to make a perception check, a verbal statement that reflects your understanding of the meaning of other people's nonverbal cues. For example, your mother uses a sharp tone of voice when she gives you instructions about the chores she would like you to do while she is at work. You say, "From the sound of your voice, I get the impression I have done something to annoy you. Have I?" The question is the perception check. She may well be annoyed with you, in which case the perception check may lead to a discussion and resolution of the problem. On the other hand, she may be concerned about an entirely different matter and inadvertently created your perception of the situation. In this case, the perception check may avoid misunderstandings and future problems.

☐ **Empathise with others** Empathising means that we evaluate our perceptions from the viewpoint of the other person. We try to understand the other's point of view and try to see the world as they see it. In addition to arriving at a more accurate perception of someone, this skill also counteracts our tendency to see the world only from our own point of view.

Scenario 7.1

Lerato was sitting in the cafeteria at work, drinking a cup of coffee and wondering why she had not got the promotion she had applied for. She was disappointed and surprised because she had been so confident that by next month she would be a supervisor in her department. She had already planned on moving to a new apartment because the increase in salary would have covered the higher rent. When Peter sat down next to her, she mumbled a greeting and hardly smiled at him. In reply to his question about what was bothering her, she started telling him about the interview with the management committee.

When she had finished, Peter said: "You know, I'm a friend as well as a work mate, and that's why I'm going to tread on your toes and perhaps sound unkind. But maybe you should think again about how you come across — how other people see you."

"What do you mean? I made sure that I answered all their questions positively and emphasised my abilities and strong points — I even told them about the changes I would implement immediately."

"Yes, but maybe they thought you were just too dominating."

"Dominating! I'm not dominating. Anyway, how can you be a supervisor unless you can show that you are in control of every situation?"

"Being in control doesn't mean that you have to always get your own way. I've seen you badger people until they agree with you — and they often don't like it." Seeing the look of amazement on Lerato's face, Peter quickly said: "Don't get me wrong. I like you. But you really tend to overpower people who don't go along with how you want to do things. You don't give them the opportunity to put across their own ideas. You even have to be in charge of our entertainment committee. What I'm trying to tell you is that management might have turned you down if that is how you came across at the interview."

Lerato was silent for a while and then said, "Funny, isn't it? I don't see myself like that at all. I thought I was always positive and helpful — actually a reasonable sort of person. I know that I am not as pretty as most of the other girls in our department, and I don't have a good figure either, so I thought that coming across as strong and helpful would make other people like me. Strange how wrong you can be about yourself."

"I'm not saying you're wrong," said Peter. "I'm only saying that other people don't see you quite the way you do." (Based on Burton & Dimbleby 1995.)

After you have studied this scenario and thought about the situation, write down your own views about how the case relates to what you have studied in this chapter: for example, perception of self and others, the development of self-concept, self-fulfilling prophecies and self-disclosure. Then suggest ways in which Lerato could create better relationships with her work colleagues and her superiors.

Summary

This chapter focused on the intrapersonal communication context and its relevance in our lives. It began by examining the concept of 'self' and its various parts: the private and public self as well as the physical, emotional, intellectual and moral self. It then went on to explain that our communication with ourselves and others depends to a large extent on the way we perceive the world around us. It first considered the way we perceive ourselves and develop a self-concept with reference to two theories: the looking-glass self and social comparison. It then showed how self-fulfilling prophecies can create problems in self-concept, and suggested some guidelines for improving one's self-concept. The five elements in intrapersonal processing were discussed: decoding, integration, schemata or perceptual sets, memory and decoding. The next part of the chapter looked at the way we perceive other people — how we form impressions of them as well as several factors that lead to the creation of inaccurate impressions. Some of the intrapersonal variables that play a role in how we see ourselves and others were briefly described: values, attitudes, beliefs, opinions and prejudices. The final part of the chapter suggested some intrapersonal skills that could improve our intrapersonal communication and the way we understand ourselves and others. The chapter ended with a scenario based on the way perception influences our concept of ourselves.

Test yourself

1. Explain how self-concept develops. Then briefly explain how the concept you have of yourself influences your communication with others.
2. What past relationships most affected the development of your self? Which present relationships are having the most influence on the current development of your self?
3. Think about a negative or positive comment that someone has recently made about you. Work through the five elements in intrapersonal processing showing how you internalised the message and the influence it had on your image of yourself.
4. Identify an instance when a comment of yours influenced someone else's self-concept. Was your comment deliberate or unintentional? How were you able to determine the impact of your communication?
5. Identify a problem you have with your self-concept. Were you made to feel inadequate by a particular person? Are you living a self-fulfilling prophecy? What do you think you should do to change this behaviour?
6. Describe three different situations in which you think you have fallen into one or more of the errors of perception about other people you have studied in this chapter.
7. Define self-disclosure and give examples of it in at least two of your relationships.

8. Identify the difference in your openness in two relationships that are important to you.
9. Job applications often ask prospective candidates to describe themselves using 10 adjectives. How would you describe yourself? Then think about five different people who know you fairly well. How do you think each one would describe you?

EXECUTIVE SUMMARY
Intrapersonal communication

1 The self
   ❑ private self, public self
   ❑ physical self, emotional self, intellectual self
2 Theories about self-concept
   ❑ the looking glass self
   ❑ social comparison
   ❑ self-fulfilling prophecies
3 Intrapersonal processing
   ❑ decoding
   ❑ schemata
   ❑ integration (perceptual sets)
   ❑ memory
   ❑ decoding
4 Intrapersonal variables
   ❑ values and attitudes
   ❑ beliefs, opinions and prejudices
5 Perceptual inaccuracies
   ❑ emotional state
   ❑ selective perception
   ❑ fundamental attribution error
   ❑ false consensus
   ❑ false consistency
   ❑ primacy effect
   ❑ recency effect
   ❑ halo effect
   ❑ stereotypes

8 Interpersonal communication

Overview

We spend a great deal of our time interacting with other people — at home, at school, work or in social situations. If you think back over the last few days, can you remember how many of your waking hours you spent completely alone? You probably spent some of your time talking to a friend, discussing an issue with a parent, or chatting to a sales assistant about a purchase you were making. In this chapter we are mostly concerned with one-to-one relationships. While you study this chapter, it is important to remember that everything you have learned about communication thus far is pertinent to interpersonal communication.

We examine communication between two people more closely by focusing on the relationships we develop and maintain in our everyday lives. We begin by giving a brief discussion of Martin Buber's description of two types of communication relationships: I-you and I-it relationships, and the consequences of each for the life of the individual. We then go on to discuss a model that describes the interaction stages of a relationship — the stages of coming together and the stages of coming apart. We also consider three factors that influence the development and nature of our interpersonal relationships. The first is self-disclosure — the way in which we reveal ourselves to others and the influence that this has on our relationships. The second concerns our interpersonal needs and is illustrated by the theories of Schutz and Homans. The third factor concerns the communication style we use in our relationships: passive, aggressive or assertive. Up till now we have been discussing close interpersonal relationships. In the remainder of this chapter we use Erving Goffman's theory of self-presentation to illustrate communication behaviour in social, rather than intimate, relationships. Throughout the chapter we provide guidelines for improving your own interpersonal relationships. There are two scenarios in this chapter. The first is based on three styles of communication behaviour: passive, aggressive and assertive. The second is based on Erving Goffman's theory of self-presentation.

Learning outcomes

At the end of this unit you should be able to:
1. Briefly describe the characteristics of I-you and I-it relationships.
2. Briefly describe the interaction stages in a relationship using an example from your own experience to illustrate each stage.

3. Define self-disclosure and give examples of it in at least two of your relationships.
4. Define the three interpersonal needs in Schutz's theory and give an example of how each one motivated you to communicate with another person.
5. Explain Homans's social-exchange theory and describe a relationship you have maintained because it provides you with greater need fulfilment than cost.
6. Define nonassertive communication and relate a personal experience to illustrate it.
7. Define aggressive communication and relate a personal experience to illustrate it.
8. Define assertive communication and relate a personal experience to illustrate it.
9. List and explain three guidelines for improving assertive behaviour.
10. Describe Goffman's theory of social interaction as a dramaturgical performance.
11. Apply the knowledge about interpersonal relationships you learn in this unit to your personal communication experiences.
12. Answer the questions based on the case studies in this chapter.

Introduction

Sociologists have noted that, as modern society becomes increasingly technological and impersonal, people seem to place a greater value than ever on meaningful relationships in their everyday lives. Research results demonstrate that the most important contributor to personal happiness — outranking money, job and sex — is a close relationship with another person (DeVito 1989). Stewart (1990:7) goes as far as asserting that "the quality of your life is directly related to the quality of your communication", an idea which Satir (1972:30) strongly reinforces in the following words: "Once a human being has arrived on this earth, communication is the largest single factor determining what kinds of relationships he makes with others and what happens to him in the world about him."

Communication scientists make the point that a great deal of time is spent in teaching children to read and write, to pronounce words and to use them correctly. But very little time at school, college or university is spent in teaching people how to communicate effectively (cf Pease & Garner 1989). Communication is the foundation for all our interpersonal relationships. Through communication we establish, develop and maintain relationships, and through communication we also withdraw from and terminate relationships. The link between communication, interpersonal relationships and the quality of life is the theme underlying the work of the philosopher, Martin Buber.

8.1   Buber's theory of interpersonal relationships

Before we discuss Buber's theory, please take note that the references to 'he' and 'him' in the discussion are not intended to be sexist. In Buber's lifetime (1878-1965), it was common practice to use the masculine form of address to refer to both men and women. We have tried as far as possible to use the masculine when Buber refers to the communicator and the feminine when he talks about the recipient, but these gender references are interchangeable.

According to Buber (1964; 1970), the basis of human existence is that people are communicating beings. Each of us is always in the process of communicating with the world (our circumstances), thereby making sense of the situation in which we find ourselves (intrapersonal communication). Other people are part of our circumstances and we enter into relationships with them as well. In Buber's view, it is the nature of the relationships that people form that determines their **mode of existence**. To express this thought simply: the meaning that life holds for each of us arises from the type of relationships we create with other people.

Buber describes two types of interpersonal relationships: **I-you relationships** and **I-it relationships**. The difference lies in the nature of the communication that takes place between the participants. To understand the difference between the two relationships, we have to explain the concepts of dialogue and monologue in interpersonal communication. A **dialogue** is a conversation between two people in which both participants have the opportunity to express themselves and to interpret each other's messages. An exchange of thoughts, feelings and meaning takes place between them. In a **monologue**, the communicator is in a sense the only participant. He or she expresses his or her point of view without taking into account the needs of the recipient or giving him or her the opportunity to respond meaningfully. It is a one-sided conversation in which no exchange of meaning between the participants is possible. Buber maintains that the attitude and intentions of the partners differ in the two ways of communicating (cf Johannensen 1971; Jansen & Steinberg 1991).

8.1.1   The I-you relationship

In the I-you relationship the partners approach each other with mutual respect, sincerity and honesty, and the intention to become subjectively involved in a reciprocal relationship. Buber says that the 'I' (communicator) reaches out to the 'you' (recipient) with his whole being and the 'you' responds with her whole being. Although interested in being understood, the 'I' does not attempt to impose his views on the 'you', or to bolster his own self-image by giving off false impressions. Each reveals the person that they really are and not the image of themselves they would like others to have. Each communicates their own feelings, thoughts and beliefs, and not opinions they have heard from others.

In addition to revealing himself as he is, the 'I' also accepts the other as the unique individual that she is. He is present to the other in the sense that he listens attentively to what she wishes to express and tries to understand her point of view. Buber explains that, in such a relationship, a space opens up between people — he calls it the interhuman domain — and it is here that dialogue unfolds and 'you' and 'I' become 'we'. The 'we', or dialogical, relationship is based on intersubjectivity — that is, the participants acknowledge the differences between them while striving to come to an understanding of each other. Buber stresses that in the 'we' relationship neither partner is taken over by the other. Although the 'we' relationship is characterised by involvement, equally important in the relationship is the idea of distance – this means that even in the closest relationship both partners retain their individuality. In the interhuman domain both participants acknowledge the other as a unique individual and simultaneously reach a deeper understanding of themselves.

8.1.2   The I-it relationship

In contrast to the I-you relationship is the I-it relationship. The main difference between the two is in the attitude and intentions of the 'I' to the other. In the I-it relationship, the attitude of the 'I' is that his partner in communication is not an equal subject in the relationship, but an object to be manipulated for personal gain. Although there are two participants, the I-it relationship is not a dialogical relationship because the distinguishing features of the I-you relationship are not present. The intention of the I is to persuade the other to his way of thinking without taking into account the views and needs of the other, as in dialogue. The communicator is conducting a monologue, a conversation in which only his point of view and needs are considered.

Words that Buber uses to characterise the I-it relationship are, among others: 'self-centredness', 'pretence', 'domination', 'exploitation' and 'manipulation'. This is not a relationship of mutual trust, openness and reciprocity, but one in which the communicator uses the recipient to achieve his own ends. There is no understanding of one another because the I-it relationship does not include the option of agreement to differ, and the recipient must always agree with the communicator's views.

Buber does not condemn the I-it relationship. He acknowledges that in order to survive in the modern world I-it relationships are unavoidable. What he emphasises, however, is that I-it should not be allowed to overtake one's life: I-it should always remain subordinate to I-you. This is because the two relationships indicate two modes of existence. The I-you relationship implies an **authentic**

mode of existence, one in which each participant individually determines the person he becomes and the meaning that life holds for him. The I-it relationship implies an **inauthentic mode of existence**, one in which the individual allows him/herself to be determined by the will of others with whom they come into contact. Ultimately, however, the type of relationship and mode of existence that predominates in each person's life remains the choice and responsibility of the individuals themselves.

While you were studying Buber's view of communication and relationships, we hope that you became aware of the importance Buber attaches to the skills of listening attentively and providing appropriate feedback to your partner. Both these aspects of communication were discussed in Chapter 4. Please refer back to this chapter if you need to refresh your memory about them. In the rest of this chapter, we move away from philosophical thoughts about communication and relationships to a consideration of some of the factors that play a role in establishing and maintaining interpersonal relationships.

Although relationships sometimes develop because people are initially attracted to one other by physical and personality factors, we do not usually form close relationships immediately upon meeting someone. Rather, we grow into a relationship gradually by getting to know more about one another through our communication. As the relationship develops, we learn about the other person as well as our reasons for forming particular relationships.

8.2   Stages in the development of interpersonal relationships

In the book aptly entitled *Bridges not Walls*, Stewart (2002) suggests that communication is the key factor that can build a bridge between people in developing and maintaining a relationship. Communication is also the factor that can create a wall or barrier between people whose relationship is deteriorating. Knapp and Vangelisti (1996:33-44) present a model that illustrates the central role of communication in all stages of a relationship. The authors make a point of bringing to our attention that the model simplifies a complex process. The stages are not as clearcut as depicted in the model — one stage merges into the next and each stage may contain behaviour from other stages. The authors also request that we resist the normal temptation to perceive the stages of coming together as 'good' and those of coming apart as 'bad'. It is not necessarily 'bad' to terminate a relationship and not always 'good' to become more intimate with someone. In addition, the authors point out that, while the dialogue in the model is oriented towards mixed-gender pairs, the model also applies to same-gender pairs. The bonding ceremony, for instance, need not be marriage. It could be an act of becoming 'blood brothers' by placing open wounds on each other to achieve oneness.

8.2.1   Interaction stages in coming together

☐ *Initiating* The *initiation* stage includes all the processes we go through when we first come together with other people, strangers or friends, either formally or informally. Perception comes into play as we consider our own stereotypes, expectations for this situation and any prior knowledge we might have about this person and previous interactions with them. We are mentally asking ourselves whether this is the sort of person we want to get to know better and whether the timing is appropriate — is the person perhaps busy, in a hurry or surrounded by others. The setting also plays a role, for instance whether we meet at the beach or in a library, as well as the amount of time that is available. We generally exercise a good deal of caution at this stage and communicate according to conventional formulas.

Table 8.1 A model of interaction stages

Process	Stage	Representative Dialogue
	Initiating	"Hi, how ya goin'?"
		"Fine. You?"
	Experimenting	"Oh, so you like to ski . . . so do I."
		"You do?! Great. Where do you go?"
Coming	Intensifying	"I . . . I think I love you."
Together		"I love you too."
	Integrating	"I feel so much a part of you."
		"Yeah, we are like one person. What happens to you happens to me."
	Bonding	"I want to be with you always."
		"Let's get married."
	Differentiating	"I just don't like big social gatherings."
		"Sometimes I don't understand you. This is one area where I'm certainly not like you at all."
	Circumscribing	"Did you have a good time on your trip?"
		"What time will dinner be ready?"
Coming	Stagnating	"What's there to talk about?"
Apart		"Right. I know what you're going to say and you know what I'm going to say."
	Avoiding	"I'm so busy, I just don't know when I'll be able to see you."
		"If I'm not around when you try, you'll understand."
	Terminating	"I'm leaving you . . . and don't bother trying to contact me."
		"Don't worry."

Source: Knapp & Vangelesti (1996:34)

☐ **Experimenting** Once communication has been initiated, we try to discover something about the other person, a process known as *experimenting*. Often this stage begins with the exchange of demographic information, like where one lives or works. The response from the other person shows the degree of interest in continuing the interaction and willingness to pursue a relationship. Small talk is the basis of experimenting — while we discuss the weather, music we enjoy, food that we like or movies we have seen, we are setting the scene for discovering more important topics of mutual interest and pave the way for future friendships. Many of our relationships remain at this stage — they are generally pleasant, relaxed, uncritical and entail limited commitments. Some of our relationships progress to the next stage.

☐ **Intensifying** When people achieve a relationship known as 'close friends' the indicators of their relationship are *intensified*, albeit that they proceed with caution at the outset. For instance, holding hands or sitting close may precede hugging. The amount of personal disclosure increases and we may reveal some previously withheld information — that my mother is an alcoholic, or that I'm scared of the dark. These disclosures make the speaker vulnerable because the other person may decide to back off and end the relationship. (See the discussion of self-disclosure in Section 8.3.) During this stage, the nature of verbal communication changes: forms of address become more informal (first name, nickname, or endearments are used) and the first person plural is used more often ('we' rather than 'I'). Words begin to take on private meanings and verbal shortcuts may replace longer sentences because the pair share assumptions, knowledge, interests, experiences and expectations. Increasingly, direct verbal commitments are voiced and the pair help each other to express thoughts and feelings. Sophistication in nonverbal communication also increases — a glance or a touch may replace the verbal message and one often notices some co-ordination in their clothing styles. As the relationship intensifies, each person is revealing his or her uniqueness while at the same time binding his or personality with the other's.

☐ **Integrating** The relationship has now reached a point where the two individual personalities almost seem to fuse or coalesce. Often, one partner will change political or religious beliefs to create unity. Verbal and nonverbal manifestations of *integrating* may take many forms. Some of these include the following:

(1) Attitudes, opinions, interests and tastes that clearly distinguish the pair from others are vigorously cultivated — "We have something special; we are unique".

(2) Social circles merge and others begin to treat the two individuals as a common package — one present, one letter, one invitation.

(3) Intimacy 'trophies' are exchanged so that each can 'wear' the other's identity — pictures, pins, rings.

(4) Similarities in manner, dress and verbal behaviour may also accentuate the oneness.

(5) Actual physical penetration of various body parts contributes to the perceived unification.

(6) Sometimes common property is designated — 'our song', a joint bank account or a co-authored book.

(7) Empathic processes seem to peak so that explanation and prediction of behaviour are much easier.

(8) Body rhythms and routines achieve heightened synchrony.

(9) Sometimes the love of a third person or object will serve as glue for the relationship — "Love me, love my rhinos". (Knapp & Vangelesti 1996:39)

Integration should not mean complete togetherness or complete loss of individuality. As Buber points out, in the 'we' relationship it is critical to maintain separate and distinct selves — even in the closest relationship both partners retain their individuality.

☐ Bonding is the institutionalisation of the relationship. At this stage a public ritual, such as engagement or marriage, announces that commitments have been formally contracted. The act of bonding sometimes changes the nature of the relationship for 'better or for worse'. Because it implies a commitment to a common future, the contract makes it more difficult to break out of the relationship. The contract often becomes a frequent topic of conversation between the participants and provides guidance for the relationship through specified rules and regulations. Bonding is also a way of gaining social support for the relationship by enabling the couple to rely on law or policy or precedent.

8.2.2 Interaction stages in coming apart

☐ ***Differentiating*** Integrating is mainly a process of coming together, whereas *differentiating* is mainly a process of disengaging or coming apart. Although individual differences may previously have been set aside, they now play a major role in creating interpersonal distance. The couple discovers how different they really are. 'We' and 'our' again become 'I' and 'my'. What causes the differences? They may be related to attitudes, interests, personality, relatives, friends or to a specific behaviour such as emotional needs or an irritating habit. The most visible communication form of differentiating is conflict which is generally expressed verbally, and ultimately ends up with an explicit or implicit "Love me (as I am) or leave me".

☐ ***Circumscribing*** In relationships that are coming apart, communication decreases quantitatively and qualitatively, or is *circumscribed*. Conversation is restricted to safe topics. Communication is superficial because the number of 'touchy' topics increases and almost anything one partner says can be interpreted by the other as being aggressive. There is generally a decrease in expressions of commitment and less conversation about the relationship. Typical phrases as this stage are "Let's not discuss that" or "Leave my mother out of this conversation" or "It's none of your business". Often it is only in public that communication increases because the couple does not want others to see that their relationship is coming apart.

☐ **Stagnating** During this stage, participants often conduct internal dialogues and conclude that, since they 'know' how the conversation will go, there is little point in initiating it in the first place. "If I say this, he'll say that" and so on. Sometimes the relationship is marked by nonverbal behaviour that more clearly indicates the unpleasant feelings of the participants than verbal interchange. Extended *stagnating* means that very few areas of conversation remain open. The situation can be seen in many relationships: between parent and child; just prior to divorce or the termination of a friendship; or following unproductive small talk. Why do people persist in a relationship that brings so little rewards? Many don't, but others are afraid that they may find it painful to terminate the relationship. Some persist because they are finding rewards outside the relationship, for example devoting more time to work and being promoted, or developing other relationships. Still others may obtain perverse satisfaction in 'punishing' the other person by not terminating the relationship.

☐ **Avoiding** implies that one or both participants no longer wish to engage in face-to-face or voice-to-voice interaction. Avoiding suggests that a permanent state of separation would be desirable. When communicating avoidance, messages may contain overtones of antagonism or unfriendliness. For example, "Please don't call me again — I do not want to see or speak to you any longer". A more subtle version of avoidance is to be consistently late for appointments or saying, "I can't stay long — I am very busy". Or, "I can't see you on Monday because...."; "I can't see you on Tuesday because...."; "I can't see you on Wednesday because....". When physical separation is not possible, a situation may arise where the participants simply ignore each other, almost as if the other person did not exist. They share the same living space, but communicate only essential messages.

☐ **Terminating** Relationships can *terminate* after one encounter or after many years of intimacy. Apart from the fact that one partner may die, termination may occur because people find themselves separated by great distances, or because they have grown socially and psychologically apart. The nature of the termination dialogue varies depending on the circumstances, but generally it is characterised by messages of distance and disassociation. 'Distance' is the attempt to create physical and psychological barriers between the partici-pants. This can be achieved through actual physical separation, or psycho-logical barriers can be embedded in other verbal and nonverbal messages. Disassociative messages prepare one or both participants for separation by emphasising differences and showing increasing concern for the one partner's own interests and points of view. Termination dialogue generally includes messages about what the future relationship (if any) is going to be like. For example, "I do respect you, but I simply must have my independence — perhaps we will still meet for coffee now and then" or "I don't ever want to see you again".

The model indicates that no single characteristic or factor can describe the complexity of interpersonal relationships.

8.3   Interpersonal communication and self-disclosure

Theorists have proposed a variety of factors that need to be taken into account in understanding the development and breakdown of interpersonal relation-ships. We have selected several theories that seem to us to be among the most important because they play a prominent role in influencing the nature and quality of our relationships: the first is your ability to reveal or disclose information about yourself to the person with whom you want to form a close interpersonal relationship.

8.3.1   Self-disclosure

Self-disclosure is defined as "revealing one's thinking, feelings, and beliefs to another" (Gibson & Hanna 1992:129), that is, revealing information about the private self to other people. Research confirms that self-disclosure is essential to the growth of meaningful interpersonal relationships. While it is in intraper-sonal communication that we decide how much information about the private self we are willing to reveal to others, it is interpersonal communication that we actually self-disclose. Telling someone something about yourself that he or she already knows would be sharing or disclosing information, but would not be regarded as self-disclosure. To qualify as self-disclosure, the information must be something that is normally kept hidden from most people, such as your deepest feelings or intimate thoughts (cf DeVito 1989). Willingness to disclose information about the private self depends on a number of factors, including your image of yourself. People with a positive self-concept are more likely to disclose information about themselves than those with a negative self-concept. People of status are usually unwilling to reveal information about themselves to people of lesser status. Generally, men are less inclined to make self-disclosures than women. And the values of your culture also play a part. Some cultures firmly discourage conversation about one's intimate feelings and personal beliefs. However, research has shown that some degree of self-disclosure not only benefits relationships, but leads to a greater degree of self-esteem (Burton & Dimbleby 1995).

The importance of self-disclosure is that it encourages the building of relationships. We know from experience that the types of relationships we share vary in quality and intensity. Some are extremely rewarding while others are casual and almost meaningless. All of us have relationships in which we reveal or self-disclose more about ourselves than in others. There are some topics we would not even think about discussing with particular people. There are some relationships in which we keep our thoughts and feelings to ourselves, and others in which we are sufficiently comfortable to allow people access to our most intimate thoughts and feelings.

Self-disclosure depends a great deal on trust. We are more likely to talk openly to people whom we have learned to trust and, at the same time, making disclosures invites trust and can bond relationships. It has been suggested that some degree of self-disclosure not only benefits relationships, but leads to greater self-esteem and develops the stability of the self-concept. However, people cannot be forced into self-disclosure. It is the type of communication that works most effectively a little at a time. Especially with new acquaintances, you need to be sensitive to the other person's nonverbal behaviour which is often an indication of their needs and feelings. Sensitivity also helps to determine whether your partner in communication will agree that certain information is intimate and highly personal. You could upset the other person if you betray his or her confidence because you failed to treat the disclosure appropriately.

8.3.2   A model of self-disclosure

A model that helps us to assess the amount of information we disclose is the Johari window (see Figure 8.21). The window is divided into four panes or quadrants. The panes represent four areas of the self which are defined in terms of what the person does and does not know about him/herself, and in terms of what others do or do not know about that person.

The **open pane** is the most public area and reflects your openness to the world and your willingness to be known. It comprises all aspects of yourself that are known to you and to others such as your name, your job or a club to which you belong. The **hidden pane** contains all the information you know about yourself that you prefer not to disclose to someone else. This area may include information about your salary, your marital problems, your failures and successes, your secret fears and so on.

The other two panes are areas where you don't know yourself. The **blind pane** represents all the things that others know about you, but about which you are not aware. This may vary from the way you twitch your nose during conversation to the way you tend to monopolise a conversation, react aggressively when people do not agree with your views, or you may be unaware of the high regard colleagues in your organisation have for the work you do. The **unknown pane** is the mystery area, known to no one. It represents information about yourself which neither you nor others have explored. It contains qualities waiting to be discovered — untapped talents or your potential for personal growth. You can only infer that it exists or perhaps confirm its existence in retrospect.

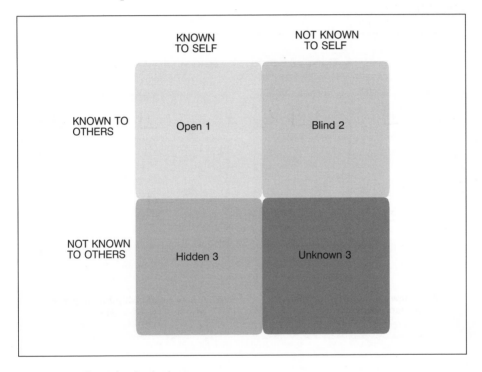

Figure 8.1 The Johari window

The four panes of the Johari window are interdependent, thus a change in one pane will affect the others. If you are open to feedback, for example, you may discover things you did not know about yourself from others, and move them into the open area. As you disclose something from the hidden area, it becomes part of the open area — the open pane enlarges and the hidden pane is reduced. Luft (1970) proposes that it is rewarding and satisfying not only to learn more about yourself and thus gain self-insight, but also to reveal enough about yourself to enable others to get to know you better. Self-disclosure however also carries a degree of risk.

We would need to draw different Johari windows to represent each of our relationships. You could try this for yourself by drawing Johari windows that depict your relationship with a good friend, an acquaintance, a teacher, a sibling and one of your parents. By looking at them, you can learn a great deal about your general approach to relationships. We can also determine the status of a particular relationship by drawing two Johari windows — one for each of the partners in a relationship. This should reveal whether one partner has disclosed more than the other (and has a larger open pane) or whether one partner has more complete self-knowledge (and a smaller unknown pane). Examples of different relationships are illustrated in Figure 8.2 (Beebe, Beebe & Redmond 1999:321-322).

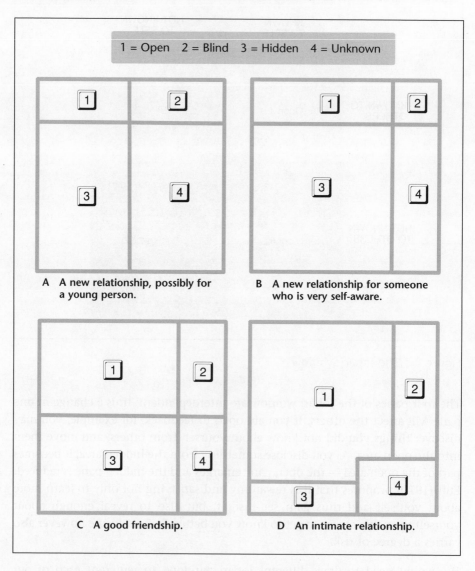

Figure 8.2 Variations on Johari windows

8.3.3 Risks of self-disclosure

Sometimes, disclosing too much of yourself to others early in a relationship may be inappropriate and costly. They may learn something about you that may stop the relationship from developing or cause it to deteriorate. Even in well-established relationships, inappropriate disclosures may have negative consequences. An admission of infidelity, for example, can cause a marriage to dissolve. The admission that you lost a job because you were accused of pilfering may cause people to reject you. According to the language theorist, Neil Postman, there is no good reason for people always to be totally honest if the relationship is going to suffer. He believes that our personal experience teaches us that "the capacity of words to exacerbate, wound and destroy is as least as great as their capacity to clarify, heal and organize" (Postman 1990:232). The point Postman is emphasising is that self-disclosure can be a two-edged sword. In some circumstances, it helps; in others, it defeats.

8.3.4 Self-disclosure guidelines

In the face of the contradictions presented between self-disclosing and withholding personal information, how are we to know how much about ourselves to reveal in a relationship? The consensus of opinion is that we have to take some risks if relationships are to grow. However, research results suggest that self-disclosure should occur only in relationships that are important to you.

Stewart (1990), for example, maintains that, while we choose to self-disclose because it will help others to know us, we should base our choices on a clear understanding of what is desirable and beneficial for the relationship. In other words, effective self-disclosure is disclosure that is appropriate to the situation and to the relationship between the people communicating.

It has been found that the most effective communication takes place between people who do not act on stereotypical expectations about self-disclosing behaviour. Beebe, Beebe and Redmond (1999) suggest that if someone's behaviour is different to yours, rather than attribute the behaviour to, for example, his or her gender, look for an explanation in the person's background, upbringing or past relationships.

DeVito (1989) and Verderber and Verderber (2002) maintain that, because of the element of risk, disclosure in a relationship should occur gradually. We should not confide intimate details about ourselves immediately upon meeting someone — information about our sex lives or financial situation or political views, for instance. Rather, self-disclosure is the kind of communication that is revealed a little at a time as we come to trust the other person. By self-disclosing, we are in effect saying to others that we trust them, that we respect them, and that we would like the relationship to develop. Thus, a successful relationship is often marked by a balance of disclosure and feedback (disclosure from the other) — that is, self-disclosure is reciprocal. This idea is explained by Myers and Myers (1992:211) in the following way:

> ... a relationship develops only when you and the other person are willing to go through the mutual process of revealing yourself to each other. If you can't reveal yourself, then you cannot be close. To be silent about yourself is to remain a stranger.

8.4   Interpersonal communication and needs

Theories that have been developed about interpersonal needs provide a way of understanding why we and others behave as we do in our relationships. They help us to gain a deeper knowledge of ourselves, our motivations for behaving in certain ways, and the manner in which we communicate. By understanding other peoples' needs and motivations, we are more likely to identify their communication priorities, learn how to attract and hold their attention, and express ourselves in ways that they understand. As the relationship between two people grows and they learn more about the needs that motivate them, it becomes easier to express themselves in ways that the other will understand.

In Chapter 2 we discussed the inner needs that motivate us to communicate with reference to Maslow's hierarchy of needs. Two theories that deal specifically with needs that are satisfied in interpersonal relationships are Schutz's (1958) interpersonal needs theory and Homans's (1959) social exchange theory.

8.4.1   Schutz's interpersonal needs theory

The major premise of Schutz's theory is that people need people. He contends that the drive to develop interpersonal relationships with others is to satisfy three basic human needs: inclusion, affection and control. We all have these needs in varying degrees and express them in different ways.

☐ *Need for inclusion* The need for inclusion reflects a desire for social contact. Schutz found that we need to be in the company of others and to establish and maintain a feeling of mutual interest with them. When the need for inclusion is met, we tend to feel accepted, understood and worthwhile. When this need is not met, we tend to feel lonely and unwanted. We all differ in the amount of interaction with others that will satisfy this need. Schutz describes people who feel little need to be included in groups and tend to avoid interacting with others — insisting that they prefer to be left alone — as **undersocial**. **Oversocial** people, on the other hand, continually seek the companionship of others and tend to join and feel part of many groups. Schutz concludes that both types fear being ignored or left out, but the overt behaviour they display to compensate for their fears is different (cf Trenholm 1991; Gamble & Gamble 1998a). In reality, most people do not belong to either of these extreme types.

They are the **adaptable-social** people who are able to balance their needs for inclusion and privacy. Such people can sometimes be comfortable being alone but at other times need and enjoy interacting with others. According to Schutz, relationships function best when people are able to achieve a balance between the need to be alone and to be with others.

❑ ***Need for affection*** Schutz found that we all need opportunities to show affection for others as well as to receive affection. This need is reflected in the development of emotionally close relationships in which affection is shown and expressed verbally and nonverbally. Again, people express varying degrees of this need by displaying different behaviour. At one extreme are the **underpersonal** individuals who value privacy and seem to have little need for affection. They avoid close ties, keep their feelings to themselves and even respond with hostility to those who want to display affection. **Overpersonal** people, on the other hand, have a high need for close relationships with others. They tend to confide in all the people they meet, express their feelings openly and freely and expect others to respond in the same way. Between these extremes are the **personal** people who are able to express and receive affection when desirable, but can also maintain a distance when necessary. Schutz maintains that personal people seem to be able to handle both close and distant (casual) relationships more comfortably than the other two types.

❑ ***Need for control*** The need for control is the desire to successfully manage and influence the events and people around you and, at other times, to allow others to establish that control. As with the other two interpersonal needs, there are differing degrees of this need and different ways of displaying it. Schutz describes **abdicrats** as people with a strong need to be controlled. They regularly assume a submissive or subordinate role in a relationship. They prefer not to make decisions or accept responsibility, but abdicate all power to their partner in the relationship. At the other extreme are **autocrats** who dominate others and feel that they must always be in charge. In fact, they become anxious if they cannot control a relationship and make every decision. The **democrat** falls somewhere between the two extremes. Such people know when it is appropriate to control and are able to do so, but they can also be comfortable submitting to others when necessary. Schutz found that relationships function best when the participants have a democratic relationship in which they share power easily and comfortably.

We can conclude from Schutz's theory that understanding our own as well as other people's needs for inclusion, affection and control can go a long way to contributing to the success of our relationships. If you have a high need for affection, for instance, you are soon going to become frustrated in a relationship with someone who prefers not to reveal feelings openly or who dislikes being touched. On the other hand, if you are the sort of person who prefers not to shoulder responsibility, but your partner is happy to do so, the matter of control in your relationship should not create a problem. We can also understand why Schutz maintains that the most successful relationships develop between people who are not extreme in their interpersonal needs.

Schutz's theory contributes to our understanding of our interpersonal needs and helps us make sense of our relationships.

8.4.2   Homans's social-exchange theory

A theory that focuses on why we maintain some relationships and terminate others is Homans's social exchange theory. According to Homans (1959), all social interactions involve some sort of exchange or barter. For example, we may offer someone help in exchange for gratitude, talk in exchange for friendship or love in exchange for security. In other words, we exchange one interpersonal need for another. In making this kind of bargain, we tend to calculate the rewards we are likely to receive and the costs we will incur on our investment. Homans maintains that, just as people pay for goods and services, they calculate the profits and losses in a relationship, and decide either to pursue or terminate it (cf Trenholm 1991).

In terms of Homans's theory, a **reward** or profit is any positive outcome resulting from a relationship. Rewards are basically the things that fulfil our needs for security, social contact, sex, financial gain, status and so forth. Rewards, however, always involve some cost or payback. For example, in order to acquire the reward of promotion at work (financial gain and status), you might have to give up some degree of freedom. The payback for the promotion could be that your social activities are curtailed and your relationships with others consequently deteriorate. Or, you might find that it is not possible to maintain a friendship which provides you with satisfaction or rewards because your boyfriend does not get on with your friends. The cost of maintaining one relationship might be that you have to give up the other.

In the same way, we calculate the **costs** incurred in maintaining our relationships and tend to terminate those that have a negative outcome: they create unhappiness, dissatisfaction and problems rather than happiness, satisfaction and pleasure. **Social exchange theory** implies that we will work to maintain a relationship only as long as the rewards or profits we perceive for ourselves are greater than the costs. According to this theory, no interpersonal relationship continues for very long unless both parties think they are making a profit.

While this economic orientation may be too rational to explain interpersonal relationships fully, it nevertheless adds to our knowledge by putting into clearer perspective the human tendency to seek profit (rewards) while incurring the least cost (payback).

8.5   Interpersonal communication and assertiveness

The third factor we have selected to explore in this chapter is the role of assertiveness in the development of interpersonal relationships. The way in which we express ourselves to others, especially in the sensitive areas of feelings, needs and opinions, can have a positive or negative effect on the quality of our interpersonal relationships. Emotions such as anger, fear, happiness or sadness, as well as the feelings that arise when confronted with adversity and conflict, are all part of meaningful relationships. To build trust, engage in self-disclosure, resolve conflicts, express our needs and influence others, we need to be able to communicate such feelings. Often, it is not the emotion itself that threatens (or enhances) the relationship, rather how you deal with the emotion and the effect that it has on you and those who are important to you. Sometimes, problems are created in relationships with friends, family or work colleagues because we lack the communication skills needed to express our emotions, needs and opinions assertively. We may choose instead to bury them or unleash them uncontrollably. The way we handle such feelings often impedes the relationship and creates additional conflicts instead of helping it (cf Gamble & Gamble 1998a).

8.5.1   Defining assertiveness

Verderber (1990:155) defines assertiveness as "verbalising your position on an issue for purposes of achieving a specific goal". The specific goal is to express yourself in such a way that you hurt neither yourself nor others. Assertiveness involves the ability to express feelings and opinions openly and honestly, to give good reasons for a belief or feeling, and to offer suggestions without attacking the other person verbally. Put another way, you have to be able to stand up for personal rights while respecting the rights of others. At the same time, the words you use and the manner in which you convey them should clearly indicate that you accept responsibility for what you say and how you say it.

8.5.2   Assertiveness styles

A study of the results of assertion training programmes leads Rakos (1986:408) to the conclusion that "assertion is a *skill*, not a 'trait' that someone 'has' or 'lacks'". As we pointed out in the Introduction to this book, skills can be learned, especially when we understand the theoretical principles on which they are grounded. While we may not be able to teach you the most appropriate language to use in each emotionally charged or adverse situation in your life, you will find that an understanding of the different ways or communication styles of coping with such situations will automatically make the choice of words much easier. The three possible communication styles in which you may express yourself are: passively (or nonassertively) aggressively and assertively (cf Dickson, Hargie & Morrow 1989; Verderber 1990; Gamble & Gamble 1998a).

☐ *The passive or nonassertive style* People who behave passively suppress their feelings to avoid conflict or rejection, or are afraid to let others know how they are feeling, even when they are being treated unfairly. They are generally reluctant to state opinions, share feelings or assume responsibility for their actions. They often submit to the demands of others even when it not in their best interests. When people behave passively, they force themselves to keep their real feelings inside and frequently end up in relationships that they do not really want. You may have noticed that people who respond in a nonassertive style often hesitate, avoid eye contact, appease others, avoid contentious issues, accept blame needlessly and generally lack confidence.

Experience shows that we hesitate to assert ourselves in our relationships for a number of different reasons which include a lack of interest in the relationship, fear at arousing the anger of our partner and subsequent reprisal, the feeling that we do not have language skills to express ourselves adequately, or because we sometimes experience feelings of personal inadequacy (a lack of self worth) (cf Zimbardo & Radl 1979).

According to Furnham (1979), cultural differences also play a part in passive behaviour in that some cultures value assertiveness whereas others emphasise values of humility, tolerance and subservience. For example, in most Western societies, nonassertive behaviour is perceived to be an asset for women but a liability for men. Thus, some women behave passively because they accept the stereotype that society has taught them. They are expected to be accepting, warm, loving and deferential to men.

On the other hand, men and women sometimes lack assertiveness as a result of childhood experiences of authoritarian parents and teachers who discouraged the expression of personal opinions and feelings. For similar reasons, many people in the work situation, for instance, believe that they must always do what their superiors tell them, irrespective of the right or wrong of the situation..

☐ *The aggressive style* People who behave aggressively lash out at the source of their discomfort with little concern for the situation or the feelings of those concerned. They insist on standing up for their own rights while ignoring or violating the rights of others. Their only concern is to dominate and 'win' in a relationship. Too many people confuse aggressiveness with assertiveness. Unlike assertiveness, aggressive behaviour is judgmental, dogmatic, fault-finding and coercive. The individual who responds in an aggressive style is often overbearing and self-opinionated, speaks loudly and abusively, interrupts others and expresses opinions vehemently. This behaviour precipitates conflict rather than resolves it. People can also be indirectly aggressive by subtly manipulating others. They very often display behaviour such as sulking, banging doors or drawers shut, or making the other person feel guilty.

According to assertiveness researchers, we tend to lash out at others simply because we have never been taught to handle our aggressive impulses, or because it acts as a form of self-defence when we feel vulnerable and powerless, or because we believe that the only way to get our ideas and feelings across to others is by being sufficiently forceful. It has also been noted that sometimes people who have repeatedly behaved in a passive manner in the past are no longer able to keep feelings of hurt and disappointment to themselves and abruptly vent them as aggressiveness (cf Lange & Jakubowski 1976).

❑ **The assertive style** The goal of assertive behaviour is neither to avoid conflict nor to dominate a relationship, but to communicate feelings and opinions honestly and clearly without hurting yourself or others. If passive and aggressive behaviour are partly due to inappropriate communication behaviour, we should be able to improve our interpersonal relationships by learning about assertive styles of behaviour.

People who behave assertively take responsibility for their actions and feelings without personal attacks on others or exaggerating for dramatic effect. They use a firm but conversational tone to express their feelings, to state what they believe to be true, to make suggestions about the behaviour or attitudes of others, and to give good reasons for their opinions and feelings. Their verbal and nonverbal messages are congruent. Thus, tone of voice, eye contact and posture match the words that are spoken. The individual who responds in an assertive style addresses contentious issues, is self-respecting, protects the rights of others, allows room for negotiation or compromise and generally conveys confidence.

You have probably realised by now that when you assert yourself, you are protecting yourself from being victimised in a relationship. At the same time, you have to understand that all people have the same fundamental right. All of us have a right to protect ourselves, to express our needs in a relationship and to influence the way others behave towards us. In essence, assertive behaviour implies that we have to have to find mutually satisfactory solutions to the problems and conflicts that arise in our relationships.

Being assertive may not always achieve the desired goal, but it is more likely to be successful than passive or aggressive behaviour. People who constantly display direct or indirect aggressive behaviour in interpersonal (or social) situations may initially get their own way, but they are generally disliked and their behaviour has a negative result on their relationships. On the other hand, people who constantly fail to assert themselves encourage others to manipulate them because they are perceived as weak and incompetent. Assertive people are generally respected and seen as competent, strong, fair and confident.

8.5.2 Developing assertive behaviour

Training yourself to improve assertive behaviour is not easy. It is certainly worth the effort. As expressed by Briggs (1986:24), "[a]ssertion training is about improving personal, and thereby professional, effectiveness. It is concerned with the building of self-confidence and esteem, and the ability to translate this into improving communications and relationships".

☐ **Knowledge** is a primary prerequisite for improving effective assertiveness in relationships. Understanding the nature of assertiveness, the different types of possible responses to adversity, and the reasons for not asserting ourselves will go a long way to help us to understand our particular problems in this regard.

☐ **Self-knowledge** is also required. The discussion of perception in Chapter 4 is pertinent here. People may be unassertive because of mistaken perceptions of others, such as perceiving a tyrant as being a 'strong leader'. One way of understanding yourself with regard to assertive behaviour is to write down several situations in the past where you were nonassertive or aggressive. Try to determine the reasons for the behaviour and then substitute an assertive response for the nonassertive or aggressive behaviour in each case. Finally, try to transfer what you have learned to situations in everyday social (and work) situations.

Assertive techniques

There are different techniques for asserting yourself in different situations:
1. **Direct assertion** involves a short, straightforward statement in support of one's opinions, suggestions or rights.
2. In **indirect assertion** the person does not actually confront the issue, but indirectly states her point of view.
3. In **complex-direct assertion**, the person uses an embellishment to soften the situation. The main types of embellishment are: showing empathy towards the other person; the use of praise; giving an apology for any negative consequences; or suggesting a compromise.

To illustrate the different techniques, we quote the examples provided by Dickson, Hargie and Morrow (1989:119-120). The scenario the authors use is that of refusing an invitation to deliver a paper at a conference, yet protecting the relationship with the other person.

1. **Direct**: "No, I can't undertake such a commitment at this time."
2. **Indirect**: "Phew . . . I've got so much on my plate at the minute. I have a deadline to meet on two books and I have another commitment at that time . . .".
3. **Complex-direct**:
   (a) "I couldn't undertake this commitment, since I am behind with the deadline on a forthcoming book, and I already have another speaking engagement in June." (explanation)
   (b) "I know you have a lot on your plate organising the Conference but . . ." (empathy)
   (c) "It's really nice of you to ask me and you if I could do it for you I would . . ." (praise)
   (d) "I'm sorry to give you more problems in organising speakers, but . . ." (apology)
   (e) "I can't undertake this but I have a colleague whom I think could . . ." (compromise).

You should also consider your **nonverbal behaviour** in assertive situations. The role of nonverbal communication (for example, eye contact, tone of voice, facial expressions, gestures and posture) in conveying attitudes and influencing relationships is discussed in Chapter 5. It is very difficult to assert yourself in a contentious situation if you constantly avoid eye contact with the person with whom you are interacting.

To conclude this section on developing assertiveness, we provide what Gamble and Gamble (1987:192) conceive as *Every Person's Bill of Rights*. The authors point out that when we sacrifice our rights, we teach others to take advantage of us. When we demand rights that are not ours, we take advantage of others. Their bill of rights offers guidelines on how to stand up for your emotional rights without being insensitive to the rights and feelings of others.

Every Person's Bill of Rights

1. The right to be treated with respect
2. The right to make your own choices and decisions
3. The right to make mistakes and/or change your mind
4. The right to have needs and to have these needs considered as important as the needs of others
5. The right to express your feelings and opinions
6. The right to judge your own behaviour
7. The right to set your own priorities
8. The right to say no without feeling guilty
9. The right not to make choices for others
10. The right not to assert yourself.

Scenario 8.1

This scenario is adapted from Verderber (1990).

Lindiwe, Shireen and Leila are first-year students who live in the same residence at the university they are attending. The three girls are very excited as they prepare for the annual dance that evening. When the three young men who are to be their partners at the dance arrive to call for them, Chris reaches into his pocket for a flask of whisky, takes a large sip and passes the bottle to Lindiwe. They all know that alcohol is not allowed in the residence rooms and, in any case, Lindiwe is concerned about anyone in the group drinking before driving. She doesn't know what to do because she does not want to precipitate an unpleasant incident before the start of what should be an exciting evening. She mutters "Uh, er, well," as she pretends to take a sip and passes the bottle on.

Shireen grabs the bottle and says: "Chris, you bloody idiot — that's damn stupid, bringing whisky into our residence. Can't anybody here have a good time without drinking? You're all impossible. Now get out of here before somebody notices, and take the bottle with you".

Seeing the angry look on Chris's face, Leila quickly says: "Chris, perhaps you didn't know that drinking is not allowed in this residence. Besides, I'd feel a lot better if we all stayed sober in order to drive to the dance. So I'd appreciate it if you'd lock the whisky in the boot of the car. We can have a great time without getting into trouble or risking an accident."

After you have studied the scenario, answer the following questions:

(1) Which of the three responses can be described as (a) assertive, (b) passive, (c) aggressive?

(2) Is the passive response in the interests of the group? What is the possible outcome?

(3) Is the aggressive response in the interests of the group? What is the possible outcome?

(4) Is the assertive response in the interests of the group? What is the possible outcome?

(5) Comment briefly on the following: the feelings you think are being expressed in the three responses; the choice of language; and the nonverbal behaviour that probably accompanied each response (including paralanguage).

8.6   The presentation of self in everyday life

Up till now we have been considering close interpersonal relationships and illustrated the nature and importance of such relationships in our lives with reference to Buber's theory. However, not all relationships are close or intimate. Some of our relationships do not progress very far beyond the experimenting stage. In fact, most of our everyday relationships are social rather than intimate in nature. We cannot form close interpersonal relationships with most of the people we meet on a daily basis — colleagues we spend a few hours with at a conference, for instance, or acquaintances we encounter at a party. To conclude this chapter we discuss a theory that describes the way people encounter one another in social situations. According to the sociologist Erving Goffman, people who meet in social situations play roles that involve socially established patterns of behaviour. In his book, *The Presentation of Self in Everyday Life*, Goffman investigates these roles and describes and illustrates them in a variety of social situations. The following is based mainly on Jansen and Steinberg (1991) and Steinberg (2000).

8.6.1   Introduction

Goffman (1922–1982) was a Canadian-born sociologist whose work focused on face-to-face (interpersonal) communication in various public and institutional contexts (eg hospitals, government departments, asylums, social situations). Goffman's approach was developed on the basis of empirical evidence he gathered through observing the conduct of real people involved in everyday social encounters. His influence is not limited to the field of sociology, but extends to various social sciences. In the field of communication science, he offers insights into the various ways in which people play social roles during interpersonal communication encounters. In other words, he is not concerned with the individual's inner self, but with the social (public) self that is presented in a specific situation. Examples of social roles include 'teacher', 'priest', 'prison warden', 'parent' and 'teenager'. In order to present a credible performance, a person has to act the role of 'teacher', 'priest', 'prison warden', 'parent' or 'teenager' in a way that is acceptable to his or her culture and society. Given this point of departure, Goffman uses metaphors from the world of the theatre to explain interpersonal communication.

8.6.2   The dramaturgical metaphor

Goffman is particularly interested in the techniques that participants use to produce, sustain and safeguard their social roleplay. He calls the way we behave in front of others a **dramaturgical performance**. He uses metaphors from the theatre to describe everyday communication encounters because he maintains that real life actors and stage actors use the same techniques to present themselves to other people. That is, communication is the performance of a 'script' by a 'team' during which we act out roles which are defined according to shared social meanings.

According to Goffman, we expect others to believe the roles we play and the attributes or characteristics we display. We learn these roles and attributes from the ritual code of the society of which we are a part. The **ritual code** defines acceptable behaviour for a particular society with reference to specific situations or settings. People know how to behave in different public contexts because they know the ritual code and the role prescriptions that derive from it. That is why people who share a culture have the same expectations about social conduct and generally act in the same way.

For each role that we play during the day, we put on a **front,** or **mask,** which hides our real identity (or inner self). These masks represent the image of ourselves that we want others to know and believe in. We behave in accordance with the role we a playing at a particular time, that is, we suit our personal appearance and manner to the requirements of the role or character we have chosen. What happens, in fact, is that we create a public self. It is as public selves that we learn to know each other. Goffman constantly emphasises that the participants in social interaction are known to one another not by their personal characteristics, but by the roles they play or by their social identity. If you think about a typical day in your own life, you will realise that you play a number of different roles and for each role you wear a different mask. You have your student mask, your best friend mask, your employee mask, your sibling mask, and so on.

In order to ensure the success of a particular performance, the people with whom you are communicating must believe that you are the character that you are playing, or the performance may fail to achieve its purpose. Therefore, Goffman emphasises the need for performers to project the correct **definition of the situation** at the outset of the performance. This includes not only behaving correctly, but also controlling your appearance and the physical setting in which the performance takes place. For example, a surgeon who is not feeling very well would not usually relate this information to the patient on whom he or she is about to perform an operation — such disclosures simply do not fit in with the behaviour prescribed by society (the ritual code) for the role of surgeon. For the same reason, the surgeon would make sure that his reception rooms are appropriately furnished to create the correct impression on his patients.

The term that Goffman uses to describe the way we convey information about the situation we are defining is impression management. **Impression management** describes the way we handle or manage the information we convey in a given situation. He distinguishes between impressions given and impressions given off. 'Impressions given' are the impressions deliberately created by the role-players in the communication encounter and must be sustained throughout the performance. This information is usually conveyed verbally. 'Impressions given off' are not intended by the role-players but are created almost without their noticing it. Such impressions are often conveyed nonverbally, in other words, such information is unintentionally 'leaked' (refer to Chapter 5). The problem with leakage is that the personal self of the performer may be revealed and contradict the carefully planned performances by the rest of the team members. If one or more performers do not play their characters convincingly, the audience may question the entire performance and it may fail to achieve its purpose.

So important is the maintenance of correct impressions that certain measures are taken to ensure success. Goffman describes two kinds of techniques which performers may use to safeguard their performance. **Defensive measures** are used by the performers themselves to save the show. For example, when a sales team is selling their product to an audience of potential customers, a member of the team who knows that the item being promoted has a limited lifespan will remain loyal to the team and not inform the audience about the consequences of purchasing the item. **Protective measures** are generally used by the audience. An audience member may, for instance, clear his or her throat when entering a room where performers are discussing a personal matter to tactfully remind them to safeguard their performance.

Despite these measures a performance may still fail because performers act out of character or perform discrepant roles. Ultimately the success of a performance depends on how well discrepant roles can be controlled. **Discrepant roles** are false or deviant roles played by participants who deliberately try to fool the team and sometimes the audience as well. They are false performances because they project the wrong impression of the characters involved and this leaves the other participants in the dark about what they should believe. We can use movies as an example to make this point clear. Many films contain characters who play discrepant roles, for example, a 'goodie' pretending to be a 'baddie' and vice versa. In real life, discrepant roles must be avoided at all costs lest the performance fails. Goffman describes several discrepant roles, for example, the 'informer', who pretends to be a member of the team in order to obtain information which he or she then passes on to the audience. Another discrepant role is that of the shill. A 'shill' is a member of a team who pretends that he or she has no connection with the team in order to make sure that the audience responds to a performance in the way the performers want. We can take an example from the mass media. Have you watched a talk show and wondered if some people have been specially placed in the audience to ask specific questions and applaud at specific times? Such people would be playing the role of a shill.

Because performers expend a great deal of effort to constantly sustain different roles, they need to relax their role-play from time to time. While a performance is given on the **front stage** of a theatre, there is also a backstage area. The **backstage** is a private area, out of sight of the audience, where the actors get ready for the role they are going to play. Goffman contends that the participants in social interaction behave as though they are in front of the stage while they are performing (engaging in communication) and then go backstage to drop their public masks and be themselves. Backstage is, for example, where the school principal can relax and smoke a cigarette even though on stage (in the school hall) he has been telling the pupils about the dangers of smoking. Because we act in various contexts and play various characters, our masks or fronts must constantly be changed and we need to prepare for the next performance. Backstage is where the preparation takes place. It is where the principal's mask is taken off at the end of the school day and he puts on his husband's mask before he goes home. Even during school time, the principal needs to switch roles — he wears a different mask in front of a pupil, or in front of the pupil's parents, or in front of a teacher. As they act out different roles in different social encounters and settings, performers continually move from front to backstage and vice versa.

8.6.3   Conclusion

Goffman's theory is concerned with the social or public self — the predictable attributes and behaviour associated with a particular role. However, we need to consider why every teacher or lawyer or salesperson shares certain character-istics but nevertheless manages to put across his or her role in a slightly different way. We must remember that within these public behaviour patterns (or social roles) there is an individual person with his or her own attitudes, experiences and responses to the situation. In other words, we all stamp our personal style on the roles we play. Although Goffman does not take the individual into account as he describes the social construction of reality, we should not dismiss his theory as superficial or artificial, as some critics tend to do. Remember that a theory can only address one aspect of communication. Goffman's interest was in the social identity rather than the inner self of people. Goffman therefore does not identify participants in communication as unique individuals. He describes types of people rather than individual persons. The participants do not meet each other on a personal level. They do not reveal their inner selves or disclose who they are really are because what is needed for communication to succeed is knowledge of what each participant represents, not of what a particular person is.

Consider the following question: How many of the people that you meet every day do you really know as individual persons and how many of them are mere types or characters defined by the requirements of a particular situation? We would say that, in fact, role-playing facilitates many of the routine activities of everyday life. Consider the time and energy you would have to expend if you had to become personally acquainted with each shop assistant who serves you in the supermarket, not to mention the waiter, postman, flower seller and so on. Our conclusion is that it is important for you as a student to consider many different views of communication. In the same way that a theorist such as Buber draws attention to the inner self, Goffman's views are equally important to an understanding of communication in modern society with its extensive and complex structure.

8.7   Presentation skills

We conclude this discussion of interpersonal communication with some ideas on how to present yourself in everyday social situations. At the outset, you would like to put across a desired image of yourself. Before going to an interview, for example, it is important for you to know what you would like the outcome of the interaction to be and to plan your performance to achieve the outcome. You could begin by assessing the situation and making sure that your appearance (clothing, makeup, grooming and so on) and communication behaviour are appropriate. You might even choose to rehearse your performance in private (backstage) before the event. To control your communication behaviour, you need the ability to use relevant verbal and nonverbal skills as well as to develop a sensitivity to aspects of communication such as active listening, appropriate feedback, assertiveness and self-disclosure. Importantly, self-knowledge and an understanding of your strengths and weaknesses will go a long way towards helping you project a desired image of yourself. Remember that you do indeed have several selves and that it is necessary to present the self that is appropriate in a given situation. Presenting a social role when you are trying to establish a close relationship, for example, simply doesn't work (cf Burton & Dimbleby 1995).

Scenario 8.2

By Fiona de Villiers

From outside, Sarah Robinson could hear the familiar sounds of school life; the insistent shrillness of the bell, the calls and easy laughter of students, and the thump of their feet on the staircase above the head's office.

In contrast, inside that office, things seemed ominously quiet, and Sarah shifted in her uncomfortable seat. She glanced down to check that the top button of her blouse was done up, then she smoothed her hair, stockings and pencil skirt, and crossed her ankles demurely, while the head's pen scratched rapidly. It was amusing, she thought to herself, that even though she was a teacher, she still felt like a naughty student whenever she was in the office. It had something to do with the enormous oak desk, the ticking clock and more especially, the principal's consistently distant, formal manner.

In the middle of Sarah's reverie, there was a respectful knock on the door, and the secretary ushered a parent into the room. It only took a second for Sarah to see that the woman was fuming. It was a clear-cut case of victimisation, she declared, her voice rising rapidly, and her face reddening. Her daughter was being bullied by the 'in-crowd' in Grade 9. Perhaps it was time to look for another school where bullying was properly dealt with This was not a new scenario for Sarah. After all, she had been head of the notoriously difficult Grade 9 for five years now. She knew exactly what was expected of her in this situation, and made suitable noises of agreement, support and understanding. She noticed admiringly the principal's method for handling these kinds of incidents: from behind his large oak desk, he nodded sympathetically while the parent gave full vent to her fury. Then, assuming complete control, in even tones and an objective manner, he sketched out the situation from the school's perspective, not once giving in to any of the wild accusations the parent had flung across the desk.

Then the head handed over to Miss Robinson to explain the 'excellent anti-bullying programme she had recently implemented in the school'. Sarah finished off the explanation — as per school protocol — by focusing on the child's own unique talents and contribution to the school, and the assurance that everything would be done to solve the problem in a constructive manner. Out of the corner of her eye, Sarah could see the head nodding her head in approval. She was even more gratified to see the parent visibly relax and smile herself.

After the meeting, Sarah felt a glow of satisfaction when the head praised the way she had affirmed both school policy, and the child in 'such a professional manner'. Sarah excused herself and went to the staffroom for a quick cup of tea before the end of the lesson. Sitting by the heater she found her good friends Stacey and Margaret. She was relieved that she could flop carelessly into a comfy armchair, undo the top button of her blouse and let off steam about the notoriously difficult parent she had just dealt with. She enjoyed the fact that she could even be a bit naughty by mimicking the woman, with her enormous cloud of teased blonde hair and wad of chewing gum in her cheek. Laughing about the matter with her friends, and kicking off her shoes for a few minutes to give her aching feet a rest, made her headache and the large pile of unmarked papers on her desk easier to bear.

She knew that once she got home she could really let off steam properly. Maybe she would call her mum over a glass of wine and have a good whinge about how tedious, petty and spoiled some parents could be. But for now, she had to rebutton her blouse, put on her shoes, go upstairs to her classroom, and face the Grade 9s.

Summary

Interpersonal communication is communication between two (or more) people in a face-to-face encounter. This chapter examined communication between two people by focusing on the relationships that we develop and maintain in our everyday lives. The link between interpersonal communication and our mode of existence was discussed by examining Martin Buber's I-you and I-it relationships. The chapter then went on to discuss a model that describes the interaction stages of a relationship — the stages of coming together and the stages of coming apart. It also considered three factors that influence the development and nature of our interpersonal relationships: self-disclosure, interpersonal needs, and the communication style we use in our relationships: passive, aggressive or assertive. We referred to the theories of Schutz and Homans to explain the role of needs in interpersonal relationships. Schutz discusses inclusion, affection and control as interpersonal needs, while Homans focuses on social exchange. This section of the chapter ended with a scenario based on the three styles of communication behaviour. The chapter used Erving Goffman's theory of self-presentation to illustrate communication behaviour in social, rather than intimate, relationships, and throughout gave guidelines for improving your own interpersonal relationships. The chapter ended with a scenario based on Goffman's theory.

Test yourself

1. Explain the following terms with specific reference to interpersonal communication:
   (a) I-you relationship
   (b) I-it relationship
   (c) interpersonal needs
   (d) passive communication
   (e) assertive communication
   (f) aggressive communication
   (g) self-disclosure.
   Give examples from your own relationships to illustrate your explanations.
2. Think about a close relationship that you have or have had with another person. Identify the stages of interaction described in this chapter and apply them to the development of your relationship. If your relationship is in the process of coming apart, identify the stage you have reached.
3. Identify the difference in your openness in two relationships that are important to you.
4. Think about some of your current and past relationships and apply the theories we have been discussing to help you gain more insight into your own and your partner's needs in interpersonal relationships. In terms of Schutz's theory, how balanced are your needs for inclusion, affection and control? How have these needs motivated you to communicate with another person? Then think about whether some of the relationships you have maintained, provide you with greater need fulfilment than cost. In those relationships you have terminated, were the costs greater than the

profits? Finally, turn your attention to the role that your communication style may have played in the maintenance or termination of some of your relationships.

5. Write passive, aggressive and assertive responses to each of the scenarios described below:

   (a) A friend invites you to accompany her to a movie you do not want to see.

   (b) Your supervisor wants you to take your annual leave at a time that does not suit you because you have already made plans to go on holiday with friends.

   (c) You have loaned a book to a friend who seems to have forgotten to give it back. You do not need the book urgently, but are worried about never receiving it if you do not raise the issue.

   (d) Your mother/father constantly makes comments that you find hurtful because he/she does not like the way you dress.

   What do you think would be the possible outcomes of each response?

6. Write two or three paragraphs on each of the following concepts in Goffman's theory, using your own examples to illustrate your discussion:

   ❑ dramaturgical performance
   ❑ roles and masks
   ❑ ritual code
   ❑ front stage and back stage
   ❑ definition of the situation
   ❑ teams.

EXECUTIVE SUMMARY
Intrapersonal communication
1 Buber's theory of interpersonal relationships
   - ☐ I-you and I-it relationships
   - ☐ dialogue and monologue
   - ☐ interhuman domain
   - ☐ mode of existence
2 The interaction stages of a relationship
   - ☐ stages in coming together
     - — initiating
     - — experimenting
     - — intensifying
     - — integrating
     - — bonding
   - ☐ stages in coming apart
     - — differentiating
     - — circumscribing
     - — stagnating
     - — avoiding
     - — terminating
3 Understanding interpersonal relationships
   - ☐ self-disclosure
   - ☐ Johari window
     - — open and closed panes
     - — hidden and unknown panes
   - ☐ Schutz's interpersonal
     - — needs theory
     - — need for inclusion
     - — need for affection
     - — need for control
   - ☐ Homans's social-exchange theory
     - — rewards and costs
   - ☐ communication styles
     - — passive, aggressive and assertive
4 Erving Goffman's theory of self-presentation
   - ☐ dramaturgical performance
   - ☐ roleplay
   - ☐ front or mask
   - ☐ ritual code
   - ☐ front stage and back stage
   - ☐ definition of the situation
   - ☐ impression management
   - ☐ teams

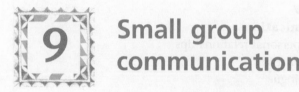

9 Small group communication

Overview

All of us spend some of our time in groups. Think for a moment about your daily activities and the different groups to which you belong. As a child, a large part of your socialisation process occurred in your family and school groups. As an adult, you probably belong to a social or sports club, religious group, study group, support group or work group at your place of employment. These examples tell us that some groups are **socially oriented** — they stem from the human need for social contact. Other groups are **task oriented** — the group works towards achieving a specific aim such as solving a problem or arriving at a decision. Of course, the categories often overlap. A social group such as a tennis club may have to solve the problem of raising funds to send a team on tour, for example, while many institutional task groups arrange social events for their members. Nevertheless, all groups, regardless of their function, have similar patterns of communication that affect how the members act, speak, and communicate with each other.

In this chapter, we focus primarily on task groups, sometimes referred to as committees. After defining a small group, we point out the advantages and disadvantages of small groups. We then consider the characteristics of effective groups and the types of roles that group members play. Our next topic deals with the stages in the formation of small groups. We then discuss different types of communication networks that operate in small groups and the consequences of each. Because the leader of a small group plays such an important role in the effectiveness of a group, we discuss different leadership styles and point out some guidelines for becoming an efficient leader. This is followed by an examination of the ways groups discuss the problems they have to address and the decisions that are made. Because conflict is inevitable in small groups, we describe different communication strategies for resolving conflict situations. The final section of the chapter points out the main differences between interpersonal and small-group communication and the chapter ends with a case study which is based on a problem-solving sequence that can be used by a small group.

Learning outcomes

At the end of this chapter you should be able to:
1. Define a small group and enumerate the advantages and disadvantages of small groups.
2. Provide examples of how 'climate' affects the operation of a group.
3. Explain how groupthink encourages conformity.
4. Define group role and give two examples of task, maintenance and self-centred roles.
5. Describe the stages in the formation of a group using an example from your own experience.
6. Distinguish among three leadership styles and give an example of each.
7. Describe how leadership theories contribute to our knowledge and understanding of leadership.
8. Describe and explain the steps in a group discussion. Use your own example of a problem-solving situation.
9. Distinguish among questions of fact, value and policy and give an example of each.
10. Define and briefly describe the technique of brainstorming.
11. Apply the different strategies for conflict resolution to examples of conflict from your own experience.
12. Answer the questions based on the two scenarios in this chapter.

Introduction

We live in a society where being part of a group, or several groups, is not a matter of choice — it is inescapable. We choose to belong to some groups (eg a sports club) and have others assigned to us by birth (eg family, age, gender). Our choice of groups and the way we behave in them depends on several factors. You may fulfil personal needs, for example, by joining a youth group, but the way you participate in the group is shaped to a large extent not only by the conventions of the group, but by your culture. As a white, Western female, your involvement in a youth group is relatively unrestricted and it is accepted that you will interact with the males in the group. But, for an Asian female, such behaviour is not always acceptable and is often forbidden (cf Burton & Dimbleby 1995).

Groups are essential in helping society to function efficiently. For example, the government achieves many of its goals by appointing groups or committees to investigate and propose legislation. On a personal level, there are also many benefits to be gained from participation in groups. Belonging to a support group such as Alcoholics Anonymous or Weigh Less, for instance, in which members of the group share experiences and offer one another support, has helped many people overcome undesirable drinking and eating habits. Professional success is often measured by how effectively a person contributes to task groups, especially in a leadership capacity.

The main form of communication in a small group is discussion. Group members in an organisation, for instance, meet to exchange information about a situation, make a decision about an issue or solve a problem. Discussion is important because it is a way for everyone to participate and voice an opinion. Barker and Gaut (1996:156) maintain that, "[t]he existence of small groups is a basic part of the democratic process".

However, people are often reluctant to attend group discussions or participate in them. One of the main complaints is that meetings are a waste of time because they seldom accomplish as much as they should. Often, the ineffectiveness of the group is blamed on the leader, but as Verderber (1990) points out, the responsibility for the 'waste of time' in fact lies with the individual members. Studying group processes, that is, how group members communicate and interact with each other, can help you make better use of the time you spend in groups and can also help you to participate more effectively in the different groups to which you belong.

9.1   Defining a group

Arriving at a scientific definition of a group is not easy. A group is not merely a random collection of individuals who happen to occupy a particular space at the same time. Thus, six people waiting at a bus stop or riding together in a lift is not considered a group. Neither are 50 or 100 people watching a film together in a cinema. A **group** is a collection of individuals who see themselves as belonging to the group, who interact verbally and nonverbally, who occupy certain roles with respect to one other, and who co-operate to accomplish a definite goal. A **small group** is composed of three to 12 people interacting face-to-face in such a way that each person influences and is influenced by every other person in the group (cf Barker & Gaut 1996; Gamble & Gamble 1987).

Let's consider the six people waiting for a bus. Certainly, they have a common goal — they are all waiting for a bus. But there is no need to interact with one another to accomplish this goal. Should an accident occur in the street where they are waiting, however, and they begin discussing how to obtain help for the accident victims, they would become a group rather than a random collection of people. During their interaction, they would decide such matters as who should telephone for an ambulance, who should fetch blankets to cover the victims and who should try to keep them quiet until help arrives. Their unified effort would make them a small group for the duration of their interaction.

The specific goals for which a small group strives may vary. For instance, a family meets to plan the household budget; a student committee meets to plan a strategy for improving hostel conditions; a study group meets to assist its members to understand course work; a board of directors meets to plan corporate policy for the coming year; union members meet to discuss contract demands. Although their goals vary, for each of these groups to succeed, its members must work together effectively. Their understanding of **group dynamics** (the scientific study of small groups), as well as the way the members communicate with each other will, to a large extent, determine the effectiveness of the group. Gamble and Gamble (1987) maintain that knowing how to communicate with others in a group setting is vital if you are to attain personal success, and critical if you are to attain professional success. While you study this section, bear in mind that everything you have learned about communication so far applies to small groups. Because small-group communication is more complex than two-person communication, additional knowledge and skills are required and are discussed in the remainder of this section.

9.2   Advantages and disadvantages of small groups

Groups that meet to solve problems and reach decisions have both advantages and disadvantages.

9.2.1 Advantages

Research shows that the advantages of small groups include the following:

- ❐ People who work in groups usually accomplish more than people who work alone because the individual members of the group can pool resources and information to achieve goals and reach decisions. Let's say that a university committee is considering the feasibility of establishing tutorial groups for students who study at a distance. Different members of the group can gather information such as: How many students would be likely to attend? In which areas? Are there tutors in the selected subjects? Is there adequate accommodation for the tutorial groups? How much would the enterprise cost? Would additional staff be required? It is often extremely difficult for one person to obtain all the information in a short time. The more information that is made available to the group, the more likely it is to arrive at a good decision or effective solution.

- ❐ Working in a group rather than alone usually results in an increase in individual motivation to find a solution to a problem as well as greater commitment to the task on hand. There seems to be a desire not to let the group down.

- ❐ Superior decisions and solutions are often reached because groups are generally better equipped than individuals to foresee difficulties, detect weaknesses, visualise consequences and explore possibilities. Often the group can pinpoint errors in an individual member's thinking and discuss and rectify them before additional problems are created.

❑ The decisions or solutions arrived at by a group tend to be better received by others than those made by an individual. The fact that a number of people came to one conclusion appears to command respect from those to whom the group reports.

❑ Many people find that working in a group is more pleasant and fulfilling than working alone. The knowledge that others respect their opinions and are willing to confirm their ideas provides a feeling of personal satisfaction.

9.2.2 Disadvantages

Despite the strong points of using groups to solve problems and make decisions, certain drawbacks have also been identified. The disadvantages of groups include the following:

❑ There is a temptation for some people to sit back and allow others to do all the work. Such people seem to have a knack for avoiding duties and responsibilities, yet still take credit for the group's achievements.

❑ On the other hand, there is a temptation for forceful people to take over and dominate the group. Such people often refuse to make compromises or allow others to be heard. The problem is exacerbated when lower-status members are reluctant to criticise the ideas of someone who is of higher status.

❑ The personal goals of group members sometimes conflict with group goals to the extent that they interfere with group objectives. An individual member who is seeking promotion, for example, might use the group to further his own ends. In the example of the university committee above, for instance, a member might recruit tutors in a particular area as quickly as possible to show how competent he or she is, without taking the main goal of the group into account — in this case, to determine the feasibility of establishing tutorial groups in the first place.

❑ It generally takes longer for a group to reach a decision than an individual working alone. In business and industry, where time is money, and where it is often essential to reach a decision quickly, the group process can be a disadvantage (cf Gamble & Gamble 1987).

The consensus of opinion is that when the problem to be solved is simple, it is more efficient for one person to work alone, but in a complex or difficult situation, there are advantages to having people pool their resources, knowledge and insight.

9.3   Group characteristics

A question that is often asked in connection with the study of small groups is: What makes an effective group? Research shows that effective small groups generally have an optimum number of members, have a good working environment, show cohesiveness, have a commitment to the task, respect norms and meet key role requirements (cf Gamble & Gamble 1987; Hamilton & Parker 1990; Verderber & Verderber 2002; Tubbs & Moss 2003).

9.3.1   Optimum number of members

Our definition of a small group in Section 9.1 makes it clear that the interactions of individual members are important for the group to function efficiently. The members must be able to talk to each other and discuss ideas that are put forward. That is why a small group is limited to about 12 people. If the group becomes too large, the members cannot fully participate in the discussion. In fact, research indicates that, although optimum size depends on the nature of the task, five to seven people is the most productive size. Such a group is large enough to supply information and share the work load, but small enough to give each member the opportunity for maximum participation. An odd number is preferable in a group of any size because, if the group finds it necessary to vote on an issue on which it cannot achieve consensus, the odd number will prevent tie votes.

9.3.2   Good working environment

A good working environment is one that promotes interaction among its members. Apart from a pleasant physical environment, such as a room with adequate heating in winter, an important consideration is seating. Seating that is too formal or too informal inhibits free discussion. The leader who sits at the head of a long table, for example, may be perceived as the 'boss' in charge of proceedings and often inhibits participation from the group. On the other hand, when the seating is too informal, subgroups of two or three people may form within the group and also not participate fully. The ideal arrangement is to have a circular table or an arrangement of tables that makes a square, so that everyone can see everyone else. In terms of seating position, everyone has equal status which establishes a 'climate' in which all members have equal opportunity to participate (see Figure 9.1).

The **group climate** referred to above concerns the atmosphere created in the group and is largely dependent on the communication styles of the members. Your own experience probably tells you that some groups have 'too hot' a climate, in that members are intolerant of each other and quickly lose their tempers, whereas others have 'too cold' a climate, in that members are aloof, sarcastic and generally unconcerned about hurting one another's feelings or ensuring that everyone gets the opportunity to voice an opinion. It has been found that members tend to act in a way that reinforces the prevailing group climate. Redding (1972) suggests that an effective group climate has the following ingredients:

(1) supportiveness
(2) participative decision making
(3) trust among group members
(4) openness and honesty
(5) high performance goals.

Group climate also affects the cohesiveness and commitment of the members to the task in hand and to group norms.

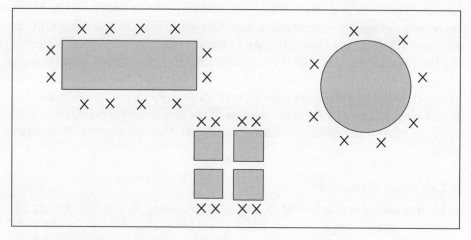

Figure 9.1 Different seating positions

9.3.3   Cohesiveness and commitment to the task

Commitment describes the willingness of individual members to work together to complete the group's task. Without sufficient commitment, there is little chance of success. People have different degrees of commitment to group work. When the group believes that what it is doing is important, members are more inclined to give fully of their time and energy. Groups that succeed in meeting their goals have members who are committed to the group in terms of attending meetings, doing what is expected of them and striving to meet the group's goals.

When members are committed, the group is likely to be cohesive. **Cohesiveness** means pulling together or uniting to accomplish a task. Effective groups are usually cohesive in that individual members actively work together as a group, and help one another as group members. A homogeneous group is generally more cohesive than a heterogeneous group. A **homogeneous** group is one in which the members have a great deal in common and pursue similar needs and purposes. A group of five women of similar age group and background who are all against abortion would be a homogeneous group. A **heterogeneous** group is one in which different ages, backgrounds and interests are represented. Cohesiveness is also directly related to the belief of individual members that they are liked, that they are accepted in the group and that their opinions are respected. Group cohesiveness usually makes it easier for the group to find ways to reach consensus when problems have to be solved and decisions made.

There is, however, the danger of too much cohesion within a group, especially if the group has a strong, dominant and respected leader. Too much cohesion can lead group members to be so concerned with maintaining good relationships within the group that they neglect the purpose for which the came together. The result is that the group is not open to new ideas and may not allow new members to join. Such groups suffer from **groupthink** — a condition in which minimising conflict and preserving harmony are more important goals than the critical examination of ideas. When groupthink predominates, the group as a whole tends to discount negative information and may even ignore ethical considerations to preserve cohesiveness. Groupthink also affects individuals within the group. Since non-conformity might damage cohesion, members who privately disagree with the views expressed by the majority may be unwilling to risk conflict by publicly admitting that they disagree. The outcome of groupthink can be that group decisions turn out to be unfair, discriminatory or insensitive (cf Janis 1972; Ellis & McClintock 1994).

Example 9.1

Groupthink has influenced decisions that range from political actions to a cult group's choice of clothing. During the Second World War, for instance, Roosevelt's close-knit presidential team ignored disturbing information that was passed on to them because, in their view, it was not possible for Pearl Harbor — the American naval base in Hawaii — to be bombed by the Japanese. Burton and Dimbleby (1995) also link groupthink with ideologies. Religious and political groups over the centuries have wanted to believe that their value system is right and all others are wrong. Jehovah's Witnesses, for instance, believe that only a select number of their followers will go to heaven on Judgement Day. The problem is that when people 'know' that they belong to the only 'right' ideological group, their belief may be used to justify all sorts of behaviour to others. Political and religious intolerance over the centuries have resulted in crimes against humanity, such as those promulgated by the Crusaders, the Nazis in Germany and apartheid authorities in South Africa.

9.3.4   Group norms

Norms are the explicit and implicit rules for behaviour that are established to enable the group to operate effectively and to develop cohesiveness. In other words, groups develop standards of behaviour that they expect members to conform to. Some norms are formal or written, such as the clearly stated codes of conduct laid down for the medical profession. Other norms are informal or unwritten, and are established early on in the group's meetings. Two important areas of norm development are group interaction and group procedure. To describe **group interaction**, think about the following examples: you may, for instance, belong to one group in which it is acceptable to interrupt the speaker to ask questions, or openly express support or disagreement with a member. On the other hand, you may belong to another group in which members are expected to be quiet until discussion is invited. Similarly, in one group the **group procedure** may be that business is not discussed unless everyone is present. In another, it may be accepted that some people come late or leave early. Norms vary from group to group and most are learned through experience with a specific group. Once established and reinforced, norms that are detrimental to the group (such as being unpunctual, using expletives and interrupting the speaker) are difficult to change. Being aware of the potential of such behaviour to detract from the effectiveness of a group encourages members to co-operate in preventing detrimental norms developing in the first place.

9.3.5   Filling role requirements

The concept of **role** is borrowed from the stage, where it refers to the character played by an actor in a play. In the social sciences, a 'role' is defined as a pattern of behaviour that is appropriate for a person's position in a group. In other words, members of a group fulfil certain prescribed roles and are accorded status according to the role they play. In every group, for instance, there is a leader who is responsible for the functioning of the group. The leader becomes the central figure in the group 'drama', with the other members as peripheral characters around him or her. In effective groups, the members understand and fill the various roles that enable the group to function. The specific role of group leadership is discussed in Section 9.5. In this section, we point out the general functions of people who fulfil task roles, maintenance roles and self-centred roles, a classification first suggested by Benne and Sheats (1948). Note that task and maintenance roles have a positive function in the group, whereas self-centred roles are dysfunctional or negative.

❑ *Task roles* reflect the work a group must do to accomplish its goals. People who fulfil task roles initiate ideas, seek and provide information, define problems, clarify and summarise suggestions and proposals and record the group's key decisions. Task roles are not limited to any one individual but are usually interchanged among the members.

❐ **Maintenance roles** reflect the group behaviour that keeps the group working together smoothly. People who perform maintenance roles fulfil the emotional needs of the group. They support and encourage others by offering praise or agreement, relieve tension by helping group members to reconcile differences, control conflict and act as gatekeeper by keeping lines of communication open and seeing that everyone has a chance to participate.

❐ Problems arise in small-group communication when members deliberately play **self-centred roles** — roles that accomplish egocentric or self-serving functions. They achieve this by being aggressive, seeking attention, promoting personal interests or not contributing at all. People who fulfil such roles dominate the discussion, verbally attack others, clown around, block suggestions and engage in point-picking — criticising everything the group attempts.

People who play task and maintenance roles are aware of the importance of participation in small groups — the need to interact with other members of the group. Responsible group members tend to plan what they are going to say in advance so that they can present their suggestions clearly and logically. They listen attentively, taking note of both the verbal and nonverbal elements of the message and they try to provide constructive feedback rather than dismiss the ideas of other group members.

9.3.6   Stages of group formation

In this section, we consider the question of how different individuals learn to work together and become a cohesive group that manages to achieve its goals. There are five developmental stages in group formation (cf Tuckman 1965; Wheelan 1994, Verderber & Verderber 2002).

❐ **Forming** This is the initial stage of group development during which the identity of the group is formed. When individuals enter a group situation, there is often a degree of tension and anxiety because of the uncertainty about a new situation. The members tend to go through a period of anxiety and dependence on the designated leader while they find out about the task, the rules and the nature of the situation.

❐ **Storming** This is a natural stage in group development marked by conflict between individual members or between a member and the leader. There is also resistance to rules and the demands of the task. However, conflict has been identified as essential to the process of cohesion because it assists in the establishment of shared norms and values. The outcome is that the members decide how the group will operate and what roles individuals will play. It has been found that when a group does not rebel, it may experience groupthink, a problem we discussed in Section 9.3.3.

❐ *Norming* During norming, conflicts are resolved and cohesiveness develops. At this stage, a degree of trust exists between group members and between the group and the leader. The group can begin to negotiate about group goals, procedures, rules and division of labour as well as standards of behaviour to which the members are expected to conform.

❐ *Co-operation* In this stage, work begins. Members co-operate to solve interpersonal problems and reach agreed goals. In order to work, members must be able to communicate openly about ideas and information. Because time and energy are directed at the task rather than at personal issues, the individuals have formed a relatively cohesive group. Groups that meet again and again without producing a report or reaching a goal are simply not working, and are most likely stuck in one of the earlier stages of development.

❐ *Adjourning* It is at this stage that the group terminates its work and members reflect on their achievements and assign meaning to their shared experiences. They also have to decide how to end or maintain the interpersonal relationships that may have formed. Ongoing groups as well as short-term groups experience endings, for instance, when a task is completed or some members are assigned to other groups. It is important for groups to have a termination ritual, which can range from an informal debriefing session to a formal gathering. It clears the way for the next challenge that an individual or the group has to deal with.

Example 9.2

This example is a practical application of the stages of group formation described in Section 9.3.6. Make sure you can recognise the five stages of forming, storming, norming, co-operation and adjourning.

A consulting team from an international organisation was brought together for the project of investigating business opportunities in Namibia. Each team member had individual expertise to contribute to the team effort. Two were fluent in the local language, and one of them knew African business culture. Another was an industry expert. A fourth knew marketing and the fifth member was a communication and negotiation expert. They met for the first time as a team in January and I sat in as they began to talk about the project. First, over coffee, they shared their backgrounds, expertise, got to know each other and shared what each of them knew about the project. It was a fun session that started quietly but soon became marked by laughter, good-natured fun, verbal repartee and jocular conversation. This was a good beginning, but as we met more times and had more serious discussions on the project, disagreements that occurred over travel plans and the structuring of the group's priorities became heated arguments. Fortunately, group members stepped in to facilitate the discussion and find ways around apparent impasses. Gradually, the parameters and pressures of the project became clear, and the group developed discussion standards and performance expectations. Even during the constant travel and tight living conditions that followed during the next four months, group members became close friends and performed together as a team to generate an outstanding and useful report. When they parted, it was with a sense of sadness as well as one of accomplishment (adapted from Harris & Sherblom 1999:53).

9.4   Communication networks in small groups

Communication is the essential ingredient for the continued existence of a group. The group's ability to accomplish a task is related to the interactions of its members. Do they feel free to express themselves openly to each other and do they have the opportunity to receive feedback about their ideas? The structure of the group, or the relationship of members to each other in the group, plays a major role in the effectiveness of communication in the group. A way of looking at group structure is in terms of communication networks. **Communication networks** are recurring patterns of interaction or, stated simply: Who talks to whom in a group? By examining networks, we examine where there are communication channels and which members transmit and receive messages to and from one another (cf Fisher 1981; Gamble & Gamble 1987; Trenholm 1991; Tubbs & Moss 1991).

We know from experience that some group members talk more than others and some are addressed more than others. This is not solely due to chance or to personality factors. It is also influenced by the individual's position in the communication network of the group.

Figure 9.2 illustrates a number of networks that might exist in a five-member group. Only individuals connected by lines can talk to each other. The wheel, chain and Y are **centralised networks**. In the wheel, A — who occupies the central position — is able to communicate with the other four, but they can communicate only with him or her. In the Y network, A, B and E can communicate with only one other person, and in the chain, the same applies to A and E. In centralised networks, the person with the most channels of communication tends to become the group leader. Unlike these networks, the circle and all-channel patterns are **decentralised networks** and are sometimes leaderless. In the circle, each member is able to communicate with two others, and in the all-channel network, each member is able to communicate with all the others.

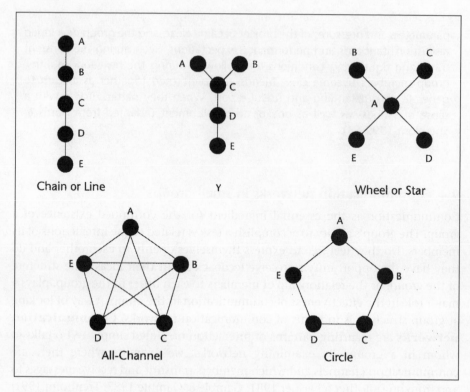

Figure 9.2 Communication networks

Two early sociologists, Bavelas (1950) and Leavitt (1951), conducted research on small groups to measure the problem-solving abilities of different networks. They studied four communication patterns: the chain, wheel, Y, and circle. Leavitt manipulated the freedom with which information could be transmitted from one subject to another in each network, and then compared the results. The wheel — the most centralised of the four networks — proved to be the fastest and most accurate in solving problems, whereas the circle — the least centralised — was slowest, used more messages and was the least accurate. However, circle groups showed the highest morale and more readily corrected their errors than the others.

Later experiments modified these early results by showing that problem-solving efficiency depends on the type of task. While they confirmed the greater speed and accuracy of centralised networks for solving simple problems, they also showed that decentralised networks are faster and more accurate in solving more complex problems (cf Shaw 1964). The reason is that decentralised networks are able to develop better plans for performing complex tasks because members can communicate their ideas and opinions directly to each other, without having to go through a central person. The later experiments also confirmed that group morale and individual satisfaction within the operation of the group are higher when people are not cut off from each other. The general consensus among researchers is that the all-channel network seems to be the most desirable. While it initially tends to be more inefficient, the opportunities for free discussion and feedback ultimately result in greater accuracy and satisfaction.

Experimental studies of communication networks are highly artificial and thus cannot be transferred directly to real-life groups. In the natural environment, factors such as noise, the location of information and members' skills and previous experience also play a role in solving problems. Nevertheless, many work groups are organised in these different ways and network research helps us more readily to understand why some group members feel frustrated while others feel content, why some groups have a higher morale than others and why some groups reach their goals more readily than others. For instance, in some work groups, individuals confer only with the group leader. In other groups, the leader receives information from upper management and then relays the information downwards. Yet other groups meet frequently to discuss and reach mutually satisfactory decisions about tasks.

A good reason for creating open channels in small groups is that, as we mentioned in the introduction to this unit, communication about the real problems and decisions with which groups are faced is done through discussion among the members. Discussion provides an opportunity for several ideas to be proposed and to be accepted, rejected or modified in response to group feedback. An understanding of communication networks can assist the leader of a group to elicit contributions from all members and encourage open communication between them.

9.5   Leadership in groups

Groups sometimes operate effectively without a designated leader. Most groups, especially those engaged in problem-solving, need effective leadership to achieve their goals. **Leadership** is defined as any behaviour that facilitates group task accomplishment, and a **leader** is any person with the ability to influence others. Influence means bringing about changes in the attitudes and actions of others. It differs from the exercise of raw power in that a good leader does not force people to submit to a particular point of view. A skilful leader guides the group through a discussion, pointing out the advantages and limitations of all the ideas suggested by the members so that the best outcome can be reached.

Leaders are either designated by the group or achieve leadership because they exhibit leadership behaviour. Effective leaders are able to help a group attain task and maintenance functions. For example, they contribute to establishing a group climate that encourages and stimulates interaction. They take responsibility for ensuring that group communication proceeds smoothly. They ask relevant questions, offer summaries as the discussion proceeds and encourage the group to continually evaluate and improve its performance (cf Gamble & Gamble 1992; Hamilton & Parker 1990; Verderber & Verderber 2002).

9.5.1   Leadership theories

Of the many theories that have been developed about leadership, we have selected two for discussion: leadership traits and leadership styles (cf Barker 1984; Verderber & Verderber 2002).

Early researchers assumed that leaders are born, not made, and looked for personality traits that distinguish leaders from nonleaders. One such study revealed that effective leaders display consistent **leadership traits** which relate to ability, sociability, motivation and communication skills. With regard to ability, leaders generally exceed average group members in intelligence, scholarship, insight and verbal facility. Sociability traits include dependability, activeness, co-operation and popularity. In the area of motivation, leaders generally exceed nonleaders in initiative, persistence and enthusiasm. Leaders also reveal a high level of competency in a variety of communication skills. A later study revealed five types of behaviour that prevent people from becoming leaders: being uninformed about the problem under discussion; being too rigid in opinions about the problem; not participating; being too authoritarian or 'bossy'; and being verbally offensive — talking too much or talking in a pompous way.

Such traits and behaviour are generalisations, and it does not follow that people who exhibit leadership traits will become group leaders. Research indicates that no one set of characteristics is common to all leaders, and that leaders and followers alike share many of the same characteristics. The particular situation appears to determine in part which individual comes forward to exert leadership. The value of trait research is that it provides 'indicators of potential leadership'. Thus, while it is not valid to say that leaders must have particular traits, it is valid to conclude that certain traits are more likely to be found in leaders than nonleaders. Regarding traits as indicators of good leadership is also useful in that it refutes the notion that some people are destined to become leaders. The prevailing view is that most people can be trained to be good leaders.

Very often, the quality of work produced by groups depends on the behaviour or style of leadership of the group leader. The assumptions we make about how people work together will influence the type of **leadership styles** we adopt. Some leaders assume that the average group member is inherently lazy, prefers to avoid responsibility and must be closely supervised. Others assume that the average group member enjoys work, is self-directed and will willingly assume responsibility (cf McGregor 1960). These assumptions have resulted in the identification of three different leadership styles: authoritarian, democratic and laissez-faire.

☐ **Authoritarian leaders** are strongly task-oriented and have firm opinions on how to achieve the group's goals. They exercise direct control over the group by determining policy and procedure, assigning tasks and roles to members, and deciding who may talk and who may not. An authoritarian leader often makes decisions without consulting the group. Although such an approach may be effective during crisis situations because it produces fast decisions, the usual outcome of this style is that it causes conflict within the group and group satisfaction is low.

☐ **Democratic leaders** are people-oriented. They guide rather than direct a group by involving all members in discussion and debate and letting everyone's points of view be heard. While such a leader may suggest alternatives, it is left to the group to decide on specific policy, procedure, and the tasks and roles of members. Democratic leadership has been proven to produce high quality results as it provides opportunities for originality and creativity, and stimulates group cohesiveness, motivation to work and achieve goals, and the desire to communicate.

The results of studies reported by White and Lippert (1968) suggest the following advantages and disadvantages of the autocratic and democratic styles:
☐ The least amount of work is done when no leadership exists
☐ More work is done under a task leader than under a person-oriented leader
☐ Task leadership may create discontent and/or result in less individuality
☐ Motivation and originality are greater under a person-centred leader
☐ More friendliness is shown in person-oriented groups.

☐ **Laissez-faire leaders** generally adopt a 'let them do their own thing' attitude and try not to direct the group at all. They supply information, advice and material when asked but do not actively participate in group decisions. The group has complete freedom in determining policy, procedure, tasks and roles. While members of a laissez-faire group feel free to progress and develop on their own, they may often be distracted from the task at hand and suffer loss of direction. The result is that the quality of work they produce suffers. On the other hand, this kind of leadership is appropriate in situations where too much direction would stifle group creativity. Support groups, such as groups for the terminally ill, seem to work well under this type of leadership because the members come together for the purpose for helping each other and prefer not be tied to a particular procedure or structure.

Although the democratic style of leadership is preferred by most people who participate in groups, all three leadership styles can be effective under the appropriate conditions. When an urgent decision is required, for example, the authoritarian style may serve the group's best interests. In situations where a minimum of interference may produce the best results, the laissez-faire style is recommended. When commitment to the group decision is of the greatest importance, the democratic style should be practised. In other words, there are no rigid rules. In this respect, consider the following thoughts on leadership provided by Trevor Manuel, South Africa's Minister of Finance:

> When the road ahead is well charted, there is a need for persistence, even stubbornness, to avoid deviating from the course when things don't go quite according to plan. But when circumstances change significantly, or you move on to new challenges, creativity and innovation come into their own.

9.5.2 Developing leadership skills

Whether you are elected as the leader of a group, or emerge as the leader, it is not possible to provide effective leadership unless you ensure that the group functions well and makes progress towards reaching its goals. Some points that group leaders should attend to in this respect include the following:

☐ having sufficient knowledge about the particular task

☐ setting an example by working harder than anyone else in the group

☐ showing sincerity by being personally committed to group goals and needs

☐ being decisive at key moments in the discussion

☐ interacting freely with all members of the group, but at the same time not dominating the discussion

☐ developing skills in maintenance functions as well as task functions so that the group remains cohesive and functional.

Some guidelines for efficient leadership

Being a good leader also means being aware of and attending to the responsibilities of ensuring that a meeting proceeds as efficiently as possible. Think about the following suggestions to facilitate efficient group leadership (cf Hybels & Weaver 1989; Hamilton & Parker 1990).

- [ ] Inform everyone involved when and where all meetings are to take place and distribute an agenda — a list of all the items that will be discussed during the meeting.
- [ ] Select a place for the meeting that will be conducive to discussion. For example, make sure that there are no distractions and that the seating arrangements invite participation by all members.
- [ ] Check the facilities shortly before the meeting to see that everything needed is in place. You may, for example, require an overhead projector, a tape recorder or a chalkboard.
- [ ] Start on time and stick to the agenda to avoid wasting time.
- [ ] Preview the agenda briefly at the start of the meeting to make sure that everyone knows exactly what is to be discussed.
- [ ] Encourage discussion but ensure that no one individual is allowed to monopolise the discussion.
- [ ] Ask pertinent questions. For example, if the group discussion goes off track, intervene with a question such as: Is this directly related to the problem we are discussing? If information is to be evaluated, ask questions such as: How recent is the information? Who is the source? Might the source be biased?
- [ ] Summarise the main points as the discussion progresses and provide an overall summary at the end.
- [ ] Thank the participants (and audience if any).
- [ ] Make sure that everyone who needs the results of the meeting is properly informed. If people are affected by the results of the meeting, inform them as quickly as possible.

9.6   Discussion in groups

Group members meet formally or informally to exchange information and ideas in order to solve problems and make decisions. For instance, a school committee discusses how to raise money for new computers, a sectional-title board discusses ways of improving the apartment complex, a security group discusses safety arrangements for political leaders, a group of judges meets to arrive at a legal decision. Most organisations in society have several groups that meet regularly to solve administrative problems that arise in the organisation.

Problem-solving and decision making are joint activities. In order to make a decision about an issue, the problem has to be investigated. Problem-solving is the process by which people generate and evaluate the solutions to an identified problem so that the best one can be chosen and implemented (cf Brilhart 1989). According to Berko, Wolvin and Curtis (1986), a good decision is one that the decision-makers feel comfortable with, the solution that the group perceives to be the best possible one for the existing problem. In other words, the group reaches **consensus**. Consensus means that group members actively participate in a discussion until they are committed to a decision. It does not mean that all agree with the decision, but that all understand the decision, accept it, and will carry out their part in implementing it. Although there are different approaches to problem-solving, researchers suggest that groups reach consensus more efficiently if they understand and follow a systematic procedure designed to lead them through the problem-solving process to a specific choice. The structure or sequence in Table 9.1 has been shown to work well in many problem-solving situations (cf Fisher 1981; Hybels & Weaver 1989; Tubbs & Moss 2003).

There are five steps in the problem-solving process described below.

Table 9.1 The problem-solving sequence

1. Identify and define the problem.	2. Analyse and research the problem.	3. Decide what the solution should accomplish.	4. Find and evaluate solutions.	5. Implement the solution.

9.6.1   Identifying and defining the problem

The first step is to recognise that a problem indeed exists and for the group as a whole to agree that it is a problem. Obvious problems, such as "We're out of money", are easy to identify and agree on. Sometimes, a symptom is mistaken for a problem. For instance, falling sales in a company may be due to a poorly designed product and not to inadequate efforts on the part of the sales team. Members must understand the specific goal of the group to avoid the waste of time mentioned earlier. An efficient way of identifying a problem is to phrase it as a question. Basically there are three kinds of question: questions of fact, questions of value and questions of policy.

1. Questions of fact deal with what is true and what is false. "Did Mr Jones steal money from the club's savings account?" is a question of fact. Jones either committed the crime or he did not. Questions of fact also describe existing conditions. For example, "Where should the company locate the new staff cafeteria?" is a question of fact which describes a matter of place.
2. Questions of value concern judgements of quality: whether something is good or bad, desirable or undesirable. "How well do adult literacy programmes work?" is a question of value because it does not ask whether such programmes exist, but questions the quality of the programmes.
3. Questions of policy are enquiries into an action that might be taken in the

future. Such questions often include the word 'should'. "Should this student be suspended for cheating in an examination?" or "Should the university build a new library?"

The type of question determines the purpose of the group and the nature of the information it requires. Of course, it may be necessary to discover facts and to clarify values before the group can decide on an action, but knowing the overall purpose helps to keep members on track in their discussion and guides them in the search for relevant information.

9.6.2   Analysing and researching the problem

☐ *Defining words and phrases* Before a group can discuss a problem or find a solution, all members must ascribe the same meaning to any word or phrase that may be ambiguous. For example, "We need to raise a lot of money" or "The company's internal mail service is too slow" or "What should the department do about people who are not getting the job done?", can mean different things to different people. The members must agree on what exactly 'too slow' means, and how much 'a lot of money' is, or what 'not getting the job done' involves.

☐ *Seeking out information* The information groups need to discuss a problem will vary. Sometimes relevant personal experience of group members is the most important source of information. Other problems can be investigated by direct observation. For example, visually inspecting traffic conditions at a school crossing can tell you the specific nature of the problem. In the case of the late delivery of mail, personal interviews with the person in charge of the mail room and the messenger who delivers the mail may yield the necessary information. Information on the value of adult literacy programmes could be obtained from a library.

☐ *Deciding what the solution should accomplish* Most problems do not have a single solution. There are usually a number of alternatives. Before a group can arrive at a decision, it must establish realistic and acceptable criteria for what the solution should accomplish. For example, in evaluating alternatives, the mail committee might decide that any solution that does not get the mail to its destination 24 hours after it was received in the mail room is unacceptable.

☐ *Finding and evaluating solutions* Often a group can find many alternatives that may lead to a decision. Some of them will have to be discarded because they are impractical, others because they do not meet the criteria that have been decided. One way of generating and evaluating solutions is to encourage the free flow of ideas by brainstorming. **Brain-storming** encourages creative thinking because it requires that everyone states ideas as they come to mind, in random order, until a long list has been compiled. In 10 to 15 minutes of intensive concentration, you may think of several solutions to a problem yourself, but a group may come up with 10, 20, 30 or more possible solutions in the same time. Brainstorming means that everyone temporarily suspends criticism and evaluation of ideas until the end of the session. If people feel free to make suggestions — even if they seem impractical or even ridiculous at the time — they tend to think more creatively than if each idea is criticised as it is presented. Only after the brainstorming session is finished is each solution evaluated as to its practicality and the degree to which it meets the criteria. The one that meets the most criteria and is the most practical is usually selected.

☐ ***Implementing the solution*** The final step in a discussion is to offer suggestions about how the solution can be implemented. Sometimes the group itself has the power to initiate the solution. At other times, it conveys its proposals and suggestions to the person or people concerned. In the case of the mail problem, the group members would recommend a solution to the head of the mail room who (hopefully) agrees to try it for a month to see if it works. If, at the end of the month, the group finds that the plan is not working, it will have to meet again to consider different solutions.

9.7 Group conflict

It is inevitable that a certain degree of conflict arises in decision making groups. Usually, when we think about **group conflict**, we assume that one party wins and the other loses, leading to a great deal of frustration. However, when handled skilfully, conflict can be constructive and lead to new ideas and innovations that are beneficial to the group. Conflict is constructive when it results in an improvement in the quality of decisions that are made or when it stimulates involvement from group members who are inclined to remain passive. Conflict can be destructive when contentious issues are not discussed and remain unresolved, creating feelings of resentment among members of the group. The key to constructive conflict lies in the group's communication processes. The key to resolving conflict is a conscious effort by group members to approach the conflict situation with respect for one another's views and with the intention to avoid aggressive behaviour.

Conflict can be defined as "an expressed struggle between at least two interdependent parties who perceive incompatible goals, scarce rewards, and interference from the other party in achieving their goals" (Hocker & Wilmot 1991:12). The important words to note in this definition are 'expressed' and 'interdependent'. For a conflict to be handled by means of communication, it must be expressed verbally or nonverbally. Also, if one party does not depend on the other for some reason or other, the two will not necessarily enter into a conflict.

9.7.1   Strategies for conflict resolution

☐ **Collaboration** The ideal conflict resolution strategy for any group conflict is one in which both parties feel satisfied with the outcome. To achieve this win-win situation requires *collaboration*, which is achieved either through consensus or negotiation. Both methods take time, energy and commitment. Collaborative communication requires the participation of all members. Each is given the opportunity to state his or her point of view as clearly and concisely as possible. At the same time, each is required to listen attentively to the views of others, without interruption or comment. Once all the perspectives have been stated, the conflicting viewpoints are discussed and explained. The important factor is that, from the outset, each person has to be open to the more rational and compelling aspects of all the arguments. The ideal resolution will combine the best elements of all perspectives, reshaping them into a new and more creative whole than any original part. When conducted fairly, each member feels empowered because he or she has been heard and has contributed to the final outcome. The greatest disadvantage of consensus is the time required to hear and discuss everyone's views and secure everyone's commitment to a final decision. Collaboration is therefore not appropriate for trivial decisions, emergency issues or decisions on which members cannot come to agreement, even after extended discussion (cf Wood 2000). Then collaboration may have to involve negotiation.

☐ **Negotiation** is frequently the method of choice in a more formal bargaining situation, such as between a labour union and a company. It is used when arguments seem unresolvable and neither side seems willing to make sufficient concessions to reach a satisfactory outcome. As a conflict resolution strategy, *negotiation* "involves forging a resolution between opposing points of view, assuring that each side 'wins' and gets the benefits most important to its overall goals" (Harris & Sherblom 1999:201). An impartial mediator is usually brought in to help the parties find areas of mutual agreement. Whether the mediator is an outsider or a group member, that person must fully understand all the issues under consideration and the different perspectives and needs of the conflicting parties. In addition, the mediator must have a high degree of integrity, competent communication and leadership skills, and the ability to set aside his or her personal views. The important part of negotiation is to achieve what is best for all without sacrificing the interpersonal relationships that bind the group together. A successful outcome will leave all parties satisfied that the resolution is fair and that all concerned got what they most needed.

☐ **Accommodation** *Accommodation* is a win-lose strategy because it means giving up all or most of one's own views and benefits for the sake of others. At its most constructive, accommodation can reduce interpersonal tension and be beneficial to the overall group effort. If the issue is a relatively minor point, for example, one person in the group wants to meet after lunch and the others prefer an early start, giving in to the majority is unlikely to create feelings of resentment. But if this person consistently has to concede on major issues merely to ensure group harmony, he or she may end up feeling so resentful and angry that he or she withdraws altogether from the group discussion process.

❑ **Compromise** *Compromise* means 'splitting the difference'. Like accommodation, as a conflict-resolution strategy, compromise can be constructive or destructive. Compromise is appropriate when the issue is not of major importance and the members agree that it would be a waste of time and energy to try to reach consensus. For instance, when some members of the group prefer Supplier A and others prefer Supplier B, and there is little to choose between them in terms of price and quality of goods, the members may agree to buy some of their supplies from A and some from B. However, compromise is destructive when, for example, someone of status in the group exercises seniority to force the issue. Should the 'loser' feel disempowered, that member may later withhold cooperation on a more important issue.

❑ **Avoidance** The *avoidance* strategy leads to a win-lose situation when the member who withdraws from the conflict does so because he or she feels threatened or disempowered. Apart from impoverishing the decision making process because opinions are withheld, the avoiding member and other group members often feel resentment and dissatisfaction. Conflict is best resolved by working through it rather than by avoiding or suppressing it. If it is not satisfactorily resolved, it may simmer beneath the surface and later disrupt the outcome that has been reached. Ideally, conflict should be faced directly and an appropriate communication strategy selected to reach a mutually satisfactory outcome (cf Harris & Sherblom 1999).

9.8   Differences between interpersonal and group communication

We conclude this chapter by pointing out that, while interpersonal and small-group communication occur in a face-to-face situation, there are differences between them. Burton and Dimbleby (1995:225) have identified the differences as follows:

> In a one-to-one situation we are presenting our Self according to our self-concept and our perception of the other person(s) and the social context. When we are part of a group, however, the dynamics of the group, its tasks and social relationships mean that we are more conscious of playing a role and of being concerned with the group. The group, when it's working cohesively, develops a life of its own of which the individual members are merely a part — we subordinate our individual needs and motives for the sake of the group.

Scenario 9.1

A company which supplies computers to a variety of businesses in a large city in South Africa has received complaints from several of its customers that only white staff are sent to install and service the computers. In response to these complaints, the company arranges for a task group to investigate whether affirmative action should be introduced in the company. During the first meeting, the leader of the task group asks for suggestions from the group members. Chaos ensues because each member of the group shouts out his or her ideas, opinions and solutions. Some of the suggestions and comments are totally impractical. Others are sound but, because most people have not had sufficient time to think about the problem before the meeting, even the best ideas are presented in a way that cannot easily be implemented. The leader asks for silence and then says: "Thank you for your enthusiasm and the variety of ideas being offered. However, if we are to reach a decision we need to thrash out all these ideas and come up with a workable solution that we can present to management. We are therefore going to follow a recognised problem-solving sequence. I will guide you as we go along."

   After you have studied this scenario and thought about the situation, write down how you would implement the five stages in the problem-solving sequence described in Table 9.1.

Summary

This chapter began by defining a small group and pointing out the advantages and disadvantages of working in small groups. It then explained that the characteristics of effective groups include having an optimum number of members, a good working environment, cohesiveness and commitment to the task and a respect for group norms. It identified the types of roles that group members play as task roles and maintenance roles. After describing the stages in the formation of small groups, it discussed different types of communication networks that operate in small groups and the consequences of each. It then examined the important role played by the leader of a group as well as two theories about leadership: leadership traits and leadership styles. The chapter also pointed out some guidelines for becoming an efficient leader. The next part of the chapter dealt with an investigation into the ways groups discuss the problems they have to address and the decisions that are made. Because conflict is inevitable in small groups, it described some communication strategies for resolving conflict situations. The chapter ended with a short note on the differences between interpersonal and small-group communication.

Test yourself

1. Select two groups to which you belong that you feel have an effective and an ineffective group climate. For each group, identify the types of behaviour exhibited by members. How did each climate affect your own participation in the group? How is each climate affected by your relationship with group members?

2. Choose a group of which you are a member and try to identify three group norms. Check your perception by asking other group members if they agree with your selection.

3. List three positive and three negative qualities you bring to groups. How could you overcome the negative qualities? Is your productivity in the group affected by your behaviour?

4. Try to determine the role each member of a group to which you belong may be playing.

5. Choose a group of which you are a member and analyse which of the following had the greatest effect on group interaction: group size; group climate; presence or lack of cohesiveness; commitment to the task; adherence to norms. On what do you base your analysis?

6. Describe the stages in the formation of a group with reference to a group of which you have been a member.

7. Observe the leaders of the small groups to which you belong and classify each leadership style as democratic, autocratic or laissez-faire. Under which leadership style do you work best? Why?

8. What is your leadership style? What are its strengths and weaknesses?

9. Use the following list of questions to judge the success of the last discussion group of which you were a member:
   (a) Did you feel comfortable in the group?
   (b) Did everyone participate and interact?
   (c) Were the group sessions enjoyable?
   (d) Did you find the task of the group enjoyable?
   (e) Was the topic adequately and efficiently covered? (cf Hybels & Weaver 1989:228)

10. Think about a conflict situation you have recently encountered in one of the groups to which you belong. Which resolution strategy do you think would have worked best in that situation and which do you think would have been the least effective? Briefly explain why.

11. How would you arrange a room for a meeting in which there is likely to be conflict? For example, which arrangement might minimise status differences?

EXECUTIVE SUMMARY
Small group communication

1 Group roles
   ☐ task, maintenance and self-centred roles
2 Stages in the formation of small groups
   ☐ forming
   ☐ storming
   ☐ norming
   ☐ cooperation
   ☐ adjourning
3 Communication networks
   ☐ centralised and decentralised networks
4 Group leadership
   ☐ leadership traits
   ☐ leadership styles
5 Group discussion
   ☐ identifying and defining the problem
   ☐ analysing and researching the problem
   ☐ deciding what the solution should accomplish
   ☐ implementing the solution
6 Strategies for conflict resolution
   ☐ collaboration
   ☐ negotiation
   ☐ accommodation
   ☐ compromise
   ☐ avoidance

10 Public speaking

Overview

"Make a speech in public! What did I do to deserve this punishment?"
"Speak in front of an audience? I'll never be able to think of anything to talk about."
"I'm too scared to speak in front of other people."

Do these statements sound familiar? Most people would rather be doing (almost) anything than giving a speech. For many of us, public speaking, particularly to large groups, is more difficult than interaction with one person or with a small group. However, to a large extent, public speaking involves the same basic techniques that we use in our daily communication with others: one person tries to get an idea across to another person, using all the skills at his or her disposal. Few people are born speakers. It is an acquired skill that everyone is able to learn to a certain degree. How to overcome your apprehension (fear) and learn to address a group of people rather than a single individual is the main theme of the rest of this chapter.

We begin by explaining the importance of public speaking skills in your professional and social life. In the remainder of the chapter we go through the steps in the speech-making process. First, you need to determine the general purpose of your speech: Is it an informative, persuasive or entertaining talk? The next step is to analyse the audience. Audience analysis requires three types of information: demographic, psychographic and sociographic. You also have to analyse the occasion that prompted the speech and the setting or venue where it will be given. You then have to select a topic for the speech. We explain how to narrow down the topic you choose to arrive at the main points that will be discussed in the talk. Your next task is to find information to support the main ideas. Good supporting materials make your ideas clear to your listeners.

A speech is structured into three parts: the introduction, the body of the speech and the conclusion. Each part has a specific purpose that is essential to the effectiveness of the speech. Regarding the body of the speech, we describe three organisational patterns that are used to present the main points in a logical and understandable way: sequential, logical and topical patterns. We then describe specific organisational features of the informative talk, the instructive talk and the persuasive talk. The final step in speech preparation is to rehearse the delivery. It is also good practice to think through the answers to possible questions that may arise at the end of the talk. We focus on the verbal and nonverbal elements of delivery that play a crucial part in determining the success of your presentation as well as the effective use of visual materials. The last part of the chapter deals with the evaluation of a speech. In other words, we try to answer the question: Why are some speeches more effective than others? The chapter ends with a scenario based on former president Nelson Mandela's first official speech as president of South Africa.

Learning outcomes

At the end of this chapter you should be able to:
1 Explain the value to yourself of a course in public speaking.
2 Describe the most important demographic, psychographic and socio-graphic characteristics of audiences.
3 Describe the main goals of a speech to entertain, a speech to inform and a speech to persuade.
4 Apply the four steps involved in selecting a topic for an oral presentation to a speech of your choice.
5 Choose and locate appropriate supporting material for your own speeches.
6 Describe three basic patterns for organising the main points in a speech, illustrating your answer with appropriate examples.
7 Briefly discuss two methods you can use in the introduction to get your listeners' interest and attention.
8 Use Monroe's motivated sequence to organise a persuasive speech on a topic of your own choice.
9 Select appropriate visuals for a talk of your choice.
10 Practise your own delivery by applying all the guidelines you have learned about in this chapter to a speech of your choice.
11 Evaluate your own and other people's speeches using the evaluation method in this chapter.
12 Answer the questions based on the case at the end of this chapter.

Introduction

You may be wondering why public speaking is important to you. It has been said that a successful, responsible, productive citizen must know how to read critically, how to write coherently and how to speak effectively. Not only does public speaking play a major role in deciding, for instance, who becomes the next president of South Africa or the United States, a cabinet minister, chairperson of a board of directors, or leader of a business, social or political organisation, but your ability to speak effectively may have a decisive influence on your success in social and work situations (cf Verderber 1990; Gronbeck et al 1992).

Most people spend the greater part of their working lives in an organisation, in either the public or private sector of the economy. In most organisations today, the ability to give oral presentations is an indication of personal and professional success. Senior personnel, for example, are expected to be able to give introductory talks to new employees, to conduct meetings, to present training sessions and to report to the board of directors. Often, a salesperson who can present a well thought-out presentation to clients has the opportunity to boost the image of the organisation as well as his or her own career. These speeches are more formal than discussions with family, friends or committee members because your purpose is more specific than in social interaction.

A great deal of our 'speechmaking' is informal and takes place in everyday social situations. For example, you might be called upon to lead the meetings of church, school or social action groups, to make a speech at a social function, or to discuss the novel you have been reading at a book club. The more confident you feel about your ability to stand up in public and deliver your address, the greater the feeling of wellbeing you are likely to experience.

Learning to speak in public also benefits you as an individual. First, training in public speaking develops your ability to investigate a topic and gather information about it. Second, the skills you learn will help you be more perceptive and more critical in your thinking and in your evaluation of your own and other people's ideas. When we listen to political speeches critically, we are better informed citizens. When we listen to advertisers critically, we are wiser consumers. The third benefit is that training in public speaking helps to develop the confidence in yourself that promotes self-esteem (cf Cohen 1983; Minnick 1983).

Even though you might say that, as a student, you have had no experience in public speaking, you should not forget the occasions when you have been a member of an audience. All of us have attended a lecture, a student gathering, a church service or even a court trial. Being a member of the audience at such occasions has already helped you form an impression of public speaking. And, from the outset, it is extremely important to know that public speaking is not only concerned with the role of the communicator (the speaker). Equally important is the role of the recipient (the listener).

At the outset, you must understand that the responsibility for an effective oral presentation rests with the speaker. You have to thoroughly prepare the talk and the delivery. The first question most people ask themselves when faced with the task of preparing a talk is: "What am I going to talk about?" Effective oral presentations involve more than selecting a topic and deciding on content. The groundwork for an effective talk is established by first thinking about the reasons for presenting the talk and the people who will be attending the talk.

Please note that the terms, 'speech', 'talk', 'oral presentation' and 'public speaking' are used interchangeably in this chapter.

10.1 Determining the purpose of your talk

Sometimes the topic will be determined by the person or organisation that has invited you to present the address. At other times, you may be free to select the topic yourself. In both cases, your first step should be to decide the purpose of your talk. Why are you speaking? What do you hope to accomplish? Most oral presentations have three purposes: to inform, to persuade or to entertain. Sometimes, two or more purposes are combined in a single presentation. For example, a speaker whose immediate purpose is to persuade the audience to register for the forthcoming general election may decide to use amusing or dramatic illustrations to entertain them at the same time (cf Gamble & Gamble 1998b).

☐ **Informative talks** In informative oral presentations, your purpose is to increase your audience's knowledge of a subject by providing information in an interesting, organised and professional manner. In a sense, an informative speaker resembles a teacher because his or her primary goal is to communicate and share knowledge that the audience does not already have. A lecture on examination preparation, a report-back on the proceedings of a club or social interest group, or on the activities of a work group in an organisation, are examples of informative talks. Sometimes, the primary purpose of an informative talk is to instruct — the emphasis is on explaining how things work, how actions are performed, or how procedures are carried out. You may want to demonstrate how to arrange flowers, paint a room or use an electric drill. In organisations, instructive talks are given to improve a skill or to train staff in new techniques or operational procedures, such as computer programmes or modifications on a machine. Most informative talks are not controversial in that they usually contain factual information presented impartially. Statistics, definitions, diagrams, pictures and demonstrations are often used to present new ideas and to make the task of explaining easier.

☐ **Persuasive talks** Persuasive presentations are intended to influence people. You go beyond giving information to adopting a cause. The information you offer is used to try to change or reinforce the attitudes, beliefs, values and behaviour of your listeners — how they feel about an issue or how they are going to act on an issue. Logical reasoning and emotional appeals are used to convince your audience to share your beliefs or follow your lead. The salesperson, for example, who demonstrates a company's product to promote sales, an architect who addresses a community group to justify building a new shopping centre, or the minister delivering a sermon, is trying to influence the audience's opinion. Sometimes an oral presentation is given to persuade people to change their political views, or to donate money or services to a cause. Have you ever thought about the fact that advertisements on television and radio are examples of short, persuasive 'speeches'? Persuasive speeches are usually more controversial than informative speeches because other people frequently hold a different view to yours. While you may deliver a speech supporting affirmative action in the workplace, a number of audience members may hold very different opinions about the topic. In persuasive talks, it is therefore important to provide evidence such as accurate and relevant statistics, the experience of others or authoritative opinions to support your assertions. You also have to be extremely sensitive to your audience's attitude towards you and your topic.

☐ ***Entertaining talks*** Your purpose in talking in front of a group may be to entertain or amuse them. The main goal is to increase the audience's feeling of enjoyment by providing humorous anecdotes and illustrations to make them laugh and relax. You want your listeners to have a good time rather than learn something or persuade them to change their attitude about an issue. You may be asked to deliver a speech at a wedding, for example, or to address your colleagues at an end-of-year luncheon. Although the listeners expend less effort during an entertaining speech, it nevertheless requires effort and preparation from the speaker. An effective humorous talk depends largely on the speaker's choice of examples and illustrations, as well as on personality, delivery and sense of humour. Think for a moment about how you would go about entertaining an audience of your fellow students on the topic, 'How to fail a course in Communication'.

Even though we identify each purpose separately, they often overlap. There are times when it is appropriate and effective to include humour in an informative or persuasive talk, and some entertaining talks may contain information that is new to the audience. Suppose that you have strong feelings about a controversial topic, and you know that most of your listeners are undecided about it, you may want to give a mainly persuasive speech. We say 'mainly' because, as an ethical speaker, you should first give them sufficient information about the topic to allow them to make a rational choice. For example, political candidates must give reasons why the audience should vote for them, or a student advisor should explain the benefits of a course in public speaking in order to convince a group of prospective students to register for such a course.

10.2 Analysing the audience

Audience analysis is the process of gathering information about the listeners whom you expect to hear your speech. This will help you decide on a topic that will capture their interest and attention, and guide you in organising and presenting the talk. Even if the topic has been selected for you by the person or organisation who invited you to speak, you will still need to be aware of who your audience is so that you can develop your talk in a direction that will hold their attention and interest. The types of information you require concern the demographic, psychographic and sociographic characteristics of your audience, as well as the setting in which the presentation will take place (cf Hybels & Weaver 1989; Gronbeck et al 1992; Lucas 1995; Beebe & Beebe 1997; De Jager 1997; Gamble & Gamble 1998b; Steinberg 1999b).

10.2.1 Types of information

❑ **Demographics** describes the profile of a group of listeners according to factors such as gender, age, nationality, language, occupation, marital status, educational level, income and/or residential area and racial, ethnic or cultural ties (cf Du Plooy 1991; Beebe & Beebe 1997). Try to find out as much as you can about the demographics of your audience as well as the churches, clubs and political groups they may have joined. This information will help you to choose examples and illustrations that will be relevant to them. Let's use gender as an example.

You need to ask yourself if your audience is predominantly male or female, or made up of both genders. Many speakers still tend to refer to doctors, engineers and breadwinners as 'he' and to teachers, nurses and homemakers as 'she'. Such speakers only succeed in offending some members of the audience. Even in a culturally diverse country such as South Africa, most people accept that social and work distinctions between the sexes have been changing over the past few years. Black women in certain rural areas in South Africa, for example, play a significant role in farming the land, whereas in other rural areas, it is mainly white men who are farmers. You would certainly start off on the wrong footing if you assumed that only men would attend your talk on farming methods in rural areas.

❑ **Psychographics** describes the profile of a group of listeners according to factors such as their interests, values, attitudes and beliefs. Information about psychographic factors will help you plan your talk because you can anticipate the audience's likely reactions. Ask yourself questions such as: "Why are they coming to listen to me?", "What are their possible interests?", "Do they have strong political or religious convictions?", "What cultural and social values can I expect from them?", "How will they react to certain topics and to me as the speaker?"

The answers to such questions will help you link your topic to their interests, and guide you in selecting your words and tone of voice. Because you cannot assume that your audience will agree with everything you say, knowledge of their attitudes, values and beliefs will help you anticipate positive and negative reactions to controversial issues and prepare for them.

Let's consider one example of how psychographic information can help you to plan your speech.

If your talk is aimed at overcoming gender bias in the workplace, you need to know whether the listeners consider the topic to be important, and how they feel about issues such as equal treatment for men and women, policies against sexual harassment and women in management positions. Acknowledging that you understand their beliefs, attitudes and values can go a long way towards persuading them to think in a different way. In cases where you believe that your audience will be negative or even hostile to your topic, you will have to be especially careful to be as objective as possible, to state your case very clearly and not to attack their point of view. It is more important in such a situation to make a hostile audience understand your position, rather than try to change a firmly held attitude.

☐ **Sociographics** describes the profile of a group of listeners in terms of group affiliations. You need to find out whether your listeners belong to groups that represent special attitudes or identifiable values. Group affiliations form a bond between people. People who belong to the same group and attend the same meetings or demonstrations, for example, often share the same interests, attitudes, beliefs and values as other members of the group. If not, they would not be willing to associate themselves with the group. Whenever you have to prepare a speech, consider how the various affiliations of your listeners could influence your topic and your approach. Ask yourself the question: "Do my listeners belong to any groups that could influence the way they respond to my speech or to me?" Think about occupational, religious, political and social affiliations. Let's take political affiliation as an example. Members of political parties tend to express relatively consistent opinions across a wide range of political issues. Such members are usually interested in policies and community issues. In South Africa, some members of political parties are very hostile towards members of opposition political parties. Public speakers may help to tone down these hostile attitudes by finding some common ground between political parties, for example that people from all parties want peace and better living conditions.

☐ **The occasion and the setting** Almost as important as the need to analyse the audience is to analyse the occasion on which you are speaking and the physical environment or setting of the speech. Because the *occasion* is what brings the audience together, it usually determines the listeners' expectations. Let's say that your topic is the horseracing industry in South Africa. Depending on the occasion, the audience might expect to hear a serious lecture or a humorous talk. If the occasion is a gathering of racehorse owners, they would probably not be impressed by a humorous speaker, whereas if the occasion is an after-dinner talk for the members of a sports club, they would probably be delighted to be entertained by listening to amusing incidents that have occurred at South African racecourses. You should also make enquiries about the venue where you will be talking. The *setting* can affect your audience's reaction and affect your presentation. Variables such as the following ultimately influence audience reaction to you and your presentation: audience size, the time of day, the type of venue, the seating arrangements, whether the room is likely to be hot or cold, and the availability of a microphone, lectern, overhead projector or other aids that will help you to deliver the talk. For example, it is too late to correct the situation when you arrive at the venue and find that there is no microphone in a large hall or that there is no projector for your laptop presentation.

10.3 Selecting a topic

Taking the audience's background, preferences and physical comfort into account is important, but it does not mean that you should only select a topic that already interests them. Analysing your audience assists your preparation and enables you to predict their reaction to your viewpoint. The final choice of subject matter is made by you. When the person or organisation that has invited you to present the address asks you to speak on a particular topic, it is usually determined by the occasion, the audience and the speaker's qualifications. A lawyer might be invited to speak to university students on crime and law enforcement on campus, a film director might be invited to talk to Communication Studies students on the latest developments in the South African film industry, or a nurse may asked to speak to athletes about sports injuries. At other times, you may be free to select the topic yourself. If you already have a topic in mind, your task is simplified. If you are finding it difficult to arrive at a topic, you could consider two broad categories of subject matter: subjects you already know a lot about, such as your hobbies, your profession or current events; and subjects that interest you and that you would like to know more about, such as laser surgery or date rape. In both cases, your choice of subject matter will be guided by your analysis of the audience, the occasion and the setting. However, this does not mean that you should only select an area that already interests your listeners. Analysing your audience assists your preparation and enables you to predict their reaction to your viewpoint, but the final choice of subject matter is made by you. Even if the topic has been determined for you, you should examine it in the light of the following steps: the subject area of the talk, a specific topic within the subject area, the purpose of the talk and the topic statement.

1. Write down the **subject** area of your talk in one sentence. As a social worker, for example, you might decide that you want to talk about social issues in South Africa that concern you. 'Social problems in South Africa' then becomes the subject area of your talk. Or the subject area of your talk could be something you know about, like home decorating.

2. Write down the **topic** of your talk in one sentence. Because each of these areas mentioned above is so vast, you then narrow the topic by identifying a

specific aspect within the area. This becomes the topic of your talk. For example, if you belong to a social organisation, you may decide that your topic will be 'Illiteracy in the workplace' or 'Street children in South Africa'. If your interest is in home decorating, you may select a topic such as 'How to re-cover furniture'.

3. Write down the **general purpose** of your talk in one sentence. Is your intention to inform or instruct the audience about the topic, to persuade them or to entertain them? In the instance of the street children, you may simply want to inform the audience about the problem of street children, or you may want to persuade them to donate money to your cause. In the case of home decorating, your goal would probably be to inform the audience about the steps involved in re-covering furniture. You may of course want to persuade them that re-covering furniture is not as difficult as most people think.

4. Write down the **specific purpose** of your talk in one sentence. The specific purpose is a concise statement that describes the exact nature of the response you want from your audience. It indicates what you want your listeners to know, feel, believe or do at the end of your speech. A useful way to arrive at your specific purpose is to write down precisely what you hope to accomplish by the end of your speech. You should be able to express your specific purpose in one sentence similar to this: *At the end of my speech, I want my audience to ...* A well-written specific purpose should meet five requirements:

    ☐ it should contain one main idea

    ☐ it should be a complete sentence

    ☐ it should be clear and concise

    ☐ it should be worded as a statement, not as a question

    ☐ it should be worded in terms of the audience response you desire at the end of the speech (cf Samovar & Mills 1989; Lucas 1995).

Here is an example based on a persuasive speech:

Example 10.1

Topic: Street children in South Africa.
General purpose: To persuade.
Specific purpose: I want my audience to donate funds to build shelters for street children. (In this case, the specific purpose indicates what you want your audience to do at the end of the speech.)

5.   Write down the **topic statement** in one sentence. Whereas the specific
     purpose of your speech indicates what you wish to accomplish, the topic
     statement is a concise statement of what you expect to say. Since it is related
     to the specific purpose of your speech, at times the two may be similar. The
     topic statement is usually expressed in a simple, complete sentence that
     refines and sharpens the specific purpose statement. You ask yourself:
     "What ideas do I need to cover in my speech to accomplish my specific
     purpose?" The best way to practise formulating the topic statement is to
     pretend that you have to explain the gist of your talk to a friend in one
     sentence. Look at the following example:

Example 10.2

Topic:	South Africa's prison system.
Specific purpose:	I want my audience to understand the three major problems in South Africa's prison system.
Topic statement:	South Africa's prison system suffers from three major problems — overcrowding, lack of reliable rehabilitation programmes, and high expense to the taxpayer.

The topic statement is a summary of what you want your audience to know.
Another way to think of the central idea is that it is your 'residual message' —
what you want the audience to remember after they have forgotten everything
else in your speech. The topic statement helps you to identify the main points
that you will develop in the body or main part of your speech (cf Lucas 1995;
Beebe & Beebe 1997).

We have now narrowed our example from the subject area to the general
purpose, to the specific purpose, to the topic statement. Look at Figure 10.1. We
have illustrated the narrowing process as an inverted pyramid — wide at the top
and narrow at the bottom. Do you see how narrowing the topic is going to help
you write the body of your speech? Because you have identified the four main
points you will be concentrating on, you can limit your research. When you are
looking for information, you will be able to eliminate everything you do not
require to achieve your purpose, and concentrate on finding material to develop
the main points in your speech — each corresponding to one of the three
factors that explain the problems of prisons in South Africa, for example. In fact,
you might find it useful to write down the main points that you will have found
information about in order to deliver your speech. This is illustrated in Example
10.3.

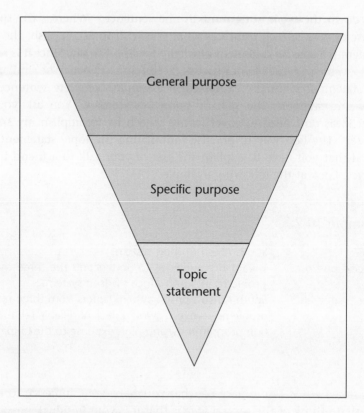

Figure 10.1 The narrowing process

Example 10.3

Topic:	HIV/AIDS in the workplace.
General purpose:	To inform.
Specific purpose:	I want my audience to understand the consequences of the problem of HIV/AIDS in the workplace.
Topic statement:	The three most important consequences of the problem of illiteracy in the workplace are: HIV/AIDS is detrimental to the individual; HIV/AIDS is detrimental to industry; HIV/AIDS is detrimental to the economy.
Main points:	(1) Why HIV/AIDS is detrimental to the individual
	(2) Why HIV/AIDS is detrimental to industry
	(3) Why HIV/AIDS is detrimental to the economy.

Notice that the topic statement provides a clear indication of the way you plan to develop your speech — it helps you identify what you want to say to your audience and focuses your attention on the information you are going to have to find.

Do not be concerned if you cannot write a complete topic statement at the outset. Sometimes you need to gather additional information to supplement the knowledge you already have, and it is not until after you have conducted some research on the topic that your topic statement can be completed.

Effective speeches begin with thorough preparation. At this stage in your speech preparation, you should feel confident that your topic and purpose are appropriate to the audience and the occasion. The process of narrowing the topic should already make you feel that you will be able to communicate your message with greater confidence and clarity.

10.4 Researching the topic

The main points you have arrived at only provide the outline or skeleton of the speech. Your next task as a speaker is to begin looking for information to support those ideas. Good supporting material indicates to your audience that you understand the topic thoroughly and that the information you provide is correct and soundly based. Supporting materials also make your ideas clear to your listeners. The word 'support' accurately describes their function because the materials you select will enable you to substantiate what you say. For example, in a persuasive speech on road safety you might say, "It is essential to drive within the speed limit. Now I will tell you why". The 'whys' are your form of support and enable you to offer reasons that might make your statement believable and acceptable to your listeners.

Generally a talk requires two sorts of material: information that you need for the content of your talk, and material such as illustrations, statistical evidence, expert opinion and quotations to support the information you provide. You can research the topic by using the material available in libraries and on the Internet, by conducting interviews, and by drawing on your personal experiences and observations.

10.4.1 Library sources

A library can be one of your richest sources of information. Libraries contain books, magazines, journal articles, encyclopaedias and other reference works, such as almanacs, biographical sources and government documents, in which you can find content information and supporting materials to integrate into your talk. Many libraries also provide information on electronic and computerised media such as film, audio- and videotapes and CDs. Finding the information is frustrating if you are inexperienced but, with a little practice, you will become familiar with the way your library catalogues books and other media. Most libraries today have fully computerised catalogue systems that record all the books and periodicals owned by the library. These systems allow you to find the book you are looking for by entering either the name of the author or the title of the book. If you do not have any specific titles in mind, you can enter the subject you are researching and the computer will generate a list of whatever books are available on that subject. If you are an inexperienced library user, your best option is to ask the librarian to explain the system they use and to help you find the information you require.

Most libraries also have computerised research services that can save you hours of work, especially if the topic of your speech is obscure and the information you require is not readily available in a book or periodical article. Make an appointment with the librarian to obtain help on how to access the databases that will provide the information you need. A database is a collection of information that can be read on a computer screen. Altogether, there are hundreds of databases covering topics from agriculture to zoology. The specific databases you can use will depend on the retrieval systems to which your library is connected. Computers are also the basis of the Internet, the worldwide network that carries information and entertainment along the Information Highway (refer to Chapter 1). You may be fortunate enough to have access to the Internet at home or at work. Otherwise, find out if your library makes provision for students to gain access to the Internet.

10.4.2 Interviews

Most people think of interviewing in terms of job interviews or interviews with celebrities. But interviewing for research purposes is an excellent way to gather information for speeches. Person-to-person contact with people who have experience in the area you are researching can provide expert opinion on a specific topic, an eyewitness account of an event or a personal testimony about a matter. Public officials, clergy, the police, school teachers and administrators, politicians, business people and, in fact, most people are willing to share information and opinions with students who confine questions to the area of the person's expertise. The interview allows you to view your topic from the perspective of the expert and often provides you with ideas and opinions that you could not have uncovered any other way. For example, if you are talking to a group of young people about the dangers of crash diets, you might want to interview a nutritionist about healthy eating habits. Or you could visit your local stamp dealer to find out what stamps are rare and why, and how stamps are collected, preserved and protected. You should be aware, however, that, while the interview can save you hours of library research, it does not entirely eliminate the need to read newspaper and magazine articles or to look for relevant books on the topic.

Interviewing requires thorough preparation if it is to be effective and yield the information you need. To have a successful interview, you need to carefully plan what to do before, during and after the interview. You should always make appointments with the people you wish to interview, inform them of the purpose of the interview, prepare the questions you need to ask to obtain the information in advance, and either tape the interview (with permission) or take notes.

10.4.3 Personal experiences and observation

The most basic source of information is yourself. Your own **experience** in the subject can provide information that is as interesting and valuable as facts and figures from books or interviews. Use your experience of, for instance, gardening, social work or home decoration to emphasise and illustrate the information you obtain from other sources.

Observation can help you and your audience picture a situation more vividly. For instance, to provide examples for a talk on dress codes in organisations, you could visit a business or professional centre and take note of the way people in different positions and departments are dressed. If you are planning to talk to a group of schoolchildren about how the fire department operates, you can learn about the operation by visiting your local fire department and observing the process in action. You could make your talk even more interesting by interviewing a fire fighter to obtain first-hand anecdotes about his or her experiences in the field.

Personal experiences and observations alone may not always convince your audience that your information is correct. It often helps to substantiate personal knowledge by supplementing or combining it with information (quotations or statistics) obtained from interviews or library sources.

10.4.4 Recording your information and citing your sources

Since library research is time-consuming, it is very important to learn to take notes as you do your reading. You also need to keep track of the information you obtain in interviews, and even from personal knowledge and observation. The reason you record information is to be able to provide its source in your speech, or tell an audience member who is interested where to find it.

Whenever you use ideas that are not your own, you need to acknowledge the source of your information. Your speeches will be far more credible if you provide the audience with the source of your information. It will also help them evaluate the content of your speech. In a written report, ideas taken from other sources are acknowledged in full. In a speech, your acknowledgement or citation need not give full biographical details — your audience will not remember them and too much detail may cause them to lose concentration. However, you must remember to have the complete biographical details available for anyone who asks for them.

10.5 Writing the talk

The written preparation for an oral presentation determines the quality of the end result. Thorough preparation enables the speaker to organise the material in a logical sequence, making it easier for the audience to follow and understand. Effective talks have three main parts: introduction, body and conclusion, each of which has a specific purpose.

10.5.1 The introduction

The introduction is a crucial part of an oral presentation. The opening comments establish the impression the audience forms of you and of the topic. Although it is only a small part of the talk, you should prepare it thoroughly and polish it until you are happy that it will have the desired effect. In the introduction, you should aim to achieve four goals: gain the audience's attention, establish your credibility as a speaker, establish rapport with the audience and state the purpose of your talk.

Telling a humorous or dramatic story, using an impressive quotation or startling statement, or asking a rhetorical question that relates to the topic are often effective openers as they gain audience attention. A rhetorical question is one to which you don't expect an answer from the audience, but which starts them thinking about the topic. For example, in a speech to high school pupils about preparing for examinations, starting your speech by saying, "Would you like to pass all your examinations this year with a distinction?" would undoubtedly grab the attention of your audience.

Having captured their attention, you establish rapport (goodwill) with the audience by indicating that you share their interests and concerns. If someone is concerned about me, the chances are I will identify more with that person. You should then establish your credentials and provide some background information so that the audience knows it can trust you. For instance, would you accept advice on lifesaving techniques more readily from a person who has had Red Cross training or from one who does not bother to explain the source of his or her expertise? Finally, the introduction should contain a brief statement of the topic and a reason for the audience to listen. You can then briefly outline the main points that are to be discussed. For instance, in a persuasive speech on the importance of voting, you could say something like this: "In this speech, I am going to explain four reasons why you should all vote in the next election." Do you see how this has created a natural transition into the body of your talk?

Writing the introduction after the body of the talk has been planned helps to ensure that all relevant information has been included.

10.5.2 The body of the talk

In the body of your talk, you will elaborate on the ideas mentioned in the introduction. The body of the talk must be organised to allow the recipients to follow the arguments easily, recognise important points, clarify abstract ideas, reinforce critical issues, and draw conclusions with confidence. Remember that, unlike written material which can be read several times, spoken material must be understood the first time. A simple technique for highlighting the main points is to number the ideas. This approach guides the listeners through the talk and helps them to write meaningful notes.

The main ideas must also be arranged in a logical pattern. Give some thought to the following three organisational techniques and then choose one which best suits your purpose: sequential, logical and topical (Abrams 1986; Steinberg 1994; Lucas 1995; Gamble & Gamble 1998b; Steinberg 1999b). When you use a sequential pattern, you discuss ideas in order of time (chronological) or in order of space (spatial). Using a time order is easily illustrated by subjects that deal with matters of history — you begin your discussion with a review of the past and move on to a discussion of the present. For example, you might describe the evolution of modern astronomy from the Chinese stargazers of the 13th century BC to the creation of the SALT telescope in Sutherland, Western Cape, in 2006. A chronological speech may span centuries or days, depending on the scope of the topic.

☐ *Sequential pattern* Speeches that are arranged in a space or spatial order focus on direction. When you use a space order you are telling the audience that there is a special significance in the positioning of the information. A space order helps your audience visualise your subject in an orderly way. You explain by arranging the main points from top to bottom (or vice versa), left to right (or vice versa), front to back (or vice versa), north to south (or vice versa), or any direction that best suits your subject. For example, you might discuss the planets in the Solar System by beginning with the one closest to the Sun and moving in order away from the Sun. Similarly, in a discussion of the stadiums hosting the different soccer matches of the 2010 World Cup, you could arrange the stadiums from north to south, starting with the FNB stadium in Soweto and moving southwards towards Bloemfontein, Durban and Cape Town (cf De Jager 1997).

☐ *Topical pattern* Sometimes the relationships among the main points of a topic may not lend themselves to a chronological or a spatial pattern — they are simply parts of a whole. Speakers who use a topical pattern of organisation divide the topic into parts or categories and then move from one part to the next showing how they are related. You can use a topical order whenever your subject can be grouped logically into subtopics, such as the component parts of a washing machine, the functions of nonverbal communication, the roles of employees in a shoe factory, the qualities or features of a product, the levels of hierarchy in an organisation and so forth. You can discuss the parts in any order as long as you do not leave any out. For example, if your specific purpose is: *'I want my audience to understand five different systems in the human body'*, you could divide your talk into five parts: nervous system, respiratory system, circulatory system, skeletal system and digestive system. Each part is a subdivision of the topic 'systems of the human body'. There is no fixed sequence for ordering the systems as long as all five are covered. Like the chronological and spatial organisational patterns, the topical pattern is most suitable for informative speeches. Because it is so versatile, it is also used more often than any other method of speech organisation.

☐ ***Logical pattern*** Although all organisational patterns are logical, the type specifically called logical emphasises the reasoning process. This is done by showing how one thing affects another, in other words, cause and effect, or problem and solution. Showing cause and effect allows you to indicate what will happen as a result of a certain event or idea. In persuasive speeches, you take cause and effect one step further and offer a solution to the result (effect) of the problem (cause). For example, you would use causal order when you want to persuade your listeners that a high-fat diet, little exercise and smoking cause heart problems. You would then use your arguments to persuade them to change to a healthier lifestyle.

10.5.3 The conclusion

The conclusion and introduction should complement one another and are best written together. The conclusion is as important as the introduction. An effective conclusion leaves the audience with the impression that the topic has been fully covered. The goals you should strive for in the conclusion are the following: to reinforce the central idea(s); to sum up and tie the main points together; to remind the audience why the information is important to them; and to motivate them to think or act on the ideas presented.

After you have completed your speech, you need to refresh your audience's memory by summarising the main points. Most of us cannot remember large amounts of new information for very long, even if we listen attentively. The summary should briefly restate the most important information. You do this by restating the purpose of your talk and the main points you used in the introduction, and then tie up the ideas by repeating two or three key words that were used in the body of the talk. Try to leave your audience with a final impression by using the same techniques as in the introduction — a quotation, rhetorical question or startling statement that leaves no doubt about your position on the topic. For example, the last sentence in the conclusion to the speech about street children could be a startling statement: "You never know — you or a member of your family might be the next victim of a neglected street child who has turned to crime in order to earn a living!"

10.6 Organisational techniques for specific purposes

The basic organisation of introduction, body and conclusion can be used to develop any of the purposes discussed earlier in this chapter. Nevertheless, each purpose has some unique features, and special techniques are used to develop each one.

10.6.1 Informative talks

Since the purpose of an **informative talk** is to increase the audience's knowledge and understanding of a topic, it is essential to use supporting details to validate main ideas. Especially if a main idea is an abstract thought or a feeling, it must be supported with concrete evidence. Ensure that the supporting information is relevant and adds to the audience's understanding of the topic.

- ❒ *Statistics* such as dates and percentages can validate your main points, but should be used sparingly. Too many statistics will make it difficult for your audience to absorb the information.

- ❒ Using specific *examples* of a person or event, or briefly relating stories, anecdotes, and personal experiences helps to explain your main ideas and personalise and humanise a talk, making it more interesting for the listeners.

- ❒ *Quotations* of an authority on the topic create impact and help establish the validity of your own ideas. Make sure that the quotation is pertinent and that you give credit to the original writer or speaker.

10.6.2 Instructive talks

When the purpose of your talk is to instruct, you usually want your audience to be able to do something. In this case, you put the information you provide into practice by using a variety of props or aids to demonstrate the procedure you are describing. Whether you are giving a cookery or flower-arranging demonstration, explaining how a machine works, demonstrating dance steps or teaching colleagues to interpret a balance sheet, you need to prepare materials to illustrate what you are saying. Often, you can gain the audience's attention and interest by involving them in the demonstration. The props you use do not replace the oral part of the talk. You continue to provide information and explain the procedure while you are busy with the demonstration.

10.6.3 Persuasive talks

In a **persuasive speech**, your goal is usually to establish a need and then show how the need can be met, or to describe a problem and then offer a solution. Certain ways of organising speeches seem to be especially effective for persuasive presentations. In Section 10.5.2 we discussed the 'cause and effect order' and 'problem-solution order' as two organisational patterns that work well for persuasive speeches. There is another organisational pattern that is especially effective for problem-solving speeches. It is called Monroe's motivated sequence and was developed by Alan Monroe in the 1930s.

Monroe's motivated sequence

Monroe's motivated sequence consists of five steps designed to persuade listeners to accept a point of view and then motivate them to take the desired action. The five steps are as follows:

1. **Attention** Begin your talk with material that satisfies the three purposes of a good introduction (gets attention, establishes rapport and states the purpose of the talk). You could, for example, create interest by beginning the speech with a startling statement.
2. **Need** To gain the sympathy and co-operation of the audience, you must prove that a problem exists by describing it with the use of relevant statistics, examples and quotations. You then relate the problem to the audience's needs or interests.
3. **Satisfaction** Present your solution to alleviate the problem and satisfy the individual's needs or interests.
4. **Visualisation** Explain what will happen if they act on the solution or if they fail to do so. In this step, the speaker often appeals to the audience's emotions by contrasting the negative results of not taking action with the positive results that acting on the solution will achieve.
5. **Action** Tell the audience what it is you want them to do to bring about the desired change. Make sure that your request is within the audience's power. You cannot expect a church group to solve the problem of street children, for instance, but you can ask them to donate money or to collect clothing.

Example 10.4

Let's look at how the student editor of a campus newspaper used the motivated sequence to develop her persuasive speech (cf Hybels & Weaver 1989). Take note of how the motivated sequence structures the main points of the speech. For each main point, the student would have to support her assertions with appropriate supporting material such as examples, statistics and expert testimony.

Topic:	Campus newspaper.
General purpose:	To persuade.
Specific purpose:	At the end of my speech I want the audience to sign a petition that suggests changes in the way the campus newspaper is funded.
Topic statement:	When the university funds the newspaper, it often tries to control the news.
Main points:	1. **Attention** This week the university said it will stop funding the campus newspaper unless the newspaper stops criticising the University Council.
	2. **Need** We have had this problem before. Whenever the university doesn't like what the paper says, it closes the paper down. The result is that you can't find out what's been happening on campus during the week.
	3. **Satisfaction** The only way to solve this problem is to charge a small fee for the paper and create our own fund.
	4. **Visualisation** The newspaper will be able to continue playing its role as watchdog of Council, and all of you will no longer find that the paper has not come out because the university has closed it down.
	5. **Action** I have a petition addressed to the principal of the university. I strongly urge all of you to sign it.

10.7 Preparing the delivery

Delivery is a practical outcome of public speaking. Therefore, a great deal of the information in this section consists of guidelines to help you present your speech successfully. Because of the practical nature of delivery, we suggest that you constantly think about well-known public speakers to whom you have listened, either on 'real' speaking occasions or on television. How does President Thabo Mbeki use language, voice and nonverbal communication? When does he read his speeches from a manuscript and when does he speak without notes? What do other politicians do? You could also think about a talk-show host like Oprah Winfrey or a TV celebrity like Gareth Cliff. In so doing, you will learn far more about effective delivery than if you only study the material in this unit.

A well-researched and prepared talk is not effective unless it is presented in a polished and professional manner. Rehearsing the talk will enable you to gain confidence, make sure that you handle any visual aids or props that are to be used, discover and eliminate any problems and check the timing of the talk. It is also good practice to think through the answers to possible questions that may arise at the end of the talk. Take the following five factors into consideration when you prepare the delivery: using notes, the language of the message, using your voice, nonverbal behaviour and dealing with questions (cf Strano, Mohan & McGregor 1989; Borcherds et al 1990).

10.7.1 Using notes

A speech that is read from a manuscript is usually boring. Organising the material into notes serves as reminders of salient points and is often the best preparation against speech apprehension or 'speaker's nerves'. This technique enables you to look at the audience and make a carefully planned talk seem spontaneous and natural. Small cards that summarise main ideas in point form are ideal for this purpose. The cards should be numbered and only one side used for writing. Good notes have headings for each main point on a separate card, followed by numbered subheadings. A brief summary of the point and essential facts, figures or examples are added under each heading, as well as reminders of any visual aids that are to be used.

Example 10.5

A notecard for a speech on street children
Topic: Street children in South Africa.
Street children need foster care to provide a family life
A   Testimony from a well-known psychologist
B   Statistics comparing juvenile offences in children from stable families and children from orphanages
    (Look up and show visual aid)
C   Question and answer session with two street children who have agreed to be interviewed in front of the audience.

10.7.2 The language of oral messages

An important reason for rehearsing the delivery is that spoken language differs from written. Language meant to be heard is personal and direct and must allow the listener instant comprehension of meaning. Directness is achieved by using the active rather than passive voice and addressing the audience as 'you'. It is important to select words that the audience will understand and to explain any essential technical terms that are used. However, it is best to avoid colloquialisms and slang.

Readers can refer back to a written message, but the audience hears the spoken word only once. The most crucial ideas should thus be restated several times during the body of the talk, using different words and examples to help the listener absorb the information. Transition words such as 'however', 'therefore', 'consequently' and 'finally', help the audience to make the connection between a new idea and one that has already been presented, and alerts them to the type of information about to be received.

10.7.3 Using your voice

Effective oral communication is more than selecting the right words. The speaker's voice should be clear and the enunciation correct and distinct. You should practise the use of intonation, stress and changes in pace and pitch, to provide variety and achieve different effects. For example, a conversational, relaxed tone of voice creates a pleasant atmosphere for the audience, whereas an animated and enthusiastic delivery causes the audience to become more attentive and creates an emotional or persuasive mood.

Pay particular attention to the volume or loudness of your voice, the rate or speed at which you speak, and decide when to introduce pauses. You also need to vary the pitch of your voice, that is, the highness or lowness of the tone of your voice, and to make sure that you articulate and pronounce all the words correctly. **Articulation** is the ability to say the individual sounds or letters in a word correctly. **Pronunciation** is the ability to say the whole word in a way that is accepted as correct. Poor articulation and pronunciation irritate listeners because they send unclear messages that take time and effort to interpret. You also need to ensure that vocal interferences do not become excessive because you have perhaps not rehearsed your speech sufficiently. **Vocal interferences** are the sounds and words we use when we hesitate or are not sure of the right word. We all use the occasional "uh, er, well" and "you know" to indicate that we are searching for the right word. Vocal interferences are part of everyday speech and are also acceptable in public speaking. But such interferences become a problem when they interrupt your listeners' concentration and comprehension.

10.7.4 Nonverbal behaviour

An awareness of how nonverbal messages, such as body movement, gestures, posture and appearance, convey meaning increases your chances of success in two ways: it helps you appear relaxed and natural, and it helps you to measure the audience's reactions. A good speaker looks directly at the audience, makes eye contact and smiles from time to time. Gestures and other body movements help you to appear more natural, provided they are not overdone and distract attention from the presentation. The way you dress is another nonverbal message. Clothing and personal appearance influence the audience's initial impression. Try to look your best regarding clothes and personal grooming, but at the same time also try to meet the norms for the occasion. Remember that a speech is a formal occasion and listeners expect the speaker to dress more formally than usual and to be well groomed. However, you also need to remember that nonverbal behaviour varies from culture to culture. Your audience analysis should help you decide what is appropriate.

10.7.5 Dealing with questions

Decide in advance whether the audience should be free to ask questions during the talk, or whether questions should be kept until the end. The question period allows the speaker to clarify or expand on points raised in the talk. It is important to listen carefully, right to the end of the question. Then repeat or rephrase the question to eliminate the possibility of misunderstanding, and to ensure that the entire audience has heard it. No matter how redundant or personal the question, you must always remain courteous and avoid sarcasm.

You cannot know exactly what questions will be asked, but you know your topic so well by now that you can anticipate some of the questions audience members are likely to ask, and you can prepare answers to them in advance. It is advisable to keep your answers simple and not to answer more than what has been asked. When faced with a question to which you do not have an answer, you should admit ignorance and offer to find out the answer, or ask for the opinion of an acknowledged expert who may be in the audience.

The question period should not be allowed to continue beyond the time limit of the talk. Should two or three people start a discussion among themselves, interrupt as politely as possible and invite those people to continue the discussion with you immediately after the presentation. Apart from questions and answers, you should take note of the general feedback from the audience (including nonverbal behaviour) and use it to improve your future presentations.

10.8 Visuals

Using visuals or graphics to illustrate your ideas can increase the effectiveness of your presentation. They help to attract and hold audience attention, speed up the comprehension process and assist the audience to retain information, clarify abstract ideas and act as guidelines to keep both speaker and audience focused on the topic.

Visuals may include charts, tables, graphs, maps, diagrams, photographs, handouts and props. You can make your own or use illustrations you find while researching your topic. It is important to select only the most appropriate visuals, that is, those that will assist in communicating the message as effectively as possible. Remember that visuals do not replace verbal information: they complement and support it. It is you, the speaker, who puts the message across.

Before deciding on which visual aids to use, consider the cost, the purpose, the time available, the venue, the audience and the situation. To be effective, visuals should serve a specific purpose, be clear and intelligible and be well integrated into the talk. You also need to develop the skills needed for the efficient operation of equipment you will require to use the visuals, such as an overhead projector or chalkboard, a tape recorder, or a laptop with presentation software. Visuals that are badly prepared, or used because it is the 'done thing' serve no purpose and create barriers to effective communication, particularly if you find difficulty in using them properly. In general, the following aspects should be kept in mind (cf Rensburg & Bredenkamp 1991):

- Visuals must be kept as simple as possible
- Visuals must illustrate the point clearly
- Decide on the best time in the presentation to show the visual
- Everybody in the audience must be able to see the visuals clearly
- The presenter must not speak to the visual. You should face the audience in order to be audible and maintain audience contact at all times
- The visuals should be in view only when they being used
- Practise using the equipment in advance so that the presentation flows smoothly. You must also make sure that the apparatus is in working order.

Figures 10.2 to 10.6 illustrate five types of visual materials which could be used to focus your audience's attention on important parts of your talk and increase the effectiveness of your presentation.

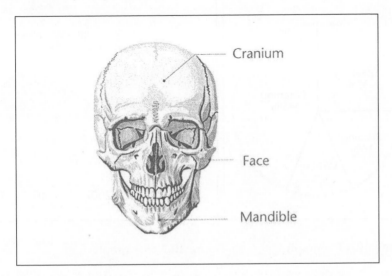

Figure 10.2 A drawing of the human skull

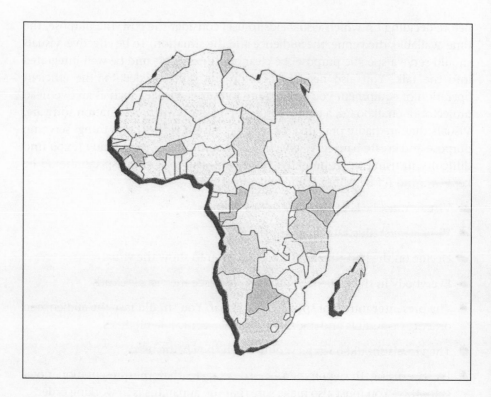

Figure 10.3 A map of Africa

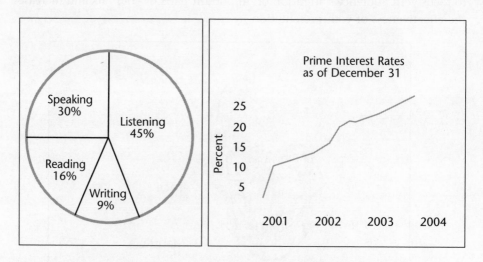

Figure 10.4 Pie graph   Figure 10.5 Line graph

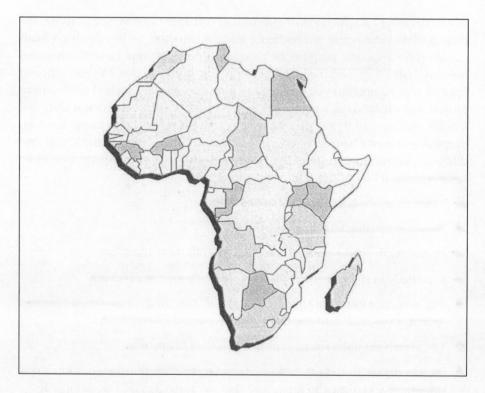

Figure 10.3 A map of Africa

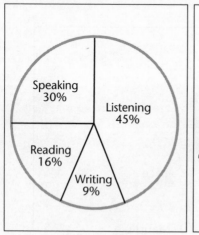

Figure 10.4 Pie graph

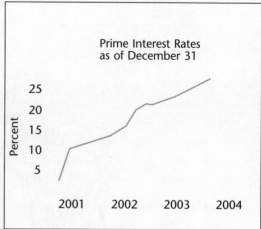

Figure 10.5 Line graph

Figure 10.6 A computer-generated graphic

10.9 Evaluating speeches

One of the most effective ways of learning what makes a good speech is to evaluate your own and other people's speeches. Evaluation does not mean that we look only for the weak points in a speech. It means that we look for the positive aspects as well. Through evaluation you will get an idea of what works and what does not work in a speech. You should be able to apply what you learn from your evaluation of other people's speeches to improving your own speeches.

10.9.1 Principles of speech evaluation

There are different systems of evaluation. A system that is recommended for beginner speakers relates the degree to which the speech conforms to the theoretical principles of public speaking, that is, to the principles we have been discussing in this chapter. We summarise the five general principles by which speeches are usually judged when using this system (cf Minnick 1983).

☐ ***What kind of speech did the occasion demand?*** Was the speech meant to inform, to persuade or to entertain? In answering this question, you can judge how well the speaker understood the topic and the occasion and whether the speaker met the requirements of each type of speech.

☐ ***Did the speaker understand the needs of the audience and did he or she adapt the message and content to those needs?*** Public speaking is a two-way process. Speakers must analyse their audiences according to the factors discussed in Section 10.2 and adjust what they say to those factors.

☐ **_The quality of the speaker's material_** Has the speaker researched the topic thoroughly? Does the speaker seem to have used the best sources available? Does the supporting material substantiate the main points? Does the evidence come from reliable sources? Are the conclusions and recommendations logical? Is the material organised in a way that is understandable to the audience?

☐ **_The impression made by the speaker_** Does he or she seem to be a person whose motives can be trusted? Does the speaker appear to be taking advantage of the audience? Does the speaker seem to respect the audience? Does the speaker appear to be knowledgeable about the topic and is he or she well prepared? Does the speaker appear to be credible?

☐ **_The speaker's delivery_**, or the way in which the message was transmitted to the audience. Was the language clear and vivid? Did the speaker make use of nonverbal communication? How did the speaker use his or her voice?

Learning to evaluate speeches takes time and practice. To encourage you to practise evaluating the speeches you listen to, we provide an evaluation form (Figure 10.7) based on the five principles discussed above.

Speech evaluation form
Speaker _____
Topic _____
Date _____
Use the following scale to evaluate the elements of the speech:
Outstanding   Good   Average   Fair   Poor
    1   2   3   4   5

Choice of topic
Was appropriate for the occasion _____
Was appropriate for the audience _____
Was appropriate for the speaker _____

Purpose
Was clear _____
Was appropriate for the audience _____
Was achieved _____

Adaptation to audience
Speaker was audience-centred _____
Speaker adapted to listeners_____

Introduction
Captured my attention _____
Established the speaker's credibility_____
Introduced the topic _____
Established rapport (motivated me to listen) _____

Quality of material
Research was thorough _____
Sources were credible _____
Speech had an introduction, a body and a conclusion_____
Main points were organised in a logical way _____
Speech was easy to follow _____
Supporting material was interesting and varied _____
Supporting material substantiated the main points_____

Delivery
Use of language _____
Use of voice _____
Enunciation and pronunciation _____
Use of nonverbal behaviour _____

Impression of speaker
Speaker showed respect for the audience _____
Speaker showed knowledge of the topic _____
Speaker had prepared thoroughly_____
Speaker appeared to be credible_____
Best aspects of speech_____
_____
_____
Improvements needed_____
_____
_____

Figure 10.7 Speech evaluation form

Scenario 10.1

Use the speech evaluation form to evaluate the following speech by former president Nelson Mandela.

Former President Nelson Mandela's first official speech as President of South Africa at his inauguration ceremony, Pretoria, 10 May 1994

Today, all of us do, by our presence here, and by our celebrations in other parts of our country and the world, confer glory and hope to newborn liberty.

Out of the experience of an extraordinary human disaster that lasted too long, must be born a society of which all humanity will be proud.

Our daily deeds as ordinary South Africans must produce an actual South African reality that will reinforce humanity's belief in justice, strengthen its confidence in the nobility of the human soul and sustain all our hopes for a glorious life for all.

All this we owe both to ourselves and to the people of the world who are so well represented here today. To my compatriots, I have no hesitation in saying that each one of us is as intimately attached to the soil of this beautiful country as are the famous Jacaranda trees of Pretoria and the Mimosa trees of the bushveld. Each time one of us touches the soil of this land, we feel a sense of personal renewal. The national mood changes as the seasons change. We are moved by a sense of joy and exhilaration when the grass turns green and the flowers bloom.

That spiritual and physical oneness we all share with this common homeland explains the depth of the pain we all carried in our hearts as we saw our country tear apart in a terrible conflict, and as we saw it spurned, outlawed and isolated by the peoples of the world, precisely because it had become the universal base of pernicious ideology and practice of racism and racial oppression.

We, the people of South Africa, feel fulfilled that humanity has taken us back into its bosom; that we, who were outlaws not so long ago, have today been given the rare privilege to be host to the nations of the world on our own soil. We thank all our distinguished international guests for having come to take possession with the people of our country of what is, after all, a common victory for justice, for peace, for human dignity.

We trust that you will continue to stand by us as we tackle the challenges of building peace, prosperity, non-sexism, non-racialism and democracy.

We deeply appreciate the role that the masses of our people and their political, mass democratic, religious, women, youth, business, traditional and other leaders have played to bring about this conclusion. Not least among them is my second deputy president, the Honourable FW de Klerk.

We also like to pay tribute to our security forces, in all their ranks, for the distinguished role they have played in securing our first democratic elections and the transition to democracy, from bloodthirsty forces which still refuse to see the light.

The time for healing of the wounds has come. The moment to bridge the chasms that divide us has come. The time to build is upon us.

We have, at last, achieved our political emancipation. We pledge ourselves to liberate all our people from the continuing bondage of poverty, deprivation, suffering, and gender and other discrimination.

We have succeeded in taking our last steps to freedom in conditions of relative peace. We commit ourselves to the construction of a complete, just and lasting peace.

We have triumphed in the effort to implant hope in the breasts of the millions of our people. We enter into a covenant that we shall build a society in which all South Africans, both black and white, will be able to walk tall, without any fear in their hearts, assured of their inalienable right to human dignity – a rainbow nation at peace with itself and the world.

As a token of its commitment to the renewal of our country, the new interim Government of National Unity will, as a matter of urgency, address the issue of amnesty for various categories of our people who are currently serving terms of imprisonment.

We dedicate this day to all the heroes and heroines in this country and the rest of the world who sacrificed in many ways and surrendered their lives so that we could be free. Their dreams have become reality. Freedom is their reward.

We are both humbled and elevated by the honour and privilege that you, the people of South Africa, have bestowed on us, as the first president of a united, democratic, non-racial and non-sexist South Africa, to lead our country out of the valley of darkness.

We understand that there is no easy road to freedom. We know it well that none of us acting alone can achieve success. We must therefore act together as a united people, for national reconciliation, for nation building, for the birth of a new world.

Let there be justice for all. Let there be peace for all. Let there be work, bread, water and salt for all. Let each know that for each the body, the mind and the soul have been freed to fulfil themselves.

Never, never and never again shall it be that this beautiful land will experience the oppression of one another and suffer the indignity of being the skunk of the world.

Let freedom reign. The sun shall never set on so glorious a human achievement. God bless Africa!

Summary

This chapter began by explaining the importance of public speaking skills in your professional and social life. It then went through the steps in the speech-making process. The first step is to determine the general purpose of your speech: is it an informative, persuasive or entertaining talk? The next step is to analyse the audience. Audience analysis requires three types of information: demographic, psychographic and sociographic. The occasion that prompted the speech and the setting where it will be given must also be analysed. The next step in the process is to select a topic for the speech. The chapter explained how to narrow down the topic to arrive at the main points that will be discussed in the talk. This step requires that we define the subject area of the talk, a specific topic within the subject area, the specific purpose of the talk and the topic statement. The next task is to find information to support those ideas. The chapter said that good supporting materials make your ideas clear to your listeners and suggested where to find information.

The next step is to write the speech. A speech has an introduction, a body, and a conclusion, each of which has a specific purpose. Regarding the body of the speech, the chapter described three organisational patterns used to present the main points in a logical and understandable way: sequential, logical and topical patterns. It then described specific features of the informative talk, the instructive talk and the persuasive talk. The final step in speech preparation is to rehearse the delivery. The chapter pointed out that rehearsing the talk enables you to gain confidence, make sure that you can handle any visual aids or props that are to be used, discover and eliminate any problems, and check the timing of the talk. It is also good practice to think through the answers to possible questions that may arise at the end of the talk. The chapter discussed the verbal and nonverbal elements of delivery that play a crucial part in determining the success of your presentation as well as the effective use of visual materials. The last part of the chapter dealt with the evaluation of a speech to answer the question: Why are some speeches more effective than others? The chapter ended with a scenario based on Ex-President Nelson Mandela's first official speech as president of South Africa.

Test yourself

1. What kind of information do you think is of more value: demographic, psychographic or sociographic? Explain your answer.
2. You have been invited to present the prizes at the end-of-year ceremony at a rural primary school in South Africa. Describe the information you would gather about the occasion and the setting. Or, choose your own example as the basis of your answer.
3. Scan the headlines of a newspaper, or listen to radio or television news, or to a talk show, and then write down three topics that would be appropriate for a speech.
4. Apply the four steps involved in selecting a topic for an oral presentation to a speech of your choice.
5. Write an outline for the body of the speech you selected in question 4. Identify the organisational technique or pattern you used. Then write the introduction and conclusion. Explain how you captured the audience's attention.
6. Choose three types of supporting material for the speech you have selected and explain where you would look for it.
7. Prepare note cards for the speech you have selected.
8. Select visuals for the talk and explain how they will increase your audience's understanding of the topic.
9. Name the five steps in Monroe's motivated sequence. Then use the sequence to develop a two-to-three minute speech to persuade your audience of fellow students to begin an exercise programme. Make clear to your listeners exactly what you want them to do and why they should do it.
10. Watch a 10-minute segment of a television drama or comedy with the sound turned off. What do the characters 'say' with their nonverbal behaviour (dress, gestures, facial expressions, and so on)?
11. Why is it important to evaluate your own and other people's speeches?

EXECUTIVE SUMMARY
Public speaking

1 Stages in preparation of speeches
   ❑ determine the purpose — to inform, to persuade and to entertain
   ❑ analyse the audience's
       — psychographics
       — sociographics
   ❑ select the topic
       — the subject area
       — a specific topic
       — purpose
       — topic statement
   ❑ research the topic
   ❑ write the talk
       — introduction, body and conclusion
   ❑ organisational techniques
       — sequential pattern
       — topical pattern
       — logical pattern
       — Monroe's motivated sequence
   ❑ prepare the delivery
       — using visuals
2 Speech evaluation

11 Mass communication

Overview

You open your favourite newspaper or magazine and your eye catches a colourful photograph of a smart hotel on a sunny beach. You spend some time studying the picture and reading the information. The next thing you know is that you are daydreaming about how wonderful it would be to go on holiday to an exotic destination like Mauritius — a place you have often heard about, but never visited. The fact that you have never been out of South Africa makes the idea of such a holiday even more appealing. Of course you are not the only recipient of this advertisement. Thousands of readers have also seen it and many of them probably had a similar response to yours. That is exactly why the hotel group chose to advertise the holiday destination in a mass communication medium.

In this chapter we discuss the mass communication context. We first explain the term 'mass' and define 'mass communication' and 'mass media' to distinguish between them. The process of mass communication is then discussed by contrasting it with interpersonal communication. We follow this with the functions that mass communication performs in society. In the remainder of the chapter we broaden your understanding of mass communication and its influence on society and people by examining the components of the mass communication process in greater detail: the mass communicator, the mass medium and the audiences of mass communication. Throughout the discussion we refer to some of the research studies and theories that contribute to our understanding of this form of communication. These theories include gatekeeping, agenda-setting, spiral of silence, magic-bullet, two-step flow and uses and gratifications theory. To show you how a theory can be applied in practice, we use a scenario to illustrate uses and gratifications theory. To conclude, we discuss the social effects of mass communication with particular reference to technological or media determinism. Technological determinism sees social change as a direct result of fundamental technological development and innovation. To illustrate this approach, we examine Marshall McLuhan's views — the power of the medium to change people's lives and the nature of society. The discussion revolves around the main concepts in his theory: the medium is the message, the global village, the ratio of the senses, hot and cool media, an eye for an ear and the Gutenberg Galaxy. We conclude with the views of two theorists who are critical of McLuhan's belief in the power of the media to bring about cultural and social changes. We end the chapter with a case based on a commentary on McLuhan's views by Baran and Davies (2003).

Learning outcomes

At the end of this unit you should be able to:

1   Define the terms 'mass', 'mass communication' and 'mass media'.
2   Describe the process of mass communication by contrasting interpersonal and mass communication.
3   Explain four functions of mass communication and illustrate each with an appropriate example.
4   Describe the role of the gatekeeper in mass communication and list some of the factors that influence the gatekeeper's choices.
5   Describe the effects of the mass media on public opinion by referring to the agenda-setting theory and the spiral of silence theory.
6   Describe how the magic-bullet theory, two-step flow theory, and uses and gratifications theory differ in explaining how the mass media influence their audiences.
7   Discuss the assumptions of media determinism.
8   Explain the following concepts in McLuhan's theory:
   ❏   the medium is the message
   ❏   hot and cool media
   ❏   ratio of the senses
   ❏   the Gutenberg Galaxy
   ❏   'an eye for an ear'
   ❏   the global village.
9   After considering the positive and negative consequences of media revolutions, give your own opinion about McLuhan's view that 'the medium is the message'.
10 Answer the questions based on the two cases in this chapter.

Introduction

Our discussion of the history of communication in Chapter 1 established that mass communication has become an integral part of life in modern societies. We are living in the Information Age, an era when communication media and the technology associated with them have become central to nearly all that we do. We would be hard pressed to imagine a day in our professional or social lives without the mass media and mass communication. In this chapter we do not study the media used for mass communication (such as newspapers, television or computers) in great depth, but concentrate rather on the nature of mass communication and its effects on society and on people. We begin with a discussion of the concept 'mass'.

11.1 The concept of mass

The word **'mass'** itself has acquired positive and negative connotations in society and therefore influences the way people define and think about mass communication and the mass media. For example, mass can be used negatively to describe a mob of unruly and ignorant people. Therefore, it is not uncommon for people who think of mass in such derogatory terms to regard the mass media as being inferior and corruptive. In a more positive sense, mass is used to describe the strength and solidarity of ordinary people. It appears, for example, in terms such as 'mass movement', 'mass action' and 'mass support' (McQuail 1987). From such a positive perspective, the mass media are considered to be instruments of enlightenment for most people. For our purposes, we pay attention to the neutral and descriptive meanings of the term. From such a perspective, mass has the following meanings:

- the multiple or mass production of messages

- the large size of the audiences that are reached by the mass media

- an amorphous group of which the individual components are difficult to distinguish from each other (McQuail 1987).

These meanings can be used to define and distinguish mass communication and mass media. **Mass communication** is a process of delivering information, ideas and attitudes to a sizeable and diversified audience through a medium developed for that purpose (Agee et al 1988). The **mass media** are the technologies and social institutions (such as newspapers, radio and TV) that are involved in the production and distribution of messages to large audiences. It is important to be aware that, while the mass media are essential in the process of mass communication, they represent the technological instruments used to convey messages to large audiences — they do not constitute the process involved.

11.2 The process of mass communication

It is perhaps easier to understand the process of mass communication by first contrasting it with something we are already familiar with — interpersonal communication — and then illustrating its complex nature with the help of a model.

In Chapter 3, we described interpersonal communication as a transactional process between two (or more) people in a face-to-face encounter. Interpersonal communication usually involves a single source (the communicator) and a single receiver (the recipient) who are known to one another and whose purpose is to engage in a meaningful exchange of messages. A characteristic of interpersonal communication is that the participants continually provide feedback or respond to each other's verbal and nonverbal messages. Feedback is immediate and gives communication its dynamic nature by allowing the participants to exchange roles while negotiating meaning to reach mutual understanding.

Mass communication has distinctive characteristics which concern the basic components in the communication process. As we discuss these characteristics, bear in mind that, unlike interpersonal communication, mass communication is mediated — it involves the use of complex technology to multiply messages and transmit them to large numbers of recipients simultaneously. The term used to describe the recipients of mass communication is the **mass audience**.

The **communicator** in mass communication is not a single individual, but a member of a team within an organisation (such as a newspaper or television station) involved in the production and distribution of messages. Listed in a newspaper, for example, you find (among others) the names of reporters, editors, photographers, layout artists, printers and salespeople, each of whom contributes to the production and distribution of the newspaper. Similarly, the **recipients** of mass communication are not single individuals but consist of large audiences who are not personally known to the communicator, or even to each other. The audience is too large for the communicator to be able to interact with personally. This does not mean that individual recipients of mass communication messages are isolated from one another. We regularly experience mass communication in dyads, small groups or organisations. You most often visit the cinema with a friend; a group of students in a residence may watch a TV programme together in the communal lounge; the entire cast of a new theatrical production may be reading the reviews in the press over breakfast the day after the opening night.

Because the demographic characteristics of audience members are diverse, messages are not personally addressed to particular individuals, but are public — they are directed at groups of people who may not have very much in common. Note the difference between public speaking and mass communication. The principal of a school addresses a meeting of parents in the school hall to discuss problems pupils are experiencing. Although she may not know all the parents personally, she knows that, as a group, they have the same purpose in attending the meeting. However, should the Minister of Education address the same problems in a television interview, the message would be received by a highly diversified audience, some of whom may not even have schoolgoing children.

There is also little or no interaction or **feedback** from the audience back to the communicator because the audience members are unable to use the same **medium** to reply to the communicator. Their access to the mass media is restricted by the media organisation, and the complex technology involved means that most people do not have the specialised skills required to **encode their messages in a mass medium.** The recipients may still provide feedback by, for example, telephoning, writing a letter to the media organisation or sending an e-mail, but such feedback is not immediate — it is delayed and is not face-to-face. Because of the time lapse, the free passage of messages that characterises face-to-face communication is lacking in mass communication. Also, not all letters, faxes or e-mails received by a newspaper, for example, get published. The 'Letters to the Editor' section of a newspaper is typically half of one page in the newspaper.

The conclusion is reached that the mediated messages of mass communication sets it apart from interpersonal and small-group communication, and even public speaking, which all occur in face-to-face situations. Consequently, mass communication has been described as an encounter with a medium and a message rather than a relationship with another person, as in interpersonal communication.

11.2.1 A model of mass communication

The model below (Figure 11.1) highlights this difference in its depiction of the process of mass communication.

The model illustrates and helps to explain the sequence of events in mass communication as well as the relationship between the basic components of the process: communicator, medium, message, audience and feedback. The model clearly shows that the media organisation occupies an intermediary position between the communicator on the one hand and the audience on the other (cf. McQuail & Windahl 1981).

In the model, A is the communicator (such as a politician or an advertiser) who would like to transmit a message (represented as X') to a mass audience (B) about a certain thing or event in the social environment (represented as X_1, X_2, X_3, X_4). If A is a politician, for example, he might want tell the audience to vote for him or her. Or, if A is an advertiser, she or he might want to persuade the audience to buy a new brand of toothpaste. But A cannot reach the audience (B) directly. He or she must first address the message to the individuals in the mass media organisation (C) who select those messages that they think will be of interest to their audiences. They encode and transmit the message (X") to the audience. Message X' and message X" are not always identical. The media organisation may, for example, decide that the politician's message is too long and they edit it to fit their schedule. A, the original source of the message, loses his or her position as the communicator. The media organisation takes over the communicative function. The audience encounters the messages of the media and not the original source of the message. A similar process occurs should members of the audience want to provide feedback (fBA) to the original communicator. Because they cannot reach A directly, the recipients may telephone or write to the media organisation (fBC) and the organisation relays the feedback (fCA) to the communicator. Note that the model also depicts a feedback loop from the audience to the original communicator (fBA). This might take the form of a vote for the politician or the purchase of the toothpaste. The model is useful in that it draws our attention to some of the characteristics of mass communication.

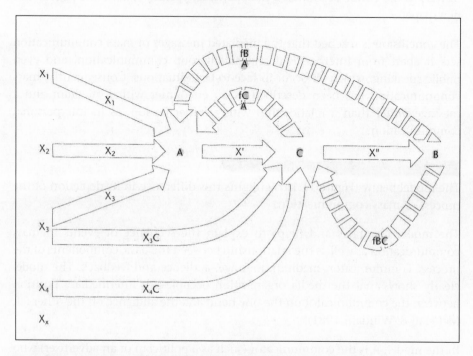

Figure 11.1 A model of mass communication
(adapted from Westley & MacLean 1957 by McQuail & Windahl 1981)

The ability of mass communication to multiply messages and transmit them rapidly to large audiences has stimulated a considerable amount of investigation by communication researchers into the functions that mass communication performs in society.

11.3 The functions of mass communication

The functions and effects of mass communication became an important field of research during the 1940s and 1950s, a period of rapid and extensive development in the mass media. This was also a time when struggling economies and other consequences of the Second World War were causing disruptions in society. Researchers, particularly in the United States, became interested in gaining insight into the effects of mass media messages on people and society, and the contributions they could make to restoring society's balance. This kind of effects approach to the study of mass communication is called functionalism. **Functionalism** provides researchers with a theoretical framework in which to investigate the social consequences of mass communication and the mass media, especially their contribution to maintaining social order.

Two theorists, Lasswell (1948) and Wright (1960), identified four basic functions of mass communication: surveillance of the environment, correlation, cultural transmission and entertainment. The following discussion of the four functions is based mainly on insights provided by Dominick (1999) and Infante, Rancer and Womack (2003).

11.3.1 Surveillance of the environment

The first function, **surveillance of the environment**, is considered the information and news-providing function of mass communication. The media keep us informed about national and international news, ranging from world stock-market prices and revolutionary uprisings to local traffic and weather conditions. In times of crisis (a national drought, for example) one of the surveillance functions of the media is to inform people what is expected of them, thereby minimising confusion and contributing to social order. The surveillance function also has to do with the transmission of information that is useful and helpful in everyday life, for example, news about where the latest movies are being screened, recipes, health issues, fashion ideas and so on.

11.3.2 Correlation

The mass media do not only supply facts and figures when they provide news and information. They also provide information about the meaning of many of those news items. Closely linked to surveillance is the **correlation** function which deals with how the mass media interpret information about the environment. Articles in newspapers, or discussions on radio and television about political, economic or social events, for example, have been selected and interpreted by the mass media, and have consequences for the way we understand and respond to these events. Our attitudes and opinions about political figures, for instance, are often influenced by the impressions we receive from the mass media. A negative impression of the African National Congress, for instance, was reinforced for many years by the South African Broadcasting Corporation (SABC) which continually portrayed it as a terrorist movement. On the other hand, the SABC in our 'new' or democratic society makes a point of highlighting the positive contributions of government departments and commercial institutions.

Interpretation can take many forms. The editorial pages of a newspaper provide comment and opinion on news stories carried on other pages. Television and radio perform a similar function in documentary and discussion programmes. The mass media also discuss and analyse issues such as the rising petrol price, the effect of drought on food prices, the Department of Health's approach to the HIV/AIDS problem, the rising crime rate and so on. Editorial cartoons, movie, book and restaurant reviews, motor and sports programmes, all form part of the correlation function.

Through the media, we can read, watch or hear the views of a variety of people: politicians, economists, cultural critics, political scientists, academics, the medical fraternity and even the man or woman in the street (in chat-back radio shows or letters to the press). There are two main advantages of the mass media performing this function. Firstly, mass audiences are exposed to a larger number of different points of view about an issue than would be possible in interpersonal communication alone. Also, the mass media make available a wide range of expertise that individuals might not otherwise have access to.

The downside to the correlation function is that there is no guarantee that interpretations by media commentators and other 'experts' are accurate and valid. There is also the danger that an individual may come to rely too heavily on the views carried by the media and become a passive and uncritical recipient of mass messages.

11.3.3 Cultural transmission

The third function, **cultural transmission** or the socialisation function, refers to the media's ability to communicate the norms, rules and values of a society so that we learn how we are supposed to act and what values are important. Cultural transmission is a teaching function of mass communication and tries to create common bonds among members of society. The next time you watch television or read a magazine, take note of, for example, how motherhood is generally portrayed in advertisements and sitcoms. We learn that motherhood and childrearing are activities that have a positive value for society and it is assumed that mass audiences will accept this value. Television shows such as *Family Ties*, the *Bill Cosby Show* and *Isidingo* have been mentioned as programmes which promote values such as respect for authority and family harmony. Many children's programmes, such as *Takalane Sesame,* are designed to encourage behaviour which is considered appropriate in a given society. You could also think about a health issue like smoking. Current concerns regarding smoking have prompted cigarette advertising to virtually disappear from television. Even though we still see cigarette advertisements in movie theatres, they carry a strong health risk warning.

11.3.4 Entertainment

The fourth function of the mass media, **entertainment**, refers to the media's ability to present messages which provide escapism and relaxation. Even though most of a newspaper concentrates on news items, newspapers also contain puzzles, comics, jokes, horoscopes, bridge and chess problems, and so on. In South Africa, most radio and television programmes are designed to entertain and amuse. When compared with live entertainment, it is apparent that the mass media can provide entertainment at relatively little cost. But entertainment that is carried by the mass media must appeal to a mass audience and the entertainment function of the media has frequently been criticised because of the low-quality content of some programmes. For example, we do not often see opera or classical ballet on television. However, many current theorists recognise its positive consequences and point out that mass communication provides relief from boredom, stimulates our emotions, helps fill our leisure time, keeps us company and exposes us to experiences and events that we could not attend in person. Another criticism of television, particularly in the USA, is that people are turning into a nation of watchers instead of doers — instead of participating in a game of tennis or soccer, or learning to play the guitar, people watch sport on television and watch music videos or listen to recordings of other people playing the guitar! (cf Dominick 1999).

The functionalist approach is still used today to study the relationship between mass communication and society. It offers researchers a theoretical framework for examining the social consequences of mass communication, especially its contribution to the maintenance of social order. With regard to changes in society, however, functionalism can only accommodate slow-moving, evolutionary change. It is incapable of accounting for sudden and fundamental change. Its application is thus limited to areas such as policy research, planning and evaluation. Functionalism has also been criticised by many theorists because it offers a limited view of communication. By concentrating on the functions that mass communication performs for society, it tends to overlook the human nature of communication and the fact that people construct meaning from messages. It has also been accused of having a conservative bias which justifies the maintenance of the existing social order and prevents any meaningful change from taking place.

The basic knowledge you have gained thus far of the process of mass communication and its functions provide the context in which we study the mass communicator, the mass medium and the audiences of mass communication in greater detail. As you study the remainder of this chapter, bear in mind that the theories we discuss were developed to meet specific concerns about mass communication. As the mass media grew in popularity during the 20th century, researchers began to show an interest in how these new forms of communication were influencing their audiences. Until the 1950s, research was concentrated on newspapers, film and radio. By the end of 1950s, when television became widely available, people grew increasingly alarmed about what this new medium was doing to them and their society, and especially what it was doing to their children. Extensive studies have been carried out in connection with the effects of television-viewing on children, but we do not discuss them here. Rather, we concern ourselves with theories that deal with the social effects of mass communication in a more general way. We have selected theories that examine the mass communicator, the mass medium and mass audiences.

11.4 The mass communicator

We said earlier that the mass communicator is usually a member of a team within an organisation involved in the production and distribution of messages. Each member of the team has a particular function to fulfil. It has been suggested that one of the primary functions of the mass communicator is that of **gatekeeping**. A **gatekeeper** refers to an individual within an organisation who has the power to select and reject messages, and even to interpret and change them, thereby influencing the information received by a recipient or group of recipients.

To understand the definition as well as the role of the gatekeeper, think about the newspaper you may read every day. All major newspaper organisations are flooded with news stories that reach them daily from sources all over the world. The items that you read have been selected and put together by media personnel (editors) who decide which items are the most relevant. The control exercised by such editors in their gatekeeping role means that what has been left out may be as important to some readers as what has been included. Gatekeeping is a necessary aspect of mass communication, and is not limited to newspapers. Gatekeepers exist in all mass media organisations, including radio, television and film. For example, the producer of a half-hour television documentary can include only a limited amount of the many hours of material that may have been filmed for the programme. Similarly, the compiler of a women's weekly radio magazine programme may have to discard some of the items that were gathered in the course of the week because of the limitations of time. The choices made by the gatekeeper concerning which information to discard and which to select and edit are influenced by other variables as well (cf Dimbleby & Burton 1992; Tubbs & Moss 2003).

A major consideration in the selection and rejection of media material is economics. The mass media are very expensive to operate and most media organisations have to show a profit to maintain themselves. One of their chief sources of income comes from the advertisers, who pay heavily for media space and time and expect to see results on their investment. A magazine advertisement for toothpaste, for example, sells not only because of the persuasive element in the advertisement, but as a result of the content in the rest of the magazine. The magazine editor tends to select material which will please the advertisers — that is, material which will appeal to the type of audiences the advertisers are aiming at.

A second major source of income comes from the audiences who, for example, buy newspapers or magazines or pay to watch a film in a cinema. To attract and satisfy large audiences, media personnel have to decide on both the news value and relevance of a particular story. **News values** (also called **newsworthiness**) are beliefs about what topics make good news, and can vary from one organisation to the next. Generally, stories that involve well-known personalities are considered to have more news value than stories about lesser-known people. Likewise, stories that portray drama, such as children being rescued from a fire, or conflict between opposing parties, are often chosen in preference to stories which portray 'ordinary' events. The relevance of a particular programme is determined by deciding, for example, whether a story about striking miners in England or a radio drama set in Alaska will interest South African audiences.

A major influence on the choices made by the gatekeeper is the **policy** and **ideology** of the media organisation. Policy refers to the criteria for news value laid down by a particular organisation, while ideology refers to the fact that most media organisations, especially newspapers, adopt a particular political point of view which is reinforced in their interpretation of news stories. You have probably noticed that, while they may cover the same events, three different newspapers interpret those events to coincide with their respective points of view. What you read in your newspaper in not an 'objective' report of the 'facts' but an interpretation of what has occurred. Public service programmes broadcast by an organisation such as the South African Broadcasting Corporation (SABC) are expected to be impartial in its news reporting. Until 1994, the SABC was criticised for supporting Nationalist government policy in its selection and interpretation of political news events, thereby directing the perceptions of its viewers in a particular direction. At the time of writing, questions are being asked about whether the SABC is again being influenced by the policies of the ruling party.

Legal restrictions and **ethics** also influence the choices made by media organisations. Every country has legal restrictions on the type of messages the mass media may communicate. The media will generally avoid reporting malicious gossip about people, unless it is verifiable, for fear of being taken to court. Most organisations also follow a code of ethics in the interests of good taste. There are exceptions of course, but most newspapers would probably decide not to publish photographs of mutilated bodies in an accident because it may offend some readers. Likewise, most television stations would not broadcast pornographic material in the early evening when children might be watching. The question of ethics in the mass media is too vast to consider in detail in an introductory text on communication. However, you might like to think about one issue — media intrusion and privacy — and the public's insatiable hunger for information about public figures such as Hansie Cronje, Princess Diana, David Beckham, Jacob Zuma, or almost any prominent politician or sports figure.

11.5 The mass medium

We mentioned in our discussion of the functions of mass communication that, as mass communication became an increasingly prevalent form of communication, a great deal of research was (and is still) conducted on the effects of the mass media and their messages on society. An influential theory in this regard is the agenda setting theory which gained prominence during the 1960s and 1970s.

11.5.1 Agenda-setting theory

Agenda-setting refers to the way the mass media create public awareness and concern about important issues, thereby contributing to the shaping of public opinion. The concept of **public opinion** represents ideas about social issues (such as political elections) that are expressed and debated in public, and the opinions of the general public as a group, rather than of individuals. The underlying argument of agenda-setting is that the public responds, not to actual events in the environment, but to "pictures in our heads" that are created by the media in their reporting of news stories (Heath & Bryant 1992:281).

Agenda-setting is an extension of the gatekeeping function we discussed earlier, in that it is concerned with the selection of news stories and the prominence given to the stories by the media. The theory proposes that, in the same way that people set an agenda for important matters that require attention, the mass media select topics, issues and individuals they consider to be important and bring them to the attention of the public. The matters that the media choose to publicise ultimately become those that we think about and talk about. According to the theory, we think these matters are important because of the **media attention** they have received, regardless of how important they may really be. The result of highlighting an issue is that it is placed on the public agenda for serious discussion (Agee *et al* 1988; Infante, Rancer & Womack 2003). An example of agenda-setting is provided by Severin and Tankard (1992), who describe how New York newspapers 'created' a crime wave in the 1930s. There were always lots of crime stories that the press did not report. On one occasion, a reporter wrote up one of these stories because it involved a well-known family.

A rival newspaper promptly looked for, and reported on, another crime. Soon, all the New York newspapers were 'finding' crimes to keep up with the others. The sudden increase in crimes reported in the press was perceived as a 'crime wave' by the public and, for a time, crime became the most discussed issue in New York. Although the crime rate had not actually risen, the public came to see crime as an important issue simply as a result of the media attention it received.

Examples of agenda-setting by the media in South Africa recently include the issues of high crime levels, corruption in government, taxi violence, HIV/AIDS, the influx of illegal aliens from other African countries and the concept of an 'African Renaissance' (Mersham & Skinner 2002). Do you think that your views on the government's controversial arms deal, for instance, were shaped to a large extent by what you heard, read and saw through the mass media?

A conclusion about agenda-setting reached by many theorists was first expressed by Cohen in 1963: "The press may not be successful much of the time in telling people what to think, but it is stunningly successful in telling its readers what to think *about*" (Agee *et al* 1988). Regarding what to think about, all recipients of mass communication should be aware that, because agenda-setting is an extension of the gatekeeping function, what is not placed on a particular mass medium's agenda may be as important to consider as what is included. How many people did not know about the gross human rights violations committed against fellow South Africans during the apartheid era because of media censorship by the Nationalist government? How did the picture change when they were exposed to television coverage of the testimonies of the people who testified in the Truth and Reconciliation Commission?

Agenda-setting is still receiving considerable attention from mass communication theorists who maintain that it is important to understand how the media shape people's views of the major issues in society, even though they may not be the dominant ones in reality. Criticisms that have been levelled against agenda-setting include the view of McQuail (1987), for example, who asserts that agenda-setting is a plausible but unproven idea, rather than a fully developed theory. He argues that research studies have not provided sufficient evidence to confirm a connection between the order of importance placed on issues by the media and the significance attached to those issues by the public.

11.5.2 Framing

Based on research conducted in the late 1990s, it has been strongly suggested that agenda-setting by the media does more than tell us what to think about. The mass media do in fact tell us how to think. The process by which this occurs is called **framing**. Tankard (in Griffen 2003:396) describes a frame as "the central organizing idea for news content that supplies a context and suggests what the issue is through the use of *selection, emphasis, exclusion* and *elaboration*". In other words, the media not only suggest which issues, events or candidates in the news are the most important. As they transfer 'pictures' into our heads, the attributes the media have given a particular 'picture' (item of interest) are simultaneously transferred. Griffin (2003:398) provides examples from political news items in the United States of America to illustrate how the media's construction of an agenda with a cluster of related attributes creates a coherent image in the minds of the audience.

> Framing is not an option. Reporters inevitably frame a story by the personal attributes of public figures they select to describe. For example, the media continually reported on the 'youthful vigor' of Jack Kennedy while he was alive, but made no mention of his extramarital affairs, which were well known to the White House press corps. The 1988 presidential race was all but over after *Time* framed the contest between George Bush and Michael Dukakis as The Nice Man vs. the Ice Man. And Republican spin doctors fought an uphill battle positioning their candidate once media stories focused on Bob Dole's lack of passion — 'Dead Man Walking' was the quip of commentator Mark Shields. Media stories in the 2000 campaign for president focused on conflicting candidate attributes. George W. Bush came across as 'likeable but lazy'. Al Gore was a 'policy wonk' and 'wooden'. Media outlets are constantly searching for material that they regard as newsworthy. When they find it, they do more than tell their audiences what to think about.

A question you might consider is whether the media in South Africa use their power in a similar way. For example, at the time of Thabo Mbeki's inauguration as president, it was said that some newspapers implied that he was a more aloof figure than the outgoing president, Nelson Mandela, who was seen as warm and friendly.

The conclusion about agenda-setting that researchers McCombs and Shaw (in Griffen 2003:396) have reached is that, "[t]he media may not only tell us what to think about, they also may tell us what and how to think about it, and perhaps even what to do about it".

11.5.3 Spiral of silence theory

Another theory that ascribes power to the mass media is the **spiral of silence theory** developed by Noelle-Neumann (1973; 1980), a German researcher. The underlying argument in this theory is that the media do have powerful effects, but that these effects have been underestimated or undetected in the past because of the limitations of research. The spiral of silence explains why some opinions are publicly expressed, whereas others are not discussed in public.

The basic assumption of spiral of silence theory is that the media effectively limit the range of opinions available to the public. Noelle-Neumann argues that because all media tend to concentrate on the same news stories, the public receives a unified picture of an issue from newspapers, magazines, television and radio stations. This unified picture creates the impression that most people view a controversial issue in the same way as the media. By paying attention to the media, people obtain an idea — often a distorted one — of the distribution of opinion in society. If people find that their own opinion on a particular issue coincides with the majority opinion expressed in media messages, they will be more likely to express and act on this opinion. If, on the other hand, their opinion is not supported by the messages disseminated by the media, they are more likely to keep quiet about it, refrain from action and thus get caught up in the spiral of silence. The more they remain silent, the more other people feel that the particular point of view is not represented, and the more they too remain silent. In political elections, for example, people are sensitive to the prevailing opinion about candidates and issues, and they are more likely to express their preferences when they know these are shared by others.

The spiral of silence is not just a matter of wanting to be on 'the winning side', but is an attempt to avoid being isolated from one's social group. Adolescents are particularly sensitive about not being different to their peers regarding the clothes they wear and the jargon they use to communicate. Have you noticed that smokers tend to express their views on smokers' rights when other smokers are present and refrain from expressing their views in a group of nonsmokers? Mersham & Skinner (2000) point out that in some cases, the threat of expressing a minority opinion is extreme. Political intolerance in South Africa, for example, has been responsible for thousands of deaths. During 2006, the attacks on security guards who refused to join the nationwide strike demonstrate how dangerous it can be to run against the prevailing climate of opinion.

The mass media affect the spiral of silence by shaping impressions about which opinions are dominant, and which opinions people can utter in public without becoming isolated. At the same time, they effectively silence the discussion of others. Noelle-Neumann believes that this influence is especially powerful today because of the pervasiveness and repetitiveness of media messages (cf Noelle-Neumann 1973; Severin & Tankard 1992; Hunt & Reuben 1993; Littlejohn 1996).

11.6 Audiences of mass communication

Some of the research into the effects of mass communication has been directed at investigating the nature of the mass audience. Prior to the 1930s, theorists assumed that individual members within the audience were passive receivers of mass media messages. Media messages were therefore capable of directly influencing the values, opinions and emotions of the audience. They took it for granted that individual audience members share the same psychological and emotional characteristics. It was also assumed that individual recipients of mass communication lived in isolation and did not interact with others. Media messages would therefore have a predictable and uniform effect on all the members. This argument of uniform and powerful direct media effects was labelled the **magic bullet** or **hypodermic-needle theory**, and later became known as the **stimulus-response theory**. Messages had only to be loaded, directed at the target and fired. If they hit their target, then the expected response would be forthcoming. For example, the results of early research studies showed that people could easily be manipulated by advertising and political propaganda messages communicated by the mass media (cf Heath & Bryant 2000). After additional investigation, mass communication theorists concluded that the earlier research results could not be substantiated, and several alternative theories about the influence of the media were put forward.

During the 1940s, researchers concluded that, while the mass media did have a profound effect on the audience, several other intervening factors modify the uniform response to messages. Studies at that time showed that recipients of mass messages are not isolated individuals, but that they interact with others — family members, friends and work colleagues — who influence their opinions on a variety of matters, such as their voting behaviour. Several people who were interviewed during the study revealed that they obtained most of their information from other people (who had received it directly from the mass media) before they learned about it on the media. Drawing on these findings, Katz and Lazarsfeld (1955) developed the two-step flow theory of mass communication.

11.6.1 Two-step flow theory

The **two-step flow theory** asserts that information from the media moves or flows in two stages. First, certain people who are heavy or regular users of the mass media, receive the information. These people, called 'opinion leaders', then pass the information along to others who are less exposed to the media, through informal, interpersonal communication. Opinion leaders, in retransmitting the information, tend to include their own interpretation of the information in addition to the actual media content, thereby modifying the influence of the mass media. The two-step flow theory is illustrated by the model in Figure 11.2.

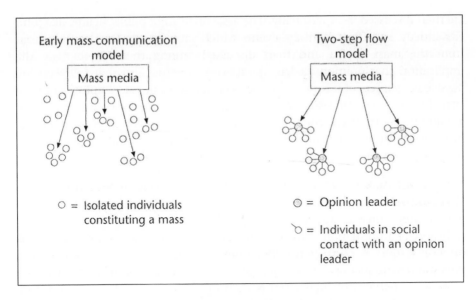

Figure 11.2 Two-step flow model of media influence compared with the traditional model of mass communication
(adapted by McQuail & Windahl 1981 from Katz & Lazarsfeld 1955)

Several characteristics of opinion leaders have been identified. For instance, they are not always prominent people in the community, but are found at all levels of society. Opinion leaders are usually well-informed people who have similar beliefs, values, education, social level and so on, to those they influence, a principle known as **homophily** (cf Barker & Gaut 1996). For example, a student is more likely to acquire information from another student, and a doctor from another doctor, and so on. Opinion leaders are reasonably successful in persuading people to change their attitudes and behaviour because they are perceived as being experts in their field. In addition, because the exchange of information takes place in an interpersonal situation, the opinion leader is able to respond to questions and discuss the matter, something the mass media are unable to do. Think about a major purchase you have to make, such as a computer. You may see a number of advertisements in the press or on television about the qualities and capabilities of different computers but, because you are not an expert on computers, the probability is that you will also seek out the advice of someone whom you consider to be an expert or opinion leader on the topic of computers and whose opinion you trust (cf Heath & Bryant 2000; Infante, Rancer & Womack 2003).

The two–step flow theory of mass communication has helped to predict the influence of media messages on audiences and to explain why certain media campaigns fail to alter audience attitudes and beliefs. It has also been criticised on the grounds that many major news stories are first heard on the media, and are then discussed interpersonally. The assassination of public figures like John F. Kennedy and Chris Hani are events which most people first learned about from the mass media and then discussed among themselves. Also, the implication that opinion leaders are active recipients, and that followers are passive consumers of information, has been found to be too simplistic and not entirely true. Nevertheless, the concept of two-step flow was instrumental in guiding future research which would lead to more complex theories about the influence of mass communication and the idea that mass audiences are active recipients of information.

More recent studies suggest that it is more accurate to talk about a **multi-step flow model**, since opinion leaders may themselves be consulting with others whom they consider to be knowledgeable. The multi-step flow model, or diffusion of information, involves change agents and gatekeepers as well as opinion leaders. A **change agent** is someone who is responsible for making policy and introducing change. Change agents are usually professionals who are more educated and of higher status than opinion leaders. They come into a community from outside — for instance, a nursing sister from the Department of Health who comes into a rural area to introduce the idea that babies should be vaccinated. Because of their position they are not usually homophilous with the people to whom they must disseminate information. The change agent prefers to interact with opinion leaders in the community. Because the opinion leaders are respected by the community, they will have considerable influence in forming and changing the attitudes of the mothers who need to bring their babies to the clinic to be vaccinated. You will recall from Section 11.4 that a gatekeeper is someone who controls the flow of information to the audience, like the editor of a local newspaper. Because gatekeepers decide which stories will reach the public, they represent another step in the flow of information between the media and the audience. There is therefore more than one intermediary and channel involved in the process of diffusion and influence (cf Barker & Gaut 1996; Infante, Rancer & Womack 2003).

11.6.2 Uses and gratifications theory

Largely in reaction to the growing dissatisfaction about the direct effects of mass communication on passive audiences, a number of recent mass media theorists have argued that the most important factors governing the effects of mass communication are the needs and interests of audience members. They have focused their attention, not on what the media do to people, but what people do with the media. In other words, they make provision for an active audience. Think about the ways in which an audience can be active rather than passive, as suggested by the stimulus-response theory. Who controls what you choose to listen to or read or watch? You buy the newspaper of your choice; you select the radio and TV programmes you want to watch; you decide which movies you will go to; you rent videos or DVDs of movies you want to watch at home. You can also choose to switch off the radio or television if a programme does not hold your interest, or even walk out of a cinema if you are not enjoying the movie (cf Tubbs & Moss 2003).

Think back for a moment to our criticism of functionalism. The four functions described by Lasswell (1948) and Wright (1960) represent functions of the content (messages) of the mass media and neglect to take into account the way audiences use that content for their own purposes. In other words, for what functions are mass media messages used by audience members? An analysis of how an audience member actively uses the media is explained by **uses and gratifications theory**.

Uses and gratifications theory suggests that basic human needs motivate individuals to attend to particular mass media, and to select and use media messages in ways they find personally gratifying. Thus, a given medium, such as radio, and a certain set of messages, such as weather information, might be used by different individuals in very different ways depending on the particular needs and interests they are seeking to satisfy. On the other hand, some audience members may have no use for this information at all (Hunt & Ruben 1993).

Perhaps the best way to understand uses and gratifications is to think about the process suggested by the theory. Acting on the basis that you have a need to satisfy, for instance the need to relax after a hard day of study, you consider all the options provided by the mass media. From these options, you first choose the medium you think will best satisfy that need and second, a particular item or programme offered by that medium. You may decide between doing the crossword puzzle in the newspaper, listening to a talk show on radio or watching a soap opera on television. Your individual characteristics, needs and interests will largely determine the choice you make. The degree of gratification (or nongratification) that results from your choice will influence decisions you make in the future.

One of the results of uses and gratifications research has been the identification of basic need categories that can be satisfied through media choices. Tan (1985) suggests five categories which show that mass communication can satisfy many of the needs we discussed in Chapter 2 with reference to interpersonal communication. Relate the list of needs below to the functions of mass communication described in Section 11.3.

☐ *Cognitive needs* Needs related to acquiring information, knowledge and understanding of our environment, as well as satisfying our curiosity. Reasons for using the media in this category can range from wanting to understand what is happening in the rest of the world to learning about other people's interests and hobbies.

☐ *Affective needs* Needs related to the pursuit of pleasure and entertainment and the satisfaction of our emotions. The choice of material in this category is highly subjective and can vary from listening to pop music to reading about astronomy or electronics or even watching a horror movie.

☐ *Personal integrative needs* Needs related to the individual's desire for self-esteem and self-actualisation. Some people tend to identify with media heroes and heroines and participate vicariously in their triumphs and successes. They might even strive to reach similar goals themselves. When interviewed by the media, some people who have climbed Mount Everest have said that they did it because watching other 'ordinary people' succeed on television made them feel that "If they can do it, so can I".

☐ *Social integrative needs* Needs related to strengthening contact with family, friends and the world. When you discuss a TV programme with a friend or go to the movies with a sibling, you are using the media to fulfil this need.

☐ *Escapist needs* Needs related to escape, tension release and the desire for diversion. Viewers report that one of the reasons for watching soap operas is that they can escape into the lives of other people (even fictional people) and forget their own problems for a while.

Think about the needs we have described in terms of your own media usage. Suppose that you and your mother often watch travel programmes together because you both enjoy them. You especially listen for information about how to reach the particular destination, what sort of accommodation is available and what there is to do and see. Your mother simply loves to relax and enjoy the beautiful scenery, smartly dressed people and exotic food. Because you plan to travel extensively as soon as you have completed your studies, your need is different to your mother's — your primary need is cognitive whereas your mother's is affective. The fact that you always try to watch together shows that you also share a common need to satisfy social-integrative needs of family life.

Uses and gratifications research has a practical application in that it assists mass media organisations to determine the motivations of their audiences and serve them more efficiently. It has, however, been criticised for being vague in defining and explaining the concept of **needs** and for producing inaccurate results. It has been suggested that respondents in research studies infer the needs they seek to satisfy from questions that are asked about why they use the media, leading to the suspicion that the need was created by the media. Like functionalism, to which it is related, uses and gratifications theory has also been criticised for being a conservative approach that looks primarily at the positive ways in which individuals meet their needs, without any attention to the possible negative effects of media in society. Nevertheless, it provides a refreshing change from the traditional viewpoint of the passive, unthinking audience (cf Severin & Tankard 1992; Littlejohn 1996).

Scenario 11.1

We said earlier that a given medium, such as radio, and a certain set of messages, such as weather information, might be used by different individuals in very different ways depending on the particular needs and interests they are seeking to satisfy. Over a period of two or three days, observe how the members of your family use the mass media. Then, for each member of the family, describe which uses and gratifications appear to be satisfied by the items or programmes they have selected. Take note of the differences in media use among the older and younger members your family, the time of day that various media are used for different purposes, and differences in weekday and weekend use of the media.

Use the table below to help you identify different types of gratifications that can be sought and obtained from the mass media.

Table 11.1 Typology of gratifications sought and obtained from the media

Gratification category	Examples
Information	❐ Finding out about relevant events and conditions in immediate surroundings, society and the world ❐ Seeking advice on practical matters or opinions and decision choices ❐ Satisfying curiosity and general interest ❐ Learning, self-education ❐ Gaining a sense of security through knowledge
Personal identity	❐ Finding reinforcement for personal values ❐ Finding models of behaviour ❐ Identifying with valued others (in the media) ❐ Gaining insight into one's self
Integration and social interaction	❐ Gaining insight into circumstances of others: social empathy ❐ Identifying with others and gaining a sense of belonging ❐ Finding a basis for conversation and social interaction ❐ Having a substitute for real-life companionship ❐ Helping to carry out social roles ❐ Enabling one to connect with family, friends and society

Gratification category	Examples
Entertainment	❏ Escaping or being diverted from problems
	❏ Relaxing
	❏ Getting intrinsic cultural or aesthetic enjoyment
	❏ Filling time
	❏ Gaining emotional release
	❏ Experiencing sexual arousal

Source: McQuail (1983:82-83)

11.7 The social effects of mass communication

The social effects of mass communication have been a topic of discussion, controversy and research since the emergence and mass distribution of newspapers, film, radio and especially television. A great deal of empirical research has been conducted on the psychological, social and political effects of television on viewers, especially young viewers. Questions such as the following (and many more) have been investigated: Is there a relationship between TV viewing and cognitive development? How does TV advertising influence young children? What is the relationship between violence on TV and antisocial behaviour in teenagers?

Another way of examining the social effects of mass communication is the **cultural studies approach**. Cultural studies has its roots in Marxist philosophy, which emphasised class differences as a cause of conflict in society. The cultural studies approach suggests that it is not only economics that maintains class differences in society, but that the content of the mass media helps to perpetuate a system that maintains the status quo of power relationships in society. It also pays attention to the fact that recipients can find different meanings in the same message. The cultural studies approach asks questions such as the following: Is it aesthetic taste or financial profits that determine whether art is considered good or bad? or What was the significance of having rock star Elton John singing at Princess Diana's funeral? (Dominick 1999).

To conclude our study of mass communication we have chosen to examine a third approach to the social effects of mass communication: technological or media determinism. **Technological determinism** sees social change as a direct result of fundamental technological development and innovation. Marshall McLuhan (1911–1980), the Canadian literary and communications scholar, was one of the best-known writers about the relationship between technology and social change. McLuhan's theory was first published in 1964 and he gained worldwide prominence as an authority on electronic media and their impact on both culture and society. As the Internet and new media have expanded, theorists today are showing renewed interest in his views. Although McLuhan made an intensive study of the history of technology from primitive times, his main interest was in print and electronic media. The theme that runs through his work is that 'we shape our tools and they in turn shape us' (cf O'Sullivan et al 1989; Griffin 2003).

Although he was interested in all communication media, McLuhan was renowned for his views on the technology and power of the electronic media to shape society. In fact, he was the first communication theorist to have directed attention to the important role of the medium in communication. To understand the main proposition in his theory — *the medium is the message* — we need to briefly explain the term 'media determinism'.

11.7.1 McLuhan and media determinism

The medium is an important component in the structure of communication because it provides the means by which the communicator is able to transmit the message to the recipient. Without the medium, communication would not be possible. **Media determinism** is an approach to the study of communication that considers the medium to play a more important role in the communication of messages than simply the technical or physical means whereby messages are transmitted in the communication process (refer to Section 3.3.5). The medium is usually regarded as a neutral 'container' that has no influence on the content of the message or the communication process itself. Media determinism asserts that the medium, because of its particular characteristics, plays an influential role not only in the communication process itself but also on how the message is formulated and understood. The main focus is often directed at ways in which a particular medium can assist the communicator to deliver a more effective (persuasive) message and the effects of the message on the recipient. McLuhan took this idea a step further and suggested that the type of medium a society uses also determines the structure of the society and shapes the way people experience their world. Consequently, media determinism tends to minimise the role of people in creating and interpreting meaning, and to ascribe to the media the power of influencing not only the message, but society itself.

McLuhan's particular interest in the characteristics of communication media was sparked off by the way that advertisements and newspapers achieve their effects. He described this as a mosaic of impressions created by the juxtaposition of pictures, words, colours, different typefaces and so on which invite participation by the recipient in the communication process. Think about an eye-catching advertisement: it often achieves its effect precisely because of the way that the different elements are placed on the page. McLuhan maintained that it is not so much the product that interests you, but the form (the shape or layout) of the advertisement that has captured your attention, and it is the form that determines how you respond to the advertisement. This assumption led him to examine the form, rather than the content, of all the different media that exist in society. He came to regard the content of messages as irrelevant and suggested that the medium and its technology was the influential factor in society. He went so far as to claim that the channels of communication we use are the primary cause of cultural change. Nothing remains untouched by communication technology — family life, schools, healthcare, friendship, religious worship, recreation, politics.

The discussion that follows is based mainly on *Understanding media: the extensions of man* (McLuhan 1974) first published in 1964; Wolfe (in Stearn 1968); Jansen & Steinberg (1991); Sonderling (1992; 1994) and Griffin (2003).

11.7.2 McLuhan's assumptions about the media

McLuhan's understanding of 'medium' or 'media' was very broad. One of his definitions is that the media are technologically created extensions of the human senses. He argued that media quite literally extend sight, hearing and touch through time and space. He maintained that people have developed extensions for practically everything they once did with their bodies. The wheel is an extension of the foot, writing is an extension of sight, clothes an extension of the skin, electronic circuits an extension of the central nervous system, and so on (McLuhan & Fiore 1967). Let's take clothing as an example. The skin is the medium for our sense of touch and is one of the ways we communicate with the environment. Clothing not only extends this form of communication, but clothing itself — for instance the way that we dress — allows us to express ourselves visually, thereby communicating a message. Similarly, McLuhan regarded the printed words that we read as an extension of our ears. The reason is that our primary mode of communication is naturally conducted by way of speech and hearing, but since the invention of the printing press, we 'see' our speech on a printed page. As print spread in society, people began to obtain more of their information by reading than listening, with the result that the sense of sight became overdeveloped. Based on these assertions, McLuhan maintained that the medium is not merely a tool invented by people, but that it has become part of the natural environment. As with any other element in the environment, the medium exerts an influence on people and on society.

11.7.3 Ratio of the senses

The core of McLuhan's theory is that people adapt to their environment through a certain balance, or **ratio of the senses**. The primary medium of an age brings out a certain sense ratio. Let's clarify what McLuhan means. We live in a world that includes our physical and social environment and we perceive or interact with our environment through our senses. We receive information from the environment through our five senses. Children, before they learn to speak, interact with people and objects that they observe in their environment by touching, tasting and smelling them. In similar manner, preliterate tribal societies, who did not have language with which to communicate, also used all their senses in their interaction with their environment and with other people. The senses of hearing, touch, taste and smell were developed far beyond the ability to see. But what happens when a new medium such as language is introduced?

The basic characteristic of language is speech, a series of sounds that people make and hear. As people became accustomed to the use of speech in their daily communication, they gradually came to depend less and less on the other senses because, to receive information through speech, they only needed to use their sense of hearing. Senses like touch, taste and smell became less important. Therefore, according to McLuhan, before printing was invented, the sense of hearing was dominant and language became part of the human environment, as natural to people as water to a fish. The environment was an **acoustic** place in which people led richer and more complex lives than their literate descendants because the ear, unlike the eye, is not able to block out stimuli in the environment.

McLuhan maintained that hearing-oriented communities tend to receive and express many experiences simultaneously. They are in touch with every aspect of the environment and with each other. People who get their information from other people are necessarily drawn closer together, in the tribal way. They have to be close to each other in order to obtain information and they have to believe what others tell them because they have no other source of information. So they are interdependent. They are also more emotional — the spoken word conveys anger, sorrow, joy, and so on, with greater intensity than the printed word.

The mechanical developments of the 20th century brought about a radical change because, as other media were invented, they became part of the human environment and exerted their influence on society. For example, the invention of the phonetic alphabet and the development of print media had great effects on the way we see and experience the world and the way that societies operate. McLuhan called the print-dominated environment the *Gutenberg Galaxy*. Consider the way he described the effects of the Gutenberg Galaxy on society and people.

Writing and printing are media with particular characteristics that are different from those of speech. Print converts audible sounds (spoken words) into visual signs (the letters of the alphabet). In order for people to communicate in written or printed media they need to learn to read and write. Reading and writing demand the use of different senses than those demanded by speech. As people began getting their information primarily by seeing it, sight replaced hearing as the dominant medium. The printed word brought a new sense ratio into being which caused a bias in human perception. In McLuhan's words, visual people have substituted "an ear for an eye" (1974:91). McLuhan proposed that Western culture developed because the requirements of the print medium forced people into a linear, logical and categorical kind of perception, rather like the string of words and letters on the printed page. When you read and write, your eyes follow each letter and word in linear succession. McLuhan maintained that, after generations of using such a medium, our thought processes have also begun to behave in the same way as we read. We think in linear fashion and that is why we work things out in logical sequences. McLuhan maintained that Western people are communicologically 'deaf' — out of touch with the environment and detached from each other. People who communicate by means of writing do not have to be in the same place at the same time — they only have to exchange written messages. Because they are alone when they express and receive messages, there is no direct interaction between them and no opportunity to see the expressions on the other's face or to exchange messages in real time. Writing and print have also changed the way people collect and store information about their environment. In oral cultures, people relied on their memory for all the information they needed, but when writing and printing became available they no longer needed to memorise information.

11.7.4 The media and social change

McLuhan maintained that each new medium influences the society as well as the people. According to McLuhan, the character of each society and civilisation is determined by the types of media that are used predominantly for communication in that society. This is based on McLuhan's assertion that the medium is the entire environment in which people live and the environment makes an impression on the human nervous system. When McLuhan said "The medium is the message" he meant that, because our environment is the medium, the messages communicated by this medium structure our percep-tions, attitudes and feelings. The introduction of each new medium changes the whole environment and influences the entire process of human thought and perception.

Each new medium also causes a revolutionary change in the whole way of life of a society. The development of writing and printing gradually brought about changes in the structure of society. The phonetic alphabet made people visually dependent and the printing press ensured that it became widespread. McLuhan pointed out that the most important characteristic of movable type is repeatability. Because the print medium demonstrated that mass production of identical products was possible, McLuhan called it the forerunner of the

Industrial Revolution. Furthermore, writing and printing became important means of administration and government and new social institutions were established, such as libraries, book stores and printing companies. Thus a whole bureaucracy developed to manage and regulate the production and distribution of written and printed messages within society.

Today, new technologies are causing yet another change. McLuhan maintained that we are in the midst of another revolution, but most people do not yet understand that the world will never be the same (remember that he was writing in the 1960s). The new technologies have ushered in a new electronic age in which the electronic media are retribalising the human race. Although modern man is literate, we obtain most of our information by hearing it — primarily through electronic sources such as the telephone, radio and television. McLuhan saw in the electronic circuit a similarity to the human nervous system. The electronic media stimulate perception by all the senses and thereby restore equilibrium. They have put us back in touch with the environment and with other people. McLuhan maintained that whereas the print revolution created an **explosion**, breaking people up into categories, the new electronic media are causing an **implosion**, putting them in touch with one another as messages are communicated instantly around the world and forcing them back into a tribal unity.

11.7.5 The global village

As a result of the expansion of the electronic media, the world has become what McLuhan called a 'global village' in which our thoughts, actions, institutions and our relationship to society have been modified. The introduction of a network of telecommunications has made possible the instantaneous transmission of information, culture, values and attitudes. Time and distance are bridged, so that what is happening in countries thousand of kilometres away can be observed in our own home, much like the situation in a small village where little happens that is not known to everybody. In fact, McLuhan pictured us all as members of a single community. You need only think about how enthusiastically we participated in televised broadcasts of the 2006 soccer World Cup, or how we eagerly watched the progress of the war in Iraq. According to McLuhan, the power of the printed word is over. By replacing books and writing as our main source of information, the electronic media have once again provided means of communication that involve the use of various senses simultaneously and, as a result, communication in the global village resembles communication in preliterate societies. The linear logic imposed by print is useless in the global village. Acoustic people no longer enquire, "Do you see my point?" Instead we ask, "How does that grab you?" What we feel is more important than what we think (cf Griffin 2003:347). And for the modern generation, ways of thinking are changing rapidly. In the hyperlinked world of the Internet, we make connections in a nonlinear network. We surf from one site to the next, backwards and forwards, up and down. Will this lead us to develop a nonlinear form of rationality, ask Baran and Davies? (2003:373).

11.7.6 Hot and cool media

Based on his view on the important influence of the media on society, McLuhan suggested that we can best understand the media by classifying them according to their effects on the human senses. His explanation of the effects of the medium on the senses is linked to the division he makes between 'hot' and 'cool' media, terms which refer to the 'temperature' of the information or the 'definition' of the image (McLuhan 1974:31). The temperature of a message is not to be confused with its content. McLuhan classified media and their messages in terms of the degree to which they involve people perceptually. Because television had become the dominant medium of the 1960s, McLuhan focused his attention on the nature and power of television.

Hot media, such as print, photographs and movies contain relatively complete sensory data so that the informational content of the message is high, or 'hot'. Hot media therefore require minimal participation from the recipient — the meaning is delivered in the message itself. McLuhan (1975:v-vi) explained that in youth culture, something 'cool' is something that one likes, and indicates commitment and involvement. Cool media, such as television, draw a person in, requiring you to participate perceptually by filling in missing sensory data.

The comparison between film and television that McLuhan (1974) made elucidates the difference. Film is a hot medium because the image projected on the screen is three-dimensional, complete in every detail, and the viewer is not required to fill in missing information in order to understand the message. A television shot is cool because it has very low definition: it is two-dimensional, rather like a comic strip cartoon. Television requires the viewer to participate in obtaining information by filling in the spaces and contours with his mind, as one does with a cartoon. The viewer is thus more involved in the television image than the film image. McLuhan suggested that when our eyes look at things on television, they behave as if they were handling or touching the image. They seem to rub over it, filling the mosaic of impressions. In this way people participate in understanding television images. The sense of touch is once again being used. McLuhan went on to say that, "Of course, packages will be obsolete in a few years. People will want tactile experiences, they'll want to feel the product they're getting" (Wolfe 1968:39).

The difference between hot and cool media is crucial because of the different impact they have on society. Because the meaning in a hot message is complete, it creates a dulling or hypnosis of the senses of the population, whereas a cool medium stimulates the senses. Paradoxically, because a cool medium demands involvement and emotion from the viewer, it results in a culture that is hot or based on greater emotional involvement. McLuhan defined Western cultures as cool, whereas developing or underdeveloped cultures are hot. He maintained that we are presently in transition from a cool to a hot culture. The change is created by the media we use for communication — books are being replaced by the electronic media, especially television, and the augmented participation required by the recipients has created a new type of tribal society and increased the level of people's involvement with their world.

Table 11.2 Features and types of hot and cool mediums

	Hot mediums	Cool mediums
Features (McLuhan, 1964:31-3)	Low participation Extends one single sense	High participation
	High definition A large amount of Information	Low definition Small amount of Information Need to be completed by the audience
	Tend to overtake cool mediums Tend to be mechanical, repetitive, uniform	Tend to be supplanted and remade by hot mediums
Examples (McLuhan, 1964:31-2)	Radio Cinema Photograph	Telephone Television Cartoon Speech
	Phonetic alphabet	Hieroglyphic and ideogrammatic written characters
	Print	Monastic and clerical script
	Paper Lecture Book	Stone Seminar Dialogue
Examples (McLuhan, 1964:36)	Past mechanical times Developed countries	The contemporary TV age Underdeveloped countries

Source: Holmes (2005:71)

But the change is not without problems — it creates tremendous stresses in society while people adjust during the transition. For example, the new environment is reshaping the perceptual life of the young. Today's children are a new tribe. They respond emotionally to the spoken word because they have tribal sensory balances. They are 'hot', they perceive in patterns rather than linearly, they want to touch, they want to be involved. But the modern acoustic child is confronted in the classroom by teachers who think in a linear fashion. Griffin (2003:349) describes how words and numbers plod along a blackboard one by one rather than prance around in patterns on a user-friendly television screen. The teacher still considers video as an audiovisual aid rather than a primary tool of learning. Belatedly, at the start of the 21st century, the change is beginning to take effect.

11.7.7 What does the future hold?

During the 1960s McLuhan became a phenomenon — a popular philosopher, a media guru and prophet. He had a strong following, especially among artists and advertising practitioners who accepted his views and pronouncements as those of an oracle. It is said that his most impressive achievement is his reputation. He was hailed as The High Priest of Popcult, the Metaphysician of Media and the Oracle of the Electronic Age. McLuhan has, however, been severely criticised for the incoherence of his ideas, his unsubstantiated statements and the lack of evidence to support his psychological arguments. His notion that literacy was obsolete and his praise of nonlinear thinking were severely criticised by other literary critics who thought nonlinear thinking was just another label for logically inconsistent, random thoughts. Empirical media researchers, who found it difficult to design research to systematically study something as amorphous as 'people's experiences' concluded that his ideas were overly speculative and empirically unverifiable (Baran & Davies 2003).

While McLuhan's pronouncements are in fact outrageous and do not form a unified theory of communication, he nevertheless succeeded in stimulating people to look at the media in a different way and raised some important issues about the influence of modern media on people and the structure of society. Everett Rogers (2000) argues that McLuhan's perspective deserves more attention by mass communication scholars, especially those interested in studying new media. It is interesting to note that, in contemporary times, he has been declared the patron saint of *Wired* magazine, the Bible of Cyberspace. McLuhan was featured on the March 3, 1967 cover of *Newsweek* and, 29 years later, despite the suspicion and outright hostility with which his views were regarded in the intervening years, he graced the cover of the January 1996 edition of *Wired* magazine (Baran & Davies 2003).

Before his death in 1980, McLuhan predicted that even the impact of computer technology as he knew it would be insignificant compared with the upheaval caused by the computer software to come. McLuhan predicted that people will work at home connected to their corporations by television. They will relay information by computer systems. The rush-hour traffic will be a thing of the past. Huge cities like New York will become obsolete. Even shopping will be done via television. It is true that we have information and entertainment at our fingertips and instant communication with people all over the world. But the question that some contemporary theorists are asking is: How does one assess qualitative changes in the lives of people in the new digital age?

Fang (1997) maintains that people today spend many hours of each day mentally or physically isolated from one another, mainly with television and computers. He explains that e-mail, home entertainment, working at home and chat rooms and bulletin boards on the WWW mean that something desirable, such as direct human contact, may be lost. He says that our generation has discovered the power of mass communication to part us from each other, and we appear to be contented.

As well as personal consequences for the individual, Fang (1997) looks at the social implications of the Digital Age. He says that the modern individual can function efficiently without often having to venture beyond his or her front door. He predicts that, in time, this could reverse the Industrial Revolution's flow of populations and wealth into cities during the past two centuries, with tremendous social consequences — both positive and negative. A further point he makes is that the values inherent in information threaten economic stagnation for large areas of the globe (eg Third World countries) where communication tools are not abundant.

Griffin (2003:350-351) cites Neil Postman, a leading media and cultural theorist, who believes that people in the Digital Age are "culturally the worse for wear". We have become a **technopoly** — his term for a society that is monopolised by technology. He maintains that we no longer use the tools we have invented, but that our tools use us. Instead of being integrated into the society's culture, our tools intrude on its belief systems and values and threaten to take it over. "The culture seeks its authorisation in technology, finds its satisfaction in technology, and takes its orders from technology" (Postman in Griffin 2003:350). Postman maintains that our reliance on technology has replaced traditional print values of propositional logic, sequential understanding, context, detachment, discipline and wisdom with the cybervirtues of speed, capacity, imagery, hypertexuality, immediate gratification and emotional involvement. We have come to rely less on logic and more on feelings.

Postman suggests that unless we assess the effects of new technologies on our lives before we adopt them, we will become "tools of our tools". Griffin (2003:351) gives us two examples. He asks: Will palm computers really make us more efficient and increase our leisure time, or will we actually become more enslaved to our schedules and lists of things to do? Will our ability to 'beam' a friend's computer simplify our lives and draw us closer together, or will that ability simply complicate our lives with new programs to learn and equipment to buy? He concludes by saying that, "Tools will do what they are designed to do. The question is, what are they ultimately doing to us?"

Scenario 11.2

The following is an extract about Marshall McLuhan's theory from *Contemporary mass communication theory* (Baran & Davies 2003:300-301). Study the text carefully and then answer the question that follows.

"Initially, McLuhan's work fit the spirit of the early 1960s . . . he was unabashedly optimistic about the profound but ultimately positive changes in our personal experience, social structure, and culture that new media technology would make possible. McLuhan was the darling of the media industries — their prophet with honor. For a brief period, he commanded huge fees as a consultant and seminar leader for large companies. His ideas were used to rationalize rapid expansion of electronic media with little concern for their negative consequences. His mantra became broadcast industry gospel: So what if children spend most of their free time in front of television sets and become functionally illiterate? Reading is doomed anyway, why prolong its demise? Eventually, we will all live in a global village where literacy is as unnecessary as it was in preliterate tribal villages. Why worry about the negative consequences of television when it is obviously so much better than the hot, old media it is replacing? Just think of the limitations that print media impose. Linear, logical thinking is far too restrictive. If the triumph of electronic media is inevitable, why not get on with it? No need for government regulation of media. The ideal form of media can be expected to evolve naturally, no matter what we try to do. No need to worry about media conglomerates. No need to complain about television violence. No need to resist racist or sexist media content. Adopt McLuhan's long-term, global perspective. Think big. Think nonlinearly. Just wait for the future to happen."

Do you agree or disagree with McLuhan's main assumptions about the mass media as outlined in the extract above? Provide reasons for your answer.

Summary

This chapter has tried to explain some aspects of mass communication. It first explained the terms 'mass', 'mass communication' and 'mass media'. The distinction between mass communication and mass media is important to our understanding of the mass communication context. The process of mass communication was discussed by contrasting it with interpersonal communication and then illustrating the process by means of a model. The next topic discussed was the functions that mass communication performs in society. The remainder of the chapter broadened our understanding of mass communication and its influence on society and people by examining the components of the mass communication process in greater detail: the mass communicator, the mass medium and the audiences of mass communication. It referred to various research studies and theories that attempt to explain the effects of mass media messages on society and on people: gatekeeping, agenda-setting, spiral of silence, magic-bullet, two-step flow and uses and gratification theory. This section of the chapter ended with a scenario based on the uses and gratification theory. To conclude our study of mass communication the chapter examined an approach known as technological or media determinism. Technological determinism sees social change as a direct result of fundamental technological development and innovation. To illustrate this approach, McLuhan's views on media determinism — the power of the medium to change people's lives and the nature of society — were examined. The discussion revolved around the main concepts in his theory: the medium is the message, the global village, the ratio of the senses, hot and cool media, an eye for an ear and the Gutenberg Galaxy. The chapter concluded with the views of two theorists who are critical of McLuhan's belief in the power of the media to bring about cultural and social changes. The chapter ended with a commentary on McLuhan's views by Baran and Davies (2003).

Test yourself

1. Differentiate between the terms 'mass', 'mass communication' and 'mass media'.
2. Contrast mass communication with interpersonal communication by describing five differences between them.
3. Explain four functions of mass communication and illustrate each with an appropriate example.
4. Briefly describe the effects of the mass media on public opinion according to
   (a) the agenda-setting theory
   (b) the spiral of silence theory
5. Briefly describe how the mass media influences its audience, according to
   (a) the magic-bullet theory
   (b) the two-step flow theory
   (c) the uses and gratifications theory
6. Compare the coverage of a major event as presented by a newspaper, a television newscast, a radio news programme and, if you have access to the Internet, a news site on the Web. Relate your findings to what you have learned about the gatekeeping function of the media.

7. Watch a television programme that deals with a controversial topic, for example, on *Special Assignment* (SABC3) or *Carte Blanche* (M-Net), with at least five other people. Take note of their comments about the programme. Did they express similar opinions about the topic? Were any opinions opposed to the stand taken by the programme presenters? Did an opinion leader emerge in the group?

8. Identify the television programmes on the channels you receive that are used primarily to inform, persuade or entertain. Do some combine two or more purposes? Which, in your opinion, are the most successful?

9. Explain the assumptions of media determinism.

10. Write two or three paragraphs on each of the following concepts in McLuhan's theory, using your own examples to illustrate your discussion:
    - the medium is the message
    - the global village
    - ratio of the senses
    - the Gutenberg Galaxy
    - an eye for an ear
    - hot and cool media.

11. What news have you seen recently on television that confirms McLuhan's belief that we live in a global village?

12. What do you think McLuhan would say about the impact of the Internet on the global village?

13. Study the way Wolfe (1968:37), the well-known author and critic, begins his essay on McLuhan:
    What if he's right   What ... if ... he ... is ... right   W-h-a-t i-f-h-e-i-s-r-i-g-h-t

W	IF	R	
H	HE	I	
A	IS	G	?.
T		H	
		T	

    What do you think Wolfe is suggesting?

EXECUTIVE SUMMARY
Mass communication

1 The concept 'mass'
2 Process of mass communication
3 Model of mass communication
4 Functions of mass communication
   ❏ surveillance of the environment
   ❏ correlation
   ❏ cultural transmission
   ❏ entertainment
5 Mass communicator
   ❏ gatekeeping
6 Mass medium
   ❏ magic-bullet theory
   ❏ agenda-setting theory
   ❏ spiral of silence theory
7 Mass audiences
   ❏ two-step flow theory
   ❏ uses and gratifications theory
8 Social effects of mass communication
9 Marshall McLuhan and media determinism
   ❏ the medium is the message
   ❏ ratio of the senses
   ❏ social change
   ❏ global village
   ❏ Gutenberg Galaxy
   ❏ hot and cool media

12 Specialisation areas in communication studies

Overview

We said in Chapter 3 that one of the important developments in the study of communication was a move away from general models and theories to an approach that deals with specific contexts of communication. We discussed these contexts in chapters 7 to 11. An even more recent development has been a need to address specific problems in the discipline by applying communication research in specialisation areas. In each specialisation area, communication has a clearly defined purpose. In this chapter, we provide a brief summary of some of the specialisation areas to extend your knowledge of the field of communication and to make you aware of some of the most recent developments in the discipline. The following specialisation areas are introduced: persuasive communication, organisational communication, intercultural communication, development communication and health communication. You will study the research that has been conducted in these specialisation areas as well as the theories that have been developed in more advanced courses in communication. Each discussion is followed by a short scenario in which the theoretical principles are applied to a practical situation.

Learning outcomes

At the end of this unit you should be able to:
1 Provide a brief overview of the historical development of persuasion from classical to contemporary times.
2 Briefly describe how each of the theoretical approaches to organisational communication discussed in this chapter views the role of communication in the organisation.
3 Explain in which type of organisation you would like to work.
4 Give your own examples of the key concepts that have been developed in intercultural communication to help explain why communication between people of different cultures is sometimes problematic.
5 Provide a brief overview of the three paradigms (approaches) in development communication.
6 Give your opinion on which paradigm you think would be best for South Africa.
7 Give examples from your own experience of each of the functions of health communication discussed in this unit.

8 Explain why effective health communication skills could help the health professional to facilitate communication with the patient.

12.1 Persuasive communication

We begin with persuasive communication because rhetoric, or persuasion, in oral communication was the basis for the earliest formal study of communication that we know about. The discussion that follows is based mainly on the succinct history of communication study provided by Ruben (1984).

Persuasion is part of everyday life. We are constantly subjected to persuasive messages by advertisers, politicians, lecturers, employers, parents and friends. We all use persuasion all the time, whether it is to coax a friend to accompany us to the cinema or to convince our parents that it is in everybody's best interests for them to stop smoking. Theorists study persuasive communication to provide communicators with knowledge that will assist them in delivering effective messages and, importantly, to provide recipients with knowledge about the strategies that persuaders use to convince them to change their attitudes or behaviour.

We think about persuasion as a modern phenomenon because we live in a world where persuasive messages are all around us and continually compete for our attention. However, a systematic study of persuasion can be traced to the classical Greeks (between the fourth and fifth centuries bc) who formalised the study of speech into an academic discipline called rhetoric (persuasion). Their focus was on the study of **oratory** — the creation and delivery of spoken messages — which reflected the essentially oral nature of Greek society. Greek interest in understanding oratory grew out of the practical needs of day-to-day life. Greece had the first true democratic government in history — the people literally governed themselves. Business, government, education and law were conducted orally in public, and every Greek citizen had the right to participate in public affairs. For example, the Assembly (seat of government) was open to all free male citizens of adult age, regardless of income or class. It met about 40 times a year and anyone present could speak about any topic — provided he could hold the audience's attention (cf Bowra 1986). The judicial system was similarly dependent upon oral communication. Greek citizens had to be their own lawyers and be able to present a case that would convince a jury of several hundred people of their innocence. Effective public speaking, or oratory, and the ability to use persuasive forms of communication therefore became a priority for most people. Consequently, a group of teachers called **sophists** became popular by teaching people the art of **rhetoric** — how to prepare a persuasive speech and deliver it eloquently. In other words, they taught people how to become effective orators.

12.1.1 Plato's and Aristotle's view of persuasion

Among the ancient theorists, Plato (427-347 BC) was sceptical of the professional sophists who earned a living by teaching orators to sway an audience. Plato maintained that the method used by the sophists — sophistic rhetoric — was not ethical because the sophists were merely interested in using rhetoric as a technical skill whereby the orator could manipulate the audience. They taught their pupils to master the stylistic aspects of oratory to be able to persuade the audience unconditionally, even if this meant manipulating the emotions of the audience or presenting a one-sided argument which was aimed at deceiving the audience.

Plato developed an alternative to the sophistic method — **philosophical rhetoric** — which was directed at persuading an audience by ethical means. Plato regarded each member of the audience as an individual and would present, for example, both sides of a discussion and give the listeners the opportunity to consider the argument in relation to their own needs and values. We could say that Plato gave the audience the opportunity to interpret the message within their own circumstances (refer to Section 3.3.10). Plato's views, together with those of his pupil, Aristotle, contributed significantly to the body of knowledge about communication in classical times.

Aristotle (385-322 BC) became one of the prominent philosophers and advocates of rhetoric in his time. Aristotle regarded rhetoric as an art (or skill) that could be taught and as a field of academic study. Of the writings that survive from classical Greece, the most important is Aristotle's *Rhetoric* — a set of lecture notes on public speaking and persuasive communication — which is still used as a reference work in departments of communication today. It is regarded as "the first orderly, systematic attempt to set down the principles of the art of public speaking" (Thonssen, Baird & Braden 1970:75). *Rhetoric* combines Aristotle's knowledge of communication with observations he made in everyday situations of the practices of speakers and the responses of audiences. Among other issues, Aristotle's *Rhetoric* contains his views about logic and truth in argumentation, various aspects of human nature and the importance of the delivery of a speech, including the orator's style of speaking. Aristotle maintained that people could be taught (and should practise) the skilful construction of an argument and effective delivery of a speech. It is remarkable how many of the principles that Aristotle stated a little over two thousand years ago are regarded as good practice today.

12.1.2 The Roman tradition and later

The ancient Romans also took public speaking very seriously, and training in rhetoric and the correct use of language began at a young age. Although the Greeks invented the science of rhetoric, Roman scholars such as Cicero (106-43 BC) and Quintilian (AD 35-95) broadened and perfected it. However, with the decline of the Classical period, democracy and the oral tradition began to wane. This can be attributed mainly to changes in society. For more than a thousand years after the fall of the Roman Empire, totalitarian regimes prevailed in Europe, and public opinion was no longer relevant in the political process. Deprived of the opportunity to sway masses of people through rhetoric, people no longer needed to be able to speak effectively and academic interest in rhetoric fell into insignificance. At the same time, the Church established complete control of religious practices, going so far as forbidding clergymen to preach. As a result, interest in rhetoric by religious scholars and other intellectuals also waned (cf Stacks, Hickson & Hill 1991).

There was a rebirth of learning during the late Medieval (7th to 13th century AD) and Renaissance (14, 15th and 16th centuries) periods, and rhetoric was once again being studied in religion. However, it was not until a new society emerged during the Industrial Revolution that the academic study of communication was revived.

12.1.3 Contemporary rhetoric

The Industrial Revolution, which began in Britain in the late 18th century and spread in the 19th century to Western Europe and the United States, created societies characterised by large-scale manufacturing industries rather than trade or farming. The invention of steam-powered machinery and the mass migration of people from rural areas to seek employment in the rapidly growing industrial cities brought about far-reaching changes in the nature of society. Although the printing press had been invented in the 16th century, it was only when the machinery that made the mass distribution of newspapers and other printed materials possible appeared that information became available to growing numbers of people. With the spread of printed materials, more and more people learned to read and write, and their thinking was freed from the restrictions of church and government. New political and religious ideas began to circulate in society, and throughout Europe and America, revolutionary movements emerged, making use of print to disseminate their ideas to increasingly receptive publics. Particularly with the spread of newspapers, public opinion once again became something that political leaders had to take into account. Scholars began to revive the art of public speaking and interest in rhetoric and speech once again became an area of academic study.

12.1.4. Digitisation

Today, the study of rhetoric embraces not only its application in the speechmaking process, but includes different types of persuasion and the various contexts in which it occurs, for example, in interpersonal relationships, advertising or politics. Any understanding of persuasion must also take into account the introduction and rapid adoption of new technologies such as personal computers and the **digitisation** of many older technologies. We could say that, even though persuasion has been used in economics, politics, religion, business and interpersonal relationships ever since humans began to interact, never before has persuasion been so effective or pervasive a tool (for good or bad) in society as today. On a personal level, persuasion influences our consumer behaviour, our interpersonal behaviour and our intrapersonal behaviour (self-persuasion). And because we spend far more time receiving persuasion than using it, modern studies of persuasion are directed as much at the recipients of persuasive messages as at the communicators — people need to learn how to become critical and responsible consumers of persuasion (cf Larson 2004). Typically, an academic course in persuasion today would include aspects such as the historical roots of persuasion, perspectives on ethics in persuasion, theoretical approaches to the study of persuasion and its application in different contexts, such as advertising and politics.

To emphasise the importance of becoming critical and responsible recipients of persuasion, consider the relevance of persuasion in your everyday life. Some ideas to get you thinking include the following: the literally hundreds of advertisements to which you are exposed every day, the political candidates who urgently want your vote, the campaigns that are developed to change your attitude to health or road safety or intercultural issues, issues revolving around religion, and of course the way that you use (and receive) persuasion in your interpersonal relationships at home, with friends or in the organisation where you work.

Scenario 12.1

After you have studied the AIDS poster below (Figure 12.1), discuss with a fellow student or family member the message the poster is trying to convey.

Figure 12.1 AIDS poster

12.2 Organisational communication

Organisational communication developed as a specialisation area in the field of communication studies in the late 1940s and early 1950s as a response to the need for organisations to become more efficient and productive in order to serve the needs of society. Organisational communication is important in businesses and industrial organisations as well as in churches, hospitals, government agencies, military organisations and academic institutions. Organisations are held together by communication. As soon as people gather together to begin organising, they need to make plans, arrive at decisions and settle disputes. Organisational communication is an umbrella term for all the communication processes that occur in the context of an organisation. Organisational communication involves intrapersonal communication (thinking to yourself), dyadic communication (say, between a manager and an employee), small-group communication (meetings), public communication (public speeches by a chief executive officer), mass communication (press releases, company newsletters, new product announcements) and digital communication (e-mail messages to staff members and other organisations or information obtained from the Internet).

Each of these forms of communication takes place both inside (internally) and outside (externally) an organisation. **Internal communication** refers to the messages that are shared among members of an organisation. Internal communication is usually concerned with work-related matters and provides the means for people to work together and co-operate with each other. An organisation, however, does not exist in isolation. It is an element in the structure of society and must adapt to social needs and changes in order to survive. An organisation may want to change its image in the community, for example, or advertise a new product. Organisations therefore establish **external communication** channels to gather information from the world outside it and to provide this world with information about the organisation.

The purpose of research into organisational communication is to help organisations operate at maximum efficiency. To this end, areas of research include theoretical approaches to organisational communication, the structure of organisational communication and the functions of organisational communication. As you study the information below, think about why each of these areas of research is important to the management of an organisation.

12.2.1 Theoretical approaches to organisational communication

☐ ***Classical approach*** The classical approach originated in the late 19th and early 20th centuries when the assembly-line technologies that were developed for factories during the Industrial Revolution were applied to other types of organisations as well. Classical theory emphasises the importance of efficient management and high productivity. In this approach communication functions mainly to establish managerial control, provide workers with job instructions, and enable managers to gather information for planning. Most of the communication in the organisation flows from management to subordinates. There is also a sharp distinction between the private and work lives of employees. What happens at home is of no concern to management, even if it has an effect on the employee's work. It has been said that classical theory regards the organisation as a machine, and the people who work in it as merely cogs in the machine. The role of the individual is not very important because, like the parts of a machine, any worker can be removed and replaced without unduly disrupting the smooth running of the organisation.

☐ **Human relations approach** Researchers in the 1930s attempted to identify the ideal work environment to encourage high productivity, loyalty and motivation among employees. They suggested that workers should not be treated as cogs in a machine, but that strategies should be developed to ensure congenial working conditions and to help employees fulfil their needs and goals. This line of study is known as the human relations approach and stresses that organisational efficiency depends on strategies for increasing the work satisfaction and personal happiness of the individual employee. It also acknowledges the importance of social relations in organisational life — cliques or informal groups are a reality that affects the organisation. The contribution of this approach is that the importance of personal interaction between the formal system and its employees was established. Organisations must provide upward channels of communication that enable employees to approach management. The human relations school has been accused of being a manipulative management strategy designed to increase worker output by pretending to be concerned about people yet still treating them as cogs in the organisational machine. However, it provided the groundwork for future theories, such as the human resources approach.

☐ **Human resources approach** The human resources perspective of organisations developed in the late 1950s in response to the shortcomings of human relations theory. According to this approach, workers are considered as sources of suggestions and ideas, and it is management's task to encourage people to contribute to the organisation in diverse ways and thereby to maximise productivity. The human resources approach particularly stresses participative decision making and effective employer-employee relations because it maintains that workers are more motivated, productive and independent, and more satisfied with their work, when they are consulted about decisions that directly affect their work activities. In respect of communication, the human resources school emphasises genuine participation by all employees. Employees' ideas and suggestions are sought and encouraged and decision making is not limited to higher management, but is encouraged at all levels of the organisation. Frequent communication is considered a necessity and management is expected to arrange group discussions, develop skilled group communication and leadership skills, and to motivate individuals towards the achievement of personal and organisational goals.

☐ **Systems approach** The systems approach considers the organisation as a whole (system) made up of separate parts, each of which has a relationship to all the other parts and to the environment in which the organisation exists. All the system parts are dependent on one another in the performance of organisational activities. Any change in one component inevitably affects the

other system components. All the parts of the system must therefore co-
ordinate their activities and functions to remain in a state of equilibrium or
balance. For this purpose, relevant information is provided through efficient
internal communication channels. Organisations also exchange information
with their environment. External communication channels in the organisation must allow a free, open and rapid flow of information between the
organisation and the society in which it exists. It is particularly important for
the organisation to establish feedback channels to gather information that
will allow it to adapt to needs and changes in the environment. In the systems
approach, communication is crucial to the organisation because it is the
unifying element that allows the system to function efficiently, achieve its
goals and remain in a state of balance.

❑ **_Cultural approach_** Utall (1983:66) defines organisational culture as "a
system of shared values (what is important) and beliefs (how things work) that
interact with a company's people, organisational structures, and control
systems to produce behavioural norms (the way we do things around here)".
Every organisation has its own cultural identity because every organisation
has a particular way of doing what it does and its own way of talking about
what it is doing. Three of the components that contribute to the culture of the
organisation are its corporate identity, image and the personality towards
which it strives. 'Corporate identity' refers to the way in which an organisation
chooses to present itself to the public through, for example, letterheads, colour
schemes, logos and so on. 'Corporate image' is the way in which the public
perceives an organisation, whereas 'corporate personality' comprises all the
characteristics that contribute to the uniqueness of an organisation, such as
original ideas that individual members contribute and the slogans that
characterise particular organisations (Du Plooy 1991; Steinberg 1999a). The
importance of making employees aware of the culture in an organisation is
that they tend to behave in certain ways because they are expected to do so. An
understanding of its culture can also help bridge cultural gaps in organisations. Instead of emphasising the differences between cultures, organisations
should strive to create a common culture (shared values and beliefs) to which
all its employees can adapt. The culture then has a unifying function in that it
is the basis for collective sense-making activities by people in the organisation
— "the way we do things around here" (cf Andrews & Baird 1992:20).

12.2.2 The structure of organisational communication

'Structure' in this context refers to the components of the communication
system in an organisation and includes the channels of communication
through which information is sent and received, the hierarchies in the
organisation, the flow of information in the organisation and communication
networks.

- ❏ **Communication channels** Channels of information in the organisation are described by distinguishing between the formal and informal flow of information. **Formal channels** are the official channels through which communication is exchanged. Formal channels may be written or oral and include personal instructions, interviews, training programmes, letters, memoranda and oral reports. However, information is also exchanged unofficially, or through **informal channels,** during, for example, conversations among employees. Such information may be work-related or may be concerned with social and personal matters. Informal channels may at times prove to be a more effective means of communication than the organisation's formal channels.

- ❏ **Hierarchies** Information is distributed throughout an organisation in a hierarchical structure. The hierarchical structure of an organisation is often depicted in an organisational chart, a linear diagram showing the status of different members of an organisation and the relationships among them. The hierarchy affects the interpersonal relations of its employees and controls the channels of communication within the organisation. The hierarchy also controls the frequency and quality of daily interactions among people.

- ❏ **Flow of information** The flow of information refers to the direction in which messages travel in the organisation and includes upward, downward and lateral or horizontal communication, and the grapevine. Downward communication flows from top to bottom in the organisational hierarchy — that is, from superiors (management) to subordinates (employees). Downward messages are usually work-related and are disseminated through formal communication channels. Upward communication flows from subordinates to superiors and usually takes place via the same channels as downward communication. Lateral, or horizontal, communication describes communication between people on the same hierarchical level and may take the form of work-related messages or may provide social interaction. The channels used for lateral communication are similar to those used for downward and upward communication. The grapevine is not prescribed by the organisation. It is an informal channel of information used to spread rumours as well as to convey important information such as news on promotions, personnel changes, annual salary adjustments and organisational policy changes. Field research indicates that grapevine communication travels very quickly and is also reasonably accurate. The dysfunctional aspect of the grapevine is that it fosters and spreads rumours. Usually characterised by prejudice, emotion, bias and partial truths, rumours arise in situations where there is ambiguity or uncertainty about issues in the organisation. In other words, an organisation with a strong grapevine could be experiencing problems with its formal communication channels and networks — organisation members are simply not receiving sufficient information through recognised channels. The trend today is to accept the existence of the grapevine as an inevitable fact of organisational life. Researchers maintain that by learning to use it to better effect, managers can build teamwork and company loyalty, increase motivation and job satisfaction and ultimately improve performance (cf Andrews & Baird 1992:80).

❑ **Communication networks** Apart from vertical and lateral communication channels, communication may also take place through communication networks in the organisation. On the most basic level, a network can be identified by establishing who communicates with whom, and who the central figures and the peripheral figures are in the communication process. Awareness of the potential networks in an organisation provides insight into what type of information is likely to be received by which people. In a university, for instance, policy decisions made by the senate about course curricula will be networked among deans of faculties and department heads (central figures), but not among the rest of the university staff (peripheral figures). Current research into communication networks examines the impact of computer technology in organisations as computers increasingly perform essential information processing functions for all employees at all levels of the organisation.

12.2.3 Functions of organisational communication

Research into the functions of organisational communication is largely concerned with the purposes that communication serves and its effects on people and activities in the organisation (cf Koehler, Anatol & Appelbaum 1981).

❑ The **informative function** is concerned with the provision of information to ensure the efficient operation of the organisation. Management and employees need accurate, timely and well-organised information to enable them to do their work efficiently, make decisions and resolve conflicts. There is also the need for organisations to obtain information to adapt to changes in environmental conditions. Most organisations have regular meetings during which information is exchanged about each area of the organisation, with a view to directing and co-ordinating behaviour towards implementing organisational changes.

❑ The **regulatory function** serves to control and co-ordinate the activities of the organisation to ensure its successful operation. Manuals, policies, memoranda, rules and instructions collectively constitute a set of guidelines for the management of the organisation.

❑ The **integrative function** is used to achieve organisational unity and cohesion by creating identity and uniformity in the organisation. As well as defining goals and tasks to facilitate the assimilation of new members, integrative messages are used to co-ordinate the work schedules of individuals, groups and departments, thereby eliminating wasted time and effort.

❑ The **persuasive function** is concerned with the way communication influences members of an organisation. Managers, for instance, have found that power and the enforcement of authority do not always achieve the desired control over employees. They have discovered that persuasion is often more effective than authoritarian methods to gain employees' co-operation. Similarly, employees may use persuasion when, for instance, requesting an increase in salary.

Scenario 12.2

Shirley is employed in an advertising firm that has to design a television advertisement for a new cleaning material. The team she works with has not been able to think of an idea that satisfies the client. Shirley is thinking about the problem while travelling to work one morning, and suddenly she thinks of a new idea which she feels sure the client will like. She happens to meet the team leader in the lift and immediately shares her ideas with him. He asks Shirley to arrange a meeting at which the entire team can discuss the idea. As soon as she reaches her office, Shirley telephones the people concerned. During the meeting, potential problems are raised and discussed. Finally, the team decides to implement Shirley's suggestion and they design an advertisement. The team leader sends an e-mail to the client suggesting several alternative dates for a presentation of the advertisement.

After you have studied the scenario, try to identify the different contexts in which organisational communication has taken place and give examples of internal and external communication.

12.3 Intercultural communication

Communication between people from different cultural groups is one of the most complex areas of human interaction. Individuals vary in their ways of looking at the world and these variations must be understood before effective communication can take place. The purpose of studying intercultural communication is to promote such an understanding. We also need to consider that in the last 30 years there has been a dramatic increase in intercultural communication, mainly due to technical developments in aviation and electronic networks. International air travel today is accessible to millions of people and satellite technology makes it possible for us to receive the news of the world at home and be linked with people all over the world (cf Tubbs & Moss 2003). Our world has become the global village predicted by Marshall

McLuhan, a world in which we know what is happening in countries all over the world, as if we were living in a small village.

12.3.1 Importance of intercultural communication

Intercultural communication can be defined as "communication between members of different cultures (whether defined in terms of racial, ethnic, or socioeconomic differences)" (Tubbs & Moss 2003:294). But what is culture? A straightforward definition is that culture describes the norms by which members of a society learn to behave. Culture can also be defined as "the total accumulation of beliefs, norms, activities, institutions, and communication patterns" (Dodd 1991:41) of an identifiable group of people. The second definition indicates that culture is "any of the customs, worldview, language, kinship systems, social organisation and other taken-for-granted day-to-day practices of a people which set that group apart as a distinctive group" (Burton & Dimbleby 1995:130). Every aspect of your life is affected by your culture: the way you dress, the food you eat, the music you enjoy, your family relationships, your expectations about marriage and a career, are but a few examples. An important point to remember is that culture is not innate, it is learned. Because it is learned, a child born in India of Indian parents, but brought to South Africa and raised by South African parents, will be culturally a South African.

For South Africans, understanding the theoretical foundations of intercultural communication and mastering intercultural communication skills are extremely important for several reasons. Economically, South Africa trades with nations as diverse as Great Britain, Israel and Japan, all with cultures and economic systems different to our own. In order to engage in successful trade relations, we have to understand their cultural expectations. In many countries, notably the United States, theories of intercultural communication have been used to train representatives of government, business and the military who have to travel or live abroad.

Importantly, South Africa is a country of diverse cultures. As well as our indigenous cultures, South Africa is home to many immigrant cultures. While we share some characteristics, each group has its own cultural characteristics which contribute in some way to our rainbow nation (cf Cleary 2003). Given the number and variety of cultures and societies in countries like South Africa, it is not surprising that communication between people of different cultures can sometimes be problematic.

A variety of theoretical approaches to and theories of intercultural communication have been developed in the last three decades. We describe three such approaches very briefly. Please note that one approach is not better than another and all three perspectives have contributed to our understanding of intercultural communication. (Refer to the research methods described in section 2.5.5.)

12.3.2 Theoretical approaches to intercultural communication

☐ The assumption of the **social science approach** is that behaviour can be observed, measured and predicted. We can therefore discover universals about the way people behave. Because culture influences communication, the primary focus is on describing and comparing cultures. For example, researchers might conduct a cross-cultural study of nonverbal behaviour among people from different countries in Africa.

☐ The **interpretive approach** concentrates on the subjective experiences of individuals and makes use of qualitative, rather than quantitative research methods, such as field studies and personal observation. The goal is to understand rather than predict behaviour and researchers might collect personal narratives and stories from members of the group. An example is an ethnographic study of speech patterns and codes in a community to find out about who speaks to whom, who initiates conversation, the degree of formality, the amount of feedback that is tolerated, and so on.

☐ The **critical approach** is primarily concerned with creating change by examining power relationships within cultures. According to this view, power relationships dominate all intercultural relationships, whether they are social, political, economic or historical. Predicting or understanding behaviour is not sufficient. The outcome of research must lead to actual change. Researchers analyse a society's cultural products, including those produced by the media, such as movies, newspapers, television and public relations manuals. Some critical studies have analysed how ethnic minorities are represented in American movies in comparison with whites. One recent study examines how the language of news reports contributes to a new form of racism (cf van Dijk 2000). You should think about why it became necessary to rewrite the history books that had been prescribed for South African school children after the change of government in 1994.

12.3.3 Key concepts in intercultural communication

Infante, Rancer and Womack (2003) describe the following as key concepts in the study of intercultural communication:

☐ **Verbal and nonverbal codes** We expect languages to differ, but we also learned in Chapter 5 that nonverbal codes are not universal, especially with regard to proxemics, haptics and chronemics. The greatest difficulties in communicating with someone who does not speak your language lies in the areas of abstraction and connotation. Please refer to Chapters 3 and 6 where these aspects are discussed.

☐ **Worldview** Values and beliefs create a worldview that may conflict with our own. For example, many Western visitors to South Africa do not understand why people from some African cultures consult a sangoma about the persistent illness or bad luck they perceive to be the result of evil supernatural forces.

☐ **Social norms and role expectations** Cultures differ about how closely a member is expected to fill his or her role expectations. It is extremely rare to find a married woman in the workplace in Japan because she is expected to be a full-time wife and mother, rather than the Western 'supermom' who often tries to combine a high-powered job with home and parental obligations. People from other cultures visiting or working in Japan may be at a disadvantage because they do not know the appropriate roles or role behaviours.

☐ **Cultural barriers** Barriers which have been identified as significantly contributing to poor intercultural relationships include prejudice, ethnocentrism and stereotyping.

☐ **High- and low-context cultures** A major contribution to our understanding of intercultural communication was Hall's (1968) distinction between high- and low-context cultures on the basis of the way information is encoded. **High-context cultures** rely on the context (the physical and emotional setting) rather than words to convey a large part of the message's meaning. It is assumed that the recipient will understand the implicit (underlying) meaning because of the context in which the message is communicated. Individuals from high-context cultures find nonverbal cues extremely important in helping them to interpret the messages of others. They are usually more skilled at decoding nonverbal messages than people from low-context cultures and the verbal message is sometimes expressed indirectly and may be ambiguous. In **low-context** cultures messages are explicit, direct and completely encoded in words because low-context cultures believe that if thoughts are not clearly expressed, they may be misunderstood. Hall also reported that people in every culture communicate in both ways. The difference is one of focus. Asian countries, such as China and Japan, are high-context and have a 'message context' orientation whereas American culture is low-context and relies more on 'message content'. In situations of intercultural negotiation or business transactions, complications arise because, in Chinese culture for instance, disagreement is shown by silence. Most Westerners, however, would interpret silence as indicating agreement — they do not instinctively know that in China it is not polite to disagree with others and that the context explains the meaning of the silence (cf Griffen 2003; Infante, Rancer & Womack 2003; Tubbs & Moss 2003).

A conclusion that many intercultural theorists have reached is that when people of different cultures encounter one another, it is important to focus more on what they have in common rather than their differences. In this vein, it is perhaps relevant to conclude this overview of intercultural communication with a statement by Hofstede (1991:237): "The principle of surviving in a multicultural world is that one does not need to think, feel and act in the same way in order to agree on practical issues and to cooperate."

Scenario 12.3

This example is taken from Beamer and Varner (2001:22) and illustrates how misunderstandings can occur in a conversation between a member of a high-context culture and a member of a low-context culture.

A Turkish male student in the United States lived in a residence where he shared a room with an American student. One day his roommate went into the bathroom and completely shaved his head. The Turkish student easily discovered this fact when he visited the bathroom and saw the hair everywhere. He returned to the room and said to his roommate, "You've shaved your head". The American replied, "Yeah, I did".

The Turkish student waited a little and said, "I discovered you'd shaved you head when I went into the bathroom and saw the hair". "Yeah", the American confirmed. The Turk was at a loss. He believed he had communicated in the strongest possible language his wish that the American would clean up the mess he'd made in the bathroom. But no such meaning was attributed to his words by his roommate. Later, he discussed the surprising episode with his friends who told him, "Listen, with Americans you actually have to say 'Clean up the bathroom!'" The Turkish student believed his message had been very clear. He was relying on the context of the communication for the message to be understood. Hair was recently and widely scattered all over the bathroom, and his roommate now had no hair.

12.4 Development communication

Development aid is the assistance offered by First World countries to improve the standard of living in Third World or developing countries. Because the participants in development settings come from different lifeworlds, communication is often difficult. The purpose of **development communication** is to find ways to avoid the one-way transmission of (usually) patronising messages from developers to recipients, and to engage recipients in a two-way transactional process in which they participate in the development projects that are planned.

The best way to understand development and development communication is by means of an historical overview of the field. The end of the Second World War saw the formation of the United Nations (UN). One of the important projects of the UN was to encourage the richer First World countries of the world to provide development aid to the poorer, underdeveloped countries of the Third World. Third World countries are underdeveloped relative to other countries in terms of physical infrastructure, agriculture, economic performance and the social and political spheres of life (cf Melkote 1991). South Africa has many characteristics of First World countries, such as a modern infrastructure and modern mass-media systems. But it also shares characteristics that are typical of Third World countries in respect of, for example, poverty, home-lessness, malnutrition, illiteracy and access to modern mass media. Development and development communication are therefore important fields of study in South Africa.

Development communication is defined as communication that promotes development. But what is development? Definitions of development have changed over the past 50 years as approaches to the conceptualisation of development have changed. Changes in thinking about development resulted from the fact that the earliest attempts at development failed. Three approaches to development are: the dominant paradigm, the alternative paradigm and the new paradigm. Think about a paradigm as a master theory that directs research and explanations in a particular field of enquiry (cf Rensburg 1996). Essentially, a paradigm is not very different from a theoretical approach.

12.4.1 The dominant paradigm

In the 1950s and 1960s, underdevelopment was seen as the result of social and cultural obstacles within the society, which prevented traditional societies from reaching their full potential. For example, it was said that members of traditional societies have an emotional, superstitious and fatalistic view of the world, whereas members of a modern society are forward-looking, innovative and free from superstition. Definitions of development emphasised the modernisation, or westernisation, of underdeveloped communities by replacing traditional ways of life with more complex and technologically advanced ways of life (cf Rogers 1969). This is the **dominant paradigm**. It was thought that, if underdeveloped societies became industrialised and urbanised, developed a Western capitalist economy, and adopted Western-style democratic politics and government, modernisation and prosperity would follow. The two main approaches to development communication that resulted from the dominant paradigm were the **diffusion of innovations approach** and the **mass media and modernisation approach**.

For the purposes of this overview, it suffices to say that 'diffusion' is the process by which new ideas (innovations) are spread (diffused) among members of a community (cf Rogers & Shoemaker 1971). An innovation can be, for example, the introduction of tractors to improve agricultural methods or the purification of drinking water to prevent disease. The mass media and modernisation approach emphasised the all-powerful role of the mass media in assisting the process of modernisation. The mass media was seen as the ideal bridge for the transmission of ideas from developed countries to the Third World and from urban centres to rural areas. It was assumed that the mass media have powerful effects on their recipients and that their messages are accepted uncritically. By introducing mass media into Third World countries, new ideas to encourage modernisation would easily be transmitted and accepted.

Criticism of the dominant paradigm was directed at ignorance of Third World realities. Researchers had an inadequate knowledge of the living conditions and cultural background of the recipients. There was an overemphasis on mass media effects and insufficient attention paid to factors such as the availability of mass media in rural areas, selective exposure — people might choose to listen to music rather than an educational programme — and the accessibility of the message in terms of language use and production techniques (cf Rensburg 1996; Sonderling 2000). Also, communication was top-down, that is, the one-way transmission of messages from specialist communicators to passive recipients. The communicators did not take into account that, even in underdeveloped communities, people want to be consulted about their needs and priorities. It might, for example, be more important for a community to have a crèche where mothers can leave their children while they seek employment on neighbouring farms than to have tractors for ploughing their small pieces of land.

12.4.2 The alternative paradigm

In the 1970s, a new group of theorists, mainly from South America, suggested an **alternative paradigm** — that the problems of the Third World did not arise from within the society but were caused by the domination of Third World countries by Western capitalist ideology. They maintained that Western countries used communication and mass media imperialism to create under-development in the Third World and thereby increase their dependency on the West. Their approach became known as **dependency theory.** As an alternative to modernisation, dependency theorists proposed that governments in the Third World promote their own form of development independently of the West. They were encouraged, for example, to adopt a communal agricultural policy based on self-reliance.

As far as communication was concerned, many Third World governments adopted the approach known as **development journalism** in response to the MacBride Commission's (1980) recommendation that Third World govern-ments should establish mass communication systems in their countries as a major development resource for national development. One of the basic principles of development journalism is that the state or government should be able to restrict the freedom of journalists and the mass media. The freedom of the media should be subordinated to their responsibility to contribute to nation-building, economic growth and cultural identity. The mass media should give priority to news and information about national, cultural and language issues and encourage national autonomy. Many African leaders supported the idea that the state has the right to intervene in media operations, impose censorship and use state subsidies to directly control the mass media (cf McQuail 1987; Sonderling 2000). Development news is, for example, information about the number of new houses built by the state, the electrification of informal settlements or the opening of a new school or clinic in a rural area.

It has been suggested that the mass media could play a positive role in transformation in South Africa and other Third World countries if certain conditions are met. The first requirement is that democracy and freedom of the press must be guaranteed. The mass media must also be accessible to most people if it is to play a meaningful development role in society. Journalists need to establish their independence from the ruling political party and should acquire specialised knowledge of development objectives. They will then be in a position to inform the public in critical but balanced reporting about development projects.

Criticism of the alternative paradigm was that, while it provided new ways of thinking about underdevelopment and using the mass media to promote change by focusing on external causes of underdevelopment, it failed to address internal causes of underdevelopment in Third World countries. Like the modernisation paradigm, it also overemphasised the role that the mass media could play in development.

12.4.3 The new paradigm

The 1980s saw a move towards a more equitable approach to development and communication. The **new paradigm** emphasises participation of recipients in development programmes, and communication as a two-way process between communicators and recipients. Participation in significant activities of the community is seen by the new paradigm as a basic human right and as a means of self-actualisation (refer to Maslow's hierarchy of needs in Chapter 2). Communication is used primarily as an instrument of **conscientisation** (the transfer of knowledge to members of the community, especially an awareness of the conditions of their existence). Through discussion, the needs and problems of the community are identified, a plan of action formulated, and the community then implements the plan. The emphasis is on self-development and cultural growth rather than on purely material assistance. For example, a discussion with a development agent about the conditions of existence depicted in a photograph of an informal settlement could lead to the community identifying problems and making suggestions about how to rectify the problems.

In the new paradigm, the mass media are still seen as important carriers of development messages, but the mass media alone are not sufficient. It is more important to use the most appropriate medium for a particular group of people. Communicators emphasise the importance of culture as a facilitator in the development process. They look at indigenous channels of communication known as **folk media**. Folk media, or "people's communication" (Jayaweera 1991:17) is a product of local culture and includes folk theatre, puppet shows, oratory, folk dances, ballads and mime. As well as fulfilling an important entertainment and religious role, folk media are used by local groups to help in their struggle for a better life. The most important features of folk media are that the community is familiar with them and they provide for a maximum amount of interactive communication. The community can discuss the message conveyed in a puppet show or dance routine with the communicators and among themselves. There is also no reason why folk media should not be integrated with mass media to provide wider geographical distribution of messages (cf Servaes & Arnst 1993:45; Rensburg 1996). For example, the types of plays that we discuss in Example 12.4 below could be videoed and broadcast on national television in South Africa.

The sharing of knowledge between communicators and recipients gave rise to the idea of **development support communication** (DSC). We need to remember that, often, communicators and recipients do not share a common language and the sharing of development knowledge sometimes involves the use of technical jargon. To promote interactive communication and the sharing of messages on an equal footing, the development support communicator (DSC) acts as a facilitator, or go-between, in the exchange of ideas. The DSC ensures that messages are made comprehensible and relevant for the recipients. The DSC might, for example, advise the leaders of a community to use pictures and posters to explain procedures such as voting or an aspect of healthcare.

While the new paradigm appears to offer the 'best' approach to development in that it is people-centred, it has not entirely replaced the other two paradigms. Even today, some of the ideas of modernisation and dependency theorists influence the approach of development communicators.

Scenario 12.4

The scenario is adapted from *When people play people: development communication through theatre* (1993:66-67) by Zakes Mda, the South African poet, artist, playwright and academic. Mda describes the different forms of folk theatre used by Lesotho's Marotholi Travelling Theatre. Topics that the theatre group deal with include strike action, migrant labour problems, health issues and political corruption, among others. After you have studied the case come up with your own ideas about the way in which folk theatre could be used for conscientisation and emancipation in a developing country.

Please note that the word 'catalyst' used in the case refers to outsiders with specialist skills in theatre and in community development who work as organised groups in communities — they must have a higher level of social consciousness than the villagers, based on their education and general social experience (Mda 1993:19).

Until 1986 Marotholi used the *agitprop* method of theatre. This means that the group toured with prepackaged productions which they created after identifying the needs of the target community. In this method the only community participation was in group discussions that took place after performances. In 1986 Marotholi changed from agitprop to participation theatre and theatre-for-conscientisation. 'Participatory theatre' is produced with and by the people with the help of catalysts. Plays are improvised within the specific parameters of the themes. The difference between this method and agitprop is that members of the community themselves are the performers, rather than a group from outside.

'Theatre-for-conscientisation' is a higher form of participatory theatre. The main difference between the two is that in theatre-for-conscientisation the spectacle is not only produced by and for the people, but during the production the spectators are invited to participate by suggesting solutions to the social problem being depicted. The 'best' solution is arrived at by trial, error, discussion, and finally audience consensus. Improvisation happens throughout the life of the production and the direction the play takes at each performance is never pre-planned.

In the type of participatory theatre known as 'forum theatre', actors and spectators converge. Any spectator may be invited to replace any actor and lead the action in the direction that is most appropriate to him or her. Consequently, if any audience members have experienced the type of social problem or situation being enacted in the performance, they replace the actors and have the opportunity to express their emotions and explain their interpretation of the events that took place. It has been argued that such theatre offers the means whereby all possible paths may be examined. The emphasis is on self-education. Consciousness is raised from inside as the group analyse social reality and power relations. When the spectators themselves become actors the catalyst group is no longer necessary. At this stage, community participation and control increase.

12.5 Health communication

Over the past two or three decades, a great deal of media attention has been paid to the state of healthcare services in South Africa. Healthcare providers or professionals, including nurses, doctors, dentists, health administrators and social workers, have been sharply criticised for their lack of communication skills. Limited human and financial resources are reflected in poor and inadequate healthcare facilities in many parts of the country. When we consider the diversity of cultures in South Africa, we can understand why differences in language and health beliefs, attitudes and behaviour can also lead to a breakdown in communication between health professionals and patients. For this reason, the study of health communication has become an extremely important field of research in South Africa.

The problems in health communication are not confined to South Africa. The media in countries all over the world are decrying the lack of effective and satisfying healthcare communication, such as insensitivity to concerns voiced by patients and their families, poor listening behaviour and a lack of empathy and respect. Even though it has been established that communication is the most important tool health professionals have in providing healthcare for their clients, many patients report that they are so intimidated by health professionals that they leave a clinic or hospital without talking, even about their symptoms (cf Infante, Rancer & Womack 2003).

Research into health communication provides us with models and skills to facilitate communication about health matters in all the contexts of communication: intrapersonal, interpersonal, in groups and organisations, and by means of the mass communication media.

12.5.1 Defining health communication

The concept of 'health' is a broad one because, according to the World Health Organisation, it refers not only to the physical state of one's body, but also includes being mentally well and socially adjusted (cf Faure 2000). A straightforward definition of health communication is "the dissemination and interpretation of health-related messages" (Donohew & Ray 1990:4). The disseminator (communicator) of the message can be an individual, an organisation or a mass medium. The interpreter (recipient) of the information can be an individual, a group, an organisation or a mass public. In terms of the definition, you can see that health communication occurs in a variety of contexts: a conversation between yourself and your doctor in a consulting rooms is an example of interpersonal health communication; the organisational health communication context refers to your experiences in a hospital, for instance; and a television campaign about dental care is an example of the mass-media context of health communication.

Health communication is a very broad area in which to conduct research and develop theories. Research into health communication has been undertaken mainly within the contexts of communication we discussed in Chapter 3. From research findings in these contexts theorists have identified the functions of health communication, health communication skills, and developed the approaches, theories and models of healthcare that are studied in more advanced courses in health communication. The discussion that follows provides a very brief discussion of some of these research contexts and findings.

12.5.2 Areas of research in health communication

☐ In the *interpersonal context*, the following relationships are studied: health professional-patient (eg between physiotherapist and patient), health professional-health professional (eg between the patient's doctor and psychologist), health professional-family (eg between the nurse and the patient's life partner) and patient-family relationships (the ways in which the patient's illness affects family members and family members affect patients).

☐ In the *small-group context* research focuses on the groups that develop in the healthcare setting, such as healthcare teams. Healthcare teams consist of groups of people with differentiated expertise who work together to provide the multiple services needed by a patient, for example a doctor, nurse, social worker and medical technologist. Effective communication between members of the healthcare team is vital if the patient is to receive the best available treatment.

☐ The healthcare *organisation* is the primary setting for healthcare practice and includes hospitals, clinics, medical centres, hospices and convalescent centres. Organisations have goals to accomplish and these goals require that staff members share information and co-ordinate their activities—that is, that they communicate effectively. Many of the problems associated with South African hospitals in recent years, such as disciplinary problems and strike action, have been attributed to poor and ineffective communication.

☐ In the *mass communication context*, health professionals can communicate publicly about health matters that concern the public in general. Television, radio, newspapers, posters, pamphlets and other media have been used to encourage the use of condoms to prevent HIV/AIDS, to quit smoking, to say 'no' to drugs, to have regular eye tests and dental checkups, to name a few (cf Rensburg 1996; Faure 2000).

12.5.3 Functions of health communication

The four functions of health communication that have been identified involve, to a large degree, the interpersonal context (cf Infante, Rancer & Womack 2003).

- ☐ **Diagnosis** This function concerns the health professional's skills of gathering and interpreting data from the patient and finding solutions to health problems.

- ☐ **Co-operation** Communication about the nature of the patient's illness and the implications of treatment prescribed for his or her care.

- ☐ **Counsel** The role of the healthcare professional in acting as a therapist and engaging in empathic listening to understand the patient's symbolic orientation, for example, cultural health beliefs about sexually transmitted diseases.

- ☐ **Education** Healthcare is not only about curing illness, but about preventing it. It is important to educate people about, for instance, nutrition, inoculation, clean water and the use of condoms in order to prevent disease. This function is carried out interpersonally as well as in small groups, in organisations and by the mass media.

12.5.4 Communication skills in healthcare

An important practical outcome of research in health communication settings is the identification of communication skills required by healthcare professionals. As well as emphasising the verbal and nonverbal skills we discussed in chapters 5 and 6, researchers have brought to the attention of health providers a variety of communication skills aimed at improving relationships with patients. For example, effective healthcare requires that patients be given the opportunity to explain their symptoms and problems accurately to the healthcare professional. In this respect it is vital to create a relationship of openness and trust with the patient and thereby encourage the process of **self-disclosure**, that is, revealing information about oneself that is not usually disclosed to others (discussed in Chapter 8). The provider must also be willing to share **control** with the patient, that is, ensuring that communication is not one-directional (from professional to patient) but an interactive or transactional process (discussed in Chapter 3). It is only by sharing control that patients are able to perceive that they can influence the outcome of their illness and that they are not merely cogs in the wheel of the healthcare system.

Empathy and confirmation are two more communication skills that influence effective health communication. As you learned in Chapter 4, **empathy** is the sharing of another's feelings from the other's point of view, not the expression of your own feelings. Empathy requires qualities such as interactive listening, observational skills, perceptual skills and sensitivity to emotions. For patients, empathy is important because illness is confusing and frightening and being understood by the health provider helps them to cope with these emotions.

Communication that is **confirmatory** allows the other person to know that he or she is acknowledged, understood and accepted as a unique individual (refer to Buber's I-you relationship in Chapter 8). Health providers have a responsibility to recognise their patients as people rather than inanimate objects. By communicating in confirming ways, health professionals help patients (and colleagues) cope with feelings of depersonalisation, rejection and even alienation (cf Rensburg 1996; Faure 2000).

Scenario 12.5

Read the following story by Kreps and Thornton (1995:1) and then answer the questions that follow.

The young woman needed four wisdom teeth extracted. The procedure was a routine one that could be performed in the dentist's office. Nitrous oxide was administered as an anaesthetic. The woman's mother accompanied her but was directed to the waiting room, with the promise that she would be called if needed. During the course of the treatment, the woman had a drug reaction. She began to experience terror and wanted her mother, only to find that she was unable to talk. Feeling helpless only increased her terror.

At no time during the one-hour dental procedure did the dentist or the dental assistant inquire into the client's comfort. After the procedure the client had several psychological reactions, including nightmares which persisted for several months. Today, almost six years later, she continues to feel aversion to dentists. The dentist and his assistant, questioned by the parent as to why they had not inquired into the client's comfort, explained that they typically become so involved in the procedure that they often do not inquire; also, they felt at a loss as to how they should approach the client during a procedure (Gamble & Gamble 1998a:386).

1   If you were the parent, how would you have responded to the practitioners?
2   How could the practitioners have ensured a more satisfactory outcome to the encounter?
3   Do you think communication skills should form part of the training of health practitioners? Explain how you think this could be done.

Summary

This chapter provided an overview of some of the specialisation areas which communication scientists are currently investigating: persuasive communication, organisational communication, intercultural communication, development communication and health communication. It also used a variety of scenarios to apply the theoretical principles discussed in each setting to practical examples.

Test yourself

1. Write down a brief overview of the historical development of persuasion from classical to contemporary times.
2. Study some advertisements from a magazine or on television and try to identify the persuasive elements that have been used to try and encourage you to buy the advertised product.
3. Briefly describe how each of the five theoretical approaches to organisational communication you have studied views the role of communication in the organisation.
4. Think of an organisation for which you have worked or with which you are familiar. Which approach to organisational communication seems to prevail? Provide examples to substantiate your point of view.
5. Give your own examples of the key concepts that have been developed in intercultural communication to help explain why communication between people of different cultures is sometimes problematic.
6. Provide a brief overview of the three paradigms (approaches) in development communication.
7. Which paradigm do you think would be best for development communication in South Africa?
8. Give examples from your own experience of each of the functions of health communication discussed in this unit.
9. Explain why effective health communication skills could help health professionals to facilitate communication with patients. Illustrate your answer with examples.

EXECUTIVE SUMMARY
Specialisation areas in communication studies
1 Persuasive communication
  - ❏ Greek and Roman traditions
  - ❏ contemporary rhetoric
2 Organisational communication
  - ❏ classical approach
  - ❏ human relations approach
  - ❏ human resources approach
  - ❏ systems approach
  - ❏ cultural approach
3 Intercultural communication
  - ❏ social science approach
  - ❏ interpretative approach
  - ❏ critical approach
4 Development communication
  - ❏ dominant paradigm
    - — diffusion of innovations
    - — mass media and modernisation
  - ❏ alternative paradigm
    - — mass media approach
    - — development journalism
  - ❏ new paradigm
    - — development support communication
5 Health communication
  - ❏ interpersonal context
  - ❏ small-group context
  - ❏ organisational context
  - ❏ mass communication context

Bibliography

Abbate, J. 1999. *Inventing the internet.* Cambridge, Maryland: MIT Press.

Abrams, KS. 1986. *Communication at work.* Englewood Cliffs, NJ: Prentice-Hall.

Adelstein, ME & Sparrow, WK. 1990. *Business communications.* (2nd ed.) Orlando, Florida: Harcourt, Brace, Jovanovich.

Adler, RB, Rosenfeld, LB & Proctor, RF. 2001. *Interplay: the process of interpersonal communication* (8th ed.) Orlando.

Adler, R B. & Towne, N. 2002. *Looking out looking in* (10th ed.) Orlando, Florida: Harcourt.

Agee, W K, Ault, PH & Emery, E. 1988. *Introduction to mass communication.* (9th ed.) New York: Harper & Row.

Albert, RE & Emmons, ML. 1986. *Your perfect right: a guide to assertive living.* (5th ed.) California: Impact.

Allport, GW. 1958. *The nature of prejudice.* Garden City, NY: Doubleday.

Andersch, EG., Staats, LC. & Bostrom, RN. 1969. *Communication in everyday use.* (3rd ed.) San Francisco: Rinehart.

Andrews, PH & Baird, JE. 1992. *Communication for business and the professions.* (5th ed.) Dubuque, Iowa: Wm C Brown.

Anstey, M. 1991. *Negotiating conflict — insights and skills for negotiators and peacemakers.* Cape Town: Juta.

Applbaum, RL., Bodaken, EM., Sereno, KK. & Anatol, KWE. 1979. *The process of group communication.* Chicago: Science Research Associates.

Arnold, W & Libby, R, 1970. *The semantics of sex-related terms* (paper delivered at the annual convention of the Speech Communication Association, Chicago, December 1970).

Aronson, E. 1980. *The social animal.* San Francisco: Freeman.

Asante, MK & Asante, KW (eds). 1990. *African culture: The rhythms of unity.* Trenton, New York: First Africa World Press.

Ayres, J. & Miller, J. 1994. *Effective public speaking.* (4th ed.) Madison, Wisconsin: Wm. C. Brown.

Baran, SJ & Davis, DK. 2003. *Mass communication theory: Foundation, ferment, and future.* (3rd ed.) Belmont,: Wadsworth.

Barker, LL. 1984. *Communication.* (3rd ed.) Englewood Cliffs, New Jersey: Prentice-Hall.

Barker, LL & Gaut, DA. 1996. *Communication.* Boston: Allyn & Bacon.

Barker, LL, Wahlers, KJ & Watson, KW. 1995. *Groups in process: An introduction to small group communication.* (5th ed.) Englewood Cliffs, NJ: Prentice Hall.

Barnlund, DC. 1970. A transactional model of communication, in *Foundations of communication theory,* edited by K K Sereno & CD Mortensen. New York: Harper & Row.

Bavelas, A. 1950. Communication patterns in task-oriented groups. *Journal of Acoustical Society of America* (22):725-730.

Beal, MB. 1983. *Exploration of agenda-setting in the news magazine "60 minutes".* MA dissertation. Arizona: University of Arizona.

Beamer, L. & Varner, I. 2001. *Intercultural communication in the global workplace.* USA: Irwin.

Beebe, SA & Masterson, JT. 1994. *Communicating in small groups: principles and practices.* (4th ed.) New York: HarperCollins.

Beebe, SA, Beebe, SJ & Redmond, MV. 1999. *Interpersonal communication: Relating to others.* (2nd ed.) Boston: Allyn & Bacon.

Benjamin, JB. 1986. *Communication: Concepts and contexts.* New York: Harper & Row.

Benne, KD & Sheats, P. 1948. Functional roles of group members. *Journal of Social Issues* (4): 41-49.

Berger, CR. & Bradac, JJ. 1982. *Language and social knowledge: Uncertainty in interpersonal relations.* London: Edward Arnold.

Berko, RM., Wolvin, AD & Curtis, R. 1986. *This business of communicating.* (3rd ed.) Dubuque, Iowa: Wm C Brown.

Bersheid, E. 1985. Interpersonal attraction, in *Handbook of Social Psychology,* edited by G Lindzey & E Aronson. New York: Random House.

Bettinghaus, EP. 1968. *Persuasive communication.* New York: Holt, Rinehart & Winston.

Birdwhistell, RL. 1970. *Kinesics and context: Essays on body motion communication.* Philadelphia: University of Pennsylvania Press.

Bittner, JR. 1985. *Fundamentals of communication.* Englewood Cliffs, New Jersey: Prentice-Hall.

Blumberg, RL. 1987. *Organizations in contemporary society.* Englewood Cliffs, New Jersey: Prentice-Hall.

Borcherds, MM. *et al* 1990. *A guide to effective spoken and written communication.* Cape Town: Arrow.

Bormann, EG. & Bormann, NC. 1988. *Effective small group communication.* (4th ed.) Minneapolis: Burgess International Group.

Botha, H. 1997. The history and development of film and television, in *Introduction to communication: Course book 6 — film and television studies*, edited by PJ Fourie. Cape Town: Juta.

Bowra, CM. 1966. *Classical Greece*. Nederland NV: Time-Life.

Bredenkamp, C. 1996. Persuasive communication, in *Introduction to communication: Course book 4 — communication planning and management*, edited by R Rensburg. Cape Town: Juta.

Briggs, K. 1986. Assertiveness: Speak your mind. *Nursing Times* (82): 24-26.

Brilhart, J K. 1989. *Effective group discussion*. (6th ed.) Dubuque, Iowa: Wm C Brown.

Brown, R. 1986. *Social psychology*. (2nd ed.) New York: Free Press.

Brownell, J. 1986. *Building active listening skills*. Englewood Cliffs, New Jersey: Prentice-Hall.

Buber, M. 1964. *Between man and man*. London: Collins.

Buber, M. 1970. *I and thou*. Edinburgh: Clark.

Burgoon, JK., Boiler, BB. & Woodall, WG. 1989. *Nonverbal communication: The unspoken dialogue*. New York: Harper & Row.

Burley-Allen, M. 1982. *Listening: The forgotten skill*. New York: Wiley.

Burton, G. & Dimbleby, R. 1995. *Between ourselves* (2nd ed.) London: Edward Arnold.

Carbaugh, D. (ed.) 1990. *Cultural communication and intercultural contact*. Hillsdale, NJ: Lawrence Erlbaum.

Chase, S. 1953. *The power of words*. New York: Harcourt Brace Jovanovich.

Clarke, AC. 1945. Extra-terrestrial relays: Can rocket stations give world-wide coverage? *Wireless World* (October): 305-308.

Cleary S (ed.) 2003. *The communication handbook*. (2nd ed.) Cape Town: Juta

Cohen, E. 1980. *Speaking the speech*. New York: Holt, Rinehart & Winston.

Condon, JC. 1975. *Semantics and communication*. (2nd ed.) New York: MacMillan.

Cook, M. 1971. *Interpersonal perception*. Baltimore: Penguin.

Crowley. D. & Heyer, P. 1991. *Communication in history: Technology, culture, society*. New York: Longman.

Dahnke, GL & Clatterbuck, GW (eds). 1990. *Human communication: Theory and research*. Belmont, California: Wadsworth.

Daly, JA., Friedrich, GW. & Vangelesti, AL. (eds) 1990. *Teaching communication: Theory, research, and methods*. Hillsdale, NJ: Lawrence Erlbaum.

Dance, FEX. & Larson, CE. 1976. *The functions of human communication: A theoretical approach*. New York: Holt, Rinehart & Winston.

Dance, FEX. 1970. The "concept" of communication. *Journal of Communication* (20): 201-210.

Daniels, TD & Spiker, BK. 1987. *Perspectives on organizational communication.* Dubuque, Iowa: Wm C Brown.

Davidoff, H. (ed.) 1953. *The pocket hook of quotations.* New York: Pocket Books.

De Beer, AS. (ed.) 1993. *Mass media for the nineties: The South African Handbook of Mass Communication.* Johannesburg: Van Schaik.

Deetz, SA. (ed.) 1993. *Communication Yearbook 16.* Newbury Park: Sage.

DeFleur, D. 1994. *Understanding mass communication.* (5th ed.) Boston: Houghton Mifflin.

De Fleur, ML. & Ball-Rokeach, SJ. 1989. *Theories of mass communication.* (5th ed.) New York: Longman.

De Jager, R. 1997. Introduction to speech communication, in *Introduction to communication: Course book 7 — speech communication, public relations and advertising,* edited by GC Angelopulo. Cape Town: Juta.

Delia, JG. 1980. Some tentative thoughts concerning the study of interpersonal relationships and their development. *Western Journal of Speech Communication* (44): 97-107.

DeVito, JA. & Hecht, ML. (eds) 1990. *The nonverbal communication reader.* Prospect Heights, Illinois: Waveland.

DeVito, JA. 1981. *The elements of public speaking.* New York: Harper & Row.

DeVito, JA. 1986. *The communication handbook.* New York: Harper & Row.

DeVito, JA. 1989. *The interpersonal communication book.* (5th ed.) New York: Harper & Row.

DeVito, JA. 1990. *Messages: Building interpersonal communication skills.* New York: Harper & Row.

DeVito, JA. & Hecht, ML. (eds). 1990. *The nonverbal communication reader.* Prospect Heights, Illinois: Waveland.

De Wet, JC. 1991. *The art of persuasive communication.* Cape Town: Juta.

Dickson, DA, Hargie, O. & Morrow, NC. 1989. *Communication skills training for health professionals: An instructor's handbook.* London: Chapman & Hall.

Dimbleby, R. & Burton, G. 1985. *More than words: An introduction to communication.* London: Routledge.

Dimbleby, R. & Burton, G. 1992. *More than words: An introduction to communication.* (2nd ed.) London: Routledge.

Dodd, C.H. 1991. *Dynamics of intercultural communication.* (3rd ed.) Dubuque, Iowa: Wm C Brown.

Dominick, J. 1999. *The dynamics of mass communication*. New York: McGraw-Hill.

Donohew, L . & Ray, EB. 1990. Introduction: Systems perspectives on health communication, in *Communication and health*, edited by EB Ray & L Donohew, Hillsdale, New Jersey: Lawrence Erlbaum.

Druckman, D. 1982. *Nonverbal communication: Survey, theory and research*. Beverly Hills, California: Sage.

Du Plooy, GM. 1991. *500 communication concepts*. Cape Town: Juta.

Du Plooy, GM. 1994. *Communication: Only study guide for CMN100-Q (Introduction to communication science)*. Pretoria: University of South Africa.

Du Plooy, GM. 1995. *Communication: Only study guide for CMN212-X (Communication semiotics)*. Pretoria: University of South Africa.

Du Plooy, GM. 1996. Nonverbal communication and meaning, in *Introduction to communication: Course book 3 — communication and the production of meaning*, edited by PJ Fourie. Cape Town: Juta.

Du Plooy GM. 2002. *Communication research: Techniques, methods and applications*. Cape Town: Juta.

Du Plooy-Cilliers, F. & Olivier, M. 2000. *Let's talk about interpersonal communication*. Sandton: Heinemann.

Ekeh, P. 1974. *Social exchange theory*. London: Heinemann.

Ekman, P. & Friesen, WV. 1969. The repertoire of nonverbal behaviour: categories, usage and coding. *Semiotica* (1): 49-98.

Ellis, R. & McClintock, A. 1990. *If you take my meaning: Theory and practice in human communication*. London: Edward Arnold.

Fabre, M. 1969. *A history of communications*. London: Leisure Arts.

Fang, I. 1997. *A history of mass communication: Six information revolutions*. Boston: Focal Press.

Faure, C. 2000. Health communication, in Faure, C, Parry, L. & Sonderling, S. *Intercultural, development and health communication*. Only study guide for COM204-8. Pretoria: Unisa.

Finlayson, R. 1991. Education in a multicultural environment. *Transvaal Educational News* (August): 6-11.

Fisher, AB. 1980. *Small-group decision making: Communication and the group process*. (2nd ed.) New York: McGraw-Hill.

Fisher, D. 1981. *Communication in organizations*. New York: West.

Floyd, JJ. 1985. *Listening: A practical approach*. Glenview, Illinois: Scott Foresman.

Fourie, PJ (ed.) 1996. *Introduction to communication. Course book 3 — communication and the production of meaning*. Cape Town: Juta.

Frey, LR. 1999. *Handbook of group communication theory and research*. London: Sage.

Furnham, A. 1979. Assertiveness in three cultures: multidimensionality and cultural differences. *Journal of Clinical Psychology* (35): 522-527.

Gamble, TK. & Gamble, M. 1987. *Communication works*. (2nd ed.) New York: Random House.

Gamble, TK. & Gamble, MW. 1998a. *Contacts: Communicating interpersonally*. Needham Heights, Maryland: Allyn & Bacon.

Gamble, TK. & Gamble, MW. 1998b. *Public speaking in the age of diversity*. (2nd ed.) Needham Heights, Maryland: Allyn & Bacon.

Gerbner, G. & Schramm, W. 1990. The international development of communication studies. *Communication* 16(1): 8-18.

Gibson, JW. & Hanna, MS. 1992. *Introduction to human communication*. Dubuque, Indiana: Wm C Brown.

Giere, RN. 1979. *Understanding scientific reasoning*. New York: Holt, Rinehart & Winston.

Glean, EC. & Pood, EA. 1989. Listening self-inventory. *Supervisory Management*.

Goffman, E. 1975. *The presentation of self in everyday life*. Garden City, New York: Doubleday.

Goldhaber, GM. 1990. *Organizational communication*. 5th edition. Dubuque.

Gombrich, EH. 1978. *Art and Illusion*. London: Phaidon.

Gorman, SR, Banks, SP, Bantz, CR & Mayer, ME (eds). 1990. *Foundations of organizational communication: A reader*. New York: Longman.

Griffin, EA. 2003. *A first look at communication theory*. Boston, Massachusetts: McGraw-Hill.

Grobler, HD, Schenck, R. & Du Toit, D. 2004. *Person-centred communication*. Cape Town: Oxford University Press.

Gronbeck, BE, German, K, Ehninger, D & Monroe, AH. 1982. *Principles of speech communication*. 11th brief edition. New York: HarperCollins.

Gudykunst, W. & Ting-Toomey, S. 1988. *Culture and interpersonal communication*. Newbury Park, California: Sage.

Gunter, B & Wober, M. 1991. *The reactive viewer: a review of research on audience reaction measurement*. London: Libbey.

Hacker, KL. & Van Dijk, J. (eds.) 2000. *Digital democracy*. London: Sage.

Hall, ET. 1968. *Beyond culture*. Garden City, New York: Anchor.

Hall, ET. 1969. *The hidden dimension*. New York: Doubleday.

Hall, E T. 1973. *The silent language*. Garden City, New York: Anchor Books.

Hall, ET & Hall, MR. 1990. *Understanding cultural differences*. Yarmouth: Intercultural Press.

Hamilton, C. & Parker, C. 1990. *Communicating for results*. (3rd ed.) Belmont, California: Wadsworth.

Harris, TE. & Sherblom, JC. 1999. *Small group and team communication*. Boston: Allyn & Bacon.

Hartley, J. 2002. *Communication, cultural and media studies: The key concepts*. London: Routledge.

Hartley, P. 1993. *Interpersonal communication*. London: Routledge.

Hawkes, T. 1985. *Structuralism and semiotics*. London: Methuen.

Hayakawa, SI. 1962. *The use and misuse of language*. Greenwich, Connecticut: Fawcett.

Hayakawa, SI. & Hayakawa, AR. 1989. *Language in thought and action*. 5th edi~tion. New York: Harcourt Brace Jovanovich.

Heath, RL. & Bryant, J. 1992. *Human communication theory and research: Concepts, contexts and challenges*. Hillsdale, New Jersey: Lawrence Erlbaum.

Heath, RL. & Bryant, J. 2000. *Human communication theory and research: Concepts, contexts, and challenges*. (2nd ed.) Mahwah, New Jersey: Erlbaum.

Herbert, RK. 1992. *Language and society in Africa*. Johannesburg: Witwatersrand University Press.

Heun, LR. & Heun, RE. 1978. *Developing skills for human interaction*. (2nd ed.) Columbus, Ohio: Merrill.

Hickson, ML. & Stacks, DW. 1989. *Nonverbal communication: Studies and applications*. (2nd ed.) Dubuque, Iowa: Wm C Brown.

Hocker, JL & Wilmot, WW. 1991. *Interpersonal conflict*. (3rd ed.) Dubuque, Iowa: William C Brown.

Hofstede, G. 1991. *Culture's consequences*. (2nd ed.) Thousand Oaks, California: Sage.

Holmes, D. 2005. *Communication theory: Media, technology and society*. London: Sage.

Homans, GC. 1959. *The human group*. New York: Harcourt Brace & World.

Homans, GC. 1961. *Social behaviour: Its elementary forms*. New York: Harcourt, Brace & World.

Hoover, K. 1979. *The elements of social scientific thinking*. (2nd ed.) New York: St Martin's Press.

Hunt, T. & Ruben, BD. 1993. *Mass communication producers and consumers*. New York: HarperCollins.

Hybels, S. & Weaver, RL. 1995. *Communicating effectively*. (4th ed.) New York: Random House.

Hybels, S. & Weaver, RL. 1989. *Communicating effectively*. (2nd ed.) New York: Random House.

Infante, DA, Rancer, AS. & Womack, DF. 1990. *Building communication theory*. Prospect Heights, Illinois: Waveland.

Infante, DA., Rancer, AS. & Womack F. 2003. *Building communication theory*. (4th ed.) Prospect Heights, Illinois: Waveland.

Innes, D., Kentridge, M. & Perold, H. (eds). 1993. *Reversing discrimination: Affirmative action in the workplace*. Cape Town: Oxford University Press.

Jakobson, R. 1958. Closing statement: Linguistics and poetics, in *Style in language*, edited by CA Sebeok (1960), Cambridge, Massachusetts: Massachusetts Institute of Technology.

Jandt, FE. 1995. *Intercultural communication*. Thousand Oaks, California: Sage.

Jandt, FE. 2004. *An introduction to intercultural communication: Identities in a global community*. Thousand Oaks, California: Sage.

Janis, I. 1972. Groupthink. *Psychology Today* (5):43-46; 74-76.

Jansen, N. 1989. *Philosophy of mass communication research*. Cape Town: Juta.

Jansen N. & Steinberg, S. 1991. *Theoretical approaches to communication*. Cape Town: Juta.

Jayaweera, N. 1991. *Folk media and development communication: Myths and realities*. Manila: Asian Social Institute.

Johannensen, RL. 1971. The emerging concept of communication as dialogue. *Quarterly Journal of Communication* 62(4):373-382.

Johannensen, RL. 1990. *Ethics in human communication*. (4th ed.) Prospect Heights, Illinois: Waveland.

Johnson, DW. & Johnson, FP. 1993. *Joining together: Group theory and group skills*. (4th ed.) Englewood Cliffs, New Jersey: Prentice Hall.

Johnson, DW. 1997. *Reaching out: Interpersonal effectiveness and self-actualization*. (6th ed.) Needham Heights, Maryland: Allyn & Bacon.

Jouard, S. 1964. *The transparent self*. New York: Van Nostrand Reinhold.

Katz, E. & Lazarsfeld, PF. 1955. *Personal influence*. Glencoe: Free Press.

Keeps, GL. 1990. *Organizational communication: Theory and practice*. (2nd ed.) New York: Longman.

Kelly, L. & Watson, AK. 1986. *Speaking with confidence and skill*. New York: Harper & Row.

Kizza, JM. 1998. *Civilizing the Internet: Global concerns and efforts towards regulation*. Jefferson: McFarland & Co.

Kleinke, C. 1986. *Meeting and understanding people.* New York: Freeman.

Knapp, ML. 1980. *Essentials of nonverbal communication.* New York: Holt, Rinehart & Winston.

Knapp, ML. 1984. *Interpersonal communication and human relationships.* Newton, Massachusetts: Allyn & Bacon.

Knapp, ML. 1990. Nonverbal communication: Basic perspectives, in Stewart, J, (ed.) *Bridges not walls: A book about interpersonal communication.* New York: McGraw-Hill.

Knapp, ML & Vangelesti, AL. 1996. *Interpersonal communication and human relationships.* (3rd ed.) Boston: Allyn & Bacon.

Koehler, JW, Anatol, KWE & Applbaum, RL. 1981. *Organizational communication: Behavioral perspectives.* New York: Holt, Rinehart & Winston.

Kramarae, C. 1981. *Women and men speaking: Frameworks for analysis.* Rowley, Mass.: Newbury House.

Kreps, GL & Thornton, B. 1995. *Health Communication.* New York: Longman.

Kreps, GL, Frey, LR. & O'Hair, D. 1991. Applied communication research: Scholarship that can make a difference. *Journal of applied communication research,* (19): 71-87.

Kreps, GL. 1990. *Organizational communication: Theory and practice.* (2nd ed.) New York: Longman.

Lange, AJ. & Jabukowski, P. 1976. *Responsible assertive behaviour.* Champaign, Illinois: Research.

Larson, CU, Backlund, PM, Redmond, MK, & Barbour, A. 1978. *Assessing communicative competence.* Falls Church, Virginia: Speech Communication Association.

Larson, CU. 1989. *Persuasion, reception and responsibility.* (5th ed.) Belmont, California: Wadsworth.

Larson, CU. 2004. *Persuasion, reception and responsibility.* (10th ed.) Belmont, California: Wadsworth.

Lasswell, HD. 1948. The structure and function of communication in society, in *The communication of ideas,* edited by E. Bryson. New York: Harper & Brothers.

Leavitt, HJ. 1951. Some effects of certain communication patterns on group perfor~mance. *Journal of Abnormal and Social Psychology* (46): 38-50.

Liebes, T. 1988. Cultural differences in the retelling of television fiction. *Critical Studies in Mass Communication* (5): 277-292.

Littlejohn, S. 1983. *Theories of human communication.* (2nd ed.) Belmont, California: Wadsworth.

Littlejohn, S. 1992. *Theories of human communication.* (4th ed.) Belmont, California: Wadsworth.

Littlejohn, S. 1999. *Theories of human communication.* (6th ed.) Belmont, California: Wadsworth.

Littlejohn, S. 2002. *Theories of human communication.* (7th ed.) Belmont, California: Wadsworth.

Louw, PE. 1993. *South African media policy: Debates of the 1990s.* Belville: Anthropos.

Lucas, SE. 1989. *The art of public speaking.* (3rd ed.) New York: McGraw-Hill.

Luft, J. 1970. *Of human interaction.* Palo Alto, California: National Press.

Lustig, MW. & Koester, J. 1993. *Intercultural competence: Interpersonal communication across cultures.* New York: HarperCollins.

Malandro, LA, Barker, L & Barker, DA. 1989. *Nonverbal communication.* (2nd ed.) New York: Random House.

Martin, LJ & Hiebert, RE (eds). 1990. *Current issues in international communication.* New York: London Press.

Maslow, AH. 1954. *Motivation and personality.* New York: Harper & Row.

Mayer, LV. 1988. *Fundamentals of voice and diction.* (8th ed.) Dubuque, Los Angeles: Wm C. Brown.

McGregor, D. 1960. *The human side of enterprise.* New York: McGraw-Hill.

McLaughlin, M. 1984. *Conversation: How talk is organized.* Beverly Hills: Sage.

McLuhan, M. 1962. *The Gutenberg galaxy: The making of typographic man.* London: Routledge & Kegan Paul.

McLuhan, M. 1974. *Understanding media: The extensions of man.* London: Abacus.

McLuhan, M & Fiore, Q. 1967. *The medium is the message.* Harmondsworth, Middlesex: Penguin.

McQuail, D. & Windahl, S. 1981. *Communication models for the study of mass communications.* New York: Longman.

McQuail, D. 1983. *Mass communication theory: An introduction.* London: Sage

McQuail, D. 1987. *Mass communication theory: An introduction.* (2nd ed.) London: Sage.

Mda, Z. 1993. *When people play people: Development communication through theatre.* Johannesburg: Witwatersrand University Press.

Mehrabian, A. 1981. *Silent messages.* (2nd ed.) Belmont, California: Wadsworth.

Melkote, SR. 1991. *Communication for development in the third world: Theory and practice.* London: Sage.

Mersham, G. & Skinner, C. 1999. *New insights into communication and public relations.* Sandton: Heinemann.

Mersham, G. & Skinner, C. 2001. *New insights into business and organisational communication.* Sandton: Heinemann.

Messaris, P. 1997. *Visual persuasion: The role of images in advertising.* Thousand Oaks, California: Sage.

Miller, K. 2002. *Communication theories. Perspectives, processes and contexts.* Boston, Massachusetts: McGraw-Hill.

Minnick, WC. 1983. *Public speaking.* (2nd ed.) Boston: Houghton Mifflin.

Myers, G. & Myers, M. 1992. *The dynamics of human communication.* New York: McGraw-Hill.

Myers, MT & Myers, GB. 1982. *Managing by communication: An organisational approach.* New York: McGraw-Hill.

Neher, WW. 1997. *Organizational communication.* Needham Heights, Maryland: Allyn & Bacon

Noelle-Neumann, E. 1973. Return to the concept of powerful mass media, in *Studies of broadcasting: An international annual of broadcasting science,* edited by H Eguchi & K Sata. Tokyo: Nippon Hoso, Kyokai.

Noelle-Neumann, E. 1980. Mass media and social change in developed societies, in *Mass communication review yearbook,* Vol 1, edited by GC Wilhoit & H de Bock. Beverly Hills, California: Sage.

Nutting, J & White, G. 1990. *This business of communicating.* (2nd ed.) Roseville. New South Wales: McGraw-Hill.

O'Barr, WM. 1982. *Linguistic evidence: Language, power and strategy in the courtroom.* New York: Academic Press.

O'Sullivan, T, Hartley, J, Saunders, D & Fiske, J. 1989. *Key concepts in communication.* London: Routledge.

Ogden, CK. & Richards, I A. 1949. *The meaning of meaning.* London: Routledge & Kegan Paul.

Pace, RW. 1983. *Organizational communication: Foundations for human resource development.* Englewood Cliffs, New Jersey: Prentice-Hall.

Packard, V. 1960. *The hidden persuaders.* Harmondsworth: Penguin.

Packard, V. 1981. *The hidden persuaders.* New York: Penguin.

Paton, BR. Griffin, K. & Linkugel, WIA. 1982. *Responsible public speaking.* Chicago: Scott Foresman.

Pavitt, C. 1990. The ideal communicator as the basis for competence of self and friend. *Communication reports* (3): 9-14.

Pearson, J. 1985. *Gender and communication.* Dubuque, Iowa: Wm C Brown.

Pearson, JC & Spitzberg, BH. 1990. *Interpersonal communication: Concepts, components and contexts.* (2nd ed.) Dubuque, Iowa: Wm C Brown.

Pease, A & Garner, A. 1989. *Talk language: How to use conversation for profit and pleasure.* London: Simon & Schuster.

Pei, M. 1965. *The story of language.* Philadelphia: Lippincott.

Perry, DK. 2002. *Theory and research in mass communication. Contexts and consequences.* (2nd ed.) New Jersey: Lawrence Erlbaum.

Peters, JM. 1977. *Pictorial communication.* Cape Town: David Philip.

Phillips, GM. 1982. *Communicating in organizations.* New York: MacMillan.

Postman, N. 1990. Crazy talk, stupid talk, in *Bridges not walls: A book about interpersonal communication,* edited by J Stewart. New York: McGraw-Hill.

Poyatos, F (ed.) 1988. *Cross-cultural perspectives in nonverbal communication,* Toronto, CJ: Hogrefe.

Purdy, M. 1996. What is listening? In M. Purdy & D. Borisoff (eds.) *Listening in everyday life: A personal and professional approach.* (2nd ed.) New York: University Press of America.

Rakos, R. 1986. Asserting and confronting, in *A handbook of communication skills,* edited by O Hargie. London: Croom Helm.

Redding, C. 1972. *Communication within the organisation.* New York: Industrial Communication Council.

Rensburg, R (ed.) 1996. *Introduction to communication. Course book 4 — Communication planning and management.* Cape Town: Juta.

Rensburg, R. & Bredenkamp, C. 1991. *Aspects of business communication.* Cape Town: Juta.

Ritzer, G (ed.) 2000. *Blackwood companion to major sociological thinkers.* Oxford: Blackwell.

Roberts, W R. 1924. *Works of Aristotle.* Oxford: Clarendon Press.

Roethlisberger, FJ & Dickson, WJ. 1939. *Management and the worker.* Cambridge, Massachusetts: Harvard University Press.

Rogers, EM. & Shoemaker, FF. 1971. *Communication of innovations: a cross cultural approach.* New York: Free.

Rogers, EM. 1969. *Modernization among peasants.* New York: Holt, Rinehart & Winston.

Rogers, EM. 2000. The extensions of men: the correspondence of Marshall McLuhan and Edward T Hall, in *Mass communication and society* (3): 117-135.

Roloff, ME & Miller, GR. 1987. *Interpersonal processes: New directions in communication research.* Beverly Hills, California: Sage.

Rosengren, KE, Wenner, LA & Palmgreen, P. 1985. *Media gratifications research: Current perspectives.* Beverly Hills, California: Sage.

Ruben, BD. 1984. *Communication and human behavior.* New York: MacMillan.

Sagan, C. 1977. *The dragons of Eden: Speculations on the evolution of human intelligence.* New York: Ballantine.

Samovar, LA. & Porter, RE (eds). 2000. *Intercultural communication: A reader* (9th ed.) Belmont, California: Wadsworth.

Satir, V. 1972. *Peoplemaking.* Palo Alto, California: Science and Behavior Books.

Schneider, DJ, Hastorf, AH & Ellsworth, PC. 1979. *Person perception.* Reading, Massachusetts: Addison-Wesley.

Schramm, W. 1954. How communication works, in Schramm, W. (ed.) *The process and effects of mass communication.* Urbana, Illinois: University of Illinois Press.

Schramm, W. 1988. *The story of human communication: Cave painting to microchip.* New York: Harper & Row.

Schutz, WC. 1958. *The interpersonal underworld.* Reading, Mass: Addison-Wesley.

Severin, WJ & Tankard, JW. 1988. *Communication theories: Origins, methods, uses* (2nd ed.) New York: Longman.

Severin, WJ. & Tankard JW. 1992. *Communication theories: Origins, methods, uses.* (3rd ed.) New York: Longman.

Severin WJ. & Tankard JW. 2001. *Communication theories: Origins, methods, uses* (4th ed.) New York: Longman.

Shannon, CE & Weaver, W. 1949. *The mathematical theory of communication,* Urbana: University of Illinois Press.

Shaw, ME. 1981. *Group dynamics: The psychology of small group behavior.* (3rd ed.) New York: McGraw-Hill.

Shockley-Zalabak, P. 1991. *Fundamentals of organizational communication: Knowledge, sensitivity, skills, values.* New York: Longman.

Shuter, R. 1984. *Communicating.* New York: Holt, Rinehart & Winston.

Smith, G (ed.) 1999. *Goffman and social organisation: Studies in a sociological legacy.* London: Routledge.

Smith, MJ. 1982. *Persuasion and Human action: A review and critique of social influence theories.* Belmont, California: Wadsworth

Sonderling, S. 1992. Murder of the combi-taxi industry by the mass media: Perceptions and realities of road safety. *Communicatio* 18(2): 57-63.

Sonderling, S. 1992. Tutorial letter for 1992. Department of Communication. Pretoria: Unisa.

Sonderling, S. 1994. Tutorial letter for 1994. Department of Communication. Pretoria: Unisa.

Sonderling, S. 2000. Development communication, in Faure, C, Parry, LL & Sonderling, S. *Intercultural development and health communication*. Only study guide for COM 204-8. Pretoria: Unisa.

Spitzberg, BH. 2000: A model of intercultural communication competence, in LA Samovar & RE Porter (eds). 2000. *Intercultural communication: A reader* (9th ed.) Belmont, California: Wadsworth.

Stacks, D, Hickson, M & Hill, SR. 1991. *Introduction to communication theory*. Fort Worth: Holt, Rinehart & Winston.

Staley, CC & Staley, RS. 1992. *Communicating in business and the professions: The inside word*. Belmont, California: Wadsworth.

Steil, LK, Barker, LL & Watson, KW. 1983. *Effective listening: The key to your success*. Reading, Massachusetts: Addison-Wesley.

Steinberg, S. 1991. Organisational communication skills: Developing a course to be taught at a distance. DLitt et Phil thesis. Pretoria: Unisa.

Steinberg, S. 1994. *Introduction to communication: Course book 1 — the basics*. Cape Town: Juta.

Steinberg, S. 1995. *Communication: Only study guide for CMN213-Y (Introduction to communication planning and management)*. Pretoria: University of South Africa.

Steinberg, S. 1996. Organisational communication, in *Introduction to communication: Course book 4 — communication planning and management,* edited by RS Rensburg. Cape Town: Juta.

Steinberg, S. 1999a. *Communication studies: An introduction*. Cape Town: Juta.

Steinberg, S. 1999b. *Persuasive communication: Public speaking*. Cape Town: Juta.

Steinberg, S. 2000. Self presentation, in Van Heerden, M, Steinberg, S & Qakisa, M. *Interpersonal communication*. Only study guide for COM 204-1. Pretoria: Unisa.

Stewart, J (ed.) 1990. *Bridges not walls: A book about interpersonal communication*. New York: McGraw-Hill.

Stewart, J. (ed.) 2002. *Bridges not walls: A book about interpersonal communication*. (8th ed.) New York: McGraw-Hill.

Stewart, J. & D'Angelo, G. 1990. Verbal communication, in Stewart, J. (ed.) *Bridges not walls: A book about interpersonal communication*. New York: McGraw-Hill.

Stewart, J. & Logan, C. 2002. Constructing selves, in Stewart, J. 2002. *Bridges not walls: A book about interpersonal communication*. (8th ed.) New York: McGraw-Hill.

Stones, R (ed.) 1998. *Key sociological thinkers*. Basingstoke, Hampshire: Palgrave.

Strano, Z, Mohan, T & McGregor, H. 1989. *Communicating!* (2nd ed.) Sydney: Harcourt Brace Jovanovich.

Straznitskas, M. 1998. *Mastering Photoshop 5 for the web*. San Francisco: Sybex.

Tannen, D. 1989. *That's not what I meant!* New York: Morrow.

Tannen, D. 1990. *You just don't understand: Women and men in conversation*. New York: William Morrow.

Terblanche, FH. 1994. Die aard en gemeenskapskulturele dimensie van nie-verbale boodskapverkeer met spesifieke verwysing na emblematiese gedrag. *Communitas* (1):32-54.

Thonssen, L, Baird, AC. & Braden, WW. 1970. *Speech criticism* (2nd ed.) New York: Ronald Press.

Ting-Toomey, S. 1999. *Communicating across cultures*. New York: Guildford.

Ting-Toomey, S. & Korzenny, F. (eds) 1989. *Language, communication and culture: Current directions*. Newbury Park, CA: Sage.

Tomaselli, KG. & Louw, PE. 1991. *The alternative press in South Africa*. Belville: Anthropos.

Trenholm, S. 1989. *Persuasion and social influence*. Englewood Cliffs, New Jersey: Prentice-Hall

Trenholm, S. 1991. *Human communication theory*. (2nd ed.) Englewood Cliffs, New Jersey: Prentice-Hall

Trenholm, S. 1995. *Thinking through communication: An introduction to the study of human communication*. Needham Heights, Maryland: Allyn & Bacon.

Tubbs, SL & Moss, S. 1991. *Human communication: principles and contexts* (6th ed.) New York: McGraw-Hill.

Tubbs, S. & Moss, S. 2003. *Human communication: Principles and contexts*. (9th ed.) New York: McGraw-Hill.

Tubbs, SL. & Carter, RM. (eds) 1978. *Shared experiences in human communication*. Rochelle Park, NJ: Hayden.

Tuckman, BW. 1965. Developmental sequence in small groups. *Psychological Bulletin* (63): 384-399.

Utall, B. 1983. The corporate culture vultures. *Fortune* (October):61-69

Van der Merwe, N. 1991. *Listening: A skill for everyone*. Cape Town: Arrow.

Verderber. RF. 1990. *Communicate!* (6th ed.) Belmont, California: Wadsworth.

Verderber, RF. 1993. *Communicate!* (7th ed.) Belmont, California: Wadsworth.

Verderber. RF. 1994. *Challenge of effective speaking*. (9th ed.) Belmont, CA: Wadsworth.

Verderber, KS & Verderber, RF. 1992. *Interact: using interpersonal communication skills.* (6th ed.) Belmont, California: Wadsworth

Verderber, KS. & Verderber, RF. 2001. *Inter-act: Interpersonal communication concepts, skills and contexts.* (9th ed.) Belmont, California: Wadsworth.

Verderber, KS. & Verderber, RF. 2002. *Communicate!* (10th ed.) Belmont, California: Wadsworth.

Watzlawick, P, Beavin, JH & Jackson, DD. 1968. *Pragmatics of human communication.* New York: Norton.

Wenburg, JR & Wilmot, WW. 1973. *The personal communication process.* New York: John Wiley.

Westrum, R & Samaha, K. 1984. *Complex organizations: Growth, struggle and change.* Englewood Cliffs, New Jersey: Prentice-Hall.

Wheelan, SA. 1994. *Group processes: A developmental perspective.* Boston: Allyn & Bacon.

Whetten, DA & Cameron, KS. 1993. *Developing management skills: Communicating supportively.* New York: HarperCollins.

White, R & Lippit, R. 1960. *Autocracy and democracy: An experimental inquiry.* New York: Harper & Row.

Whorf, BL. 1956. *Language, thought and reality.* Cambridge, Massachusetts: MIT.

Whorf, BL. 1966. Science and linguistics, in Carroll, B.J. (ed.) *Language, thought and reality: Selected writings of Benjamin Lee Whorf.* Cambridge, Massachusetts: MIT.

Wilmont, W. 1975. *Dyadic communication.* Reading, Massachusetts: Addison-Wesley.

Wilson, GL, Hantz, AM & Hanna, MS. 1989. *Interpersonal growth through communication.* (2nd ed.) Dubuque, Iowa: Wm C Brown.

Wolfe, T. 1968. suppose he is what he sounds like, the most important thinker since newton, darwin, freud, einstein, and pavlov — what if he is right? in *McLuhan: hot and cold*, edited by GE Stearn, Harmondsworth, Middlesex: Penguin.

Wolff, FI, Marsnik, NC, Lacey, WS & Nichols, RG. 1983. *Perceptive listening.* New York: Holt, Rinehart & Winston.

Wolvin, AD & Coakley, CG. 1982. *Listening.* Dubuque, Iowa: Wm C Brown.

Wood, JT. 2000. *Communication in our lives.* (2nd ed.) Belmont, California: Wadsworth.

Wood, JT. 2002. *Interpersonal communication: everyday encounters.* (3rd ed.) Belmont, California: Wadsworth.

Wright, CR. 1960. Functional analysis and mass communication. *Public Opinion Quarterly* (24): 605-620.

Zannes, E. 1982. *The widening circle*. Reading, Massachusetts: Addison-Wesley.

Zimbardo, PG & Radl, SL. 1979. *The shyness workbook*. New York: The A&W Visual Library.

Addendum

Useful electronic addresses

Following is an alphabetical list of electronic addresses (fax, e-mail or the Internet) that apply mainly to South Africa, and which are useful for scholars, researchers and communication practitioners in retrieving up-to-date information.

(South African) Communication Services:
http://www.gcis.gov.za

(South African) Department of Communications (Government):
http://www.doc.org.za

(South African) Independent Broadcasting Authority:
http://iba.org.za

(South African) National Information Technology Forum (NITF):
http://www.sn.apc.org/nitf/

(South African) Press Association (SAPA):
http://www.sapa.org.za

America-On-Line/Time Warner:
http://www.corp.aol.com/whoweare.html

Cable News Network (CNN):
http://edition.cnn.com/INDEX/about.us/

Europe Media: the latest developments in the European media:
http://www.europemedia.net

Globalvision New Media:
http://www.mediachannel.org

International Communications Forum:
http://www.icforum.org

Institute for Global Communications:
http://www.igc.org

International Telecommunication Union (ITU):
http://www.itu.int

Media Institute of Southern Africa:
http:www.misa.org.na

National Information Technology Forum:
http://wn.apc.org/nitf

Journal of International Communication:
   http://www.uta.fi

Information, communication and society:
   http://www.infosoc.co.uk

News: latest news with direct links to leading newspapers, such as *The Mail & Guardian; The Sowetan; Beeld* and *City Press*
   http://www.news24.com/News24/Home/

South African Broadcasting Corporation
   http://www.sabc.co.za

South African Independent Media
   http://www.southafrica.indymedia.org/

South African National Editor's Forum (Sanef)
   http://www.sanef.org.za

Unesco: Communication, Information and Informatics Sector:
   http://www.unesco.org/webworld/

University of South Africa (Unisa):
   http://www.unisa.ac.za

World Wide Works: South African Independent Technology Research Organisation:
   Internet, ICT:
   http://www.theworx.biz

Index

Note: Page numbers in italics refer to Tables and Figures.